P9-DTZ-673

The
Social Work
Dictionary

THE

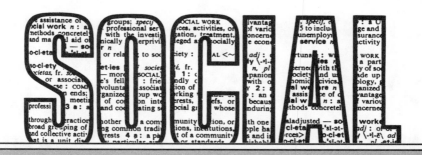

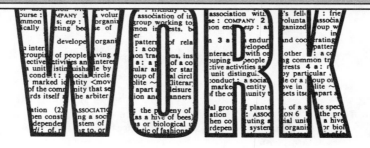

SOCIAL WORK

by
ROBERT L. BARKER

NATIONAL ASSOCIATION
OF SOCIAL WORKERS
Silver Spring, Maryland

Copyright © 1987 by the National Association of Social Workers, Inc.

First Impression, 1988.

All rights reserved. No part of this book may be reproduced or transmitted in any form or by any means, electronic or mechanical, including photocopying, recording, or by any information storage and retrieval system, without permission in writing from the publisher.

Library of Congress Cataloging-in-Publication Data

Barker, Robert L.
    The social work dictionary.

    1. Social service—Dictionaries. I. National
Association of Social Workers. II. Title.
HV12.B37 1987   361.3 '03 '21   87-5501
ISBN 0-87101-145-X

Printed in the United States of America

Cover designed by Dan Hildt
Interior designed by Margo Dittmer

 3

CONTENTS

FOREWORD

One of the characteristics of a profession is that it develops its own distinctive vocabulary. In describing their activities, members of a profession coin new words and develop new meanings for existing terms. The extensive history of the social work profession and the variety of approaches used by its practitioners indicated a compelling need for a comprehensive dictionary of social work terms. The National Association of Social Workers commends Dr. Robert L. Barker, the author of this present volume, for his professional contributions as a social worker, scholar, trailblazer, and innovator in taking on this formidable task.

The creation of a social work dictionary was indeed a challenge. First, there was the sheer amount of work entailed in assembling a set of terms that captures the richness and diversity of the profession. Second, there was the need to achieve consensus among practitioners and scholars on the meanings of many terms and on which terms should be included. To accomplish the second task, Dr. Barker convened an extensive group of experts to review the definitions he had written. In our opinion, Dr. Barker and his consultants have succeeded admirably in fulfilling the need for a comprehensive dictionary, and we hope their efforts will stimulate social workers to examine the way they think about their activities and how they express their professional opinions.

NASW is pleased to publish this important reference work. We are proud to add the *Social Work Dictionary* to the basic source materials of social work and the other social sciences.

Dorothy V. Harris
President, NASW

Mark G. Battle
Executive Director, NASW

PREFACE

The language of social work, like the profession itself, is growing and becoming more sophisticated and refined. This is a positive trend because it is the result of both increased social work knowledge and the profession's desire to communicate with greater precision. It is also the product of closer relationships with other professions and segments of society, each of which has its own jargon and terminology.

Although this trend is positive, it nevertheless presents a formidable challenge to social workers. To express themselves effectively and to comprehend the words of their colleagues and members of other professions, they have to be familiar with a growing and divergent body of complex terms. They are also expected to have ready access to a variety of resources, organizations, and services that can be utilized to meet the needs of their clients.

Another challenge to clear communication arises from the divergent specialties and conceptual orientations within the profession itself. For example, social workers who are policymakers or social advocates do not usually share identical vocabularies with their colleagues in clinical work. Even within a single social work practice specialty there is risk of misunderstanding because of the many different theoretical perspectives in current use. Clinical social workers with psychodynamic orientations, for example, may have considerable difficulty interpreting the words used by their colleagues with behaviorist, psychosocial, systems, existential, or cognitive perspectives, and vice versa.

Although these trends increase the potential for communication problems, social workers face mounting pressure to minimize such difficulties. Legal actions and professional sanctions against professionals who misinterpret or improperly disseminate information are becoming more frequent. Society is more insistent in demanding that professionals prove they are competent and up to date. More than ever, this proof takes the form of licensing and certification exams and, to a great extent, passing these exams requires the worker's understanding of the terms and concepts used in the profession.

It is in this context that the *Social Work Dictionary* has been developed. Its aim is to give the social worker an abbreviated interpretation of the words, concepts, organizations, historical events, and values that are relevant to the profession. As such, it is not designed to provide encyclopedic detail but rather a concise overview of social work's terminology.[1]

Over 3,000 terms are defined here. They are the words used in social work administration, research, policy development, and planning; in community organization, human growth and development, and health and mental health; in macro and micro social work and clinical theory and practice; and words that relate to social work's values and ethics, to its historical development, and so on. The terms are those that have developed within the profession as well as those that social workers have adopted for their own use from sociology, anthropology, medicine, law, psychology, and economics. The symptoms and diagnostic labels for various forms of mental disorders are defined as they are understood by social workers, psychiatrists, psychologists, and other mental health professionals. Many terms are derived from the theoretical orientations of psychodynamic, cognitive, behavioral, and existential as well as systemic and linear approaches. Also included are concepts in social work practice with individuals, groups, families, and communities.

The definitions comprise descriptions of some of the organizations, trends, philosophies, and legislation that have played major roles in the development of social work and social welfare. In addition, the dictionary contains a chronology of the milestones in social work and social welfare and presents the text of the NASW Code of Ethics.

Some readers may find that one or more of their favorite terms have been excluded. Other readers may have a different interpretation of the meaning of a term than is offered here. Naturally, it is hoped that such omissions, discrepancies, and errors are minimal. But, in a dynamic field, populated by intelligent professionals with divergent views, it is probable that there will be differences of opinion about what words should be included and how they should be defined. This dictionary does not purport to present all the words used by social workers or to present any "official" definitions of such terms. In fact, it is inevitable that additional knowledge and different perspectives will necessitate commensurate revisions of the *Social Work Dictionary*.

As the author of this work, I assume full responsibility for the words that have been included and excluded as well as for the way they are defined. Choosing what terms to include was done by listing the words that appeared in the indexes of the major social work journals and textbooks of the past two decades. (The major textbooks were the ones in

---

[1] At least one other dictionary of terms in the general area of social welfare has been published, but it consists largely of terms from related fields and does not focus exclusively on social work. See Erle Fiske, *The Dictionary of Social Welfare* (New York: Social Sciences Publishers, 1948).

most general use in graduate and undergraduate schools of social work.) I also went through the indexes of the most important textbooks and journals of disciplines that are related to social work.

To write the definitions I found it necessary to review how each word was used by several authors. As often as not, there were slight differences in their interpretations of a given word. I tried to provide a definition that was closest to the majority view and to the mainstream of social work thinking. I also tried to make each definition original for this dictionary. No definitions have been deliberately quoted from any copyrighted sources.

Once my definitions were completed they were examined by many colleagues. More than 300 of my MSW and DSW students reviewed definitions for clarity and conciseness. The definitions were then submitted to members of an Editorial Review Board whose names and affiliations follow this preface. The members of this board were chosen for their considerable expertise in at least one area of social work knowledge or a related field such as medicine, law, administration, or economics. Each of them reviewed 50 to 100 of the definitions within their realm of expertise for accuracy, clarity, conciseness, and relevance of examples. Each reviewer was also given a list of all the terms to be included in the dictionary and asked to suggest any other terms that should be included.

The result is this work. It uses the standard format for professional dictionaries and glossaries. The terms are listed in alphabetical order (letter by letter, without regard for intervening spacing, hyphenation, or punctuation) and are expressed in the way readers are most likely to look for them. Many terms permit cross-referencing, and the words that appear in italics in the text refer to terms that are defined elsewhere in the dictionary.

NASW and I plan to issue future editions of the *Social Work Dictionary*. We invite anyone who uses this work to write NASW to recommend changes, additions, deletions, or corrections. In this way the dictionary will be a living, constantly improving document—the product of input from the widest possible range of social workers. I hope that the *Social Work Dictionary* will be a useful tool for social workers in their efforts to achieve clear communications and better professional understanding.

Robert L. Barker, DSW, ACSW
Washington, D.C.
January 1987

EDITORIAL REVIEW BOARD

Donald R. Bardill, Ph.D., Florida State University, Tallahassee

Mark Battle, MSSA, National Association of Social Workers, Silver Spring, Maryland

Richard Bateman, DSW, Social Research Center, Baltimore, Maryland

Barbara Berkman, DSW, Massachusetts General Hospital Institute of Health Professions, Boston

Thomas L. Briggs, MSW, Syracuse University, Syracuse, New York

Beulah R. Compton, Ph.D., University of Alabama, University

Larry L. Constantine, LCSW, Adolescent and Family Institute of LUK, Fitchburg, Massachusetts

Claudia Coulton, Ph.D., Case Western Reserve University, Cleveland, Ohio

Ronald B. Dear, DSW, University of Washington, Seattle

Hon. Ronald V. Dellums, MSW, U.S. House of Representatives, Washington, D.C.

James R. Dumpson, Ph.D., Commonwealth Fund, New York; Fordham University, New York

Courtney Elliott, Ph.D., Catholic University of America, Washington, D.C.

Hans S. Falck, Ph.D., Medical College of Virginia, Virginia Commonwealth University, Richmond

Owen W. Farley, Ph.D., University of Utah, Salt Lake City

Nina S. Fields, Ph.D., California Institute for Clinical Social Work, Los Angeles

Sophie Freud, Ph.D., Simmons College, Boston, Massachusetts

Carel B. Germain, DSW, University of Connecticut, West Hartford

Neil S. Gilbert, Ph.D., University of California, Berkeley

David Guttmann, DSW, Catholic University of America, Washington, D.C.

Ronald Harman, MSW, MD, Psychiatric and Family Consultants, Washington, D.C.

Karl D. Hawver, MD, Georgetown University Medical School, Washington, D.C.

June Gary Hopps, Ph.D. Boston College, Chestnut Hill, Masschusetts

Mónica Jiménez de Barros, MTSW, Escuela de Trabajo Social, Pontificia Universidad Católica de Chile, Santiago

Lloyd A. Johnson, MSS, JD, Howard University, Washington, D.C.

Alfred Kadushin, Ph.D., ACSW, University of Wisconsin, Madison

Jill Doner Kagle, Ph.D., University of Illinois at Urbana-Champaign

Alfred J. Kahn, DSW, Columbia University, New York

Rosalie A. Kane, DSW, University of Minnesota, Minneapolis

Tobe Schwaber Kerson, DSW, Ph.D., Bryn Mawr College, Bryn Mawr, Pennsylvania

Larry W. Kreuger, Ph.D., University of Missouri—Columbia

Armand Lauffer, Ph.D., University of Michigan, Ann Arbor; Brookdale Institute, Jerusalem, Israel

Arnold M. Levin, Ph.D., Institute for Clinical Social Work, Chicago, Illinois

Karen Gail Lewis, ACSW, Medical Center and Department of Psychiatry, University of Cincinnati Medical School, Cincinnati, Ohio

Florence Lieberman, DSW, Hunter College, CUNY, New York

Maryann Mahaffey, MSW, City Council of Detroit; Wayne State University, Detroit, Michigan

Henry W. Maier, Ph.D., University of Washington, Seattle

Jesse F. McClure, Ph.D., Arizona State University, Tempe

Carol H. Meyer, DSW, Columbia University, New York

Ruth R. Middleman, Ed.D., University of Louisville, Louisville, Kentucky

Alehé Mirdjalali, MS, Institut de Psychologie Clinique, University of Paris, France

Edward J. Mullen, DSW, University of Chicago, Chicago, Illinois

Kenji Murase, DSW, San Francisco State University, San Franscisco, California

Elizabeth Thompson Ortiz, DSW, California State University—Long Beach

Frederick G. Reamer, Ph.D., Rhode Island College, Providence

Helen Rehr, DSW, Mt. Sinai School of Medicine, CUNY, New York

Jackson Rose, MBA, JD, George Washington University, Washington, D.C.

Lawrence Shulman, Ed.D., Ph.D., Boston University, Boston, Massachusetts

Joseph Shields, Ph.D., Catholic University of America, Washington, D.C.

Frances Simsarian, DSW, Private Practitioner, Washington, D.C.

Max Siporin, DSW, State University of New York at Albany

Herbert S. Strean, DSW, Rutgers—The State of University of New Jersey, New Brunswick

Martin Sundel, Ph.D., University of Texas, Arlington

Yecheskel Taler, Ph.D., University of Haifa, Mount Carmel, Haifa, Israel

Francis J. Turner, DSW, York University, Toronto, Ontario, Canada

John B. Turner, Ph.D., University of North Carolina, Chapel Hill

Ione D. Vargus, Ph.D., Temple University School of Social Administration, Philadelphia, Pennsylvania

Joseph L. Vigilante, DSW, Adelphi University, Garden City, New York

Charles Zastrow, Ph.D., University of Wisconsin, Whitewater

ACKNOWLEDGMENTS

Many people have made valuable contributions to the development of the *Social Work Dictionary*. The members of the Editorial Review Board were always supportive, generous in sharing their ideas and expertise, and prompt in responding to specific questions. The many baccalaureate, MSW, and doctoral students who reviewed selected terms and definitions provided essential guidance in making sure that concepts were defined with clarity and relevance to their needs. Faculty as well as staff and students at the National Catholic School of Social Service also contributed many useful ideas and suggestions. Dean Frederick J. Ahearn and former dean Joan W. Mullaney gave much-needed encouragement and expertise during the three years devoted to this project. The NASW Publications Department was also extremely supportive. Director of Publications Jacqueline M. Atkins, who for many years had planned a social work dictionary, worked collaboratively on all phases of this project. She helped plan the format, suggested additional terms to be defined, coordinated communications with editorial reviewers, and made sure that everyone involved kept to their schedules. Editor Susan H. Llewellyn was especially helpful for the care, expertise, and good humor she exercised in going over every word herein. Kenneth R. Greenhall and Bradley Frome of the Publications Department also contributed their skills to the project.

A

AASW: See *American Association of Social Workers (AASW)*.

abnormal: A term denoting atypical functioning that is usually seen as maladaptive or destructive. In social work the term usually refers to behaviors rather than people. There is rarely a clear and consistent demarcation between *normal* and abnormal, but rather a continuum. In a *pluralistic society* some behaviors that are considered normal by some people are often seen as abnormal by others.

abortion: Termination of pregnancy before the fetus has developed enough to survive outside the uterus.

abstinence: Voluntary avoidance of such physical activities as eating, drinking alcoholic beverages, taking drugs, or sexual intercourse.

abuse: Improper behavior intended to cause physical, psychological, or financial harm to an individual or group. See also *child abuse, drug abuse, elder abuse, spouse abuse,* and *substance abuse.*

Academy of Certified Social Workers (ACSW): A program established by the *National Association of Social Workers (NASW)* in 1962 to evaluate and certify the practice competence of individual social workers. Social workers are eligible for ACSW membership if they obtain an *MSW* or doctorate from an accredited school, have two years of supervised full-time or 3,000 hours of part-time practice experience, provide three professional references, and successfully pass the ACSW examination. NASW membership is required for admission to and continued participation in the academy. Exceptions to these requirements are sometimes made under certain specific circumstances.

acceptance: Recognition of an individual's positive worth as a human being without necessarily condoning the individual's actions. It is considered one of the fundamental elements in the social worker's helping *relationship.*

accessibility of service: For people in need, the relative opportunity of obtaining relevant services. For example, social agencies with greater accessibility are located near their natural clientele; are open at convenient hours; maintain shorter waiting lists; have affordable charges; and have personnel, resources, settings, and policies that make clients feel welcome. Also, appropriate ramps and doors to permit entrance by handicapped persons are essential to an agency's accessibility.

access provision: The actions and procedures of a social program or service provider organization to ensure that its services are available to its target clientele. Three of these procedures are (1) educating the public about the existence of the service, (2) establishing clear and convenient referral procedures, and (3) obtaining legal or *ombudsman* services to overcome obstacles to getting the service.

accident prone: A term applied to individuals who tend to become injured because of supposedly chance occurrences. Being accident prone is thought to be the result of personality factors.

accommodation: A term that has three different meanings to social workers: (1) in *community organization,* the ability of one group to modify aspects of its culture to deal better with other groups or aspects of the environment; (2) in health care and work with the aging, a property of visual perception in which the lens of the eye is able to change its shape to permit focusing on objects at difference distances from the observer; (3) in developmental and *Piagetian theory,* an individual's growing ability to modify current thought structure to deal with new or newly perceived features of the environment.

accountability: The state of being answerable to the community, to consumers of a product or service, or to supervisory groups such as *boards of directors*; also, a profession's obligation to reveal clearly what its functions and methods are and to provide assurances to clients that its practitioners meet specific standards of competence. See also *quality assurance.*

accreditation: The acknowledgment and verification that an organization (such as an educational institution, social agency, or care facility) fulfills explicit specified standards. For example, schools of social work in the United States are evaluated periodically by the *Council on Social Work Education (CSWE)* and certified for accreditation if they meet CSWE standards.

accrual accounting: In social service administration and management, an alternative to the cash accounting system. Each expenditure is recorded and considered a liability when the obligation is established rather than when the cash has been disbursed. Each item of revenue is recorded and considered an asset when the obligation has been incurred rather than when the actual cash has been received.

acculturation: The adoption, by one cultural group or individual, of the culture of another; also, the process of conditioning an individual or group to the social patterns, behaviors, values, and mores of others.

acting out: Expressing strong emotions through overt behavior rather than words; when an individual's outward response to inner feelings cannot be revealed directly, the behavior is often destructive or maladaptive.

ACTION: The federal government program established in 1971 as an umbrella organization that includes the *Peace Corps, VISTA,* and *Foster Grandparents* programs and the Office of Volunteer Liaison.

action research: In *social planning* and *community organization,* the linking of the data-gathering process with the development of a program designed to alleviate the problem that has been identified. *Mobilization for Youth* is one example.

action system: The people and resources in the community with whom the social worker deals in order to achieve desired changes. For example, the action system for a client who is being evicted might include the other residents of the apartment building, local city housing officials, and the newspaper reporters contacted by a worker in an effort to change a landlord's policies.

action theory: The group of concepts used by social scientists to understand social and personality systems by analyzing "acts" and the individuals who perform them, called "actors." In assessing an act, the investigator considers the actor's values and goals in carrying out the act, as well as overt behaviors. Action theory differs from classical *behaviorism* in that it empha-

sizes the value-motivated behavior of individuals and the subjective meanings attached to an action. Behavior is seen as occurring within culturally defined situations and relationships and includes the actor's internalized values and expectations of the reactions of others.

action therapy: Treatment procedures and intervention strategies based on direct alterations of behaviors or of obstacles to change. Such therapies include *behavior modification,* some *cognitive therapy* methods, and *experiential therapies.* The term "action therapy" is often used to make a distinction from so-called "informational therapies," which are oriented toward helping clients gain insight and other forms of self-awareness that foster changes indirectly.

activism: Planned behavior designed to achieve social or political objectives through such activities as *consciousness-raising,* developing *coalitions,* leading *voter registration drives* and political campaigns, producing propaganda and publicity, and taking other actions to influence social change.

activist role: In social work, a rejection of the so-called objective, neutral, or passive stance in favor of taking specific actions in behalf of the *client system.* These actions may include overt *side-taking,* making specific recommendations to clients, leading campaigns to change social institutions, or exerting an influence on client value orientations.

activity group: A form of group involvement, which may or may not have a specifically designed therapeutic purpose, in which the participants work on programs of mutual interest. The members engage in activities as diverse as cooking, folksinging, carpentry, or crafts. Historically, activity groups were prevalent in early *social group work,* especially in *settlement houses* and *youth service centers.* Their primary orientation was not therapeutic per se, but as a means for learning *social skills,* democratic decision making, and developing effective relationship capacities. More recently, activity groups are found in nursing homes, mental hospitals, and recreation centers.

acute: A term pertaining to intense conditions or disturbances of relatively short duration. Mental disorders lasting under six months are often considered to be acute, and those lasting more than six months are considered chronic.

acute care: A set of health, personal, or social services delivered to individuals who require short-term assistance. Such care is usually provided in hospitals or community social agencies where the extended treatment that exists in *long-term care* is not expected.

adaptation: The active efforts of individuals and species over their life spans to achieve *goodness of fit* with their environment in order to survive, develop, and fulfill their reproductive functions. According to Carel B. Germain *(Social Work Practice: People and Environments,* New York, Columbia University Press, 1979), adaptation is also a reciprocal process between the individual and the environment, often involving changing the environment or being changed by it. Social workers oriented to *systems theories* consider that helping people move through stressful life transitions by strengthening or supporting their adaptive capacities is a central part of their intervention strategy.

adaptedness: The degree to which an individual, group, or social system is able to adjust to changes in the system or the environment.

addiction: Physiological dependence on a chemical that results in *tolerance* and in *withdrawal symptoms* when the substance is unavailable. Addictive substances include alcohol, tobacco, *narcotics,* and many sedative drugs. Most professionals now use the term *substance dependence.*

ad hoc coalition: A group of people sharing a mutual interest or problem who form a temporary alliance to address their concern. The group dissolves when the goal is reached or the members no longer share the concern.

adhocracy: A type of administrative organization characterized by minimization of personnel hierarchies, theoretically in order to achieve greater program flexibility; in social agencies, an alternative to *bureaucracy.*

adjudication: A court decision and the process of reaching that decision through a legal hearing or trial.

adjustment: An individual's activities to satisfy a need or overcome an obstacle in order to return to a harmonious fit with the environment. These activities may become habitual responses. Successful adjustment results in *adaptation;* unsuccessful adaptation is called *maladjustment.*

adjustment disorder: A maladaptive pattern of behaviors that occurs in a individual within approximately three months of experiencing some psychosocial *stress.* The disturbance is more serious than the normal or expected reactions to stressors and may result in impaired social functioning. Eventually, the symptoms usually cease or decrease when the stressors are eliminated or the individual reaches a new level of adaptation.

Administration for Children, Youth, and Families (ACYF): The federal organization within the *Office of Human Development Services* of the U.S. *Department of Health and Human Services*

(HHS). ACYF facilitates programs that provide social services to families, including *day care, adoption,* and *foster placement* for children, particularly those with special needs.

Administration for Native Americans: The organization within the *Office of Human Development Services* of the U.S. *Department of Health and Human Services (HHS)* whose responsibilities are to assure that American Indians and Alaska Natives have the same access to the nation's health and welfare provisions as do all other Americans and that their unique needs are addressed. The functions of the Administration for Native Americans are different from but compatible with those of the *Bureau of Indian Affairs* with the U.S. Department of the Interior.

administration in social work: The coordinated totality of activities in a social welfare organization that is necessary for transforming policies into services; also, a method of practice used to plan, assign, coordinate, evaluate, and mediate the interdependent tasks, functions, personnel, and activities that are called upon to achieve specified organizational goals. Social workers tend to use the term "administration" to refer to a cooperative, relatively democratic process of mutuality in not-for-profit organizations and the term *management* to refer to control, direction, and authoritarianism in for-profit organizations, even though the two terms are essentially synonymous.

Administration on Aging: The organization within the *Office of Human Development Services* of the U.S. *Department of Health and Human Services (HHS)* that oversees and facilitates the nation's programs for the elderly. The organization monitors the overall condition of aged Americans, facilitates research, helps develop legislation, disseminates relevant information, and coordinates programs designed to foster the well-being of elderly Americans.

admissions: In a social agency or health care facility, the department or administrative unit that implements the procedures for bringing the client or patient under the care of the organization's system.

admissions procedures: The explicit rules and modes of action for bringing an individual under the care of an organization, social agency, or health care facility. Such procedures often include getting consent from the client (or those responsible for the client) to provide the appropriate care, obtaining pertinent background information about the client from a variety of sources (that is, interviews with the client or client's family, medical records, social histories, and medical and psychological tests), contracting with the client or third parties to provide financing for the care, advising the client about when to go to the appropriate place, and coordinating the initial information exchanges between the client and those concerned about the client. Admissions procedures often include criteria for screening in or screening out applicants for the service.

adolescence: The life-cycle period between childhood and adulthood, beginning at puberty and concluding with young adulthood.

adoption: Taking a person, usually an infant or child, into one's home and treating him or her as though born into the family. A legal as well as a *child welfare* function and process, it includes changes in court records to show the legal transfer of the individual from the birth parents to the adopting parents. Adoption gives the individual the same rights of inheritance as other children and the adoptive parents the same responsibilities and rights of control as other parents. See also *subsidized adoption.*

adult: A fully grown individual who has reached the legal age of maturity; in most states this age is 18.

adult day care: Programs that provide personal, social, and homemaker services to adults who are unable to care for themselves when their primary guardians are unavailable. Those most likely to require such care are physically and mentally handicapped people whose caregivers must be away every day for extended time periods. Facilities providing such care may include private homes, nursing homes, and other institutions.

adult development: Normal changes that occur in the individual from the age of maturity to death. These include the physical, cognitive, social, emotional, and personality changes that occur after adolescence.

adult education: The process—with people who are beyond the age of general public education—of acquiring and imparting knowledge, skills, and values. Adult education programs have been used to eliminate illiteracy, improve vocational and economic opportunities, and enhance human potential. The Adult Education Association of the United States sponsors research, issues publications, and maintains standards for those who provide such services.

adult foster care: Programs in which adults who are unable to care for themselves because of handicaps or health problems—and who have no suitable family members to provide the care they need—are placed with other families on a relatively permanent basis. Usually these families are selected and monitored by workers from relevant public agencies and are paid for providing the care.

adulthood: The life cycle stage in human development that begins at maturity (age 18 in most states) and ends at death. Social scientists often divide adulthood into several periods, such as "early adulthood" (18 to 44), "middle adulthood" (45 to 64), and "late adulthood" (65 to death).

adult protective services: Human services—often including social, medical, legal, residential, and custodial care—that may be provided for adults who are unable to provide such care for themselves or who have no *significant others* who might provide it. Such persons are often incapable of acting judiciously in their own behalf and are thus vulnerable to being harmed by or to inflicting harm on others. In such situations, and typically after a legal decision has been made, the social agency or other care facility provides the relevant service until it is no longer deemed necessary. The 1975 *Title XX* legislation mandated that adult protective services be provided without regard to a person's financial or residency eligibility.

adversarial process: A procedure for reaching decisions by hearing and evaluating the presentation of opposing viewpoints. The adversarial process is most notably seen in courts of law, where opposing attorneys present evidence and arguments in support of their respective views or clients.

advice giving: A type of social work intervention in which the worker helps the client to recognize and understand the existence of a problem or goal and to consider the various responses that might be made to deal with it. The worker then recommends actions that are considered to be the best way to accomplish the objectives.

advisory board: A committee that provides needed information, expert opinion, and recommendations about how to achieve an organization's goals or how to do so according to some predetermined criteria. Members of the advisory board are consulted as a group or as individuals for their expertise. Members may be elected, hired, or serve as volunteers and may or may not be the same as the organization's *board of directors.*

advocacy: The act of directly representing or defending others; in social work, championing the rights of individuals or communities through direct intervention or through *empowerment.* According to the *NASW Code of Ethics*, it is a basic obligation to the profession and its members.

AFDC: See *Aid to Families with Dependent Children (AFDC).*

AFDC-UP: See *Unemployed Parent Program of (AFDC-UP).*

affect: An individual's expression of mood, temperament, and feelings; an individual's overt emotional state.

affective congruency: Feelings that are consistent with the feelings most other people have about the same thing. For example, a social worker who is distressed at seeing an abused child has affective congruency with most other people.

affective disorders: Emotional disturbances characterized primarily by chronic or episodic changes of mood, such as *depression, euphoria,* or *mania.* In *DSM-III* these disturbances are listed under *major affective disorders* and include such illnesses as *major depression, bipolar disorder,* and *cyclothymic disorder.*

affirmative action: Positive steps taken by an organization to remedy imbalances in minority employment, promotions, and other opportunities; also, measures designed to change the ratio of minority to nonminority employees in an organization.

AFGE: See *American Federation of Government Employees (AFGE).*

AFL-CIO: See *American Federation of Labor–Congress of Industrial Organizations (AFL-CIO).*

Afro-American: A term used by some people in referring to black citizens of the United States.

AFSCME: See *American Federation of State, County, and Municipal Employees (AFSCME).*

aftercare: A term pertaining to the continuing treatment, physical maintenance, and social support of formerly hospitalized or institutionalized clients during extended convalescence or social transition back to the community.

aged: Very old. In the United States, this term is generally appied to people who have reached 60 or 65. Developmental psychologists identify three groups who make up the aged population as the "young old" (60–64), the "middle old" (65–74), and the "old old" (over 74).

ageism: Stereotyping and generalizing about people because of their age; commonly, a form of discrimination against the elderly.

agency: See *social agency.*

Agency for International Development (AID): The U.S. government program created in 1961 by a consolidation of other international relief organizations to administer and coordinate economic and social welfare assistance to other nations.

Agent Orange: A herbicide used most notably in the Vietnam War to defoliate areas where enemy troops were thought to be hiding. Some veterans have claimed that their exposure to Agent Orange resulted in their subsequent contracting of various diseases, including cancer.

age segregation: Isolating people from one another based on their ages. This may occur as a result of *ageism,* personal preferences, social convenience, or the necessity of providing different services to people with different needs and lifestyles. Examples occur in a *gray ghetto,* in public elementary schools, and in mandatory retirement programs. When a community or society discourages this type of segregation it is seeking a high degree of age integration.

aggression: Behavior characterized by forceful contact and communication with other people. Human aggression is most directly observable in such expressions as verbal or physical attacks and indirectly through competition, athletic endeavors, and similar activities. Aggression may be appropriate and used for self-defense or self-enhancement, or it may be destructive to oneself and others. Some social scientists use the term "aggression" to refer only to harmful behaviors and the term "assertiveness" for behavior that is not intended to harm others.

agitator: In community organization, a role in which an individual or group confronts and challenges existing social structures by such means as publicity, public debate, *voter registration drives,* and organizing active and *passive resistance* campaigns. The goal of the agitator is usually to create new institutions or to change the ways in which established ones operate.

agoraphobia: An irrational and persistent fear of being in unfamiliar places or of leaving one's home. Most people with this disorder make special efforts to avoid crowded rooms, public transportation facilities, tunnels, and other environments from which escape seems difficult and where help is unavailable. Agoraphobia is the most pervasive and among the most severe of the *phobic disorders.*

AICP: See *Association for Improving the Condition of the Poor (AICP).*

AID: See *Agency for International Development (AID).*

AIDS: Acquired Immune Deficiency Syndrome, a viral disease that prevents the body's immune system from working and is almost always fatal. The AIDS virus, HTLV-III (Human T-Cell Lymphotropic Virus), is transmitted through exchanges of body fluids such as infected blood or semen or occasionally from mother's milk to infants. People with AIDS become susceptible to a variety of illnesses such as a rare form of pneumonia or cancer of the blood vessel walls.

Although most victims have been homosexual and bisexual men with multiple sex partners (70 percent) or abusers of intravenous drugs (17 percent), men and women who engage in intercourse with AIDS carriers or who receive infected blood transmitted through needles (as in recreational drug use or blood transfusions) are also at risk. No cases have been found in which AIDS has been transmitted by casual contact with an AIDS patient or person in the high risk groups. Once an individual has been infected with the AIDS virus, the incubation period, before any symptoms appear, may be five years or more.

Aid to Families with Dependent Children (AFDC): A *public assistance* program, originating in the *Social Security Act* of 1935, funded by the federal and state governments to provide financial aid for needy children who are deprived of parental support because of death, incapacity, or absence. AFDC is administered on the state and local levels, usually through county departments of public welfare (or human or social services). At the national level it is administered by the *Family Services Administration (FSA)* of the U.S. *Department of Health and Human Services (HHS)*. Eligibility is determined on the individualized basis of need compared to assets (that is, a *means test*). Many states provide benefits when the father is home but unemployed. See also *Unemployed Parent Program of AFDC (AFDC-UP)*.

Aid to the Blind (AB): A *categorical program* for the needy blind, originating in the *Social Security Act* of 1935. The program was administered at the state and local levels before 1972, when it was consolidated, with *Old Age Assistance (OAA)* and *Aid to the Permanently and Totally Disabled (APTD)* programs, into the *Supplemental Security Income (SSI)* program.

Aid to the Permanently and Totally Disabled (APTD): A program that was established by a 1950 amendment to the *Social Security Act* to provide financial assistance to needy people with serious and permanent physical or mental handicaps. In 1972, with passage of the federal *Supplemental Security Income (SSI)* program, the program was consolidated with the *Old Age Assistance (OAA)* and *Aid to the Blind (AB)* programs.

Al-Anon: A voluntary *self-help organization* comprising primarily the relatives of alcoholics who meet regularly to give each other mutual support and to discuss ways to help solve common problems. Al-Anon is a national organization with chapters in most communities in the United States.

Alaska Natives: The ethnic-racial group of American citizens, many of whom are commonly known as Eskimos and Aleuts, whose ancestors lived in the area now known as Alaska before Europeans explored and settled the Western Hemisphere.

alcohol abuse: Consumption of alcohol in such a way as to harm or endanger the well-being of the user or those with whom the user comes in contact. Such consumption often leads the abuser to cause accidents, become physically assaultive and less productive, or to deteriorate physically. Alcohol abuse is the nation's and the world's greatest drug problem.

Alcohol, Drug Abuse, and Mental Health Administration (ADAMHA): The federal organization within the U.S. *Public Health Service* that coordinates the nation's effort to reduce and eliminate health problems caused by abuse of drugs and alcohol and to improve people's mental health.

Alcoholics Anonymous (AA): A voluntary *self-help organization* comprising people who have experienced problems related to alcohol consumption. Founded in 1935 by two alcoholics, the organization functions through 17,000 local groups. None of the local groups have formal officers, consitutions, or dues, and all are open to anyone with a drinking problem.

alcoholism: Physical or psychological dependence on the consumption of alcohol; can lead to social, mental, or physical impairment.

alien: One who resides in a country but is not a citizen or national of that country. See also *undocumented alien*.

alienation: The feeling of apartness or strangeness experienced in cultural or social settings that seem unacceptable or unpredictable.

Alien Labor Certification Division: A division of the U.S. Department of Labor that authorizes workers from foreign nations to remain in the United States for a specified time to help meet labor needs. See also *green card*.

alimony: Money paid by one ex-spouse, in accordance with legal requirements, to the other to provide for separate maintenance. Alimony payments are most commonly made by ex-husbands to their former wives, although increasingly, ex-wives are required to make such payments to their former husbands. Alimony is distinct from the obligation of child support payments. See also *palimony*.

almshouse: A home for the poor; a form of *indoor relief*, prevalent before the twentieth century, in which shelters funded by philanthropists were provided for destitute families and individuals. In recent decades, almshouses have largely been replaced by *outdoor relief* programs in which the needy are provided with money, goods, and services while living in their own homes. See also *workhouse.*

altruism: Unselfish regard for the well-being of others, accompanied by motivation to give money, goods, services, or companionship.

Alzheimer's disease: An organic mental disease characterized by confusion, forgetfulness, impaired ability to learn, disorientation, and *dementia,* thought to be the result of diffuse brain atrophy, especially in the frontal lobes.

ambivalence: Contradictory emotions, such as love and hate, that occur simultaneously within an individual. In its extreme form it is related to indecisiveness and rapidly shifting emotional attitudes toward someone or some idea.

ambulatory care: Medical treatment and health care in outpatient clinics, dispensaries, and physicians' offices; noninstitutional health care.

American Association for Marriage and Family Therapy (AAMFT): An inter-disciplinary professional association founded in 1942 (as the American Association of Marriage Counselors). Its functions and goals include the professional development of its members through conferences, training programs, and publications and the enhancement of the well-being of families and couples in America.

American Association for Organizing Family Social Work: See *Family Service America (FSA).*

American Association of Group Workers (AAGW): An organization of professional social workers who specialized in working with small groups. AAGW was formed in 1936 and discontinued as an autonomous entity in 1955 when it merged into the then newly created *National Association of Social Workers (NASW).*

American Association of Hospital Social Workers (AAHSW): The organization, established in 1918, comprising social workers employed in medical facilities and hospital social service departments. In 1934 it was renamed the American Association of Medical Social Workers (AAMSW) to reflect its growing membership of workers employed in nonhospital medical facilities. In 1955 it merged with six other professional groups to form the *National Association of Social Workers (NASW).*

American Association of Industrial Social Workers (AAISW): The organization of professional social workers who provide occupational social work services through employment with business organizations or through *employee assistance programs (EAPs).* The association develops and maintains standards of quality assurance and encourages more effective utilization of industrial social workers.

American Association of Medical Social Workers (AAMSW): See *American Association of Hospital Social Workers (AAMSW).*

American Association of Psychiatric Social Workers (AAPSW): The professional membership association, founded in 1926, comprising social workers who specialized in clinical work with the mentally ill or who served in mental health settings. AAPSW merged with six other social work membership organizations in 1955 to form the *National Association of Social Workers (NASW).*

American Association of Retired Persons (AARP): The largest U.S. senior citizens' group, founded in 1958 to provide social, economic, and recreational services to persons over 50 (retired or not).

American Association of Schools of Social Work (AASSW): (1) The organization founded in 1985 to enhance the quality and focus of social work education and the educational institutions that provide it. Formerly an organization of deans of social work schools, the association comprises deans, faculty, and other concerned professionals. (2) An earlier organization by the same name, established in 1919, was the forerunner of the *Council on Social Work Education (CSWE).*

American Association of Sex Educators, Counselors, and Therapists (AASECT): The multidisciplinary professional organization founded in 1967 that advocates for greater public knowledge about and healthy expressions of human sexuality. The association, which publishes the *Journal of Sex Education and Therapy,* educates the general public and professionals about aspects of sexuality and treatment of its problems. It also defines and maintains standards for professionals who provide sex education in public schools, churches, and private institutions. Its major focus is on establishing standards for therapists and counselors who treat sexual dysfunctions and help people achieve sexual fulfillment.

American Association of Social Workers (AASW): A professional membership organization of social workers, founded in 1921 and incorporated into the *National Association of Social Workers (NASW)* in 1955.

American Association of State Social Work Boards (AASWB): An organization comprising social workers who serve as members of the boards of state licensing bodies in those states that have legal regulation for social work. In most such states, board membership is achieved by gubernatorial appointment. This association permits those who serve on such boards to communicate with their counterparts in other states about such matters as developing competency tests, continuing education requirements, recertification policies, reciprocity, and other mutual concerns.

American Civil Liberties Union (ACLU): A voluntary citizens' organization formed in 1920 and dedicated to the restraint of governmental interference with individuals' personal freedom.

American Family Therapy Association (AFTA): A professional association whose members treat couples and families who are experiencing relationship problems. AFTA helps maintain standards pertaining to the education, skills, and values of members who work with families.

American Federation of Government Employees (AFGE): A labor organization founded in 1932, with local chapters throughout the nation and headquartered in Washington, D.C., whose members are employed by the government of the United States. Many AFGE members are social workers employed by the federal government as administrators, researchers, supervisors, and providers of direct social services.

American Federation of Labor–Congress of Industrial Organizations (AFL-CIO): The oldest and largest labor union organization in the United States. AFL was founded in 1886 to help assure workers of fairer and more stable working conditions. In 1935, several AFL unions —unhappy with the emphasis on skilled craftsmen—broke away and formed the CIO to give greater voice to industrial workers. The two groups merged in 1955 and now include nearly 100 distinct unions, including AFGE and AFSCME, with which many social workers are affiliated.

American Federation of State, County, and Municipal Employees (AFSCME): A labor organization founded in 1936, with headquarters in Washington, D.C., and chapters throughout the nation, whose members are employed by nonfederal governments. Many of its members include state and county public assistance workers, child welfare workers, and other social service personnel. Other membership groups include police personnel, firefighters, and public agency administrators.

American Hospital Association (AHA): An organization founded in 1899, comprising more than 5,500 hospitals and other patient care institutions in the United States. AHA establishes and sanctions standards and guidelines to maintain *quality assurance.* One of its many affiliated membership groups is the *Society for Hospital Social Work Directors (SHSWD).*

American Indian Movement (AIM): A *civil rights* organization, founded in 1968 and headquartered in Minneapolis, Minnesota, whose purposes include encouraging self-determination among American Indians and gaining recognition of American Indian treaty rights. AIM also conducts research, maintains historical archives, and sponsors educational programs.

American Indians: Also known as *Native Americans,* the ethnic-racial-cultural groups of American citizens whose ancestors lived in the Western Hemisphere before its exploration and settlement by Europeans.

American Public Welfare Association (APWA): A voluntary organization of individuals and social agencies interested in maintaining effective administration and improved delivery of publicly funded human services. Founded in 1930, it includes more than 1,200 local, state, and federal public welfare organizations.

amnesia: Inability to recall some or all past experience, due to emotional or organic factors or combinations of both. Retrograde amnesia is the inability to recall events occurring before a specific time. Anterograde amnesia is the inability to recall events occurring after a specific time, usually after the amnesia itself has started.

amnesty: A pardon granted to a person or members of a group that excuses them for committing offenses that were illegal. For example, Vietnam draft evaders were subsequently granted presidential amnesty.

amniocentesis: A test to determine, by extracting and examining a sample of the amniotic fluid, the presence of some specific defect in the developing fetus. See also *chorionic villi sampling (CVS).*

amphetamine: A drug that stimulates the cerebral cortex, tends to increase one's mental alertness temporarily, produces a sense of *euphoria* and well-being, and reduces fatigue; sometimes used clinically by physicians in treating children's *hyperkinesis* and in weight control. Popularly known as "bennies," *uppers,* and *speed,* they are addictive and usually require increasingly large doses as *tolerance* develops. *Addiction* can and frequently does result in psychosis or death from overexhaustion or cardiac arrest.

anaclitic: A term for a form of dependency, such as that experienced by an infant for its caregiver. A typical characteristic of young children, it indicates pathology when excessive in adults. It is most commonly seen as a form of depression that one experiences when fearing the possible loss of an important source of nurturance.

anal personality: A descriptive term from *psychoanalytic theory*, referring to an individual who is excessively fastidious, miserly, rigid, and compulsively obsessed with orderliness; also known as "anal character."

anal phase: The second stage in *psychosexual development theory*, which occurs between the ages of 2 and 3. During this stage of personality development the child becomes oriented to the functions of the anus and learns to have more control over the environment by giving or withholding feces.

analysand: One who is being psychoanalyzed.

analysis: A systematic consideration of anything in its respective parts and the relationship of those parts to one another. The term is commonly used to indicate *psychoanalysis.*

analysis of variance (ANOVA): A statistical procedure commonly used in social work research for determining the extent to which two or more groups differ significantly when one is exposed to a *dependent variable.*

analyst: See *psychoanalyst.*

anarchism: A doctrine and social movement that espouses the abolition of formal government and freedom from controls on individual actions.

andragogy: The practice of helping adults (rather than children, to whom the term "pedagogy" applies) to learn. The concept is important in social work education, which usually seeks to use the "adult learner model" in teaching social work students. The model recognizes adult learners as being responsible, self-directing, and autonomous and as people who have already accumulated many life experiences that can usefully be shared with fellow students. It also views adult learning as being more effective when students experience immediate and direct application of their developing problem-solving skills.

androgyny: A sex role orientation in which mannerisms, appearance, and behaviors that are usually considered either male or female are both incorporated into one's behavioral repertoire.

anemia: A disorder in which the blood is deficient in red cells or hemoglobin. The most apparent initial symptom is a feeling of tiredness resulting from the blood's inability to transport enough oxygen through the body.

angel dust: A slang term for the psychedelic or hallucinogenic drug *PCP (phencyclidine).*

anger: A common and usually normal emotion that occurs in response to an individual's perception of being threatened or harmed. Its manifestations often include irritability, physical or verbal attacks, increased heart rate and respiratory activity, and rage and negativism. Anger may be continuous or intermittent, directed inward or outward, intense or mild, and, according to some psychologists, conscious or unconscious. It is considered maladaptive or pathological when it is relatively continuous or occurs even when there is no immediate source of threat.

angina pectoris: Sharp pains in the chest that occur when the heart muscle receives insufficient blood. Caused by sudden closure of the coronary arteries, often brought on by excitement or physical exertion, angina is treated with drugs that dilate the blood vessels.

anhedonia: Lacking the full capacity to experience pleasure in situations that seem pleasurable to others. It is a symptom frequently seen in clients with *depression.*

anomie: Normlessness; the elimination or reduction of social and personal *values, mores, norms,* and codes of conduct. Anomie frequently occurs in rapidly changing societies and communities or groups subject to catastrophic stress. In such circumstances individuals often become alienated, apathetic, and devoid of previously valued goals.

anorexia nervosa: An *eating disorder* most often encountered in girls and young women whose extended refusal to eat leads to severe weight loss, malnutrition, and cessation of menstruation. The usual medical criteria for this diagnosis include the loss of one-fourth or more of one's body weight. This life-threatening condition is thought to be related to a disturbed body image and an exaggerated fear of becoming obese.

Antabuse: A drug that—when it is in the bloodstream of an individual who ingests alcohol—induces nausea. It is used to facilitate *aversion therapy* in the treatment of *alcoholism.*

antecedent: In *behavior modification* and *social learning theory,* an event (*stimulus*) that precedes a behavior (*response*) and is thought to influence it.

anterograde amnesia: See *amnesia.*

Anti-Defamation League of B'nai B'rith: A *civil rights* organization founded in 1913, the Anti-Defamation League works to end anti-Semitism, improve intergroup relations, and promote the democratic process. The league is headquartered in New York City.

antidepressant medication: *Psychotropic drugs* used by psychiatrists and other physicians to help their patients achieve relief from the symptoms of *depression.* Some of the major drugs of this type are known by the trade names Elavil, Norpramin, Pertofrane, Adapin, Sinequan, Imavate,

Janimine, Tofranil, Aventyl, Vivactil, Parnate, Marplan, and Nardil. Doctors point out to their patients that relief through antidepressant medication is not usually expected until several days after it has been taken regularly according to prescription.

antipoverty programs: The generic term for public and private associations and activities devoted to the eradication of poverty. As well as direct help to poor individuals, such activities include research into the causes and consequences of poverty and actions that may eliminate economic inequality and instability.

antipsychotic medication: The group of *psychotropic drugs* used by physicians to control certain symptoms seen in *schizophrenia* and other psychoses. These drugs include Compazine, Haldol, Mellaril, Navane, Prolixin, Serentil, Stelazine, Thorazine, and Trilafon.

antisocial behavior: A pattern of actions that results in an individual's isolation from other people or frequent conflict with others and with social institutions.

antisocial personality: A maladaptive pattern of relating to others characterized by irresponsibility, inability to feel guilt or remorse for actions that harm others, frequent conflicts with people and social institutions, the tendency to blame others and not to learn from mistakes, low frustration tolerance, and other behaviors that indicate a deficiency in *socialization*. This is one of the more common of the *personality disorders*. The term replaces the less precise labels *psychopathic personality, psychopath,* and *sociopath.*

anxiety: A feeling of uneasiness, tension, and sense of imminent danger. When such a feeling occurs within a person with no specific cause in the environment, it is known as *free-floating anxiety.* When it recurs frequently and interferes with effective living or a sense of well-being or is otherwise maladaptive, it is known as *anxiety disorder.*

anxiety disorder: A chronic or recurring state of tension, worry, fear, and uneasiness arising from unknown or unrecognized perceptions of danger or conflict. The major types of anxiety disorders include *generalized anxiety disorder, obsessive-compulsive disorder, posttraumatic stress disorder, agoraphobia,* and *social phobia.*

anxiety hysteria: A psychoanalytic term referring to psychoneurosis in which there are intense anxiety-induced dramatic behavior, *free-floating anxiety,* and phobias. Analytically oriented therapists consider this condition to be the result of repressed sexual conflict.

anxiety neurosis: See *generalized anxiety disorder.*

apartheid: An official policy in the Republic of South Africa separating racial groups and permitting discrimination against nonwhites.

Apgar rating: A score, devised by Dr. Virginia Apgar in 1954, to indicate the relative health of a baby at birth. This measure is now commonly used in neonatal care facilities. Five factors are each assigned the values 0, 1, or 2, so that a baby in ideal health would achieve an Apgar rating of 10. The criteria are heart rate (absent = 0, slow or irregular = 1, rapid = 2), respiratory effort (absent = 0, slow or irregular = 1, good, crying = 2), reflex irritability (absent = 0, grimace = 1, cough, sneeze = 2), color (blue = 0, body pink, extremities blue = 1, completely pink = 2), and muscle tone (flaccid = 0, weak = 1, strong = 2).

aphasia: The inability to use previously possessed language skills. Specific types of aphasia may include loss of ability to utter words, loss of ability to understand written or spoken words, inability to put words and phrases together properly, or various combinations of these.

aphonia: Loss of ability to speak normally as a result of physiological or emotional disorders.

APM: Annual Program Meeting, the name social work educators use to refer to the *Council on Social Work Education (CSWE)*–sponsored conference that meets in a different U.S. city every March.

apnea: A disturbance in the respiratory mechanism, usually resulting in temporary cessation of breathing. In some infants the disturbance may be related to crib death. See also *sudden infant death syndrome (SIDS).*

appeal: In the legal justice system, a resort to a higher (appellate) court in order to cause a judicial decision to be reviewed and possibly reversed or a case to be retried.

applied research: Systematic study in which the potential findings are to be used to solve immediate problems.

appointment: The designation of a specified period of time during which the social worker or other professional and the client have agreed to meet. Clinical social workers typically maintain calendars to list their appointments for each day. These appointments commonly last 50 minutes or one hour for individuals and couples, 90 to 120 minutes for groups, and longer for home visits.

apprenticing: Putting one person under the care and tutelage of another, ostensibly for the purpose of learning certain skills. This process is historically significant in child welfare in that it was widely practiced in the United States in the eighteenth and nineteenth centuries as a way to care for homeless youth. As such, it was a major precedent for the subsequent system of *foster care.*

appropriation: An allocation of funds, usually made by a government legislative body, to an organization or program empowered by that governmental body to accomplish a specific goal.

APTD: See *Aid to the Permanently and Totally Disabled (APTD).*

arbitration: A decision-making mechanism called for when two or more opposing factions cannot achieve consensus or continue working toward complementary goals. The disputing parties agree to appoint a neutral person and to abide by that person's judgment.

arousal: A state of becoming excited into action. Social workers in community organization activities sometimes seek to provoke arousal in client groups by making them aware of a relevant problem and its potential solution. In human sexuality, the term refers to physiological and psychological changes in response to stimulation and leading to preparation for sexual intercourse. Sexologists William Masters and Virginia Johnson described arousal as occurring primarily in the first of the four stages of sexual response (excitement, plateau, orgasm, and resolution). They indicated that arousal begins in the excitement phase, in which vasocongestion (swelling of the blood vessels) commences, the heart and pulse rates increase, and the skin becomes flushed.

arteriosclerosis: Hardening of the arteries, a condition that makes it difficult for the blood to circulate. This can result in *hypertension, stroke,* and brain cell destruction, with consequent loss of memory, confusion, and inattention.

arthritis: Painful inflammation of the joints of the body. Causes include dysfunction of the endocrine glands, nerve impairment, or degeneration due to infections and old age. The major types include rheumatoid arthritis, osteoarthritis, and gout. Arthritis disables more people in the United States than any other disorder.

articulation disorder: A speech problem characterized by the inability to pronounce certain sounds clearly. The individual may have difficulty pronouncing one or more sounds such as *r, sh, th, f, z, l,* or *ch,* often making substitutions for these sounds and giving the impression of "baby talk." The disorder is not caused by mental retardation or physical conditions.

artificial insemination: The joining of sperm and ovum, for the purpose of reproduction, by means other than sexual intercourse. Many women who had been unable to conceive naturally have become pregnant through this process. Using surgical instruments, the physician implants semen taken from the woman's husband, or sometimes from an anonymous donor, into a fallopian tube or into the uterus, where sperm can form a union with the ovum. See also *in vitro fertilization.*

art therapy: The use of paintings, sculpture, and other creative expressions in the treatment of people with emotional problems. Art therapy is often used in *social group work* and in *group psychotherapy.* Often used with institutionalized people or inpatients, it is also considered to be effective with healthy people who wish to share art as a means of enhancing personal growth and development. In some forms of art therapy, clients create their own works and discuss the results with the therapist or with other members of an art therapy group. In other forms, the clients are exposed to works of art by a variety of artists and asked to assess how the works affect their own feelings and understandings. See also *bibliotherapy.*

Asian Americans: Residents or citizens of the United States whose racial background and sometimes ethnic identification is with the peoples of Pacific-Asian areas, including Chinese, Japanese, Vietnamese, Koreans, Filipinos, and others.

Asian American Social Workers (AASW): The national professional association established in California in 1968 by social workers of Pacific-Asian background. It sought to develop and promote social welfare programs that benefit Asian Americans and to protect their rights, as well as to enhance its members' professional development.

assertiveness: See *aggression.*

assertiveness training: A program designed to teach individuals to express their feelings, needs, and demands directly and effectively.

assessment: The process of determining the nature, cause, progression, and prognosis of a problem and the personalities and situations involved therein; the social work function of acquiring an understanding of a problem, what causes it, and what can be changed to minimize or resolve it.

assimilation: The social integration or adoption of one group's *values, norms,* and *folkways* by another group. For example, a group of immigrants may eventually integrate with or adopt the culture of their new society. Also, in *Piagetian theory,* the individual's act of incorporating an aspect of his or her environment into an existing thought structure.

Association for Improving the Condition of the Poor (AICP): An organization founded in New York by Robert Hartley in 1843 to combat poverty primarily through "character-building" activities. Volunteers tried to get poor people to abstain from alcohol, become more self-disciplined, and acquire the work ethic. Many of the methods and goals of AICP were later adopted by some *Charity Organization Societies (COS)*, and by *friendly visitors*.

Association for the Study of Community Organization (ASCO): Organization established in 1946 by social workers specializing in or interested in community organization. In 1955 it was merged into the newly established *National Association of Social Workers (NASW)*.

Association of American Indian Social Workers (AAISW): See *National Indian Social Workers Association (NISWA)*.

Association of Women in Social Work (AWSW): A professional association that advocates equal opportunities, rights, and benefits for female social workers. The association also brings together social workers to consider the special needs and concerns of women social workers and their clients.

asthma: A pulmonary disorder in which the muscles in the walls of the bronchi contract, causing the individual to have difficulty breathing.

asylum: A refuge or sanctuary; also, an institution for the care of people suffering psychiatric disorders, certain physical illnesses, or economic destitution.

atherosclerosis: Artery wall congestion caused by accumulation of fats, cholesterol, and calcium salts and resulting in increased risk of hypertension, impaired circulation, and *stroke*.

at-risk population: Those members of a group who are vulnerable to, or likely to be harmed by, a specific medical, social, or environmental circumstance. For example, overweight people or those who smoke are an at-risk population because they are more likely to have heart attacks or cardiovascular problems. Infants born to women who drank heavily while pregnant constitute a population at risk for birth defects.

atrophy: Wasting away of body tissues.

attachment: An emotional bond between individuals, based on attraction and dependence, which develops during critical periods of life and may disappear when one individual has no further opportunity to relate to the other.

attention deficit disorder: A disorder that occurs in infancy, childhood, or adolescence, characterized by impulsive behavior, inattentiveness, and excessive motor activity. The term "attention deficit disorder" is now used in place of several less accurate and less precise terms, including "hyperactive child syndrome," "minimal brain dysfunction," and "hyperkinetic reaction of childhood." Attention deficit disorder comprises "attention deficit disorder with *hyperactivity*," "attention deficit disorder without hyperactivity," and "attention deficit disorder, residual type."

audit: An inspection of the accounting records of an individual or organization in order to verify their accuracy and completeness. For example, a social agency's records might be audited annually by representatives of those who provide funding.

authoritarian: Pertaining to a system in social organizations and administration characterized by the relative absence of democratic decision making and implementation processes and the requirement of submission to higher-ranking members of the organization. Punishments or sanctions are often imposed on those members of the organization who do not comply, and rewards are given to those who do.

authoritarian management: An administrative style sometimes used in social welfare organizations by leaders who tend to make most of the decisions unilaterally and use their power to demand that the members of the organization accept and support these decisions.

authority: Expertise or power.

autism: A *developmental disorder* in which the individual appears to have little interest in the external world or capacity to relate effectively to people or objects and is presumed to be devoting full attention to inner wishes and sensations. Other symptoms may include deficient social and communication skills, abnormal ways of relating to others, and unusual responses to sensations. This condition is most commonly seen in young children and infants, in whom it is referred to as "infantile autism."

autonomous practice: Professional activity and decision making that takes place in relative independence of social agency auspices, supervision, and organizational requirements. The practitioner sets the standards of performance and self-monitors the work done. This is a relative concept, in that all professions and professional activities are regulated and influenced to some extent by social, ethical, legal, political, and economic forces. Some social workers use this term to indicate *private practice*.

autonomy: An individual's sense of being capable of independent action; ability to provide for one's own needs; also, independence from the control of others.

autonomy versus shame and doubt: The basic conflict found in the second stage of human psychosocial development, according to Erik Erikson, occurring approximately between ages 2 and 4. During this stage the toddler may come to feel more in control of the environment and exhibit growing independence of actions or may be overcome with feelings of guilt if independent actions are inconsistently tolerated by others.

aversion stimulus: In *behavior modification,* an object or situation that the subject identifies as being painful or unpleasant and attempts to avoid whenever possible. See also *social learning theory.*

aversion therapy: A procedure commonly used in *behavior therapy* designed to eliminate a maladaptive behavior, such as overeating or abusing drugs and alcohol, by associating the behavior with some real or imagined *aversion stimulus.*

avoidance: (1) In *behavior modification* procedures, an individual's response that postpones or averts presentation of an aversive event; (2) in *psychodynamic theory,* an ego *defense mechanism* resembling *denial,* involving refusal to face certain situations or objects because they represent unconscious impulses or punishments for those impulses.

avoidant personality disorder: One of the *personality disorders,* in which the individual is hypersensitive to potential rejection, has low self-esteem, is socially withdrawn, and is generally unwilling to enter social relationships unless there is assurance of uncritical acceptance. Avoidant personality disorder is an *Axis II disorder.*

Axis II disorder: A classification of mental disorders in *DSM-III* (the *Diagnostic and Statistical Manual of Mental Disorders*). These disorders are usually considered to be deeply embedded in the individual's psychic apparatus and originate during the formation of the basic personality. Axis II disorders are viewed as belonging to a separate layer or axis of behaviors so deeply embedded that they might be overlooked in assessing an individual regarding other symptoms of psychiatric disorder. In adults and adolescents they consist of twelve specific *personality disorders* including *borderline, avoidant, paranoid, schizoid, histrionic, antisocial, dependent, compulsive, passive-aggressive, schizotypal, narcissistic,* and atypical personality disorders. Axis II disorders of children include developmental disorders of reading, language, articulation, and arithmetic.

B

baby boom generation: The men and women in the United States who were born in the decade immediately following World War II. Demographers indicate that many more than the usual number of births occurred during these years because many people had postponed having children during the war. This "bulge" in the population necessitates many adjustments in social and economic planning as the baby boomers move through the life cycle. When this group reaches retirement age in the years 2010–2020, it is anticipated that the *social security* system will be severely strained.

"bag lady": A term often applied to impoverished, homeless women, many of whom are mentally ill and carry their possessions in shopping bags.

bail: A monetary or other form of security posted by or for someone accused of a crime. The purpose is to ensure that the accused will appear at subsequent legal proceedings, to enable the accused to avoid imprisonment while awaiting trial, and to relieve the authorities of the costs of incarcerating the accused during this period.

barbiturates: Drugs that act as central nervous system depressants. Physicians often use them clinically to facilitate their patients' sleep and to control convulsive disorders. In slang they are known as *downers.*

Barclay Report: The 1980 British government–sponsored study evaluating and delineating the role of social workers in providing social services. The report recommended increased involvement in counseling, social planning, promoting community networks, negotiating, and social advocacy.

bargaining: In community organization and planning, the negotiating of agreements between various factions so that the parties can compromise and make equitable exchanges. A plan to bring together the parties in such negotiations is called a bargaining strategy.

barrio: A neighborhood whose residents are predominantly Hispanic.

basal metabolism: The amount of energy used by an individual at rest.

baseline: The frequency with which a specific behavior or event occurs in a natural state, measured before any attempts are made to influence it.

battered child: A youngster who has been physically abused or injured. The injury is usually inflicted on the child by a parent, other adult *caregiver,* or older sibling and may occur intentionally or impulsively in episodes of uncontrolled anger.

battered spouse: A husband or, more often, a wife who has been physically injured by the other. Battering is a physically violent form of *spouse abuse.*

Batterers Anonymous: A national *self-help organization,* with chapters in most larger communities, whose members (most of whom have been wife abusers) help one another to end abusive behavior. They have regular meetings to provide support and encouragement, and they maintain a "buddy system" and telephone hot lines.

battery: A form of illegal abuse that involves physical force or injury.

bed-wetting: *Enuresis,* the involuntary discharge of urine, usually by a child who had formerly achieved bladder control, during sleep or bed rest.

behavior: Any reaction or response by an individual, including observable activity, measurable physiological changes, cognitive images, fantasies, and emotions. Some scientists consider even subjective experiences to be behaviors.

behavioral assessment: In *behavior modification* and *social learning theory,* the delineation of undesired behavior patterns and their controlling conditions. The description of these patterns is based on direct observation rather than on inference about underlying pathology based on surface cues. Contrast with *psychosocial assessment.*

behavioral family therapy (BFT): The use of *social learning theory* and the therapeutic techniques of *behavior modification* to help families achieve specific goals. The behaviorally oriented family therapist helps the client-family members define their problems clearly in terms of overt actions and develop problem-solving behaviors to which all agree. Homework assignments, quantifying specific actions, and maintaining certain communications activities are frequently part of this form of intervention.

behavioral rehearsal: The technique used by social workers and other helping professionals, especially those with behaviorist orientations, in which the professional suggests or demonstrates desired behavior to a client and then encourages the client, through description, role-playing, and other demonstrations, to behave similarly. With practice, feedback, and repetition of the behavior in the relatively "safe" environment of the worker's office, the client is more likely to be successful in achieving the desired behavior at the appropriate time.

behaviorism: The school of psychology and related sciences, founded by Ivan Pavlov, J. B. Watson, B. F. Skinner, and others, which seeks to explain behavior in terms of observable and measurable responses. Basic tenets of the orientation are that maladaptive behavior patterns are learned and can be unlearned and that introspection, cognition, and the *unconscious* are unscientific hypotheses. Behaviorism has led to theoretical concepts and therapeutic methods such as *behavior modification* and *social learning theory.*

behavior modification: A method of assessing and altering behavior based on the methods of applied behavior analysis, the principles of *operant conditioning, classical conditioning,* and *social learning theory* (for example, *positive reinforcement, extinction,* and *modeling*).

behavior therapy: Application of *behavior modification* principles in clinical settings to assess and alter undesired behaviors such as fears, anxiety, depression, sexual deviations, and other problems, using techniques based on empirical research.

Bender gestalt test: A test used in diagnosing certain psychological and neurological disorders. After the subject has copied several designs, the results are analyzed, usually by a trained psychologist or neurologist, for spatial errors that help locate and determine the type of disturbance.

benefits: (1) Cash benefits, payments in the form of money or redeemable vouchers. (2) In-kind benefits, services or goods, rather than money. In-kind benefits might include food baskets, agricultural surpluses, housing, and personal counseling.

bereavement: The process of reviewing memories of a lost loved one and the adjustment to the deprivation of that loss.

Beveridge Report: A 1942 report, by economist Sir William Beveridge (1879–1963), that proposed a plan providing for "cradle to grave" economic protections. The report formed the basis for much of the current British social security system. An early settlement house leader and social worker, Beveridge served as director of *Toynbee Hall.*

bias: An attitude that can influence feelings, usually resulting in an individual's having positive or negative predispositions about a particular group, individual, idea, or thing; also, in research, a tendency for the results to lean in one or another direction because of improper *sampling,* misuse of statistical or research tools, or other improper methods.

bibliotherapy: The use of literature and poetry in the treatment of people with emotional problems or mental illness. Bibliotherapy is often used in *social group work* and *group therapy* and is reported to be effective with people of all ages, with people in institutions as well as outpatients, and with healthy people who wish to share literature as a means of personal growth and development. See also *art therapy.*

bigamy: The illegal offense of having more than one wife or husband at the same time. Bigamous marriages have no legal validity in any state in the United States.

Big Brothers/Big Sisters of America: Organizations of volunteers who work under professional supervision, usually by social workers, providing individual guidance and companionship to boys and girls deprived of a parent. Big Brothers was founded in 1946, especially to provide role models for fatherless boys. Big Sisters was formed in 1971, primarily to provide role models and positive female images for youngsters. The two groups were merged in 1977.

bimodal: In frequency distributions, two categories whose values occur most frequently. For example, in a city where the delinquency rate peaked every January and July, there would be a bimodal distribution of delinquency.

bioethics: The analysis and study of legal, moral, social, and ethical considerations involving the biological sciences. Issues of particular interest include genetic engineering, *birth control, euthanasia,* cloning, and transferring body parts from one person or animal to another.

biofeedback: A method of training people to modify their own internal physiological processes, such as heart rate, muscle tension, blood pressure, and brain wave activity, through self-monitoring. Usually this is done by using mechanical instruments to provide information about variations in one or more of a subject's physiological processes. The resulting information is displayed to the subject (*feedback*), helping the individual to control these processes even though he or she may be unable to articulate how the learning was achieved.

biogenic: Originating physiologically or biologically rather than psychologically.

biopsy: Removal and examination of body tissue samples to detect the presence of cancer and other diseases.

biopsychosocial: Biological, psychological, and social in nature; a term applied to phenomena that consist of biological, psychological, and social elements, such as stress.

bipolar disorder: A category of mental illnesses in which mood and affect are maladaptive. Formerly known as *manic-depressive illness,* the category may be subcategorized as *manic* type (symptoms often include *hyperactivity, euphoria,* distractibility, pressured speech, and grandiosity), depressed type (symptoms often including deep sadness, apathy, sleep disturbance, poor appetite, low self-esteem, and slowed thinking), and mixed type (frequently alternating patterns of manic and then depressed traits).

birth control: Limiting or preventing reproduction by various means. These include contraceptive (antipregnancy) devices such as condoms, contraceptive pills, diaphragms, intrauterine devices (IUDs), and spermicides. Another type of birth control occurs through the more-or-less permanent surgical sterilizations of men (as in *vasectomy*) or women (as in *tubal ligation*). Among the more common efforts to control conception is "natural family planning," in which there is awareness of the fertility cycle and sexual intercourse occurs only during those times in the cycle believed to be less likely to result in pregnancy. Abstinence from sexual intercourse and *abortion* are other methods some people use to avoid conception and giving birth.

birth-order theories: Hypotheses to explain apparent differences among siblings depending on whether they are oldest, youngest, or middle children. Some theorists suggest that the personalities of first children are influenced by the fact that more is usually expected of them, so they tend to become achievers but also tend to have more feelings of insecurity and failure. Middle children, on the other hand, are often made to feel inferior to their older siblings, so they may try harder to catch up or display traits of inadequacy or anger in interacting with others. Youngest children, according to many of these theorists,

may refine attention-getting skills and narcissistic traits. The research on such hypotheses is still inconclusive and somewhat contradictory.

birthrate: The ratio of the number of births in a given population and period of time to the total population, usually expressed in terms of the number of births per 1,000 or 100,000 of the population.

bisexuality: Erotic attraction to both males and females; also, the coexistence in an individual of homosexuality and heterosexuality.

bivariate analysis: Statistical analysis focusing on the simultaneous relationship between two variables. One example is *cross-tabulation.*

Black Lung program: A federally regulated workers' compensation program for coal miners disabled by tubercular-type illness associated with working in underground mines. The program is financed primarily through a tax on mineowners.

black market adoption: The illegal *adoption* of children by childless couples or individuals who are unable to adopt through legitimate public or private adoption agencies. Typically, the party who wants a child contracts with an intermediary to obtain a child and makes monetary payments to the intermediary and indirectly to the child's legal guardian. See also *gray market adoption.*

black power: The social movement whose goal is the achievement of greater racial equity in economic, political, and social influence. A basic premise of the movement is that black influence will grow as more black people gain positions of leadership in elective office, government, and business and acquire enough money to use in seeking legal rights and educational opportunities. The movement seeks to get black people who achieve these positions to work together in pursuit of these goals rather than dilute such efforts by working in disparate directions.

blacks: The term often used for racial *minorities of color* who come from, or whose ancestors came from, middle and southern Africa.

blamer role: A recurrent pattern of interpersonal communication characterized by acting superior, finding fault, behaving dictatorially, and attributing one's problems to others. The role was delineated by Virginia Satir (*Peoplemaking,* Palo Alto, Calif.: Science and Behavior Books, 1972, p. 66), who described the blamer as a person who conceals inner feelings of loneliness and failure by making persistent accusations. Other roles are the *computer role,* the *distracter role,* and the *placater role.*

blended family: A family that is formed when separate families are united by marriage or other circumstance; a stepfamily. The term is also used to refer to various kinship or nonkinship groups whose members reside together and assume traditional family roles. Some family therapists also apply this term to family groups whose individual members have not achieved distinct or autonomous roles or identities for themselves.

block grant: A system of disbursing funds to meet a locality's health, education, and social welfare needs while permitting the recipient organizations to determine how best to distribute the money. Used mostly by the federal and sometimes state governments, the system is designed to consolidate budget itemization and eliminate the necessity of earmarking funds for every individual program and *categorical program*. The system was a major provision of the Omnibus Budget Reconciliation Act of 1981 (P.L. 97-35). Proponents say it increases efficiency and local control, and opponents suggest that it is a covert way of reducing expenditures for social welfare needs.

blocking: A temporary failure of memory, interrupting one's flow of speech or thought.

block organizations: Formal or informal social groups who live in close physical proximity to one another (as in a city block); have shared values, problems, and vulnerabilities; and meet to achieve their mutual goals.

block placement: In social work education, an alternative to the traditional format for *field placement*. In the traditional model the student alternates classroom experiences with work in a social agency on different days of each week. In block placements the student attends classes only for several months and then works virtually full time in a social agency, under academic and professional supervision, for several months. The amount of time spent in the agency during a block placement is the same as in the traditional approach.

blue collar: A term used to describe members of a wage-earning *socioeconomic class*. The term originally applied to people who worked in factories or manual labor settings in which blue or dark clothes were worn, and was used to distinguish these workers from those employed in offices or retail stores (white-collar workers).

board of directors: A group of people empowered to establish an organization's objectives and policies and to oversee the activities of the personnel responsible for day-to-day implementation of those policies. Social agency boards of directors are often made up of volunteers who are influential in the community and reflect the views prevalent in the community.

body language: See *kinesics*.

bonding: The development by one person of attachment for another. The process begins when the individual has needs that are regularly fulfilled by the other and his or her identity is partially shaped by the interrelationship.

borderline: A descriptive term applied to any phenomenon located between two categories. Social workers and mental health personnel often use the term informally in describing individuals who are at or near the dividing line between psychosis and nonpsychosis or normalcy and mental illness; not to be confused with *borderline personality disorder*.

borderline personality disorder: One of the more common of the *personality disorders*, it is characterized by some of the following symptoms and traits: deeply ingrained and maladaptive patterns of relating to others, impulsive and unpredictable behavior that is often self-destructive, lack of control of anger, intense mood shifts, identity disturbance and inconsistent self-concept, manipulation of others for short-term gain, and chronic feelings of boredom and emptiness.

Borstal system: British penal program for young offenders (ages 15 to 23) in closed or open prisons that emphasize education, training, and rehabilitation. The system has undergone many changes and is now merging with the British corrections system for adult and youthful offenders. See also *reformatory*.

boundaries: Regions separating two psychological or social systems. A central concept in *family systems theories*, pertaining to the implicit rules that determine how the family members or subsystems are expected to relate to one another and to nonfamily members. A function of boundaries, which are analogous to the membranes of living cells, is to differentiate systems and their subsystems and permit the development of *identity*. Healthy family functioning largely entails clear boundaries; less healthy functioning is seen where boundary subsystems are either inappropriately rigid or not consistently clear (that is, in a *disengaged family* or an *enmeshed family*).

boycott: An organized refusal to maintain certain relationships with a person, organization, or government body. For example, a community organizer might convince all residents of a neighborhood to stop patronizing a store that discriminates against minorities.

brainstorming: In social work administration, a method of stimulating the development of ideas by assembling certain staff and board members and encouraging open discussion while postponing criticism or analysis of the ideas proposed.

brief therapy: Any form of psychotherapy or clinical social work intervention in which specific goals and the number of sessions are predetermined. Brief therapy is usually goal oriented, circumscribed, active, focused, and directed toward specific problems or symptoms.

broken home: A family in which at least one parent is absent because of divorce, death, or desertion. Social workers now generally prefer the term *single-parent family.*

broker role: A function of social workers and community organizers in which clients (individuals, groups, organizations, or communities) are helped to identify, locate, and link available community resources and various segments of the community are put in touch with one another to enhance their mutual interests.

Brown v. Board of Education: The 1954 U.S. Supreme Court ruling that the "separate but equal" interpretation of the Fourteenth Amendment was unconstitutional and that racial segregation of public schools was illegal. See also *Plessy v. Ferguson.*

BSW: A bachelor's degree awarded to qualified students who majored in social work in CSWE-accredited undergraduate colleges.

budget: An itemized list of the amount of all estimated revenues a social agency or organization anticipates receiving and the delineation of the amount of all estimated costs and expenses necessary to operate the organization; a statement of probable revenues and expenditures during a specified time period.

bulimia: A pathologically excessive appetite with episodic eating binges, sometimes followed by purging through such means as self-induced vomiting, laxative abuse, and diet pills or diuretics. Bulimia usually starts as a means of dieting. Then, when hunger occurs, the person eats, feels guilty, and purges, which leads to more eating, more dieting, and so on.

bureaucracy: A form of social organization whose distinctive characteristics include a task-specific division of labor; a vertical hierarchy with power centered at the top; clearly defined rules; formalized channels of communication; and selection, promotion, compensation, and retention based on technical competence.

bureaucratization: The trend in social institutions and organizations toward more centralized control and enforced conformity to rigidly prescribed rules and channels of communication.

Bureau of Health Professions: The bureau within the U.S. *Public Health Service* whose function is to facilitate the training and coordinate the distribution of people in the health care professions.

Bureau of Indian Affairs: A federal organization, now within the U.S. Department of the Interior, created in 1824 to provide social services, health and educational programs, agricultural and economic assistance, and civil rights protections to *American Indians* and *Alaska Natives.*

Bureau of Labor Statistics (BLS): A research agency of the U.S. *Department of Labor* that compiles and publishes statistics about many variables of interest to social workers and social planners, including employment and unemployment rates, consumer prices, and wage rates.

bureaus of public assistance: State and county organizations that administer programs to provide economic and social services to needy families; funded from local, state, and federal revenues, these bureaus often help administer such programs as *Aid to Families with Dependent Children (AFDC)* and *general assistance (GA).* In some jurisdictions these bureaus are known as the Department of Welfare, the Department of Social Service, or the Bureau of Health and Human Services.

burnout: A form of depression and apathy related to on-the-job stress and frustration. The worker becomes bored, unmotivated, and uncreative and is often unresponsive to improved conditions.

busing: The transporting of students across school-district boundaries, usually court-ordered, to facilitate more equitable racial balance.

C

Canadian Association of Schools of Social Work (CASSW): The organization whose membership comprises the professional schools of social work in Canada and whose purpose is to facilitate communication between schools and to maintain standards through accreditation reviews.

Canadian Association of Social Workers (CASW): The professional organization of qualified Canadian social workers whose purposes include professional development of its membership through educational programs, conferences, publications, and the development and enforcement of ethical standards.

cancer: A malignant tumor; uncontrolled growth of abnormal cells. Unlike normal body cells, cancer cells do not stop growing when in contact with other cells and thus may spread in the body. The cells spread either by invading surrounding tissue or by metastasis (movement by way of the blood or lymph system to other organs or tissues). Cancer cells compete with normal tissue for nutrients and eventually kill normal cells by depriving them of nutritional needs. Causes, specific symptoms, prognosis, and treatment vary considerably.

cannabis: See *marijuana*.

capitalism: An economic system in which the production and distribution of goods and services are controlled through private ownership and open competition for consumers.

capital punishment: Government-sanctioned implementation of the death penalty, imposed on some criminals convicted of capital crimes, which may include murder, rape, or treason.

carcinogen: A cancer-causing substance.

care-and-protection proceedings: The legal intervention on behalf of a dependent whose parents or guardians no longer seem willing or able to provide for the dependent's needs.

CARE: Cooperative for American Relief Everywhere, Inc., a voluntary organization founded in 1945 through which gift parcels are sent from the United States to needy people in other nations. Its original name was Cooperative for American Remittances to Europe.

career counseling: The procedure used by social workers, personnel and guidance advisors, educational specialists, and other professionals to provide information, advice, support, and *linkage* of resources to people who are deciding about future vocations or workers who seek to improve their current employment circumstances. Career counseling is most commonly offered to students in high schools or colleges to help them learn about existing opportunities and to help them recognize their assets and limitations. Such counseling is also offered in work organizations to help employees maximize their vocational potential.

caregiver: One who provides for the physical, emotional, and social needs of another person, often one who is dependent and cannot provide for his or her own needs. The term most often applies to parents or parent surrogates, day care and nursery workers, and health care specialists. The term is also applied to all people who provide nurturance and emotional support to others, including spouses, clergymen, and social workers.

case aide: In social work, a *paraprofessional* who helps the worker, as a member of a *social work team*, to provide specified services for the client. Frequently the aide has developed expertise in accomplishing a set of specific functions and is called on to fulfill those functions when they are deemed important by the social worker in charge of the case. For example, the aide might be asked to telephone members of the client's family to obtain additional information or accompany a client to a clinic. Most case aides are paid employees of the worker's agency, but some are volunteers or part of the *natural helping network*. See also *social work associates*.

case conference: A procedure often used in social agencies and other organizations to bring together members of a professional staff to discuss a client's problem, objectives, intervention plans, and prognoses. The participants in the conference may include the social workers who are providing the direct service to the client or client system and the professional supervisor of these workers. Additional participants might include other agency workers who have special expertise or experience with similar problems or populations, members of other professional groups or disciplines who can provide further information and recommendations, and sometimes personal associates or relatives of the client who may be asked to provide information or helping resources.

case finding: Searching out and identifying those individuals or groups who are vulnerable to or experiencing problems for which the social worker or agency has responsibility in order to provide needed help and service.

case integration: Coordination of the activities of social workers and service providers from other relevant auspices who are simultaneously serving the needs of a client. This coordination means that the respective providers' services are consistent, additive, nonduplicative, and directed purposefully toward achieving the same goals. See also *case management.*

caseload: All the clients for whom a given social worker is responsible.

case management: A procedure to coordinate all the helping activities on behalf of a client or group of clients. The procedure makes it possible for many workers in the agency, or different agencies, to coordinate their efforts to serve a given client through professional teamwork, thus expanding the range of needed services offered. Case management may involve monitoring the progress of a client whose needs require the services of many different professionals, agencies, health care facilities, and human services programs. It typically involves *case finding,* comprehensive multidimensional assessment, and frequent reassessment. Case management can occur within a single large organization or within a community program that coordinates services between agencies. Federal legislation enacted in 1981 enabled states to pay for case management for Medicaid recipients under waiver of the usual rules. Social workers and nurses are the professional groups most often called upon to fulfill this function. Case management is seen as an increasingly important way of limiting problems arising from fragmentation of services, staff turnover, and inadequate coordination between providers. See also *case integration.*

case-mix reimbursement: A system in which government or third-party organizations pay an institution, such as a nursing home or hospital, for their expected services to a group of people over a specified period of time. Typically, the amount paid to the institution depends not on the individual's specific health care requirements but on the variety of services likely to be required for the group for which care is provided. The system of *diagnostic related groups (DRGs)* is one form of case-mix reimbursement.

case record: Information about the client-situation and the service transaction that is documented by the social worker during the intervention process and retained by the agency or in the worker's files. The purpose of case records is to coordinate, communicate, set goals, and remember intervention strategies. According to Jill Doner Kagle (*Social Work Records,* Homewood, Ill.: Dorsey Press, 1984), case records also exist to demonstrate accountability, justify funding, and support supervision and research. See also *problem-oriented record* and *SOAP charting method.*

case study: A method of evaluation by examining systematically many characteristics of one individual, group, family, or community, usually over an extended period of time.

casework: See *social casework.*

cash benefits: See *benefits.*

catalyst role: The social worker–community organizer's function of creating a climate of introspection and self-assessment for the client or community and facilitating communication, stimulating awareness of problems, and encouraging belief in the possibility of change.

cataract: Cloudiness in the lens of an eye, resulting in impaired vision. Surgical treatment for cataracts has become relatively convenient and inexpensive.

catatonic: A term used to describe certain mentally ill people who seem detached from reality and oblivious to environmental stimuli. Typically, these people move very slowly and rigidly or may be stiff and statuelike. On some occasions, and with no apparent provocation, their movements may become active and uncontrolled, and their moods may become excited. This is usually followed by a return to the more characteristic state of stupor.

catchment area: The geographic region in which all potential clients are served by a given social agency.

categorical assistance: Welfare programs for specific groups of people identified in the *Social Security Act.* Originally the programs were *Old Age Assistance (OAA), Aid to the Blind (AB), Aid to Dependent Children (ADC), and Aid to the Totally and Permanently Disabled (ATPD).* Needy people in these categories could receive financial assistance from their respective states, supplemented by federal grants. In 1974, responsibility for the three adult categories was assumed by the federal *Supplemental Security Income (SSI)* program.

categorical grant: Payment of funds or goods made by an organization, agency, or individual (grantor) to a recipient (grantee) for agreeing to accomplish some specified objective. For example, public assistance programs such as *Aid to Families with Dependent Children (AFDC)* are categorical grants made by the federal government to state governments in consideration of the state governments' distribution of funds to needy families in a prescribed way.

categorical program: The provision of social services and other benefits to people who belong to specifically designated groups that are particularly at risk, such as the aged, parentless children, and the blind and disabled.

catharsis: Verbalization of ideas, fears, past significant events, and connections, the expected result of which is a release of anxiety or tension, resulting in improved functioning; also called *ventilation.*

cathexis: The concentration of emotional energy and feelings onto a person, idea, object, or onto oneself.

Catholic Charities USA: An organization founded in 1910 to coordinate the 3,000 Catholic church–related local organizations and individuals who provide such voluntary social services as *family therapy, child welfare,* vocational and economic counseling, and recreational and educational services. The organization was formerly known as the National Conference of Catholic Charities.

CAT scan: Computerized axial tomography, a medical diagnostic tool for taking pictures of the interior of a patient's head and body.

cause-oriented organization: A formal or informal group comprising individuals who are united by shared values and goals and devoted to achieving specific social change or solving certain problems.

cause-versus-function issue: The controversial historic dichotomy in social work involving practice, the orientations of social reform, and case services. Some early social workers, such as Jane Addams, advocated a cause orientation, emphasizing societal change through political action and community organization. Others, such as Mary Richmond, stressed the function of individual betterment through the worker's technical skills, such as interviewing and advice giving. The current view among most social workers is that the field must include both cause and function orientations.

cease and desist order: A statement made by a court or judicial authority prohibiting an individual or organization from starting or continuing a particular activity. For example, a social work activist might help the tenants of an apartment building get such an order from the court to stop a landlord from converting units to condominiums or unaffordable dwellings.

Census Bureau, U.S.: The federal bureau, functioning within the U.S. Department of Commerce, that carries out the constitutional requirement that all the people in the nation be counted every decade. The bureau, centered in Suitland, Maryland, conducts surveys and analyzes and disseminates resulting data about individuals, population groups, and social trends.

Center for Health Statistics: See *Department of Health and Human Services (HHS), U.S.*

Centers for Disease Control: A U.S. *Department of Health and Human Services (HHS)* organization based in Atlanta, Georgia, that coordinates efforts throughout the nation to prevent and minimize the spread of disease. The center acquires, analyzes, and disseminates data about the incidence of disease and its etiology, progression, and elimination.

centralization: The concentration of administrative power within a group, organization, or political entity. For example, public assistance programs—which had been managed primarily at the state and local levels—became more centralized with the passage of the *Social Security Act* and later the *Supplemental Security Income (SSI)* program.

centrifugal family structure: In family systems theory, the pattern of relationship among family members in which there is little cohesiveness or attachment and each member feels compelled to seek emotional support from outside the family. This structure may also occur in nonfamily relationships.

centripetal family structure: In family systems theory, the pattern of relationship among family members in which each person is bound into the family and relatively isolated from outsiders. For example, the children remain at home even after reaching adulthood, and all family members encourage each other to remain highly interdependent. This structure may also occur in nonfamily relationships.

cerebral palsy: A disability of muscle control and coordination caused by brain damage that occurred before or during the birth process. The degree of severity depends on the extent of the brain damage. Although no cure exists, treatment involving physical, occupational, speech, and psychosocial therapy and appliances such as braces is often effective in minimizing disability.

cerebrovascular accident: See *stroke.*

certification: An official assurance that someone or something possesses the attributes it is claimed to have. Legal certification of a profession is the warranting by a state that the persons certified have attained a specified level of knowledge and skill. Professional certification is such warranting by a professional association. Certification typically does not prohibit uncertified persons from engaging in the specified behavior (as does a *license*), but it prevents their use of the title "certified." Certification is usually considered to be a stronger form of regulation than *registration* but weaker than the license.

certified social worker: A social work practitioner who is warranted by a professional association or legal body to have attained a specified level of education, knowledge, and skills; the title "certified social worker" is protected by statute in some jurisdictions and by professional associations in others, so that its use is restricted to those who qualify. See also *Academy of Certified Social Workers (ACSW)* and *legal regulation.*

CETA: The Comprehensive Employment and Training Act (P.L. 93-203), a federal program begun in 1973 to retrain and place long-term unemployed, inefficiently employed, or disadvantaged people in more suitable jobs and jobs with a future. The public service job program sponsored by CETA was replaced in 1982 by the *Job Training Partnership Act,* which encouraged more private-sector, local, and state involvement in employment training programs.

chaining: In *behavior modification,* a specific and complex series of connected or associated stimulus-response units that terminate with the delivery of a reinforcer. Social workers using behavioral techniques also use "backward chaining," in which the last stimulus-response unit of a chain is established first and the other units are added in reverse order until the desired chain is complete.

CHAMPUS: The Civilian Health and Medical Program of the Uniformed Services, a federally funded health insurance program for the dependents of active duty and retired U.S. military personnel. CHAMPUS pays a significant proportion of the health care costs for the beneficiary in the private health care service delivery system when such care is not available or accessible in military medical facilities. In certain circumstances, qualified social workers are directly reimbursed by CHAMPUS for providing their professional services in the care of people with some mental disorders.

change agent: A social worker or other helping professional or group of helpers whose purpose is to facilitate some improvement.

change agent system: The organizations, agencies, and community institutions that provide the auspices and additional resources through which the worker (*change agent*) provides service.

channeling: A *case management* administrative procedure in which social agency workers remain aware of the community's resources and often direct their clients to relevant programs for additional or supplementary service during the ongoing helping process. See also *linkage.*

character: The most deeply ingrained aspects of personality and the resulting habitual modes of response.

character disorder: A maladaptive personality pattern involving inflexibility in thinking, perceiving, and reacting; also known as character neurosis. Individuals with this dysfunction are often obsessively meticulous, pedantic, and cruel in an intellectual way. Psychoanalytically oriented professionals also describe certain specific maladaptive character traits, such as the "oral character" (demanding), "anal character" (emotionally constricted), and "genital character" (excessively preoccupied with sexuality).

charette: A technique used by community organizers and disaster relief planners to stimulate citizen participation during crisis planning. Professionals and community members (especially those most likely to be affected by the crisis) work together intensively to plan means of coping with the situation.

charity: Literally, love for one's fellow humans; the donation of goods and services to those in need.

Charity Organization Societies (COS): Privately administered and philanthropically funded organizations that were the essential forerunners of modern social service agencies. First established in Buffalo, New York, in 1877 and duplicated in most larger eastern cities soon thereafter, COS were staffed by volunteer workers who provided direct services to clients and coordinated community efforts to deal with social problems. As more COS workers, sometimes known as *friendly visitors,* gradually became professionalized, they were called social workers. By the 1930s, as government assumed more responsibility for people's economic and social security, the original COS goal was reached and most of the organizations discontinued operations or were merged into other private social work agencies such as the Family Service Association of America. See also *Family Service America (FSA).*

chemotherapy: The treatment of a disease, such as cancer, with chemicals.

Chicano: A term sometimes used to describe American citizens of Mexican birth or ethnic heritage.

child abuse: The recurrent infliction of physical or emotional injury on a dependent minor, through intentional beatings, uncontrolled corporal punishment, persistent ridicule and degradation, or sexual abuse, usually committed by parents or others in charge of the child's care. Many state laws now require social workers and other professionals to report instances of suspected child abuse to the appropriate authorities.

child advocacy: Championing the rights of children to be free from abuse or exploitation by others. Since the beginning of their existence, social workers have led in this effort by fighting for child labor laws; calling public attention to inadequate care facilities and orphanages; and working to set up juvenile justice programs, to expand foster and adoption care, and to eradicate child snatching, kidnapping, and child abuse.

child care: Nurturance and management of children's day-to-day requirements for life and successful development. Although the term can apply to any activity in which a youngster's needs are provided for by a parent or guardian, it is specifically applied to children in institutions or 24-hour group living situations. In this context, child care activities include physical care (such as feeding and clothing), habit development (such as personal hygiene and socialization), self-management (discipline), therapeutic care (counseling), tutoring, and first aid as well as running the living group as a cohesive unit and managing the institutional program.

child care worker: A professional or *paraprofessional* who is responsible for the daily care and nurturing life experiences of a group of youngsters who reside in an institution. Such workers are often known as houseparents, residential workers, or group living counselors. They fulfill the activities of institutional *child care* and are employed primarily in residential settings for emotionally disturbed and dependent children and for the mentally retarded, in corrections facilities, in institutions for the physically handicapped, and in homes for unwed mothers.

child custody: See *custody of children.*

Child Health and Human Development, National Institute of: The organization within the *National Institutes of Health (NIH)* that provides information and expertise on such factors as *sudden infant death syndrome (SIDS)*, birth defects, *developmental disabilities,* and human reproduction and fertility.

childhood: The early stage in the human life span characterized by rapid physical growth and efforts to learn how to assume adult roles and responsibilities, mostly through play and formal education. Many developmental psychologists say this stage takes place after infancy and lasts until *puberty* (that is, from approximately 18–24 months to 12–14 years) or until *adulthood* (18–21 years). This stage is sometimes divided into early childhood (from the end of infancy to about age 6) and middle or late childhood (from 6 to, or through, adolescence).

childhood schizophrenia: A chronic psychotic disorder, involving disturbances in thought, perception, affect, and behavior, that appears in an individual before puberty. The schizophrenic youngster typically shows extremely withdrawn behavior, gross immaturity, and failure to develop much autonomy or identity separate from parents or surrogates.

child neglect: The failure of those responsible for the care of a minor to provide the resources needed for healthy physical, emotional, and social development. Examples of neglect include inadequate nutrition, improper supervision, deficient health care, and not providing for educational requirements.

child protective services: Human services, often including social, medical, legal, residential, and custodial care, which are provided to children whose *caregivers* are not providing for their needs. Social workers who work in child protective service units of government agencies often help legal authorities with investigations to determine if children are in need of such services, help them to get them when needed, and may provide such services themselves.

child psychoanalysis: The use of psychoanalytic theory and methods in helping children overcome psychic conflicts and emotional disturbances that impede their healthy development. Practitioners of this discipline, also known as child analysis, are usually physicians with education in psychoanalysis and added training for work with children.

child psychotherapy: Treatment, by trained professionals, of youngsters for mental illness, emotional conflict, impaired psychological development, or behavioral maladaptations. Psychotherapy with children includes all the theory and method applied to other psychotherapies but may emphasize *play therapy*, small-group therapy, and supportive and reeducative therapies. Professionals who provide child psychotherapy services include specially trained psychiatrists, social workers, psychologists, mental health nurses, educational specialists, and other mental health professionals.

children: Youngsters who are under the legal age of responsibility or emancipation; in most states this age is 18.

Children's Aid Society: The private organization founded by Charles Loring Brace in 1853 in New York to provide shelter, education, care, and family placement for homeless and destitute children. The society's methods greatly influenced modern child welfare programs and the foster care system.

children's allowances: A *demogrant* for children; an income-providing program, not based on need, in which children's families receive periodic cash or in-kind *benefits* to supplement the costs of their care. This system does not exist in the United States but is common in other industrialized nations of the world.

Children's Bureau: The U.S. government organization, created in 1912 and now part of the *Administration for Children, Youth, and Families (ACYF)* of the U.S. *Department of Health and Human Services (HHS)*, which plans, integrates, and advocates national programs on behalf of children.

Children's Defense Fund: An advocacy and lobbying organization on behalf of the nation's children that scrutinizes government agencies and legislation affecting children and proposes new programs and changes in old ones. It strives to create and enforce child welfare laws and to support organizations that serve the special needs of children.

child sexual abuse: A form of *child abuse* in which a dependent child is compelled, by manipulation or force, to fulfill the erotic demands of an older person, often a family member.

child snatching: The term generally used to describe the illegal act of removing a dependent child from the care and authority of the legally authorized parent or guardian, usually by another of the child's relatives. Most typically, child snatching takes place among families that are dissolving, as in divorces or foster home placements, and one of the former caregivers does not accept the legal ruling granting custody to someone else. The unauthorized person takes the child and often conceals its whereabouts or keeps moving so that the authorities have difficulty returning the child to the rightful custodian.

Child Support Enforcement Office, U.S.: The organization within the *Family Services Administration (FSA)* of the *Department of Health and Human Services* that helps states and local jurisdictions compel parents to meet their obligations to their children. The office helps plan and manage programs to locate absent parents, establish paternity, coordinate activities between states, and bring to justice parents who do not fulfill their obligations.

child welfare: That part of human services and social welfare programs and ideologies oriented toward the protection, care, and healthy development of children. Child welfare measures are found in national, state, and local programs and are usually designed to prevent conditions that interfere with the healthy and positive development of children.

Child Welfare League of America (CWLA): The major national voluntary organization for promoting the interests of children. Founded in 1920, it is a federation of accredited child welfare agencies that provides standard setting, accreditation, technical leadership to local governments, and advocacy for children.

CHINS: See *persons in need of supervision (PINS)*.

chlorpromazine: See *antipsychotic medication.*

chorionic villi sampling (CVS): A medical procedure for detecting chromosomal abnormalities and inherited metabolic disease in the fetus by removing and examining a small amount of placental tissue. See also *amniocentesis.*

chronic: Pertaining to problems, abnormal behaviors, and medical conditions that have developed and persisted over a long period of time; many helping professionals consider problems that have lasted over six months to be chronic and those that last less than six months to be *acute.*

CIO: See *American Federation of Labor–Congress of Industrial Organizations (AFL-CIO).*

circular causality: The concept, particularly in *systems theories,* that describes the cause of an event, behavior, problem, or pattern as being part of a complex sequence of reciprocally influential interactions. Behavior in one component of an organized system affects behavior in another component, which affects behavior in the first, and so on, in a recurring circular fashion. In this view, the *linear causality* concept is an epistemological error.

cirrhosis: The scarring of body tissue, most commonly the liver. Those most susceptible to cirrhosis are middle-aged males with a nutritional (protein) deficiency brought about by alcoholism. The damage to the liver may result in such symptoms as emaciation, jaundice, gastrointestinal disturbances, hepatitis, enlargement of the liver and spleen, and distension of the veins. Treatment usually includes a diet with adequate protein, vitamin supplements, and sometimes blood transfusions and excess fluid removal. Social and psychotherapy, including alcoholism treatment, are also usually indicated to prevent recurrence of the symptoms.

citizen participation: Involvement of members of the general public who are likely to be affected by a changed social policy, law, or circumstance in the process of planning and implementing that change. Skilled community organizers usually attempt to facilitate citizen participation in change efforts. Many laws dealing with the public welfare (such as *Title XX* of the *Social Security Act*) require citizen participation in the development and implementation of certain social service plans. Some social workers identify various types of citizen participation, including agencies or bureaucracies that initiate the involvement and those in which citizen groups and individuals themselves initiate the involvement.

city planning: Systematic efforts to order urban development, establish priorities, and implement goals pertaining to the overall well-being of a city, town, neighborhood, or metropolitan region. City planners were originally oriented toward the physical development of a city, including development of its infrastructure and aesthetic amenities. Later their objectives expanded to include developing sound land use patterns, improving governmental procedures, and enhancing the quality of life and welfare of citizens.

civic associations: Private voluntary organizations whose members meet regularly for socialization and to plan and implement activities for the benefit of the community. These associations vary considerably in their goals, methods, and membership requirements. Some of these associations, which have chapters in most communities, include the Lions Club, Jaycees, Rotarians, Junior League, and the Business and Professional Women's Clubs.

civil defense: Procedures, structures, plans, and systems designed to protect the lives and property of the nonmilitary population from enemy attack or natural disaster.

civil disobedience: Noncompliance with a government's laws or demands, usually to call attention to those laws that are considered unfair and to bring about changes or concessions in them. Civil disobedience often takes the form of group actions such as marches and assemblies, deliberate nonpayment of taxes, and obstruction of the free movement of others. See also *passive resistance.*

civil disorder: A public disturbance in which a group is involved in violent activity causing danger, injury, or property damage to others.

Civilian Conservation Corps (CCC): A federal program established in 1933 to conserve and develop U.S. natural resources and to create jobs for unemployed young men. The program was abolished in 1942. It was used, in part, as a model for the 1964 *Job Corps* program.

civil liberties: Certain freedoms that may not arbitrarily be taken away or denied by society or external authority. The freedom to act according to one's own conscience, to worship, speak, and travel without restriction, and to choose one's own profession or associates are examples of civil liberties.

civil rights: Rights of citizens to be protected against discrimination or arbitrary treatment by government or individuals and to engage in certain behaviors as long as they do not infringe on the rights of others. In the United States, these rights include those guaranteed in the Consitution's Bill of Rights (such as freedom of speech, religion, and the press) and others instituted since the adoption of the Bill of Rights (such as due process and equal protection under the law). Several civil rights acts and constitutional amendments have sought to bestow specific protections on blacks and other minority groups. This legislation includes such acts as the *Civil Rights Act of 1964,* the *Voting Rights Act of 1965,* and the 1968 housing acts designed to eliminate discrimination in housing and real estate. See also *civil liberties.*

Civil Rights Act of 1964: The comprehensive federal legislation (P.L. 88-352) prohibiting discrimination for reasons of race, religion, or national origin in schools, employment, and service in places of public accommodation including restaurants, theaters, and hotels.

civil rights groups: *Cause-oriented organizations* whose members share the goal of achieving equality of opportunity for all people including members of minority groups and women. They seek changes in the sociopolitical system that fosters discrimination, ethnic stereotyping, and inequitable treatment in legal institutions. Some of the major national civil rights groups include *NAACP,* the *Urban League,* the *American Civil Liberties Union (ACLU),* the *American Indian Movement (AIM),* the *Anti-Defamation League of B'nai-B'rith,* the *National Organization for Women (NOW),* the *Congress of Racial Equality (CORE),* *Operation PUSH,* the *Southern Christian Leadership Conference (SCLC),* and *Concern for the Dying* as well as the National Abortion Rights Action League and the National Right to Life Committee. There are also many state and federal organizations concerned with the enforcement of civil rights laws, including the U.S. *Commission on Civil Rights.*

civil servants: A term pertaining to government employees below elected or policymaking ranks whose employment is based on specified and needed skills and performance of certain duties. See also *Office of Personnel Management (OPM).*

Civil Works Administration (CWA): A federal program established in 1933 to provide employment for millions of citizens in public works projects and to stimulate depressed industries such as construction. The program was abolished at the beginning of World War II.

class action suit: A civil legal action taken by or on behalf of a group, community, or members of a social entity against an alleged perpetrator of harm to that group or some of its members.

classical conditioning: See *respondent conditioning.*

classification: The process of organizing information into categories or class intervals so that the data can be more readily analyzed and understood. For example, a social worker might plan for the needs of potential clients in the agency's *catchment area* by categorizing the area's population as to age groups, gender, economic well-being, recent visits to hospitals, and incidence and type of mental illness.

client: The individual, group, family, or community that seeks and is provided with professional services.

client-centered therapy: A form of *psychotherapy* originated by psychologist Carl Rogers. Its central hypothesis is that clients are inherently motivated to develop and maximize their capacities (that is, to self-actualize) and can resolve their own problems provided that the therapist establishes a caring, warm, empathic, permissive, and nonjudgmental atmosphere. The client-centered therapist assumes a nondirective stance and usually does not advise, interpret, or challenge, except to encourage the client or to restate the client's remarks to clarify them.

client system: The *client* and those in the client's environment who are potentially influential in contributing to a resolution of the client's problems. For example, a social worker may see a *nuclear family* as the client and the *extended family* and neighbors, teachers, and employers as making up part of the client system.

clinical social work: A specialized form of direct social work intervention with individuals, groups, and families that takes place, for the most part, in the worker's office. Some professional social workers use the term as a synonym for *social casework* or *psychiatric social work*, although others believe that each of these terms has a somewhat different meaning. According to Herbert S. Strean (*Clinical Social Work,* New York: Free Press, 1978), most clinical social workers consider that their professional responsibility includes an interest in and intervention with aspects of the client's environment that produce the difficulty, as well as *intrapsychic* material.

clinician: A professional person, working directly with clients, whose practice occurs primarily in an office, hospital, clinic, or other controlled environment. In such settings the practitioner studies the problem, assesses and diagnoses the client-situation, and directly treats or helps the client to achieve prescribed goals. The social work clinician is generally one who provides direct helping services to the client (individual, family, or group), usually in the worker's office.

closed family: A family structure whose members maintain highly interdependent relationships, providing little opportunity for relationships with people who are not family members.

closed system: In *systems theories,* a self-contained system that is organized to resist change and maintain the status quo. For example, a closed family system is relatively uninvolved with non-family members, less tolerant of ideas that differ from the *family myths*, and structured to maintain its interrelationships with minimal outside interference. See also *open systems.*

coalition: An alliance of various factions or ideological groups in a society brought together to achieve a goal. Social workers in *community organization* often attempt to form such alliances among influential groups or among less powerful groups in order to increase their influence. Coalitions may be ad hoc (organized to address a specific goal or single issue and expected to disband when it is achieved), semipermanent (more formally organized around broader and longer-range goals), or permanent (such as political parties).

cocaine: An illicit drug derived from the leaves of the coca plant that gives the user feelings of euphoria, energy, alertness, confidence, and heightened sensitivity. Sometimes known as "coke" or "snow," the drug is usually taken through the nostrils ("snorting") and sometimes injected in combination with other drugs such as heroin ("speedballing") or chemically converted and smoked ("freebasing"). Many researchers claim that it is not physically addictive and that the body does not develop *tolerance* but that it is psychologically habit-forming. Repeated use can produce marked deterioration of the nervous system and general physical deterioration, destruction of the mucous membranes, paranoia, depression, and hallucinations. See also *crack.*

codeine: A *narcotic* analgesic (pain-relieving drug) found in some prescription medications, and, in certain states, in over-the-counter medications, such as some cough syrups. Like all narcotics, codeine is addictive when used with some degree of frequency.

code of ethics: An explicit statement of the values, principles, and rules of a profession, regulating the conduct of its members. See also *NASW Code of Ethics.*

coding: The social research procedure in which numbers or other symbols are assigned for each variable or category of answer in a survey or other study. For example, a 1 may be assigned for every yes response and a 2 for every no.

coercion: Forcing or compelling an individual or group to perform (or stop performing) some activity. This may occur through legal actions, government interventions, social influence, or political pressure, as well as through threats of violent harm. An important role of social workers, especially those in *community organization,* is to bring people together so that they can resist the attempts of others to coerce them into actions they do not want to take.

cognition: The mental process of recognizing, understanding, remembering, and evaluating relevant information.

cognitive-behavioral therapies: Approaches to treatment and to helping people resolve specific problems using selected concepts and techniques from *behaviorism, social learning theory, action therapy, functional social work, task-centered treatment,* and therapies based on *cognitive models.* These forms of therapy are contrasted with the therapies known as *insight therapies* and tend to be comparatively short term, focused on the here and now, and fairly limited and specific in goals. The therapist with a cognitive-behavioral orientation tends to be fairly directive and focused on the client's *presenting problem.*

cognitive development: The process by which individuals acquire the intellectual capacity to perceive, evaluate, and understand information. Jean Piaget (1896–1980) formulated the most complete cognitive theory to date. He divided human development into four typical stages, the *sensorimotor stage,* (birth to age 2), the *preoperational stage* (ages 2 to 7), the *concrete operations stage* (ages 7 to 11), and *formal operations* (age 11 to adulthood). See also *Piagetian theory.*

cognitive dissonance: The mental state in which a person experiences two or more incompatible beliefs or *cognitions* simultaneously. In the healthy individual this state usually leads to psychological discomfort that remains until the person acts to clarify the discrepancy.

cognitive map: An individual's image or perceptual picture of the environment.

cognitive models: Representations of the ways by which people come to know, perceive, or understand phenomena. Such models can be used to envision or describe how human individuals develop their abilities to organize knowledge and understand their worlds, as in *Piagetian theory.* Such models can also be used to describe certain treatment approaches, such as *rational-emotive therapy* (Albert Ellis), *reality therapy* (William Glasser), *individual psychology* (Alfred Adler), and *rational casework* (Robert Sunley and Harold D. Werner).

cognitive style: An individual's preferred way of organizing and processing information. There are individual differences in how people perceive, remember, understand, and solve problems that influence the way information is organized and processed. For example, some people are more analytical and others have more global approaches to their environments.

cognitive theory: A group of concepts pertaining to the way individuals develop the intellectual capacity for receiving, processing, and acting on information. Cognitive concepts emphasize that behavior is determined by thinking and goal determination, rather than primarily resulting from instinctive drives or unconscious motivations.

cognitive therapy: Clinical intervention using *cognitive theory* concepts that focus on the client's conscious thinking processes, motivations, and reasons for certain behaviors. Alfred Adler is said to have been a major originator of cognitive therapy. Current forms of this approach include *rational-emotive therapy, reality therapy, existential therapy,* and *rational casework.* The psychosocial orientation of early, "pre-Freudian" social workers was considered to have much in common with the cognitive approach.

cohabitation: The term that is commonly applied to a man and woman residing together in husband-wife roles without formal marriage; however, it also applies to others, such as homosexuals, and to more than two people living together.

cohort: In research and demographic studies, a group of subjects who were born during a specific time period or who share another characteristic that is related to the subject being investigated. For example, when life expectancies are being calculated, one cohort might be a group of 100,000 people who were born in the same month.

cohort sequential analysis: A research method that systematically evaluates selected age groups of people over a staggered period of time. This helps correct any bias inherent in a *longitudinal study.*

COLA: Cost-of-living adjustment; an increase or decrease in benefits based on changes in the relative purchasing power of money (*inflation* or *deflation*).

colitis: Inflammation of the large intestine.

collaboration: The procedure in which two or more professional persons work together to serve a given *client*. The client may be an individual, family, group, community, or population. The professionals may work relatively independently of one another but communicate and coordinate their respective efforts to avoid duplication of services, or they may work as members of a single helping team. Collaboration also takes place among agencies and other organizations on a variety of projects. See also *interdisciplinary activity, interprofessional team, and linkage.*

collaborative therapy: A treatment format in which two or more social workers or other professionals each treat a single member of a family and, to some extent, coordinate their efforts. For example, a husband might be seen by one social worker and the wife by another, or a disturbed child might be seen by a *child psychoanalyst* and the parents treated conjointly by a social worker.

collective bargaining: A coordinated activity undertaken by a group of people who share a common interest or objective to influence change in some policy, law, or type of payment. The term most commonly applies to the efforts of organized labor in negotiating contracts.

collective responsibility: Assignment of obligation, trust, or blame to more than one person or organization. For example, all the "smokestack industries" of a region may be considered responsible for acid rain, and special taxes might be levied on them to be used for cleaning up the problem.

"coming out": The process of self-identification as a lesbian woman or gay man, followed by revelation of one's sexual orientation to others.

Commission on Civil Rights, U.S.: The independent federal body whose mission is to advance the cause of equal opportunity and investigate alleged denials of civil rights because of race, color, religion, gender, age, handicap, national origin, or the administration of justice. The commission does fact-finding on voting rights and equality of opportunity in education, employment, and housing.

commitment: The act of consigning an individual to a hospital or prison, usually after undergoing due legal process; also, a pledge or obligation. For example, social work students, to fund their educations, sometimes accept "commitment scholarships," in which a social agency or organization provides financial support in exchange for agreement to work for that organization for a predetermined period of time after graduation.

Committee for the Advancement of Social Work with Groups: An international organization of social work educators and practitioners affiliated for the purpose of developing effective social work practice with groups. The organization seeks to secure a more prominent place for work with groups in the curricula of social work schools and the programs of professional organizations. The committee sponsors an annual symposium at which scholarly papers about social work with groups are presented.

Commodity Supplemental Food Program (CSFP): A federally funded food assistance program that provides monthly packages of food to women of low-to-moderate income who have children under the age of 6.

Common Cause: A voluntary membership organization founded in 1970 and known as the "citizens' lobby." Its primary goal is to represent the interests of the public and to counterbalance special-interest lobbies. Its role is to inform the public about legislation and act as a watchdog over the lawmaking process and its implementation.

common-law marriage: *Cohabitation* by a man and a woman who consider themselves, and are generally considered by others, to be married but who have not had a civil or religious marriage ceremony. This marriage is recognized by law for some purposes in some jurisdictions.

communication: The exchange of information, including all the ways in which knowledge is transmitted and received.

communication theory: The body of concepts that pertains to the way people exchange information. Some major elements of communication theory are *content analysis, cybernetics, decoding, feedback, kinesics, metamessage, paralinguistics,* and *proxemics.*

community: A group of individuals having common interests or living in the same locality.

Community Action program (CAP): The neighborhood organizations established in 1965 under the *Office of Economic Opportunity (OEO)*. The goal of the program and its agencies was to develop the social and economic resources in poor communities and help find alternative ways to attack the forces that perpetuate poverty. CAP originally was responsible for the *Head Start* program, the *Legal Services Corporation,* and other programs that have since been transferred to other government agencies or disbanded. At first, in order to develop a variegated series of innovations, each Community Action Agency was somewhat independent of local and federal control. Subsequently, the agencies were led by elected officials with only a minority of poor people in leadership positions. The Community Action program established about 3,000 neighborhood service centers in poor communities to provide counseling, employment placement, legal advice, and, in some, health and child facilities.

Community Chest: An organization working for or in behalf of *private social agencies* in various geographic areas to raise and distribute funds through unified campaigns. The name originated in 1913, but the organization has since been renamed *United Way.*

community decision network: The aggregate of key organizations and individuals who have the formal or informal power to determine the course of action to be taken by a community. The decision network may include political leaders and legislative bodies, industrial leaders, religious groups, and civic associations. Its composition varies depending on the specific issue or community.

community development (CD): Efforts made by professionals and community residents to enhance the social bonds among members of the community, motivate the citizens for self-help, develop responsible local leadership, and create or revitalize local institutions. Community development workers have been active in *Third World* nations at least since the 1920s, especially in consciousness-raising, helping community residents to achieve greater collective participation, and developing local leadership. In the United States, CD workers have worked especially in underdeveloped rural settings and poor urban neighborhoods to facilitate the efforts of the residents to work together to increase their influence, self-sufficiency, and economic and educational opportunities.

community mental health center: A local organization, partly funded and regulated by the federal government, that provides a range of psychiatric and social services to people residing in the area. These include inpatient, outpatient, partial hospitalization, emergency, and transitional services, programs for the elderly and for children, screening and follow-up care, and programs that deal with alcohol and *substance abuse.*

community organization: An intervention process used by social workers and other professionals to help individuals, groups, and collectives of people with common interests or from the same geographic areas to deal with social problems and to enhance social well-being through planned collective action. Methods include identifying problem areas, analyzing causes, formulating plans, developing strategies, mobilizing necessary resources, identifying and recruiting community leaders, and encouraging interrelationships between them to facilitate their efforts.

Community Planning and Development Office: The federal organization within the U. S. *Department of Housing and Urban Development (HUD),* responsible for stimulating growth, rehabilitation, and new development in urban areas, especially those that are economically distressed. The office seeks to provide adequate housing and suitable environments, especially for people of low or moderate incomes. Grants and loans are provided through state agencies.

community property: Assets jointly owned by a husband and wife by the fact of their marriage. In states that have community property laws, both spouses are generally considered by law to share all property either has acquired during the marriage.

community self-help: The process of involving volunteers and other citizens in a community in decision making, social service planning, and coordination with professionals and agency employees. This process includes decentralization of responsibility and control from national, state, or local agencies to individuals and community groups.

Community Services Block Grant program: The U.S. *Department of Health and Human Services (HHS)* program that began its existence as the *Office of Economic Opportunity (OEO).* In 1969 many OEO programs were curtailed or placed within other government agencies. The emphasis of the remaining programs was changed to planning and research and overseeing and funding local Community Action Agencies. Community Services Block Grants were incorporated into the *Family Services Administration (FSA)* in 1986.

comparative social welfare: Analysis of the alternatives for providing the social service, economic, educational, and health care needs of a nation or social group by reviewing how different societies have addressed the same objectives.

comparable worth: The concept that payment or salary is to be based solely on the value of the work performed instead of on such considerations as the employee's sex, minority status, or need; also known as *pay equity.*

compensation: (1) A mental mechanism in which one tries to make up for imaginary or real characteristics that are considered undesirable. When this occurs unconsciously it is considered a *defense mechanism.* (2) The term also refers to payment for services rendered.

compensatory education: Special school and preschool programs designed to improve the educational readiness of children in poor neighborhoods. Examples include the *Head Start* program and Project Follow Through.

competence: The ability to fulfill the requirements of a job or other obligation. Competence in social work includes possession of all relevant educational and experiential requirements, demonstrated ability through passing licensing and certification exams, and the ability to carry out work assignments and achieve social work goals while adhering to the values of the profession. In the legal system, the term "competence" refers to the capacity to understand and act reasonably.

competency-based practice: In social work, the demonstrated ability to fulfill the professional obligations to the client, the community, the society, and the profession. This demonstration occurs through acquisition of *certification* (and *licensing* where applicable), maintaining currency by adhering to *continuing education* requirements, and participating in agency *supervision* and *in-service training.*

competent evidence: In the legal justice system, the facts about a case that are admissible in courts of law as well as convincing, reliable, and valid. Such information is to be distinguished from the opinions, guesses, or secondhand data offered by a professional expert witness. For example, a social worker's assessment that an infant's bruises were probably the result of child abuse because there was a past history of similar events in the family would not be considered competent evidence.

complementarity: The fit of two or more *roles* within an individual; also, the way certain roles of one individual fit with the roles of a relevant other person. For example, the social worker–client roles are usually complementary because the behaviors expected of each are compatible.

Comprehensive Employment and Training Act: See *CETA.*

comprehensive planning: Efforts by policymakers to coordinate knowledge, influence, and resources on a broad (rather than piecemeal) scale in order to achieve overall goals. This includes looking for the underlying causes rather than the overt symptoms of human problems. Comprehensive planning also considers and seeks to facilitate the reaching of human potential rather than confining itself to eliminating problems. To achieve this, comprehensive planning seeks to coordinate program resources not according to the specialized functions of existing agencies and professions, but across organizational lines of responsibility.

compulsion: (1) A strong and repetitive urge to act in a certain way. It is frequently a means of relieving anxiety that results from conflicting ideas and wishes that cannot be directly expressed. (2) The term also refers to forcing a person to act according to the wishes of another.

compulsive personality disorder: A type of *personality disorder* that has all or many of the following characteristics: perfectionistic behavior, insistence on having others submit to a certain way of doing things, limited ability to express warm feelings or tenderness, preoccupation with trivial details and rules, stinginess, stiff formality in relationships, and poor ability to prioritize and make decisions.

computer role: A recurrent pattern of communication in relating to others, characterized by very correct and proper behavior and calmness without apparent feeling. This role was delineated by Virginia Satir (*Peoplemaking,* Palo Alto, Calif.: Science and Behavior Books, 1972, p. 68), who described the person playing this role as one who feels vulnerable and responds to the perceived threat by pretending it is harmless and by hiding feelings of inadequacy through the use of big words. Other roles are the *blamer role,* the *distracter role,* and the *placater role.*

conation: That part of the mental function involving will or volition.

concentrations: The term used by social work educators for clusters of courses, parts of courses, or other formal learning experiences that provide the social work student with deeper and more focused knowledge and skill in certain areas of professional concern. After students have acquired formal education in basic areas of social work knowledge, they are often required, as part of their education, to select one or more concentrations that reflect their own interests and professional directions. Different schools of social work have different concentrations and ways of defining their concentrations. In most schools of social work, concentrations are defined according to specific *methods, fields of practice,* special populations, and special problems. Methods concentrations may include casework, group work, *community organization,* research-evaluation, direct clinical practice, administration–policy-planning combination, family–marital treatment, and *generic social work* practice combining macro and micro orientations. *Fields of practice* concentrations include *child welfare,* mental health, health, *school social work,* criminal justice, gerontology, rural social work, *industrial social work,* family and children's services, and various combinations. Special problems concentrations include *substance abuse* and *poverty,* and special populations concentrations include *minorities* and women.

Concern for the Dying: See *living will.*

conciliation: A mediation process in which two or more parties seek to minimize or eliminate their differences. The social worker's role in such instances is usually to advise, referee, and arbitrate. See also *mediator role* and *mediation, divorce.*

concrete operations stage: The phase of cognitive development that, according to *Piagetian theory*, occurs between ages 7 and 11, in which the individual learns to apply logic to observable and manipulable physical relationships.

concurrent therapy: The treatment format in which the social worker or other helping professional sees different members of a family or client system separately in individual sessions. This format has been used most commonly in marital therapy to maintain confidentiality and to encourage the participants to reveal their thoughts and behaviors when they might not feel able to do so in front of their spouses. This format is the opposite of *conjoint therapy.*

conditioned inhibition: In *behavior modification*, the pattern in which the subject is taught not to respond to a stimulus that previously elicited a response.

conditioned response (CR):   In *behavior modification*, a classically conditioned response that has been learned after being associated repeatedly with a *conditioned stimulus (CS).*

conditioned stimulus (CS):   A previously neutral event in the environment that begins to elicit a learned or *conditioned response (CR)* when paired with an *unconditioned stimulus (US)*. For example, seeing a dog does not elicit fear in an individual, but if the individual associates dogs with being bitten, the sight of a dog can elicit fear.

conditioning: A process through which behavior is learned. The two major types of conditioning, *respondent* (also known as classical) and *operant*, are differentiated by the sequence in which the stimulus is presented. In respondent conditioning the stimulus is presented in advance in order to elicit a behavior or response. In operant conditioning the subject's behavior must occur first and is then rewarded (*reinforcement*). See also *conditioned stimulus (CS), unconditioned stimulus (US), operant conditioning,* and *respondent behavior.*

conduct disorder: A maladaptive behavior pattern that becomes evident during childhood or adolescence and is characterized by persistent and repeated violations of the rights of others or the violation of age-appropriate *norms* and social rules. The four subtypes of conduct disorder are "undersocialized" (poor peer relations, little affection or bonding, indifference to the feelings of others, egocentrism), "socialized" (attachment to some but callousness toward outsiders), "aggressive" (physical violence to others and criminal behavior), and "nonaggressive" (persistent lying, *truancy*, running away from home, and *substance abuse.*)

confabulation: The act of making up for gaps in memory by fabricating stories or details.

confidentiality: A principle of ethics according to which the social worker or other professional may not disclose information about a client without the client's consent. This information includes the identity of the client, content of overt verbalizations, professional opinions about the client, material from records, and so on. In some jurisdictions, in very specific circumstances, social workers and other professionals may be compelled by law to reveal to designated authorities some information (such as threats of violence, commission of crimes, suspected child abuse, and other client behaviors) that would be relevant to legal judgments. See also *Tarasoff.*

conflict: (1) In groups or communities, the striving by two or more parties to achieve opposing or mutually exclusive goals; (2) in psychological terms, the mental struggle of two or more mutually exclusive impulses, motives, drives, or social demands.

conflict induction: The technique used especially by social workers in *community organization* and *family therapy* in which issues and value discrepancies are introduced to force members of the group into active confrontation, debate, and new coalition building. The families and citizens' groups with whom this is effective tend to be those that habitually avoid conflict and social discomfort, thus maintaining a stalemate that is unhealthy for some or all of their members.

conflict management: A conflict resolution procedure in organizational development in which the organization's members are helped to define the nature of their relationships, remove barriers to communication, define where they are interdependent, identify problems and resources, and work together to solve specific problems.

conflict resolution: The process of eliminating or minimizing the problems that result when different parties or groups compete with one another for the same limited objectives. This process most commonly occurs by facilitating compromises, achieving accommodation, or sometimes by the total surrender of one group to the other. Social workers often engage in this process when they help clarify, educate, mediate, and propose compromises or alternative solutions to clients or client systems who are contesting some mutual objectives.

conflict theories: Explanations about the nature, progress, and consequences of social conflict. The most prominent theories have been developed by Karl Marx, Georg Simmel, Lewis

Coser, and others. Marx hypothesized that conflict would eventually lead to an overthrow of the power group, leading to a classless, conflict-free society. Simmel and Coser suggest that conflict is not inherently bad and serves such important functions as solidifying the in-group, increasing group cohesiveness, and mobilizing the energies of group members.

conformity: Behavior that is consistent with the norms and expectations of the relevant social group.

confrontation: The act of bringing together opposing ideas, impulses, or groups for the purpose of systematic examination or comparison.

congenital: Existing since birth; term applied to a disorder or condition that originated during fetal development or the birth process.

Congressional Budget Office (CBO): The organization within the legislative branch of government that provides Congress with basic budget data and analysis of alternative fiscal and programmatic policy issues. CBO prepares an annual budget report to Congress that includes a discussion of alternative spending and revenue levels and allocations. CBO monitors the results of congressional action on individual authorizations and appropriations and provides five-year projections of the costs of continuing current policies on taxes and expenditures. See also *Office of Management and Budget (OMB).*

Congress of Racial Equality (CORE): The civil rights organization founded in 1942 to ensure fair application of the law to all races and to promote opportunities for minorities.

conjoint therapy: A type of intervention in which a therapist or team of therapists treats a family by meeting with the members together for regular sessions; also, a type of intervention in which the husband and wife are treated as a unit and seen together by the marital therapist or therapy team.

conscience: A person's system of moral values, standards of behavior, and sense of right and wrong. See also *superego.*

conscientization: A term coined by educator Paolo Freire; the process of helping clients and others become aware of, and feel concern about, a problem, objective, or value.

conscious: Mental awareness; that part of the mind that is aware of the immediate environment and of feelings and thoughts.

consciousness-raising: The process of helping an individual or group become aware of and more sensitive to a social condition, cause, or idea that had been of little prior interest.

consensual validation: The use of mutual agreement as the criterion for the truth or reality of a phenomenon; often used in *community organization* and in *clinical social work* as the objective or goal and to demonstrate progress toward that goal.

consensus: The process in which individuals and groups achieve general agreement about goals of mutual interest and the means to achieve them. Consensus is often facilitated by the community organizer by focusing first on goals and methods of high acceptability, by emphasizing common values, and by mediating and circumventing conflicts.

consequence: In *behaviorism,* an event that follows a behavior and that may increase or decrease the probability of that behavior's recurrence. A consequence may also have no effect on the behavior.

conservation: In *cognitive theory,* the ability to remember or retain relevant information and the ability to ignore irrelevant cues. For example, conservation was seen in Piaget's experiments when developing children began to retain the idea that water does not change when it is poured into pitchers of different shapes.

conservatism: An ideological orientation that tends to oppose change from previously established social values, mores, and structures. Many conservatives justify their ideology by presuming that traditional mores and structures are based on accumulated wisdom and are more effective than anything available to replace them.

conservator: A court-appointed guardian or custodian of the assets or property belonging to someone who is judged unable to manage them properly. The conservator may be an individual or, in some jurisdictions, a public or private agency.

constituency: A group of supporters, customers, voters, or clients whose interests are served by someone with the authority to represent them in seeking to meet their collective needs and interests.

constraint: In social planning and policy development, any general limitation on the level of rights. For example, zoning laws accompanied by fines, jail terms, and other penalties limit the rights of landowners.

construct validity: In social research, a method for assessing the validity of an instrument or scale. The scale or instrument is administered to two groups known in advance to be different. If the instrument is valid it should show different results.

consultation: An interpersonal relationship between an individual or agency possessing special expertise (for example, a consultant) and someone who needs that expertise to solve a specific problem. Alfred Kadushin (*Consultation in Social Work*, New York: Columbia University Press, 1977, p. 37) describes social work consultation as a problem-solving process in which advice and other helping activity from the consultant is offered to an individual, group, organization, or community that is faced with a job-related problem. Unlike *supervision*, which is relatively continuous and encompasses many areas of concern, consultation occurs more on an ad hoc or temporary basis and has a specific goal and situation focus. The consultant, unlike the supervisor, has no special administrative authority over those to whom advice is given.

consumerism: A social movement and orientation designed to advocate for and protect the interests of people in their roles as users of services or commodities and to scrutinize the activities, skills, training, effectiveness, outcomes, and products of those who provide these goods or services.

Consumer Price Index (CPI): A measure of the cost of living issued monthly by the *Bureau of Labor Statistics (BLS)*. It shows changes in the expenses for goods and services purchased by moderate-income families.

Consumer's League, National: See *National Consumers League (NCL)*.

consumption-versus-investment concept: See *investment-versus-consumption concept*.

containment: Efforts to maintain boundaries and reduce movement beyond them; a method of social control in which a group of people who are separated from their peers are given special benefits so that they have less incentive to challenge their separation.

content analysis: In *communication theory*, the systematic study of some group interaction, written document, or other communication primarily by evaluating the frequency with which certain ideas, reactions, or expressions occur.

content validity: In social research, a method for assessing the *validity* of an instrument or a scale. Items that actually exist on a scale are compared with items that could have been used.

contextual theory: The family systems concept, originated by Boszormenyi-Nagy, that seeks to understand family interactions, conflicts, and loyalties in terms of the legacy of accumulated obligations, debts, and hurts that occur in a family system through several generations.

contingency: In social research and statistics, a term connoting an association or correlation between variables, as in contingency tables. In *behaviorism*, the consequences that are expected to follow behaviors.

contingency contracting: In *behavior therapy*, a technique in which an agreement is made spelling out the behaviors to be performed in order for a certain consequence to follow. The technique is used particularly by behavorial family therapists who help family members carry out "if-then statements."

continuing education: Training taken by social workers and other professionals who have already completed formal education requirements to enter their field. Most professions require their members to keep up with current knowledge by participating in specified additional training within certain time limits. For example, state licensing boards for social workers may require them to obtain a specific number of CEUs (continuing education units) by successfully completing qualified academic or professional courses.

continuity of care: Coordination of the efforts made by different organizations, or divisions within one organization, to provide for the client's needs with a minimum of duplication or gaps in service. See also *case integration*.

continuous reinforcement: In *behavior modification*, a *schedule of reinforcement* in which *target behaviors* are reinforced each time they occur (compared to the less frequent *intermittent reinforcement*).

continuum: A phenomenon that has variability even though no discrete gaps or separate parts are evident.

contraception: See *birth control*.

contract: A written, oral, or implied agreement between the client and the social worker as to the goals, methods, timetables, and mutual obligations to be fulfilled during the intervention process.

contracting: The therapeutic procedure of discussing with the client the goals, methods, and mutual obligations of treatment to obtain a clear verbal understanding or to establish a formal agreement about them.

control: To regulate; to exercise direction or restraint over another. In social research, a standard for comparison. In social welfare management, a procedure for regulating the flow of information and activity so that efforts to achieve goals are coordinated.

control group: In research, a group of subjects who are matched in every possible respect with an *experimental group*, except that they are not exposed to the variable being tested.

controlled substances: Drugs that, because of their potential for abuse or addiction, have limited availability and are strictly regulated or outlawed. These substances include *marijuana, narcotics* (opiates such as opium, heroin, morphine, and *codeine* and nonopiates such as *methadone*), stimulants (such as *cocaine* and *amphetamines*), depressants (such as *barbiturates* and *tranquilizers*), and *hallucinogens* (such as *LSD*, mescaline, and peyote).

control variable: A variable introduced by a researcher to check the apparent relationship between independent and dependent variables.

conversion: A *defense mechanism* is which anxiety or emotional conflict is transformed into overt physical manifestations or symptoms such as pain, loss of feeling, or paralysis.

conversion disorder: One of the *somatoform disorders* (those involving physical symptoms for which there are no organic findings). The condition generally includes symptoms suggesting neurological disease, such as paralysis, coordination disturbance, anesthesia, blindness, or seizures. The psychological purpose of the disorder is primarily to achieve some *primary gain* (keeping the originating conflict out of awareness; for example, becoming "blind" while witnessing a traumatic event) or *secondary gain* (getting sympathy or an excuse to avoid an unpleasant obligation).

conversion symptoms: Somatic complaints that are *psychogenic*. The term derives from psychodynamic theories that hypothesized that unconscious and intolerable thoughts or drives are converted into physical manifestations, most commonly involving the nervous system (for example, paralysis, blindness, and so on).

Cooperative for American Relief Everywhere: See *CARE*.

cooptation: A community organizer's strategy for minimizing anticipated opposition by absorbing or including the opponent in the group's membership. Once a member of the group, the opponent has less ability to criticize the program in public. Opposition within the organization is also less effective because the person is in the minority. The term is also used to indicate any election of a person or group into another group's membership.

copayment: A provision in some insurance programs that requires the policyholder to share the cost of any loss or claim. In many health insurance programs the beneficiary is required to pay a percentage of the provider's bill before reimbursement is made for the rest. The major purpose of this arrangement is to discourage inappropriate use of resources and encourage responsible participation.

coping mechanisms: The behavioral and personality patterns used to adjust or adapt to environmental pressures without altering goals or purposes.

corporal punishment: Inflicting physical pain for the purpose of punishment, as in spanking a misbehaving child.

corporate welfare: Providing services, financial assistance, subsidies, or other benefits to organizations to help them maintain their viability or profitability. For example, a national government might reduce the tax rates or subsidize part of the expenses of a labor-intensive industry because it supposedly provides many jobs for citizens. A municipal government might offer to give land at low or no cost to companies that relocate to the area, in order to enhance the local economy. Some of the people who are most strongly opposed to governmental welfare benefits for individuals favor corporate welfare programs for businesses.

corrections: The professional specialty that seeks to change and improve the behaviors of convicted law offenders through imprisonment, parole, probation, and—ideally—educational programs and social services.

correlation: In research, a mutual relation; a pattern of variation between two phenomena in which change in one is associated with change in the other. High correlations are not necessarily indicative of causality.

correlation coefficient: A numerical index of the extent to which two variables are related. When the score is positive ($+0.1$ to $+1.0$), it indicates that the frequency of one phenomenon is associated with the frequency of the other. When the score is negative (-0.1 to -1.0), it indicates that a high frequency on one phenomenon is associated with a low frequency on the other. Perfect agreement between two variables is expressed as $+1.0$. Perfect inverse relationships are expressed as -1.0. A correlation coefficient of 0.0 indicates no apparent relationship.

cost-benefit analysis: An administration and management procedure in which various goals of the organization are evaluated systematically along with the expenses and resources required to achieve them.

costing: Estimating the total expenditure of a program or plan that would be necessary to reach a specified goal. Costing is also referred to as "costing out."

cost of living: A relative term pertaining to the amount of money required to purchase the goods and services needed to live adequately in a given society.

cost-of-living allowance: An increased *cash* or *in-kind benefit* based on the amount of money deemed necessary to live according to a specified economic standard. For example, members of such groups as retired military personnel, federal employees, and social security recipients are sometimes paid a sum in excess of their originally contracted income to take into account the increased amount of money necessary for them to maintain their living standard.

cost-of-living index: A measure to determine the relative purchasing power of money at a given time in a given society. In the United States, the index is calculated by weighting the average prices of 296 commodities that are considered important or representative of people's overall needs.

cost sharing: A budgeting and administrative procedure that occurs when two or more governments or other organizations divide certain financial obligations. Each participating organization agrees to pay a portion of the total outlay, the amount usually depending on its own needs, resources, and expected benefits from the expenditure. For example, the federal government and a state government agree to share the costs of public assistance payments to eligible recipients in that state. In another example, two social agencies that provide similar services in the same area agree to employ one consulting firm to provide both agencies with information about the area's demographic characteristics. See also *revenue sharing.*

cotherapy: Psychosocial intervention on behalf of a client conducted by two or more professionals working in *collaboration.*

Council on Governments (COG): Comprehensive planning organizations comprising representatives of several local governments that are usually in geographic proximity (that is, several towns, cities, and counties in an area). COG members meet periodically to consider the mutual needs of the people in the area and ways of combining resources to meet those needs. Their purposes include planning, coordination, integration of their respective efforts, and achieving more influence with their state governments and at the national level than could be achieved through their isolated efforts. Typical service-planning activities include transportation, water and sewage treatment, and services to the elderly.

Council of Nephrology Social Workers (CNSW): A professional association of social workers that is an advisory unit and integral part of the National Kidney Foundation. Founded in 1973, the council comprises primarily medical and health care social workers who are concerned about social services for people with kidney disease, urinary system disorders, diabetes, collagen disease, and related disorders.

Council on International Programs (CIP): A social work organization that helps social workers from other countries come to the United States for additional training in U.S. schools of social work and other educational facilities.

Council on Social Work Education (CSWE): An independent organization comprising social work educators, professional organizations, social agencies, and academic institutions for the purpose of establishing and maintaining standards in social work education. The parent organization of CSWE was established in 1919 and later became known as the American Association of Schools of Social Work (AASSW). In 1952, AASSW merged with the National Association of Schools of Social Administration (NASSA) to form CSWE. The organization is the primary body for accrediting schools of social work in the United States. CSWE also sponsors an annual program meeting every March in different cities and publishes books, pamphlets, and the *Journal of Education for Social Work.* See also *curriculum policy statement.*

counseling: A procedure often used by clinical social workers and other professionals from various disciplines in guiding individuals, families, groups, and communities by such activities as giving advice, delineating alternatives, helping to articulate goals, and providing needed information.

countertransference: A set of conscious or unconscious emotional reactions to a client experienced by the social worker or other professional, usually in a clinical setting. According to psychodynamic theory, these feelings originate in the worker's own developmental conflicts and are projected onto the client. Freud also used this term to refer to the therapeutic actions the analyst might take in response to the client's *transference* feelings.

couples group therapy: A *family therapy* strategy and *group psychotherapy* format in which several couples meet on a regular basis with a therapist to work systematically on resolving marital and family problems.

CPT: *Current Procedural Terminology,* a physician's manual that systematically lists and codes the services and procedures performed by physicians. CPT, first published in 1966, is periodically revised. The part of CPT that lists and codes the services and procedures commonly used by psychiatrists is also published separately as *Procedural Terminology for Psychiatrists.* Better known as PTP, it lists such activities as diagnostic interviews, medical psychotherapy with drug management, electroconvulsive therapy, and so on. PTP or CPT codes do not include, and should not be used to report, services of nonphysicians.

"crack": A highly addictive form of *cocaine* made by mixing small amounts of it with baking soda and water. When dry, the substance is broken or cracked into small pebbles and usually smoked in special pipes. Crack is relatively inexpensive, highly potent, and can be lethal. Users tend to become obsessed about getting additional supplies.

creaming: A term referring to the use of social services and programs, presumably available to all, by people who are most likely to succeed with the help of a given intervention program. The term is also used to describe the process in which such programs are most often used by the more knowledgeable, sophisticated, and less needy, so that they are less accessible to others.

crib death: See *sudden infant death syndrome (SIDS)*.

crime: Any behavior that violates a law. Some social scientists extend this definition to include any behavior that is contrary to the society's moral codes for which there are formalized group sanctions, whether or not they are institutionalized as laws.

criminal justice policy: The society's guidelines and established procedures to be considered when deciding how to cope with illegal conduct. Elements of current U.S. criminal justice policy include the right to trial by jury, the right to competent counsel, rights of appeal and *habeas corpus*, determinant sentencing, probation rather than incarceration for less serious crimes with no prior convictions, and parole for appropriate conduct during incarceration.

criminal justice system: The programs, policies, sociopolitical and legal institutions, and physical infrastructure designed to help prevent and control crime and to adjudicate, incarcerate, and rehabilitate people engaged in illegal behavior.

crisis: A term used by social workers in two different ways: (1) as an internal experience of emotional change and distress and (2) as a social event in which a disastrous event disrupts some essential functions of existing social institutions. When seen as a period of emotional distress, it is considered to be precipitated by a perceived life problem or obstacle to an important goal resulting in internal discord for which the individual's typical coping strategies are inadequate. The outcome of the crisis can be positive if the individual eventually finds new *coping mechanisms* to deal with the unfamiliar event, thus adding to the repertoire of effective adaptive responses.

crisis bargaining: Actions taken by people during times of upset or duress to ameliorate the situation or minimize the conflict. The concept is most clearly delineated in the *Kübler-Ross death stages* theory. In this theory, bargaining is the third crisis stage in responses to impending death. After the individual typically goes through a period of *denial* and then *anger*, he or she attempts to avoid or delay death by making promises or "deals" or by conforming to different standards.

crisis care centers: Facilities in social service and health care organizations oriented toward providing short-term emergency assistance and helping individuals and groups return to precrisis functioning. These centers provide such services as disaster relief, suicide prevention, emergency food and shelter, counseling victims of rape or other crimes, sheltering victims of spouse or child abuse, detoxification for substance abusers, and many other activities.

crisis hot line: See *hot line*.

crisis intervention: The therapeutic practice used in helping clients in crisis to promote effective coping that can lead to positive growth and change by acknowledging the problem, recognizing its impact, and learning new or more effective behaviors for coping with similar predictable experiences.

crisis sequence: A series of predictable changes experienced by the person in crisis: (1) hazardous event (a stress producer that may be a single catastrophic event or a series of mishaps that have a cumulative effect); (2) vulnerable state (heightened tension and anxiety caused by the hazardous event, intensified as the individual uses the entire repertoire of coping techniques before seeing they do not work in this new situation); (3) precipitating factor (the "last straw," often seen as the presenting problem or event that brings tension to a peak); (4) active crisis state (disequilibrium has set in and is manifested by psychological and physical turmoil, aimless activity, disturbances in mood and intellectual functioning, and painful preoccupation with events leading to the crisis event); and (5) reintegration (the individual adjusts or accepts and learns new and effective coping techniques, a phase that may be adaptive or maladaptive).

crisis theory: A group of related concepts pertaining to people's reactions when confronted with new and unfamiliar experiences. These experiences may come in the form of natural disasters, significant loss, changes in social status, and life-cycle changes. See also *crisis sequence* and *crisis intervention*.

cross-sectional research: A research design whereby the researcher collects data on the phenomenon under investigation at one point in time, as in a one-time survey; also, a comparison of subjects who represent different aspects of a single variable, such as "upper class," "middle class," and "lower class."

cross-tabulation: A method for assessing the joint relationship between two variables by using tabular methods.

CSWE Curriculum Policy Statement: See *curriculum policy statement.*

cult: A group whose members hold strong beliefs associated with the teachings of a leader; a body of beliefs and rites practiced by a group that usually attributes religious, mystical, or magical powers to its leader.

cultural deprivation: The absence of certain socialization experiences that an individual may need to cope effectively in new social situations. One who has been deprived in this way often lacks the social skills, values, or motivations necessary to deal with the relevant environment.

cultural lag: The retention of customs, habits, and technologies even though they have become obsolete or irrelevant to the new standards set by the prevailing culture.

cultural relativism: The view that specific norms or rituals can only be understood accurately in the context of a culture's goals, social history, and environmental demands.

culture: The customs, habits, skills, technology, arts, science, and religious and political behavior of a group of people in a specific time period.

culture of poverty: A premise according to which the poor are impoverished because their values, norms, and motivations prevent them from taking advantage of widespread opportunities to achieve economic independence.

culture shock: The experience of temporary confusion, depression, and anxiety when an individual enters another cultural or subcultural group environment and is uncertain about the expected roles and norms. See also *anomie.*

Current Procedural Terminology: See *CPT.*

curriculum: The defined program of study in an educational institution. In schools of social work, the curriculum includes a prescribed number and variety of required and elective courses, field placement, and other educational experiences.

curriculum policy statement: A document that formally and officially describes the educational objectives, standards, and required outcomes of affiliated institutions. In social work in the past 50 years many curriculum policy statements have been issued by various social work education groups. At present, most social work educators use this term when referring to the curriculum policy statement adopted by the

Council on Social Work Education (CSWE) in 1982. This document delineates the official criteria for accrediting *MSW* and *BSW* social work programs. The statement does not prescribe any particular curriculum but does specify certain content areas to be covered and how they are to be related to each other; to the purposes and values of social work; and to the mission, resources, and educational content of each professional program. The curriculum policy statement is revised and updated periodically.

custodial care: The provision of shelter, food, and basic physical needs without amenities.

custody: A legal right and obligation of a person or group to possess, control, protect, or maintain guardianship over some designated property or over another person who is unable to function autonomously (for example, children and certain handicapped adults).

custody of children: A legal determination in divorce cases specifying which parent or other guardian will be in charge of the children. This determination is based on what is considered to be in the best interests of the children. In some circumstances, *joint custody* is awarded so that responsibility is shared between both parents. Typically, in joint custody the child lives with each parent for fixed periods of time.

cutback: Reduction in service, funding, or budget or resource allocation usually related to declines in demand, cessation or reduction of former sources of revenue, inaccessibility of personnel, or discontinued support.

cybernetics: The study of the processes that regulate or control systems, especially the flow of information. See also *communication theory.*

cyclical unemployment: Loss of jobs caused by periodic downward trends in the business cycle. Usually this type of unemployment affects more workers for longer periods of time than the other types of unemployment (*frictional, seasonal,* and *technological*).

cyclothymic disorder: A mood disturbance that has lasted more than two years and includes periods of *depression* and *hypomania*; a mild form of *bipolar disorder* (manic-depressive illness).

cystic fibrosis: A hereditary disease of the endocrine glands that causes them to produce abnormally thick and sticky secretions that form cysts and often cause obstructions in the pancreas, liver, and lungs. Symptoms vary according to the severity of the condition and the organs particularly involved, but they most often include nutritional deficiency, diarrhea, distended abdomen, and respiratory infections.

D

day care: Facilities and programs that care for children or other dependents when their parents or guardians are not available for their care. The term also applies to health and physical care programs for people of all ages who return to their homes each evening.

day hospital: Facilities primarily for the elderly and handicapped who sleep in their own homes but receive medical and social services during the day.

death: The total and permanent cessation of vital functions; currently, in humans, the determining factor is the absence of measurable brain wave activity.

death rate: The ratio of the number of deaths in a specific time period to the total population or to an identified segment of that population; it is usually expressed in terms of the number of deaths per 1,000 or 100,000 people. It is also known as *mortality rate.*

death wish: A person's behavior or thought patterns that become self-destructive, physically harmful, and oriented toward death. According to some psychoanalytic theorists, every individual has a certain degree of unconscious desire to die that may be consciously manifested in *masochism,* masochistic tendencies, or self-destructive behavior.

decentralization: Diffusion of responsibility, planning, and implementation of change from the highest levels of an organization's authority toward those closer to the problem or area of action. An example is the federal government's *revenue sharing* with states and municipalities.

decertification: The process of removing the title and commensurate responsibility and privileges from an identified individual or group because they have not complied with predetermined qualifications or criteria or because they no longer want the designation.

decision theory: A mathematical approach to decision making using such devices as *gaming,* modeling, and simulation.

declassification: A policy used by governments and other employers, often as a means of reducing personnel expenditures, to eliminate educational and experience requirements for holding a job and performing its functions. For example, some professional social work positions were declassified when agencies no longer required that specific jobs had to be done only by social workers with *MSW* degrees.

decoding: In *communication theory,* the process of translating verbal and nonverbal cues, body gestures, and other signals into messages that are comprehensible to the one receiving them.

decompensation: The progressive loss of normal mental functioning, *defense mechanisms,* or coherent thought processes, often culminating in a form of *psychosis.*

decriminalization: The repeal or adoption of legislation, the result of which is that an action formerly considered to be a crime is no longer so regarded and legal punishments can no longer be imposed.

deductible: A provision in health and other insurance coverage in which a beneficiary is required to contribute a specified sum per claim in a given period, before the insurer pays the remaining amount of the claim.

deductive reasoning: The process by which particular conclusions are reached by starting with general principles believed to be true. For example, a social worker believes that all rape victims subsequently suffer some degree of emotional distress. The worker sees a client who was raped and deduces that she is experiencing some distress even without her saying so. See also *inductive reasoning.*

de facto: In actual fact; regardless of legal or normative standards. for example, de facto segregation occurs when a neighborhood is underrepresented by ethnic minorities even though it has no legal provision to exclude minorities.

default judgment: In the legal justice system, a decision made against a defendant who fails to appear for a court hearing.

defense mechanism: A mental process that protects the personality from anxiety, guilt feelings, or unacceptable thoughts. Psychoanalytic theorists consider such mechanisms to be generally unconscious. Some of the best-known defense mechanisms include *denial, displacement, idealization, substitution, compensation, overcompensation, conversion, sublimation, reaction formation, projection, rationalization,* and *intellectualization.*

defensiveness: Excessive sensitivity to actual or potential criticism or disapproval; also, behavior that attempts to avert criticism or embarrassment.

deficit: The excess of expenditures and liabilities over income and assets during a specific budgetary period.

deflation: A reduction in the cost of living and general price levels of an economy.

defrauding: Criminally depriving a person of his or her rightful property through deception or misrepresentation.

deinstitutionalization: The process of releasing patients, inmates, or people who are dependent for their physical and mental care from residential-custodial facilities, presumably with the understanding that they no longer need such care or can receive it through community-based services.

de jure: According to law; by statute. For example, "de jure segregation" refers to the legally enforced separation of groups of people (by race, sex, age, and so on.) This condition existed in U.S. public schools before the 1954 Supreme Court decision (*Brown v. Board of Education*) and exists through *apartheid* in South Africa. See also *de facto.*

delinquency: The failure to fulfill one's duties or obligations. This term is most often used by social workers in referring to the actions of youngsters who violate laws or fail to conform to the reasonable demands of *caregivers* and other authorities.

delinquent: (1) A law offender who is considered to be a minor (in most states, under 18, in some up to 22) by the jurisdiction of residence or where the offense is committed; (2) a term applied to a debt that has not been paid when due or an agreement that has not been fulfilled.

delirium: A state of confusion, often accompanied by *hallucinations, delusions, emotional lability,* and *anxiety.* It is an acute disorder, usually reversible, caused by changes in cerebral metabolism typically induced by drug or alcohol ingestion, shock, or fever.

delirium tremens (d.t.'s): A form of *delirium* resulting from withdrawal from excessive consumption of alcohol. The victim often develops such symptoms as fever, convulsions, tremors, and hallucinations, generally occurring between one and four days after the drinking has stopped.

Delphi conferencing: A procedure, especially in social planning and community organization, that uses a highly structured, multistage questionnaire with a group of experts or panelists so that they can make focused assessments about the desirability, value, and feasibility of a proposed plan or policy.

delusion: An inaccurate but strongly held belief retained despite objective evidence to the contrary and despite cultural norms that do not support such beliefs. It is often a characteristic of *psychosis* or *paranoid ideation.* Major types include delusions of grandeur (an exaggerated sense of self-importance) and delusions of persecution (the mistaken belief that one is being threatened or harmed by others).

demand subsidy: The concept of providing cash or vouchers to economically disadvantaged clients so that they can purchase needed services or products through the existing marketplace. This is in contrast to the concept of *supply subsidy,* in which funds are provided to organizations so that they may provide their services to those in need. Food stamps and Medicaid are programs that use the demand subsidy principle, whereas community mental health centers and public hospitals are examples of supply subsidy.

dementia: An organic deterioration of the mental processes, usually characterized by memory loss, personality change, and impaired judgment and ability to think abstractly or systematically; a manifestation of certain types of *psychosis,* including *senile psychosis.*

demogrant: A benefit provided to those in specified population categories (for example, children, mothers, the elderly, or citizens) without regard to need. Rare in the United States, this type of benefit is a common form of income redistribution in many other nations. See also *maternity benefits* and *Medicare.*

demography: The systematic study of population variables and characteristics.

demonstration: (1) In social change efforts, a group action designed to call public or political attention to a problem or issue of interest to the participants. This typically takes the form of massing or marching together in highly visible settings or picketing the entrances of buildings where objectionable behavior is believed to be taking place. (2) The term also applies to behaviors intended to show how something can be done effectively, such as when a social worker shows a client how to communicate better with others by role-playing.

demonstration programs: Service delivery programs that are usually limited by time and geographic range but are designed to test whether measures proposed for solving specific problems are desirable and effective. In theory, programs that are demonstrated as effective can then be made permanent and expanded for a larger population. Examples of demonstration programs are *Mobilization for Youth* in New York City and the NASW Mental Health Manpower studies.

demonstrative: A term applied to behavior that is outwardly expressive of emotions and to persons who exhibit such behavior.

denial: The *defense mechanism* that protects the personality from anxiety or guilt by disavowing or ignoring unacceptable thoughts, emotions, or wishes.

Department of Health and Human Services, U.S. (HHS): The federal agency formed in 1979 when the *Department of Health, Education, and Welfare* was divided into two cabinet-level agencies. The principal components of the department now include the *Social Security Administration (SSA)*, the *Office of Human Development Services*, the *Health Care Financing Administration* (including *Medicare* and *Medicaid*), the *Public Health Service*, and (since 1986) the *Family Services Administration (FSA)*.

Department of Health, Education, and Welfare, U.S. (HEW): A federal agency formed in 1953, replacing the Federal Security Agency, to administer, develop, and improve the national programs for social welfare, health, and education. When the separate Department of Education was created in 1979, the remaining components of the agency became known as the *Department of Health and Human Services (HHS)*.

Department of Housing and Urban Development, U.S. (HUD): The federal agency formed in 1965 to administer, develop, and improve the national programs in housing, urban renewal, and community development. Its major divisions include the Office of Fair Housing and Equal Opportunity, New Community Development, Community Planning and Development, and the *Government National Mortgage Association (GNMA)*.

Department of Labor, U.S.: The federal agency created in 1913 to improve working conditions, job safety, and employee welfare; to secure employee benefits; to enhance employment opportunities; and to acquire and disseminate information about social conditions affecting employment. Its major offices and organizations include

the *Occupational Safety and Health Administration (OSHA)*, the Labor-Management Services Administration, the Employment Training Administration, and the *Bureau of Labor Statistics (BLS)*.

dependency: A state of reliance on other people or things for existence or support; a tendency to rely on others to provide nurturance, make decisions, and give protection, security, and shelter. Some of this reliance is natural, but in most adults, when it becomes excessive, it is often symptomatic of neurosis, regression, or emotional insecurity.

dependent personality disorder: One of the *personality disorders,* in which the individual is generally passive in most relationships, allows others to assume responsibilities, lacks self-confidence, feels helpless, and tends to tolerate abusiveness from others.

dependent variable: In research, the phenomenon or reaction to be tested or measured when a new stimulus or condition is introduced.

depersonalization: A feeling of being in an unreal situation or a sense that one's self or body is detached from the immediate environment. This experience is often found in individuals who are subjected to inordinate *stress* or are in *crisis* as well as individuals with specific mental disorders such as *neurosis* and *psychosis*.

depersonalization disorder: A type of mental disturbance in which the individual copes with internal conflict and anxiety through psychological detachment or by experiencing the feeling of being in an unreal situation. It is one of the *dissociative disorders.*

depression: A group of emotional reactions frequently characterized by sadness, discouragement, despair, pessimism about the future, reduced activity and productivity, and feelings of inadequacy, self-effacement, and hopelessness. In some individuals, such traits may be mild, intermittent, and undetectable by observers, but in others they may be constant and intense. In its more pathological forms it may be a manifestation of a *major affective disorder, bipolar disorder,* or *cyclothymic disorder.*

depression, economic: A socioeconomic condition in which business activity is lowered for a prolonged time, unemployment rates are high, and purchasing power is greatly diminished. See also *stagflation and recession.*

depressive reaction: A term indicating sadness, pessimism, and lowered activity often precipitated by an actual or perceived severe loss. The term is now replaced by *bipolar disorder, major depression, dysthymic disorder,* or *cyclothymic disorder,* depending on other symptoms.

deprivation: A state of unfulfilled, unmet, or incompletely met physical, social, or emotional needs.

desegregation: The act of abolishing *segregation,* whether *de facto* or *de jure,* that has been imposed on certain minority groups.

desensitization: The elimination or minimization of physical or psychological reactions to stimuli. Behaviorally oriented social workers use a form of this, known as *systematic desensitization,* especially to help some clients overcome certain fears or ineffective behavior patterns.

desertion: The act of abandoning a person or position to whom or to which one has certain obligations. In marriage, desertion occurs when one spouse leaves the other, without the other's consent, and has no intention of returning. Desertion may or may not be accompanied by nonsupport (intentional failure to provide food, shelter, and maintenance when legally obliged to do so). Desertion is usually grounds for divorce.

detention: The act of restraining a person, usually in an institution, jail, or other holding facility, for some legal purpose.

deterrence: In the legal justice system, a policy that uses fear of restraint and punishment to attempt to discourage criminal activity.

detoxification: The process of removing drugs or other harmful substances from the body for a sufficient length of time to permit the restoration of adequate physiological and psychological functioning. This is achieved by withholding the abused substance from the individual while providing rest, proper diet, nursing care, suitable medication, and social services.

developmental approach: In *direct practice,* an orientation toward or focus on the predictable changes that occur throughout the human life cycle, including physical, mental, social, and environmental changes.

Developmental Disabilities Administration: An agency within the U.S. *Department of Health and Human Services (HHS)* that provides information and coordinates expertise about the causes, prevention, and treatment of human developmental disabilities, such as *mental retardation, autism, seizure disorders,* and *cerebral palsy.*

developmental disability: A condition that occurs as a result of disease, genetic disorder, or impaired growth pattern before adulthood. Some of the conditions classified as developmental disabilities include *cerebral palsy, Down's syndrome, epilepsy, mental retardation,* and *autism.*

developmental disorder: A group of physical and mental dysfunctions that appear before the individual reaches maturity. Professionals dis-

tinguish between "pervasive" and "specific" developmental disorders. Specific developmental disorders include developmental reading, arithmetic, and *language disorder* and developmental *articulation disorder.* Pervasive disorders include infantile *autism* and "childhood onset pervasive developmental disorder," which is characterized by gross and sustained impairment in social relationships, multiple oddities of behavior, and lack of appropriate *affect.* These characteristics become evident after 30 months of age and before 12 years.

developmental stages: The progression of physical and mental changes over time resulting in clusters of identifiable and predictable characteristics that tend to occur during specific time periods.

deviance: The act of differing sharply from normal behavior or maintaining standards of conduct, norms, and values that are in marked contrast to accepted standards; the term was formerly used to indicate sexual *perversion.*

diabetes: A disease, caused by a disorder in the islands of Langerhans in the pancreas, in which an insufficient amount of insulin is produced or secreted so that the body cannot process sugars properly.

diagnosis: The process of identifying a problem (social and mental as well as medical) and its underlying causes and formulating a solution. In early social work delineations it was one of the three major processes, along with study and treatment. Currently, many social workers prefer to call this process *assessment* because of the medical connotation that often accompanies the term "diagnosis." Other social workers think of diagnosis as the process of seeking underlying causes and assessment as having more to do with the collection of relevant information.

Diagnostic and Statistical Manual of Mental Disorders: See *DSM-III.*

diagnostic related groups: See *DRGs.*

diagnostic school in social work: The name given to the orientation in social work that emphasized psychodynamic and social change theories and insight-oriented treatment procedures. The term was first used to distinguish this group of social workers from colleagues who were identified with the *functional school in social work.*

dialysis: Treatment for *kidney disease.* The various types of dialysis include *hemodialysis,* peritoneal dialysis, and chronic ambulatory peritoneal dialysis. Dialysis can be performed in hospitals, special outpatient centers, and, in some cases, in the patient's home. Dialysis has no curative value but substitutes for the function of the kidneys.

didactic analysis: Psychoanalysis oriented primarily toward instruction rather than therapy.

differential response: In *behaviorism* and *social learning theory*, a response that is elicited by a particular *stimulus* among many possible different stimuli. For example, a child may learn to smile when a parent smiles.

differentiation: In family systems theory, the ability of family members to distinguish or separate their identities, thoughts, and emotions from those of other members of the family. See also *fusion*.

diphtheria: A contagious disease that occurs mostly in preschool children and is transmitted by droplets of moisture exhaled by infected individuals. The bacteria that cause the disease lodge in the mucous membranes of the throat, producing tissue-destroying *toxins*. Diphtheria deaths are caused by tissue damage, particularly in the heart. The disease was once common in the United States and elsewhere, but injections of diphtheria *toxoid* routinely given to infants have minimized its incidence rate.

direct cost: The amount paid by a recipient of any goods or services—a sum that may only partially cover the expense of producing those goods or services. See also *indirect cost*.

direct influence: A treatment procedure in *social casework* or *clinical social work* in which the worker attempts to promote a specific type of behavior in the client. It is done systematically and cautiously, often by offering suggestions and advice about how best to reach the client's own goals.

directive therapy: An approach in counseling in which the social worker or other mental health care provider offers advice, suggestions, information about resources, and prescriptions for more effective behavior.

direct practice: The term used by social workers to indicate their range of professional activities on behalf of clients, in which goals are reached through personal contact and immediate influence with those seeking social services. It is to be distinguished from *indirect practice* (activities aimed at achieving social goals or developing human opportunities).

direct treatment: A group of intervention procedures used in *social casework* or *clinical social work* in which the worker seeks to implement specific changes or improvement through personal contact with the client. The term was first used by Mary Richmond to designate a social worker's face-to-face interactions with individual clients, as distinguished from "indirect treat-

ment" or problem solving and developmental work in the environment.

disability: Inability to perform activities, usually due to a physical or mental condition or infirmity that lasts or is expected to last continuously for life, indefinitely, or for a specific time.

disability benefit: The provision of cash, goods, or services to one who is not capable of performing certain activities because of a physical or mental condition; a form of *categorical assistance* based on incapacity. In the United States the *Supplemental Security Income (SSI)* program for the needy disabled is currently the most extensive example of this type of program.

disabled: A term applied to someone who is incapable of carrying out certain duties or functions because of a specific physical or mental condition or infirmity. The condition may be temporary or permanent; it may be partial or total.

disarmament: The intentional decisions and actions that bring about a reduction in or elimination of the weapons possessed by a nation or group. Many social workers have been active in the *peace movement*, in which nations are encouraged to lay down their arms or discontinue supplying arms to others.

disaster: An extraordinary event, either natural or human made, concentrated in time and space, that often results in damage to property and human life and health and is disruptive of the ability of some social institutions to continue fulfilling their essential functions.

disaster syndrome: The psychological and social relationship problems typically experienced by victims of a crisis or calamity. Social workers who specialize in disaster relief identify several phases of the syndrome: preimpact (apprehension and anxiety accompanying the threat or warning); impact (the hazard strikes and the community organizes its relief effort); postimpact (often characterized as a "honeymoon" phase of high energy for coping and mutual cooperation); and disillusionment (when people encounter the long-term obstacles brought about by the disaster).

discharge planning: A social service in hospitals and other institutions that is designed to help the patient or client make a timely and healthy adjustment from care within the facility to alternative sources of care or to self-care when the need for service has passed. When practiced by skilled social workers, discharge planning helps the client and relevant others to understand the nature of the problem and its impact, facilitates their adaptations to their new roles, and helps arrange for postdischarge care.

discretionary funds: The money available after purchase of necessities; also referred to as disposable income. In budgeting, the term also refers to funds put aside for allocation outside rigid *categorical grants.* The use of these funds is generally determined by persons empowered to choose how to spend them.

discrimination: (1) The process of distinguishing between two objects, ideas, situations, or stimuli; (2) the prejudgment of people based on identifiable characteristics such as race, gender, religion, or ethnicity.

disengaged family: A family whose individual members and *subsystems* have overly rigid *boundaries* that result in restricted interaction and psychological isolation from one another. Some disengaged families may also have diffuse as well as rigid boundaries. See also *enmeshed family.*

disengagement theory: The perspective, held by some experts on the process of aging, that says that as some older people slow down they gradually become more self-preoccupied, lessen emotional ties with others, have less interest in world affairs, and slowly withdraw from society. The theory also holds that society disengages from the older individual. The resulting mutual disengagement results in a decrease in life satisfaction. This theory is controversial, and some researchers point out that many older people maintain very active lives in late adulthood and show no decrease in life satisfaction.

displaced homemaker: A woman who becomes widowed or divorced after spending years as her family's caretaker and who usually has not developed other marketable skills to facilitate economic independence.

displacement: A *defense mechanism* used to reduce anxiety accompanying certain thoughts, feelings, or wishes by transferring them to another thought, feeling, or wish that is more acceptable or tolerable.

disposition: The arrangement made on behalf of a client or patient by the provider of a health or social service to conclude the intervention. This may include referral to a more appropriate resource, follow-up care, or successful achievement of goals so that help is no longer needed. In many types of case records, professionals conclude entries by writing "Disposition" (or "Disp."), followed by the course of action recommended for the ongoing care of the client.

disruptive tactics: Actions that interfere with the normal operations of social institutions to bring about changes in laws, norms, or social structures. These activities are undertaken and coordinated, especially by *social activists* and com-

munity organizers, to call public attention to problems and injustices and to put pressure for change on the organization. Examples include sit-downs in the offices of corporate executives, picket lines on roads leading to nuclear reactors, organized heckling of political candidates during their speeches, and *greenlining.*

dissociation: A *defense mechanism* in which the individual segregates or postpones the feeling, tone, or *affect* that would ordinarily accompany a situation, thought, object, or person, which would otherwise lead to intolerable anxiety. The term is also known as "disassociation."

dissociative disorder: A type of psychiatric illness characterized by a sudden, temporary change in the normally integrative functions of consciousness, identity, and motor behavior. Specific forms of the disorder include psychogenic amnesia (which may be selective or generalized, continuous or intermittent), psychogenic *fugue, multiple personality,* or *depersonalization disorder.*

distracter role: A recurrent pattern of communication in relating to others, especially family members, characterized by evasiveness, diverting attention, bringing in irrelevant statements, changing the subject, and moving in such a way that the focus of attention is changed. The role was delineated by Virginia Satir (*Peoplemaking,* Palo Alto, Calif.: Science and Behavior Books, 1972, p. 70), who described the distracter as a person who fears the threats of close relationships and prevents them through these diversionary tactics. Other roles are the *blamer role, computer role,* and *placater role.*

distribution: In research, the frequency with which a given variable or demographic factor appears in an identified category, geographic area, map, or graph.

divorce: The legal dissolution of a marriage. Each state establishes its own laws determining the criteria (grounds) for dissolution. Adultery, incompatibility, and living apart for specified periods of time are the grounds most commonly accepted. Many marriages are also dissolved through *no-fault divorce.*

divorce mediation: See *mediation, divorce.*

divorce therapy: A type of clinical intervention designed to help couples who have decided to dissolve their unions. Divorce therapy includes helping the couple consider alternatives to divorce, minimize adjustment problems, and discuss rationally how to disengage in the healthiest way possible. This therapy also deals with practical and legal aspects of the dissolution, such as child custody and property decisions. Divorce therapy also helps people learn to manage relationships with their former spouses and adjust to new lifestyles.

DNA: Deoxyribonucleic acid, a complex molecule found in living cells, whose components are arranged in particular sequences, the pattern of which determines the genetic information carried by the chromosomes.

doctoral programs: In social work education, the professional and academic training that culminates in the Ph.D. or *DSW* degree. Doctoral education in social work has tended to emphasize development of the student's research and knowledge-building skills and advanced practice competence. The DSW and Ph.D. degrees are equivalent and have virtually the same requirements. It was sometimes erroneously believed that DSWs would be for those seeking increased professional practice competence and Ph.D.s for those more involved in research, theory building, and knowledge building. However, the differences are more related to the preferences of the particular institution than to different requirements. See also *GADE.*

do-gooder: A term often applied, pejoratively, to social workers and other people whose jobs or personal consciences require them to do what is necessary to uphold the legal statutes and ethical values of a society and to protect the disadvantaged from exploitation by the privileged.

dole: A pejorative term once commonly applied to *public assistance* payments.

domestic violence: Abuse of children, elders, spouses, and others in the home, usually by other members of the family or other residents. The term also refers to the social problem in which one's property, health, or life are endangered or harmed as a result of the intentional behavior of another family member.

donor constituency: The contributors of funds and resources to a social agency or other organization. These people and groups may exert an implicit or formal influence on the priorities, values, and programs of the organization.

double bind: A form of paradoxical communication in which one person expresses a message that can be interpreted in two or more contradictory or mutually exclusive ways, and the recipient of the message is prevented from escaping the consequences or commenting on the contradiction.

double blind: In research, a technique in which neither the subject nor the experimenter knows whether a real change was actually introduced. For example, in researching the effects of drugs, the experimenter and the subjects do not know whether inert drugs (placebos) or active drugs are being administered.

double-entry bookkeeping: An accounting procedure, used in most social agency budget records, in which every transaction is recorded twice and the resulting increase or decrease in one account is reflected by a decrease or increase in another account.

"downers": A slang term referring to *barbiturates, tranquilizers,* or other central nervous system depressants often used by certain drug abusers to induce a state of deep relaxation. Some abusers become highly dependent on these substances, often leading to increased *tolerance.*

Down's syndrome: A congenital form of mental retardation, often characterized by a flattened face, widely spaced and slanted eyes, smaller head, and lax joints. Genetically determined by the presence of an extra chromosome, the disorder was formerly known as "mongolism."

DRGs: Diagnostic related groups, the name applied to a federally mandated prospective payment mechanism designed to control the costs of medical and hospital care for *Medicare* recipients. The system is administered by the U.S. *Health Care Financing Administration.* Payments made to the hospitals caring for Medicare patients are determined in advance, based on which one of 467 discrete categories of disorder—or diagnostic related group—the patient has at the time of admission, as well as on the patient's age, whether or not surgery is necessary, and, in some cases, the presence of complications. Each category, with relevant additional factors, is equated with a flat sum. If costs for care exceed the predetermined amount, the hospital is expected to bear the excess, but if they are lower than the predetermined amount, the hospital may keep the difference. This is supposed to encourage shorter hospital stays, a less extensive mix of services per hospitalization, and diminished likelihood of rehospitalization.

drive: In *psychoanalytic theory,* a basic impulse or urge that motivates overt behavior.

drug abuse: The inappropriate use of a chemical substance in ways that are detrimental to one's physical or mental well-being. See also *substance abuse.*

drug abuse detection: Efforts, usually by those with certain types of authority over others (for example, parents and employers), to assess the possibility that illegal or controlled substances are being used. Such efforts include urine sampling, confinement to observe the presence of *withdrawal symptoms,* covert investigation, and many other activities. Experts suggest that the presence of several of the following indicators can be clues to *substance abuse* in youngsters: long- or short-term forgetfulness; aggressiveness and irritability; school tardiness, truancy, or declining grades; difficulty in concentration; lowered energy; reduced self-discipline; uncaring or sullen behavior; constant disputes with family members; disappearance of money and valuables; unhealthy appearance, including bloodshot eyes; changes in and evasiveness about friendships; and trouble with the authorities.

drug addiction: The abuse of chemical substances that results in a physiological dependence in which the body tissues require the substance in order to function comfortably. In the absence of the substance the individual experiences *withdrawal symptoms*. See also *substance dependence*.

drug dependence: The misuse of and reliance on chemical substances, resulting in *drug addiction* or *drug habituation*.

Drug Enforcement Administration, U.S. (DEA): A unit of the U.S. Justice Department charged with enforcing the regulations that apply to *controlled substances*. DEA is responsible for overseeing and managing the legal production and use of narcotics, amphetamines, and barbiturates handled by pharmacists, doctors, and hospitals.

drug habituation: The abuse of chemical substances that results in psychological dependence, a pathological craving for the drug that is unrelated to physical dependence and that, by itself, leads to psychological discomfort in the absence of the drug but not to *withdrawal symptoms*.

drug tolerance: See *tolerance*.

DSM-III: The third edition of the American Psychiatric Association's *Diagnostic and Statistical Manual of Mental Disorders,* published in 1980. This manual represents the *American Psychiatric Association's* official classification of mental disorders. Each disorder is labeled and given a numerical code and systematic criteria for distinguishing it from other mental disorders. *DSM-III* calls for the subject to be evaluated on each of five levels, or axes. Axis I disorders include clinical syndromes as well as certain conditions that are not due to mental illness but are the focus of attention or treatment, referred to in this dictionary as the *V Codes. Axis II disorders* are the personality disorders and specific developmental disorders. Axis III is used for the subject's physical diseases and conditions that may be relevant to psychological health. In Axis IV the psychiatrist provides a coded number to indicate the overall severity of stresses that are judged to contribute to the current disorder.

Axis V is used to indicate the subject's highest level of functioning (socially, vocationally, and in use of leisure time) during the past year.

DSW: Doctor of Social Work (or Doctor of Social Welfare), an advanced professional degree in social work education. The DSW degree requirements typically include several years of previous social work practice experience, acquisition of required preliminary degrees such as the *MSW,* successful completion of prescribed doctoral-level course work in a qualified school of social work, passing written and oral comprehensive examinations, and successful completion and defense of a dissertation. Most DSW programs are affiliated with professional schools of social work that are part of accredited colleges and universities. See also *doctoral programs*.

dull-normal: A term sometimes used by educators and educational psychologists in describing an individual whose IQ scores are between 70 and 90; an individual with slightly limited intellectual capacity but not of such deficiency as to require extensive care and protection by others.

dyad: Two people or objects in a relationship or interacting system.

dynamic: In personality theory, an orientation that emphasizes intrapsychic influences, conscious and unconscious thought processes, and nonobservable mental phenomena such as *drives, conflicts, motivations,* and *defense mechanisms*. In field theory, the forces that act on a psychological field. In social systems theory, the term refers to the process of striving for and maintaining homeostatic stability.

dysfunction: A deficiency in a system that precludes its optimal performance; synonymous with "malfunction."

dyslexia: An impairment of reading and writing skills, often with the tendency to reverse letters or words while reading or writing them or not noticing certain letters or words.

dyspareunia: A woman's (occasionally, a man's) experience of pain during the act of sexual intercourse.

dyssocial: A term pertaining to an individual who behaves according to the norms of the immediate peer group or subculture but contrary to the norms of the larger society, or to one who engages repeatedly in criminal and destructive activities. This term is now used by professionals to replace the term *sociopathic*.

dysthymic disorder: A type of mental illness characterized by certain degrees of sadness, pessimism, hopelessness, and despair, it is usually thought to be the result of *anxiety* or internal conflict. The condition was formerly known as *depressive neurosis*.

E

EAPs:　See *employee assistance programs (EAPs)*.

earmarked taxes:　Income, whose purpose has been designated in advance, received by a government body from citizens and corporations. For example, gasoline sales taxes are largely designated for highway maintenance, and construction and *payroll taxes* for unemployment benefits.

earned income credit:　A measure used in the *OASDHI (social security)* system to determine the amount of benefits for which an individual is eligible, based on the contributions that were made during his or her highest income periods. Theoretically, workers whose income is highest contribute the most to the system through social security payroll taxes and receive the highest possible benefits when they retire.

Earned Income Tax Credit:　A provision in the U.S. Internal Revenue tax code to give cash supplements to working parents whose incomes are relatively low. The parent or parents file federal income tax statements, and if their taxable earnings are below a specified amount, they receive a check for the difference. This is the first form of *negative income tax* in effect in the United States.

Easter Seal Society:　The organization, founded in 1919, that coordinates fundraising and disbursements on behalf of crippled children and adults in the United States.

eating disorders:　A group of mental disturbances—usually first evident in infancy, childhood, or adolescence—involving maladaptive or unhealthy patterns of eating and ingestion. Major types include *anorexia nervosa, bulimia,* pica (repeated eating of nonnutritive or inorganic substances), and rumination disorder of infancy (repeated regurgitation with no evidence of nausea or gastrointestinal illness).

echolalia:　Repetitive imitation of the speech of another, often seen in people with certain types of schizophrenia.

eclectic:　Composed of those aspects of various theories or practice methods that appear to be most useful for current needs.

ecological perspective:　An orientation in social work and other professions that emphasizes the environmental contexts in which people function. Important concepts include the principles of *adaptation, transaction,* and *goodness of fit* between people and their environments, *reciprocity,* and *mutuality.* In professional interventions the *unit of attention* is considered to be the interface between the individual (or group, family, or community) and the relevant environment. See also *life model.*

ecomap:　A diagram used by social workers, family therapists, and other professionals to depict a variety of reciprocal influences between the client and those related to the client, relevant social institutions, and environmental influences.

econometrics:　Statistical analysis of economic trends and problems.

Economic Opportunity Act:　The major legislation (P.L. 88-452) of President Lyndon B. Johnson's *War on Poverty.* Enacted in 1964, it established the *Office of Economic Opportunity (OEO)* and helped created such programs as *VISTA,* the *Job Corps, Head Start, Upward Bound,* the *Neighborhood Youth Corps,* and the *Community Action program (CAP).* Many of these programs were subsequently dismantled.

economies of scale:　A tendency for some costs of providing services to increase less than proportionally with increased output. For example, in certain circumstances, a social agency might be able to triple its service output while only doubling its budget.

ecosystem:　The physical and biological environment and the interaction between every component thereof.

edema:　Accumulation of fluid in the body tissues and cavities, leading to swelling. Edema may be symptomatic of a variety of disorders, including heart failure, kidney disease, pneumonia, and infection.

educable: Having potential for learning, especially for formal education and basic survival skills. Professionals often use the term in referring to mentally retarded individuals whose retardation does not preclude learning certain social or academic skills.

Education for All Handicapped Children Act: The federal law (P.L. 94-142) enacted in 1975 that mandates and distributes funds for public schools so that they may provide equal educational opportunities and free special services for all handicapped children, including those with learning disabilities. Such services may include special testing, remedial lessons, counseling, and tutoring.

educator role: In social work, the responsibility to teach clients necessary adaptive skills. This is done by providing relevant information in a way that is understandable to the client, offering advice and suggestions, identifying alternatives and their probable consequences, modeling behaviors, teaching problem-solving techniques, and clarifying perceptions. Other social work roles are identified as the *facilitator role,* the *enabler role,* and the *mobilizer role.*

EEOC: See *Equal Employment Opportunity Commission (EEOC).*

efficacy: The degree to which desired goals or projected outcomes are achieved; in social work, the capacity to help the client achieve, in a reasonable time period, the goals of a given intervention.

egalitarianism: A social value; a belief in human equality leading one to treat others as peers or equals.

ego: The self; the part of the mind that mediates between the demands of the body and the realities of the environment, consisting of *cognition, perception, defense mechanisms,* memory, and motor control. In *psychodynamic* theory, one of the three major spheres of the psyche, along with the *id* (biological and primitive drives) and the *superego* (internalized system of social prohibitions). The healthy ego finds ways to compromise between these competing pressures and enables the person to cope with the demands of the environment.

ego alien: A synonym for *ego dystonic.*

egocentrism: Excessive preoccupation with oneself; an exaggerated view of one's importance. Also, in *Piagetian theory,* the normal state of the child under the age of 6 who has not yet learned to take another person's perspective.

ego defense: See *defense mechanism.*

ego dystonic: Traits of personality, behavior, thought, or orientation considered to be unacceptable, repugnant, or inconsistent with the individual's overall "true" nature; a synonym for *ego alien.* For example, someone who is considered to be an "ego dystonic homosexual" is one who does not accept his or her sexual orientation.

ego functioning: The manner in which the ego deals with the demands of society and mediates between internal psychological conflicts.

ego ideal: An individual's goals, positive standards, and highest aspirations; also, one or more significant others in a person's life who are emulated.

ego integration: Achievement of inner harmony and compatibility of the various aspects of one's personality as a unified whole.

ego-oriented social work: Clinical social work that incorporates the principles of *ego psychology* into professional practice.

ego psychology: Psychosocially oriented concepts that build on *Freudian theory* but emphasize the individual's adult development and ability to solve problems and deal with social realities more than instincts and drives.

ego strengths: In psychodynamic theory, the degree of psychic energy available to the individual for problem solving, resolving internal conflicts, and defending against mental and environmental distress; also, the individual's capacity for logical thinking, intelligence, perceptiveness, and self-control over impulses to achieve immediate gratification.

ego syntonic: Traits of personality, thought, behavior, and values that are incorporated by the individual, who considers them acceptable and consistent with his or her overall "true" self; the opposite of *ego dystonic.* For example, a person considered to be an "ego syntonic homosexual" is one who accepts his or her sexual orientation.

ELAN: The Educational Legislative Action Network, a program within the *National Association of Social Workers (NASW)* that was established in 1971 to coordinate efforts to inform national and state legislators about issues of concern to social workers. ELAN has been reconstituted in recent years, and its functions are achieved through local NASW chapters and in other political action activities at the national level.

elder abuse: Mistreatment of aged and relatively dependent people. Elder abuse includes physical battering, neglect, exploitation, and psychological harm and is often inflicted by the elderly person's adult children, other relatives, legal custodians, or others who provide for their care.

elderly: Advanced in age. This term is commonly used to designate persons beyond a nation's official retirement age. The term "pre-elderly" is used for people who are less than a decade from reaching retirement age.

elective mutism: The refusal to talk in almost all social situations even though the ability to speak and comprehend language exists and there is no organic or physical cause. This condition is most commonly found in younger children during the time they are compelled to participate in social situations such as school.

Electra complex: The term used in early *Freudian theory* for the unconscious sexual attraction girls, especially from ages 3 to 7, have for their fathers. The term is roughly analogous to the *Oedipus complex* for boys.

electroshock therapy (EST): Treatments administered by physicians, primarily neurologists and psychiatrists, in which convulsions are induced in patients by applying small amounts of electrical currents to the brain. Although its use has been significantly curtailed because of the increased use and development of *psychotropic medications,* EST (or ECT, for electroconvulsive therapy) is reported to be effective with certain patients, especially some with *affective disorders.*

eligibility: The meeting of specific qualifications in order to receive certain benefits; the criteria used in welfare systems to determine which people may receive help. For example, to be eligible for food stamps a person must meet certain income requirements, and to be eligible for *Medicare* a person must be above a certain age.

Elizabethan Poor Laws: The statutes, codified in 1601 during the reign of Queen Elizabeth I, that established many of the principles that are still influential in dealing with the economically disadvantaged. Among their provisions were local rather than national responsibility for the care of the poor, the distinction between the *worthy poor* and the *unworthy poor,* punitive measures for those refusing to work, standards of responsibility for relatives, and the *means test* to determine need for assistance.

emancipation: Freeing an individual or members of a social group from the control of another or others. For example, a minor child may become emancipated from parental control (and from the right to parental support or maintenance) on getting married.

embezzlement: The crime of willfully appropriating money or property that is in one's control but belongs to another. The embezzler has possession of the property by virtue of a business relationship or through some office, employment, or position of trust with the owner. For example, if the treasurer of a social agency uses funds that were donated to the agency to pay personal expenses, that individual is guilty of embezzlement.

Emergency Relief Administration: See *Federal Emergency Relief Administration (FERA).*

emit: To respond, as in *operant conditioning.*

emotion: A feeling, mood, or *affect;* a state of mind usually accompanied by concurrent physiological and behavioral changes and based on the perception of some internal or external object.

emotional divorce: A distancing between members of a *dyad,* usually a married couple, because they have experienced considerable pain, anxiety, anger, or other similar reactions in their previous encounters. Typically, the resulting behavior includes avoidance of one another's physical presence, avoidance of discussions about certain emotionally charged events, or refusal to provide needed emotional support.

emotional lability: A tendency to change moods rapidly and frequently. This is a commonly encountered symptom of *affective disorders* and of immaturity.

empathy: The ability to perceive, understand, and experience the emotional state of another person.

emphysema: A disorder of the respiratory system in which the alveoli in the lungs become enlarged or inflexible, making it difficult and uncomfortable to breathe.

empirical: Based on direct observation or experience.

empirically based practice: A type of professional social work intervention in which the worker uses research as a practice and problem-solving tool; collects data systematically to monitor the intervention; specifies problems, techniques, and outcomes in measurable terms; and systematically evaluates the effectiveness of the intervention used.

employable: A term applied to those in the population who are potentially able to work. Economic planners sometimes identify this group as being within certain age parameters and without incapacitating infirmities.

employee assistance programs (EAPs): Services offered to employees to help them overcome problems that may have a negative impact on job satisfaction or productivity. Services may be provided on-site or contracted through outside providers. They include counseling for alcohol and *drug dependence, marital* or *family therapy,* and *career counseling.*

employment: The state of working in exchange for money.

employment policy: The principles, guidelines, goals, and regulations pertaining to the way a nation or an organization deals with its actual and potential *work force*. Aspects of an employment policy include hiring and firing rules and procedures, salary and benefits structure, occupational safety and health provisions, and economic programs to stimulate the creation of more jobs.

employment programs: Programs at the federal, state, and local levels and in private industry designed to secure more jobs for more people and to ensure that those jobs include decent wages and benefits and equal opportunities. In the United States, in addition to the *unemployment insurance* program, these programs have included the provisions of the *Job Training Partnership Act*, the *Job Corps*, and the *Neighborhood Youth Corps*.

Employment Retirement Income Security Act: See *ERISA*.

empowerment: In *community organization* and social activist social work, the process of helping a group or community to achieve political influence or relevant legal authority.

empty nest: A term applied to the nuclear family after the children have matured and left the home.

enabler role: In social work, the responsibility to help the client become capable of coping with situational or transitional stress. Specific skills used in achieving this objective include conveying hope, reducing resistance and ambivalence, recognizing and managing feelings, identifying and supporting personal strengths and social assets, breaking down problems into parts that can be solved more readily, and maintaining a focus on goals and the means of achieving them. Other primary social work roles are identified as the *facilitator role*, the *educator role*, and the *mobilizer role*.

encopresis: The inability to control bowel functions.

encounter group: An intense, short-term group experience—using some *gestalt therapy, group psychotherapy*, and *humanistic orientation* principles and techniques—designed to promote the personal growth of the participants. The emphasis is not on correcting disorders but rather on increasing the emotional and sensory aspects of being and increasing open communication and self-awareness.

endemic: A term applied to a phenomenon, social problem, or disease that is peculiar to a given population group, culture, or geographical area.

endogamy: The practice of confining marriage to members of one's own social or ethnic group.

endogenous: Pertaining to disorders or problems that come from within the individual rather than from environmental or situational stress factors. For example, endogenous depression comes from unresolved emotional conflict or physiological imbalances instead of actual sad experiences.

endowment: A fund, consisting of money or property, established by or on behalf of a person or institution (such as a social cause or social service agency), the income from which is to be used to achieve certain specified purposes.

end stage renal disease (ESRD): Irreversible loss of kidney function, caused by genetic or metabolic factors or by external factors such as trauma or infection. ESRD patients require artificial *dialysis* treatment or a kidney transplant to survive.

enmeshed family: A concept used in the *structural family therapy* orientation to designate an unhealthy family relationship pattern in which the role boundaries between various family members are so vague or diffuse that there is little opportunity for independent functioning. This condition is contrasted with the *disengaged family*, in which the role boundaries of the various members are so rigid and inflexible that members withdraw from the relationship.

entitlement: Services, goods, or money due to an individual by virtue of a specific status.

entrepreneurial practice: In social work, the activities involved in the provision of human and social services for profit. Such activities include private clinical social work practice, providing consultations to social agencies and community organizations for fees, and establishing for-profit social service facilities such as private schools for disturbed children, employment agencies for unemployed social workers, training facilities for business organizations, and homes for such *at-risk population* groups as the *frail elderly*, unwed mothers-to-be, and unplaced foster-care children.

entropy: A concept used in *systems theories* pertaining to the dissolution or deorganization of a system. It is hypothesized that systems are always going through this process in their movement toward and away from *equilibrium*.

enuresis: The involuntary discharge of urine.

environmental modification: See *environmental treatment*.

Environmental Protection Agency (EPA): The federal organization established in 1970 to develop and enforce standards for controlling water, air, and noise pollution and to promote those activities that result in a healthy habitat for wildlife and human well-being.

environmental treatment: The *social casework* concept that recognizes the impact of forces outside the individual and strives to modify this impact through such techniques as providing or locating specific resources, interpreting the client's needs to others, advocacy, and mediation. Some social workers call this activity *indirect treatment* or "environmental modification."

epidemic: The occurrence of a disease, disorder, or social problem that spreads rapidly and affects many people in a community within a relatively short time period.

epidemiology: The study of the frequency and distribution of a specified phenomenon, such as a disease, that occurs in a population group during a given period of time. Usually this is expressed in terms of an *incidence rate* (number of new cases in a time period) and *prevalence rate* (the total number of those who currently have the specified problem). Other commonly used terms in epidemiology are *point prevalence* (the number of cases measured at one point in time), *period prevalence* (all cases occurring in a specified time frame, such as one year), and morbidity risk (any individual's lifetime risk of having a specific illness). See also *morbidity rate.*

epigenesis: Emergence; the perceived original occurrence of a phenomenon.

epilepsy: A disorder characterized by recurrent, involuntary episodes of altered states of consciousness, frequently but not always accompanied by convulsive body movements. Most professionals now refer to this condition as a *seizure disorder.*

episode of service (EOS): A specific social service goal and all the alternative means used by a *social work team* and its client to achieve it. According to Robert L. Barker and Thomas L. Briggs (*Differential Use of Social Work Manpower*, New York: National Association of Social Workers, 1968, p. 214), the team members first assess the client's need and then, often with the client, translate this into specific and realistic goals. The team then discusses the variety of techniques and resources that might be utilized and selects those that are most feasible.

epistemology: The study of the nature, methods, and limits of knowledge.

Equal Credit Opportunity Act (ECOA): The federal legislation (P.L. 93-495) enacted in 1974 that requires retail firms and lending institutions to use the same criteria for everyone in deciding whether to grant credit, regardless of gender, marital status, or minority or ethnic background. To protect the economic rights of women, the act gives wives as well as husbands the right to have credit records in their own names.

Equal Employment Opportunity Commission (EEOC): The five-member federal panel that administers Title VII of the *Civil Rights Act of 1964*, prohibiting discrimination by employers, unions, or employment agencies and striving to promote fair practices in the workplace.

equality: A fundamental social work value; the principle that individuals should have equal access to services, resources, and opportunities and be treated the same by all social, educational, and welfare institutions.

equal rights: The obligations of a society or organization to afford the same opportunities and access to all, regardless of status.

equifinality: The property of living systems that permits them to reach identical points, although by different routes; a concept in *systems theories* stating that different behaviors by living organisms can lead to the same or "equal final" results. In systems theories, the opposite of equifinality is *equipotentiality*.

equilibrium: A concept in *systems theories* in which opposing forces and elements achieve balance; also, a state or condition that is never truly reached because each variable continues to change, requiring some offsetting or equivalent change in another variable.

equipotentiality: The property of living systems in which subsystems may have identical origins or beginnings but achieve different outcomes. This is the opposite and corollary principle to *equifinality*.

equity: The state of fairness or impartiality, including any systems (for example, the *criminal justice system* and the *social welfare* system) that determine how one's rights and claims are fulfilled.

ergonomics: The analysis of working conditions, employee relations, tools, and working patterns in order to fit the person with the job and the job with the person.

ERIC: Educational Resources Information Centers; Department of Education centers in over 500 locations across the United States that provide data about the nation's educational programs and facilities. Information covers such topics as resources for exceptional children, handicapped persons, people unable to speak English, and people seeking to become teachers.

ERISA: The Employee Retirement Income Security Act of 1974 (P.L. 93-406), a federal program administered by the U.S. *Department of Labor* and other agencies, which protects the interests of workers who participate in private pension and welfare plans.

erogenous zone: Any area of the body whose stimulation leads to sexual arousal.

estrangement: The loss of contact with or antagonism toward one's relatives or associates because of apathy or active disagreement.

ethics: A system of moral principles and perceptions about right versus wrong and the resulting philosophy of conduct that is practiced by an individual, group, profession, or culture. See also *code of ethics.*

ethnic group: A distinct group of people who share a common language, set of customs, history, culture, race, religion, or origin.

ethnicity: An orientation toward the shared national origin, religion, race, or language of a people; also, a person's ethnic affiliation, by virtue of one or more of these characteristics and traditions.

ethnic-sensitive practice: Professional social work that emphasizes and values the special capabilities, distinctive cultural histories, and unique needs of people of various ethnic origins. When a practitioner's work adheres to social work values, it is automatically ethnic-sensitive practice.

ethnocentrism: An orientation or set of beliefs that holds that one's own culture, ethnic or racial group, or nation is superior to others.

ethnology: The scientific study of humanity's division into racial groups and the history, characteristics, and culture of the races.

ethology: The scientific study of the formation of human character and animal behavior by assessing the genetic, physiological, and evolutionary development and adaptation to the environment of living organisms.

ethos: The moral beliefs or ethical character of a people or culture.

etiology: The underlying causes of a problem or disorder; also, the study of such causes.

ET programs: Employment training programs, used in many states to help public assistance recipients become economically independent by training them to get and keep jobs and to help them learn marketable skills. In most states where ET programs exist, the children of the recipients are provided with health and day care services while the parent is in the training program. See also *GAIN programs.*

eugenics: The theory and practice of "improving" human qualities genetically or minimizing genetic disorders. The practice may be negative,

(discouraging or preventing parenthood among those who are considered biologically deficient), or positive, that is, (encouraging reproduction among healthy people).

euphoria: A perception of extreme well-being, excessive optimism, and increased motor activity. It is often pathological and indicative of such problems as *bipolar disorder,* manic states, *organic mental disorder,* and drug-induced states.

euthanasia: Putting to death or permitting the death of an incurably ill person; also known as "mercy killing."

evaluation research: Systematic investigation to determine the success of a specific program. For example, a social work researcher might conduct a study of the incidence of nutritional deficiency in an Appalachian town before and after its citizens are made eligible for an antipoverty program.

eviction: Forcing an individual, family, or business to discontinue its occupancy of housing, land, or other real property, usually by due process of law.

exceptional children: A designation applied to dependent youngsters who, because of unusual mental, physical, or social abilities or limitations, require extraordinary forms of education, social experience, or treatment. These children include mentally retarded youngsters who can benefit from educational training facilities designed to help them reach their potential. Other such children may be those with physical disabilities and deformities, mental disorders, special talents, very high intelligence, or unusual physical abilities.

exceptional eligibility: A social service policy in which services or benefits are established for people who constitute a special group even though they may not have unique or special needs and although others outside the group may have the same needs or be in the same circumstances. Such programs are often developed because of strong political pressure or public sympathy for the group. Some veterans' programs are a notable example.

exclusion allowance: A portion of some benefit that may not be counted as taxable income. Examples include certain tax-deferred retirement annuity plans and some social security benefits.

exhibitionism: The tendency to show off one's real or imagined traits and talents to gain the attention of others; frequently, the display of one's genitals or sexual characteristics in socially unacceptable circumstances.

existential social work: A philosophical perspective in social work that accepts and emphasizes the individual's fundamental autonomy, freedom of choice, disillusionment with prevailing social mores, a sense of meaning derived from suffering, the need for dialogue, and the social worker's commitment to the concept of client self-determination.

ex officio member: Someone who belongs to a group or board by virtue of holding another office or status. For example, an ex officio member of the board of a *sectarian social agency* might be the highest-ranking local clergyman of that denomination.

expenditure: A payment, or obligation to pay, for some goods or services received. For example, a social agency budgets for specific anticipated operating expenses. Capital expenditures are those the social agency makes to acquire or improve a relatively permanent asset such as the building where the agency's activities take place. Revenue expenditures are those the agency makes from its operating budget for such purposes as expendable supplies.

experience rating: (1) A measure of a corporation's employee retention-layoff rate. Employers with high ratings—that is, those who lay off fewer employees than their competitors in similar industries—may be rewarded with payroll tax benefits; (2) a measure used by the insurance industry to indicate the probability of risk to a specified group.

experiential therapy: A form of psychosocial intervention or clinical treatment that emphasizes activity, acting out of conflicts and situations, role playing, confrontation, and simulating situations that are similar to the client's frequent life experiences. Experiential therapies focus on the "here and now" and discourage the client from relying solely on description of past circumstances. Experiential therapies often occur in *group* or *family therapy* settings.

experiment: A systematic project to test a *hypothesis.*

experimental group: In research, a collection of subjects who are matched and compared with a *control group* in all relevant respects, except that they are also subject to a specific *variable* being tested.

expert witness: One who testifies before a lawmaking group, or in a court of law, based on special knowledge of the subject in question, enabling the decision makers to make a better assessment of the evidence or merits of the issue. Social workers are often called as expert witnesses before legislative bodies that seek to draft legislation to enhance the public welfare. Social workers are also frequently asked to testify as expert witnesses in court hearings, especially in disputes over *custody of children, child neglect, welfare rights,* marital dissolution, landlord-tenant controversies, and care for the mentally and physically handicapped. See also *forensic social work.*

ex post facto experiment: In research, an *experiment* conducted after the event being tested has already occurred. The experimenter thus cannot introduce the experimental stimulus but attempts to control, sometimes statistically, all extraneous factors.

extended care facilities (ECT): Nursing homes for patients who need to remain in a facility for extended periods of time, up to 100 days. To receive the ECT designation and thus be eligible for *Medicare* reimbursement, the facility must meet special federal and state certification standards. They must have staffs that usually include a medical director; an RN nursing director, nursing supervisor, and skilled nursing staff; dietician; physical therapist; occupational therapist, and a director of social services. ECTs are subject to *utilization review* by government bodies and third parties. See also *skilled nursing facility.*

extended family: A kinship group comprising relatives of a *nuclear family* (parents and their children), such as grandparents, uncles, aunts, second cousins, and so on.

externalization: The projecting of one's own thoughts or values onto some aspect of the environment; also, the distinction young children make between themselves and their environments.

extinction: In *behavior modification,* the elimination or weakening of a *conditioned response (CR)* by discontinuing *reinforcement* after the response occurs (*operant conditioning*). In *respondent conditioning* this occurs through repeated presentations of a *conditioned stimulus (CS)* without the *unconditioned stimulus (US).*

extrapolation: Making inferential estimations based on, but beyond the scope of, available data.

extrovert: An individual who tends to be outgoing and directs attention to others. The opposite of an *introvert.*

F

face sheet: A page, usually in the front of a client's case record or in front of a question-naire, on which specific identifying data about the subject are recorded, such as age, gender, income, family members, prior contacts with the agency, and so on.

face validity: A simple method for assessing the *validity* of a scale or instrument, in which the researcher—using his or her professional judgment alone—accepts the instrument as valid if it looks or sounds valid.

facilitation: An approach to social work in-tervention in which the worker stimulates and mediates *linkages* between client systems, helps develop new systems, or helps strengthen exist-ing ones. The worker acts as an enabler, sup-porter, mediator, and broker for the client, pav-ing the way for the client to reach desired goals. According to Allen Pincus and Anne Minahan (*Social Work Practice: Model and Method*, Itasca, Ill.: F. E. Peacock Publishers, 1973, p. 113), facilitation activities might include eliciting in-formation and opinions, facilitating expressions of feelings, interpreting behavior, discussing al-ternative courses of action, clarifying situations, providing encouragement and reassurance, prac-ticing logical reasoning, and recruiting mem-bers, usually within the context of a collaborative or bargaining relationship.

facilitator role: In social work, the respon-sibility to expedite the change effort by bring-ing together people and lines of communica-tion, *channeling* their activities and resources, and providing them with access to expertise. Other primary social work roles are identified as the *enabler role,* the *educator role,* and the *mobilizer role.*

fact-gathering interview: An interview in which the social worker seeks predetermined and specific data from the client. The worker asks specific questions and records relevant answers, often on *face sheets* or forms. Its purpose is not primarily therapeutic and thus gives relatively little opportunity for the client to ventilate feel-ings or work through problems.

factitious disorder: Behavior that appears to be abnormal or symptomatic of mental illness but that is probably under the subject's volun-tary control. It is similar to *malingering* except that in factitious disorder there is no apparent benefit to be gained from the problem.

failure to thrive: See *marasmus.*

Fair Debt Collection Practices Act: Federal legislation, passed in 1978 (P.L. 85-109), to con-trol abusive behavior, late evening telephoning, warnings about loss of reputation, and threats of job loss made by debt collectors.

Fair Employment Practices Committee (FEPC): The first federal program to monitor and eliminate discrimination in the U.S. labor force, created in 1941 by executive order of Presi-dent Roosevelt. The program was opposed by Congress and finally abolished in 1945.

Fair Labor Standards Act: Federal legisla-tion, enacted in 1938 (52 Stat. 1060) and ad-ministered by the U.S. *Department of Labor,* that sets minimum wages, payment of time and a half for work beyond 40 hours in a week, and provisions of equal pay for equal work.

family: A primary group whose members are related by blood, adoption, or marriage and who usually have shared common residences, have mutual rights and obligations, and assume responsibility for the primary *socialization* of their children.

family allowance: A *demogrant* form of benefit in many nations, not including the United States, in which every eligible family, regardless of financial need, is allocated a specified sum of money. There are many variations to this system depending on the nation's social policy goals. These include making higher payments for families with more children, reducing payments if families have more than a prescribed number of children, and requiring families whose income exceeds a certain amount to pay back the family allowance at tax time.

Family Assistance Plan (FAP): A proposal to reform part of the U.S. social welfare system by guaranteeing every employed American family an annual income above the specified amount considered necessary to maintain an adequate standard of living. The proposed legislation was developed in 1969 by the Nixon Administration but was not passed by Congress.

family court: A court of law that hears cases pertaining to conflicts among family members, such as divorce, custody, and meeting financial obligations to members of the family.

family, extended: See *extended family.*

family map: A pictorial representation of the way a family is structured around a specific problem or concern. Each member of the family is represented by circles or squares, and the type of relationship that tends to exist between them is illustrated by drawing various types of lines.

family myths: A *family therapy* term that refers to a set of beliefs, based on distortions of facts or history, shared by members of a family. These beliefs serve to enforce the *family rules* that influence the way the members interact and ensure cohesiveness and stability in the family. (For example, one family might believe and communicate the view that its male members are less assertive than its female members.) The family members may be aware that these ideologies are inaccurate, but they are allowed to go unchallenged in order to preserve the existing family structure.

family, nuclear: See *nuclear family.*

family of orientation: A kinship group united not necessarily by blood but by such factors as common residence, shared experiences and backgrounds, mutual affection, and economic dependency.

family of origin: A kinship group united by blood or genetic similarity.

family of procreation: A family begun by an adult couple.

family planning: Making deliberate and voluntary decisions about reproduction. A couple practicing family planning decides to have only a certain number of children after considering economic circumstances, life goals, the nature of the reproductive process, and *birth control* methods.

family policy: A nation's principles and planned procedures that are intended to influence or alter existing patterns of family life. Technically, all of a nation's social policy concerns (such as income maintenance, housing, education, and defense) affect families. Thus, the term "family policy" generally focuses more on such issues as fertility rates and family size, child care for working parents, care of the elderly, foster care programs, and income maintenance programs for families, as in *family allowances.* A nation's family policy may be explicit or implicit.

family projection process: A *family therapy* term, developed by Murray Bowen, referring to the way some members of a family, especially parents, attribute sources of conflict to other members of the family, especially children. This process frequently results in one or more of the children in a family becoming the symptom-bearers for the family's ills.

family rules: A *family therapy* term that refers to repetitive patterns of behavior and mutual expectations regulating that behavior in a family. One family, for example, might maintain a mutual expectation that none of its members are to express outwardly any feelings of affection for one another. Another family might have a rule that every dispute is to result in threatened or actual physical violence.

family sculpting: A technique in some forms of *family therapy* in which family members are asked to position and choreograph the movements of other family members to demonstrate clearly how they perceive communication and relationship patterns.

family secrets: A *family therapy* term that refers to beliefs and perceptions some or all of the family members may hold, share with, or conceal from from one another to achieve certain family relationship goals.

Family Service America (FSA): The national organization comprising privately funded, local family service agencies in most larger communities in the United States, plus professionals and private citizens interested in social services for families. Formerly known as the Family Service Association of America (FSAA), it was established as an outgrowth of the National Association of Societies for Organizing Charities in 1911 and took its present name in 1983. Its member agencies provide *family* and *marital therapy,* guidance and counseling, educational programs, and social services to the community. The national organization sets standards for member agencies, provides public relations and educational programs, sponsors research and publications (including *Social Casework*), and its board helps set policy and advise lawmakers about family needs.

family service organizations: Social agencies that provide a variety of human services, especially to couples, families, and extended family units. These organizations are most often funded through grants and private donations and follow policies established by independently elected or appointed boards of directors. Services include *family* and *marital therapy*, family life education, and community activities to enhance healthy family development. Many of these agencies are affiliated with national organizations such as *Family Service America (FSA)*, Jewish family services, and LDS *Social Services*.

Family Services Administration (FSA): An organization within the U.S. *Department of Health and Human Services (HHS)*, created in 1986 through a consolidation of federal programs to aid low-income families. The six major programs included in FSA are *Aid to Families with Dependent Children (AFDC)*, the *Work Incentive program (WIN)*, the *Community Services Block Grant program*, the *Low Income Home Energy Assistance program*, the *Refugee Assistance program*, and the *Child Support Enforcement Office*. FSA is one of the major units of HHS, which also includes the *Health Care Financing Administration*, the *Office of Human Development Services (OHDS)*, the *Public Health Service*, and the *Social Security Administration (SSA)*.

family therapy: Intervention by a professional social worker or other family therapist with a group of family members who are considered to be a single unit of attention. Typically, the approach focuses on the whole system of individuals, interpersonal patterns, and communication patterns. It seeks to clarify roles and reciprocal obligations and encourage more adaptable behaviors among the family members. The therapist concentrates on verbal and nonverbal actions and on the "here and now" rather than on family history. Variations in family therapy techniques are practiced by proponents of psychosocial, behavioral, systems, and other orientations. Some of the more influential family therapy "schools" have been influenced by Salvador Minuchin (*structural family therapy*), Jay Haley (*strategic family therapy*), Virginia Satir and the Palo Alto Group, Murray Bowen, Carl Whittaker, Henry V. Dicks, Mara Selvini-Palazzoli, Peggy Papp, and many others.

family violence: Aggressive and hostile behaviors between members of a family that result in injury, harm, humiliation, and sometimes death. These behaviors may include physical abuse, rape, destruction of property, and deprivation of basic needs.

family welfare: One of professional social work's first designated *fields of practice*, a type of skilled intervention with members of families. The activities include *marriage counseling*, instructing parents about effective child rearing, child protective services, and helping clients get ac-

cess to financial assistance, health care, educational provisions, and employment. Family welfare work took place in public and private agencies such as departments of public assistance, and *family service organizations*.

fear: The emotional and physical reaction to an identifiable or perceived source of danger.

feasibility study: A systematic assessment of the resources needed to accomplish a specified objective and concurrent evaluation of an organization's existing and anticipated capabilities for providing those resources.

fecundity: A given population group's potential for reproduction, determined by counting the number of fertile women of childbearing age.

Federal Crime Insurance Program: A program established in 1971 and administered by the U.S. *Department of Housing and Urban Devlopment (HUD)* that provides insurance against the risks of crime when it is not available from commercial insurance companies.

Federal Deposit Insurance Corporation (FDIC): A government corporation that insures people's deposits in national and some state banks in the Federal Reserve System. Depositors are assured that their funds, up to an amount specified in advance, will be returned to them in the event that the bank fails or has insufficient resources to meet all its obligations.

Federal Emergency Management Agency (FEMA): An independent agency of the U.S. government designed to organize and coordinate the nation's emergency preparedness. It oversees civil defense programs, urban riot response, and disaster relief.

Federal Emergency Relief Administration (FERA): The government organization established during the Roosevelt Administration in 1933 with social worker Harry Hopkins as its director. The program distributed federal funds to the states for emergency unemployment relief and required every local administration to have at least one experienced social worker on its staff. FERA and other *New Deal* programs were terminated as World War II began.

Federal Housing Administration (FHA): The national program implemented in 1938 to encourage home ownership. Its most important feature has been to guarantee loans to finance individual homes, permitting homeowners to make lower down payments (5 and 10 percent) and to take longer to pay the balance (30 and sometimes 40 years).

Federal Insurance Contributions Act (FICA): The federal program through which social security taxes are deducted from employees' paychecks.

Federations of Social Agencies: Organizations comprising private welfare agencies in a given community that combine some of their resources and efforts for fundraising, public relations, lobbying, and educational activities.

feedback: Transmitting information about the results of an action to the individual who performed that action. This permits a more objective evaluation of the action's effectivness. It also permits modifications in the ongoing action to increase the likelihood of success. In social work administration, feedback is often used in supervision, personal evaluations, client reports, and objective outcome measures to help workers achieve desired improvements or to give them positive indicators when they are doing good jobs.

fee for service: A charge made to clients or their *fiscal intermediaries* in consideration for the social worker's provision of a specified service (such as an hour of counseling).

felonies: Crimes that are more serious than *misdemeanors*. Felonies include *burglary,* some categories of *larceny, homicide, rape,* and *assault.*

feminism: The social movement and doctrine advocating legal and socioeconomic equality for women. The movement originated in Great Britain in the eighteenth century.

feminist social work: The integration of the values, skills, and knowledge of social work with a feminist orientation to help individuals and society overcome the emotional and social problems that result from sex discrimination.

feminist therapy: A psychosocial treatment orientation in which the professional (usually a woman) helps the client (usually a woman) in individual or group settings to overcome the psychological and social problems largely encountered as a result of sex discrimination and *sex role stereotyping.* Feminist therapists help clients maximize potential, especially through *consciousness-raising,* eliminating sex role stereotyping, and helping them become aware of the commonalities shared by all women.

fence: One who receives stolen property and sells it for a profit.

fertility: The biological capacity to reproduce.

fertility rate: A demographic characteristic indicating the number of live births that occur in a population group during a specific time period.

fertilization in vitro: See *in vitro fertilization.*

fetal alcohol syndrome: Various forms of damage to an unborn infant due to heavy maternal alcohol consumption. Potential problems include retarded growth, mental retardation, and sometimes craniofacial and limb anomalities.

fetology: The medical specialty that deals with the care and treatment of the *fetus* during prenatal development.

fetus: An unborn infant; usually the term is applied to developing human organisms from the third month after conception until birth. Development from the ninth week consists primarily of the refinements of existing organ systems and increases in size.

FICA: See *Federal Insurance Contributions Act (FICA).*

field instruction: In social work education, an integral part of the *BSW* and *MSW* educational curricula, providing students with supervised opportunities to engage in direct social work practice. Students are helped to refine professional skills, acquire and solidify social work values, and integrate elements of knowledge acquired in the academic setting with those obtained in the field.

field placement: A part of the social work student's formal educational requirement, consisting of ongoing work in a relevant community social agency. The *MSW* student typically is given a work assignment (of 16 to 20 hours weekly) in one agency during the first training year and assigned to another agency, with about the same time requirements, during the second year. The student receives close supervision by agency personnel and has the opportunity to integrate, utilize, and apply classroom content to practical experiences. Field placements also exist in undergraduate *(BSW)* social work training programs and in certain circumstances in some doctoral programs.

fields of practice: The social work term pertaining to the profession's various practice settings and the special competence needed to work in those settings. Fields of practice were established by the 1920s, when it became apparent that social work practice itself was so far-reaching that it was becoming difficult for individuals to encompass. The first fields of practice included *family welfare, child welfare, psychiatric social work, medical social work,* and *school social work.* These fields have, to some extent, subsequently changed in their focus and new ones have emerged. They now also include *industrial social work, occupational social work, gerontological social work, rural social work, police social work,* and *forensic social work.*

field study: A social research method of investigating subjects in their natural environments instead of in a laboratory or clinician's office. For example, a social worker doing research in a ghetto neighborhood would stay in that neighborhood making systematic observations for an extended period of time.

filial responsibility: See *relative's responsibility.*

financial management: The planning, control, and direction of one's income and expenditures. This includes appropriate recording and bookkeeping, establishing and implementing consistent priorities and timing for purchasing decisions, minimizing waste, and budgeting. Social work administrators are concerned with financial management as an integral part of their managerial responsibilities. Social workers in direct practice often teach or help some of their clients to plan and control their finances.

first-order change: In *systems theories,* a temporary or superficial change in a system and the way it functions. See also *second-order change.*

fiscal intermediaries: Organizations that provide third-party and fourth-party financial services between recipients and providers of a benefit. For example, a government organization (third party) provides funds for *Medicaid* health care providers, whereas a private insurance company such as Blue Cross–Blue Shield (fourth party) may provide the related administrative support.

fixation: A continuing mode of behavior, persistent thought, or enduring emotional attachment that has become inappropriate for one's present circumstances; in *psychodynamic* theory, the partial or complete arrest of personality development at one of the *psychosexual* stages.

fixed assets: An organization's or social agency's financial holdings, such as land, buildings, and properties, that are not readily negotiable. Fixed assets exclude such values as accessible cash, expertise of personnel, and the agency's reputation or goodwill factors.

fixed-interval schedule: A procedure used in *behavior modification* in which a *reinforcement* is delivered when a specified period of time has elapsed after a response has occurred. For example, a child may be given a reward 10 minutes after completing a homework assignment.

flat affect: The appearance of apathy in mood. For example, an individual may show no emotion when told of bad news or frown when told good news. It is sometimes a symptom of *schizophrenia* or *depression.*

flat-rate fee: A predetermined amount of money charged by a social worker or other professional for providing a particular service. The amount assessed is related to the service itself rather than to the client's unique economic circumstances. See also *sliding fee scale.*

Flexner Report: An influential paper delivered to social workers in 1915 by Dr. Abraham Flexner that declared that social work was not yet a profession because it lacked a unique technology, specific educational programs, a professional literature, and practice skills. Although it was controversial, the report stimulated social work to make the changes that eventually resulted in the fulfillment of Flexner's criteria of professionalism.

flight into illness: A phenomenon commonly seen in clinical social work and other psychotherapies, wherein the client whose therapy is coming to an end suddenly exhibits new symptoms of the *presenting problem.* It is considered a manifestation by the client of *dependency* on the worker or a *transference* experience.

flight of ideas: Rapid skipping from one thought or mental association to another without much basis for connection. It is sometimes symptomatic of *hyperkinesis, bipolar disorder* (manic type), and drug-induced *euphoria.*

flooding: A procedure used in *behavior therapy* in which anxiety-eliciting stimuli are presented, either in reality or in imagery, with such regularity or intensity that the subject eventually stops responding with anxiety. See also *implosion.*

folie à deux: The sharing of delusions by two people. For example, a husband and wife may come to believe, and help reinforce one another's conviction, that they are being ridiculed secretly by their neighbors. This phenomenon is also known as *shared paranoid disorder.*

folkways: Informal, traditional, and not strongly enforced patterns of behavior and standards of conduct in a culture.

Food and Agricultural Organization (FAO): An agency of the United Nations, established in 1945, to improve the world's agricultural production and distribution and the nutritional level of all peoples. It devises plans for improving yields in agriculture, oceans, and forests and supervises research in improving seeds and hybrid crops and developing more fertilizers and pesticides.

Food and Drug Administration (FDA): A federal program, established in 1931 and now part of the *Department of Health and Human Services (HHS),* that maintains standards and conducts research on the safety, reliability, and value of food and drug products available for human consumption.

food assistance programs: *Social welfare* benefits for eligible people to assure that their nutritional requirements are met. The major food assistance programs in the United States are managed by the U.S. Department of

Agriculture (USDA) and include the *Food Stamp program,* the school breakfast and *school lunch programs,* and the *WIC program* to provide special supplemental food for women, infants, and children considered at risk for nutritional deficiencies. USDA also arranges to donate surplus agricultural products to some charitable institutions and nonprofit summer camps.

Food Stamp program: A federal *food assistance program,* enacted in 1964 and administered by the U.S. Department of Agriculture through state welfare departments. Coupons are distributed to needy eligible individuals and families to be used like cash in participating stores to purchase most foods, plants, seeds, and sometimes meals-on-wheels, but not alcohol or tobacco products. The objective is to improve the diets of low-income households by supplementing their food-purchasing ability.

force field analysis (FFA): A problem-solving tool often used in social welfare planning, administration, and community organization for assessing the degree of resistance or receptivity to a proposed change. The analysis includes listing the social forces that push for change (such as high costs of the existing program or structure or ineffectiveness in reaching stated goals) and then listing those forces expected to obstruct change (such as the existing personnel's fear of losing job security or authority). FFA analysis then delineates actions that can be taken to increase or decrease certain forces so as to facilitate movement toward the desired goal.

foreclosure: The legal termination of the right to a specified property, usually as a consequence of nonpayment of the obligation.

forensic social work: The practice specialty in social work that focuses on legal matters and educating law professionals about social welfare issues and social workers about the legal aspects of their objectives. The activity also includes providing expert testimony (or preparing other social workers to provide such testimony) in courts of law on such disputes as child custody, divorce, delinquency, nonsupport, relatives' responsibility problems, and welfare rights.

formal operations stage: In *Piagetian theory,* the developmental stage that occurs during adolescence and that is characterized by greater flexibility in thought, increasing ability to use logic and deductive reasoning, the ability to consider complex issues from several different viewpoints, and a reduction of *egocentrism.*

foster care: The provision of physical care and family environments for children who are unable to live with their natural parents. Foster care is typically administered by county social service departments. Their workers evaluate children and their families to help legal authorities determine the need for placement, evaluate potential foster homes as to appropriateness for placing the particular child, monitor the foster home during the placement, and help the legal authorities and family members determine when it is appropriate to return the child to the natural family. The precedent for foster care in the United States originated largely in the procedures known as *apprenticing* and *indenture,* in which homeless youths were placed in the care of a merchant or craftsperson for instruction and lodging in exchange for work. The term "foster care" also applies to full-time residential care for elderly, developmentally disabled, or mentally ill adults.

Foster Grandparents: A federal program, administered by *ACTION,* that employs low-income senior citizens to provide care and emotional support for deprived, retarded, or neglected children.

foundations: Institutions through which private funds are distributed for public purposes such as education, international relations, health, welfare, research, the humanities, and religion. Those foundations that have funded social welfare research and service provision have included the *Russell Sage Foundation,* the Kellogg Foundation, the Robert Wood Johnson Foundation, the Carnegie Endowment, the Ford Foundation, the Rockefeller Foundation, and the Commonwealth Fund.

foundling hospitals: Institutions that receive and care for abandoned children. Traditionally, they have been financed by philanthropic contributions and later by local taxpayers. St. Vincent's Infant Asylum was established in 1856 as the first such facility in the United States. For the most part they have been replaced by *foster care* programs.

fourth party: A *fiscal intermediary* between the provider of a health care or social service, the consumer of that service, and the organization that pays for the service. The fourth party does not provide the cash to cover the charges but provides administrative services for the cash provider (third party). For example, the U.S. government is the third party for the *CHAMPUS* program, which pays health care providers for their treatment of dependents of military personnel. But in most locales *CHAMPUS* contracts with a private insurance company, such as Blue Cross–Blue Shield (the fourth party), to process the administrative details.

frail elderly: Aged men and women who suffer from, or are vulnerable to, physical or emotional impairments and require some care because they have limited ability or opportunity to provide entirely for their own needs.

franchising: The process by which one organization grants another organization, group, or individual the right and obligation to fulfill one of its customary functions. For example, a state government might contract with a private company to provide penal facilities and services to some of its convict criminal population. Or a county government might engage a group of private social work practitioners to conduct all the investigations for foster care placements.

fraud: A criminal act involving intentional deception that results in loss of property by an individual or group.

fraudulent contract: (1) An explicit or implied agreement between two closely related people that is repeatedly violated by one person, forcing the other to adopt new behaviors to accommodate; (2) a written document, to which parties agree, that contains deceptive statements or information.

free association: A therapeutic procedure, most commonly used in psychoanalysis and other insight-oriented therapies, in which the professional encourages the client to express whatever thoughts or emotions come to mind. The client verbalizes at length and is given no distracting external cues by the therapist that could influence the material being presented.

Freedmen's Bureau: Originally known as the Bureau of Refugees, Freedmen, and Abandoned Lands, this U.S. War Department organization was established in 1865 and was the nation's first federal welfare agency. Its major purpose was to assist former slaves in the transition to freedom by distributing food rations to the needy, finding employment opportunities, developing educational and medical institutions, and providing legal assistance. The bureau was eliminated in 1872.

Freedom of Information Act: Federal legislation enacted in 1966 (P.L. 89-554) to establish the right of citizens to know (with specific exceptions) what information the government and some other organizations are keeping about them. For example, under certain circumstances it gives clients of federally administered health and welfare agencies the right of access to their case records.

free enterprise system: An economic orientation of a nation or community that permits open competition for customers with minimal government regulation or involvement in the economy. This is a relative concept, because any social system except anarchy must have some public regulation or controls.

free enterprise system: An economic orientation of a nation or community that permits open competition for customers with minimal government regulation or involvement in the economy. This is a relative concept, because any social system except anarchy must have some public regulation or controls.

free-floating anxiety: Pervasive tension not attached to specific threats, situations, or ideas.

freestanding social services: Social service agencies and programs that operate independently of other service provider organizations and usually offer a wide range of personal social services. Examples include child welfare and family service agencies. Freestanding social services are contrasted with social service programs that operate as components of other organizations such as the social service departments of hospitals, schools, industrial organizations, and the military.

Freudian slip: See *parapraxis.*

Freudian theory: An integrated set of principles about human behavior and the treatment of personality disorders based on the ideas of Viennese neurologist Sigmund Freud (1856–1939) and his followers. Central concepts about personality development include the growing organization of drives (*instincts, libido, pleasure principle,* and the *reality principle*), personality structure (*unconscious, preconscious,* and *conscious*), personality dynamics (*id, ego,* and *superego*), and the stages of psychosexual development (the phases known as *oral, anal,* and *phallic*). Treatment concepts include *free association, catharsis, transference,* and *countertransference.* See also *psychoanalytic theory.*

frictional unemployment: One of the four kinds of unemployment (the others being *seasonal, cyclical,* and *structural*), which occurs when people are moving geographically or occupationally from one job to another with only slight intervals of time with no work.

friendly visitors: Volunteers and, later, paid employees of the *Charity Organization Societies (COS)* who eventually became known as *social workers.* Their primary job was to investigate the homes of the needy, determine the causes of problems, provide guidance for solving problems, and—as a last resort—provide material assistance to those clients deemed "worthy." Friendly visiting was supplanted by casework as it developed greater professionalism, more thorough training, and better understanding of the causes of problems.

frigidity: An early term used to describe sexual disorders of women who do not experience sexual desire or orgasms. The terms now used to describe these problems include *orgasmic dysfunction, dyspareunia,* and *functional vaginismus.*

frustration: A state of tension that occurs as a result of some goal-directed behavior being thwarted or postponed.

frustration tolerance: The capacity to endure having a goal thwarted or postponed.

fugue: Amnesic flight; a *psychogenic* condition in which an individual, usually after experiencing intolerable internal or external stress, develops *amnesia* and abandons home, job, or familiar environment.

functional assessment: Systematic procedures and criteria used by social workers and other professionals, especially in health care and institutional settings, to determine the capacity of clients to provide for their own care and well-being. The client is evaluated as to the ability to carry out needed activities for daily living and possession of the tools needed to fulfill those activities.

functional impairment: The inability of an individual to meet certain expectations or responsibilities due to temporary or permanent physical or mental incapacitation. The term is used by some social workers to refer to a situation in which an individual is only partially disabled and can effectively carry out most but not all functions that are ordinarily expected. The term is also applied to situations in which an individual lacks the ability to control certain vital functions.

functional mental illness: A term that pertains to psychological disorders for which there is no apparent physical or organic base.

functional requisites: In social policy development, the delineation of anticipated program activities and services, identification of targets of service, and specification of anticipated types of intervention to be used.

functional school in social work: A theoretical and practice orientation in social work based partly on the "will" concept of Otto Rank and the ideas of Virginia Robinson and Jessie Taft. It is also known as the "Pennsylvania School" and the "Rankian School," to distinguish it from the *diagnostic school in social work.* Most influential from 1930 to 1950, the approach deemphasized diagnostic inquiry, history taking, and *Freudian theory* and stressed a strategy that was time-limited and focused on those issues that came within the agency's function.

functional vaginismus: A psychogenic sexual disorder in women in which continuing involuntary spasms of the musculature of the outer third of the vagina interfere with coitus.

function-versus-cause issue: See *cause-versus-function issue.*

funding: Allocation of a specific amount of money to be used in carrying out an organization's program for a certain amount of time.

fundraising: The process of soliciting and acquiring income through philanthropic contributions, private donations, grants, fees for service, investment, and other means.

fusion: In family systems theory, the obscuring of separate identities between the family members. See also *differentiation.*

G

GADE: See *Group for the Advancement of Doctoral Education in Social Work (GADE)*.

GAIN programs: State welfare programs, originating in California, in which public assistance recipients are provided with training, education, job counseling, and employment placement. If the services are not successful in getting an eligible AFDC family head into the work force, the recipient is provided with up to a year of employment in relevant public service positions. See also *ET programs*.

Gamblers Anonymous: A self-help organization for compulsive gamblers and all people who experience problems as a result of gambling. Patterned to some extent after the *Alcoholics Anonymous (AA)* program, it was founded in 1957 and now has chapters in major cities throughout the United States.

gambling, compulsive: A disordered behavior in which the individual becomes preoccupied with wagers and develops a progressively worsening urge to bet money. The urge often becomes uncontrollable and occurs even when funds for making bets are not available.

gaming: A process in which participants are *role playing* potential or actual life simulations in which problems occur that must be resolved. The term "simulation" refers to an analogy of something or some process in the real world, however it is perceived. Unlike other role-playing situations, gaming has specified rules that are used to govern actions. According to Armand Lauffer (*Social Planning at the Community Level*, Englewood Cliffs, N.J.: Prentice-Hall, 1978, pp. 305–307) there are "move rules" (which specify who can do what, with or to whom, and with what resources) and "termination rules" (which define who has won and when the game is over). Games and simulations, as herein defined, are social, as contrasted to such physical simulations as wind tunnels in aircraft design centers.

gang: In sociological terms, a group that originally forms spontaneously and whose members maintain a relationship because they share certain attributes. These attributes include age, ethnicity, residence in a neighborhood, or common values that lead to mutual bonding. Social workers and legal authorities often use the term to refer to a fairly cohesive group of young people who support one another in various antisocial pursuits.

GANTT chart: A scheduling technique commonly used in social work and social planning to show graphically each of the activities of an organization and the time taken to complete each of them. For each activity there is a horizontal line drawn under calendar dates, and a horizontal bar is drawn to show the duration of time spent on the task. Because the GANTT chart does not show interconnections between activities, the *PERT* chart tends to be used for more complex planning.

garnishment: A legal process in which a debtor's money or other property (such as wages, salary, or savings) in the possession or control of another person is applied to a debt owed to a third party. Due process requires that the debtor be given notice and an opportunity to be heard by a court, which may order the employer, banker, or other holder of the property to remit such funds to an agent of the court or to the person to whom the money is owed until the obligation has been fulfilled. For example, an employer may be required to withhold a portion of an employee's salary and remit it to the court to meet the employee's child support obligation.

gatekeeper: One who facilitates or obstructs social movement from one status to another or communication between one group and another. In social work the term has several specific uses. In *community organization* it refers to an indigenous member of a community who permits or precludes real access by the organizers to those in the target population. In this sense, gatekeepers are typically the natural leaders of a community or they work in key positions that permit them to know what and who is influential. These people may be playground workers, traffic patrol people, gang leaders, bartenders, or neighborhood "busybodies." The term is also used in social work education in referring to the role of the faculty person who is instrumental in including or excluding certain students as members of the profession. The gatekeeper role is also performed by formal organizations and social agencies that evaluate potential clients for certain eligibilities.

Gault: The 1967 decision rendered by the U.S. Supreme Court (*In re Gault*) that affirmed the right of juveniles to the same legal protections as adults in criminal court proceedings. This gave juveniles the right to proper advance notification of the charges, the right to counsel, freedom from self-incrimination, and the opportunity to have their counsel confront witnesses. Prior to *Gault*, juvenile proceedings were regarded as civil, not criminal, and the state was supposedly acting in the interests of the child. As a result of the decision, social workers and other nonlegal persons often made or influenced decisions regarding the rights and liberty of children.

gay: The term preferred by many homosexuals in describing themselves and their sexual orientation.

gender identity: The relative degree to which an individual patterns him- or herself after members of the same sex. This is a synonym for *sexual identity.*

General Accounting Office (GAO):   The independent federal agency within the legislative branch of government that assists the U.S. Congress in determining whether public funds are efficiently and economically administered and spent and in evaluating the results of existing government programs and activities. As such the GAO has general rights of access to and examination of any records of the federal departments and agencies for which Congress has allocated funds.

general assistance (GA):   A residual or emergency welfare program operated under state and local auspices to provide *means-tested* financial and other aid to individuals who are not eligible for any of the *categorical programs* such as *social security (OASDHI), Aid to Families with Dependent Children (AFDC),* or *Supplemental Security Income (SSI).* Local departments of public welfare (also called departments of human services or social services in some counties) determine eligibility

and help coordinate the distribution of these funds.

generalist: A social work practitioner whose knowledge and skills encompass a broad spectrum and who assesses problems and their solutions comprehensively. The generalist often coordinates the efforts of specialists by facilitating communication between them, thereby fostering *continuity of care.* See also *specialist* and *generic social work.*

generalization: (1) The process of forming an idea, judgment, or abstraction about a class of people, things, or events, based on limited or particular experiences; (2) an act or pattern of behavior in which an individual avoids discussing personal problems by characterizing them as being universal. For example, a client may say, "Every couple fights," to conceal current marital conflicts. Generalizations are also used in social work practice to connect or clarify a client's experiences with others. For example, the worker might say, "Everyone feels depressed at times."

generalization, behavioral: In *behaviorism* or *social learning theory,* the tendency of a *response* to occur in the presence of a *stimulus* that is similar to one that was present when the response was learned.

generalized anxiety disorder: One type of anxiety neurosis (or anxiety state), this disorder is characterized by such symptoms as motor tension (shakiness, trembling, inability to relax, and restlessness), apprehension (fear and worry), autonomic hyperactivity (sweating, clammy hands, dizziness, light-headedness, upset stomach, flushing, and increased pulse and respiration rate), inability to concentrate, insomnia, irritability, and general impatience.

general systems theory: A conceptual orientation that attempts to explain holistically the behavior of people and societies by identifying the interacting components of the system and the controls that keep these components (*subsystems*) stable and in a state of *equilibrium.* It is concerned with the *boundaries, roles, relationships,* and routes of information flow between people. General systems theory is a subset of *systems theories* that focuses on living entities, from microorganisms to societies. See also *ecological perspective* and *life model.*

generativity: In Erikson's *psychosocial development theory,* a term pertaining to an individual's interest in parenting, establishing, and guiding the next generation; also, becoming interested in the welfare of others and in exploring one's one creative efforts.

generativity versus stagnation: According to Erikson's theory, the longest stage of a person's psychosocial development, occurring roughly from age 24 to 54. In it, the individual tries to reconcile conflicts between egocentric desires and the need to contribute to the well-being of future generations.

generic social work: The social work orientation that emphasizes a common core of knowledge and skills associated with social service provision. A generic social worker possesses basic knowledge that may span several methods. Such a worker would not necessarily be a specialist in a single field of practice or professional technique but would be capable of providing and managing a wider range of needed client services and intervening in a greater variety of systems.

generic-specific controversy: A debate among social workers that has existed since at least the 1920s. One faction sees the profession as comprising a group of different specialists, each with a unique body of knowledge and highly refined professional skills that require considerable training and practice to master and that are applied to a specific and relatively narrow part of the total spectrum of social welfare needs. The other faction sees professional social work as being made up of generalists—people who have a *macro orientation* and who can be useful by developing and integrating services and *channeling* people to them. The generalist faction also believes that social work skills are sufficiently similar from one specialty to another so that a worker can be effective in a variety of settings. Since the 1929 *Milford Conference* was convened to attempt to resolve the controversy, most social workers have taken positions that fall somewhere between these extremes.

genetic counseling: The specialty in medicine and related fields that helps people who have, or risk having, physical problems due to inherited defects. Such problems include *Down's syndrome, cystic fibrosis, diabetes, sickle-cell anemia, hemophilia,* and *Huntington's chorea.* Counseling includes prevention of new problems by advising individuals about their reproductive risks and alternatives.

genetic diseases: Inherited diseases such as *sickle-cell anemia, Tay-Sachs disease, Huntington's chorea,* and so on.

genital stage: In *psychodynamic theory,* the last significant phase of psychosexual development, that begins with *puberty* and continues for several years thereafter. Freud postulated that, with the onset of adultlike sexual feelings, the individual has an opportunity to resolve the *Oedipus complex* conflicts, sever erotic attachments to opposite-sex parents, and transfer sexual drives to peers of the opposite sex.

genocide: The systematic elimination of racial, religious, ethnic, or cultural groups, usually through mass extermination by the government of the nation in which they reside.

genogram: A diagram used in *family therapy* to depict family relationships extended over at least three generations. The diagram uses circles to represent females and squares for males, with horizontal lines indicating marriages. Vertical lines are drawn from the marriage lines to other circles and squares to depict the children. The diagram may contain other symbols or written explanations to indicate critical events, such as death, divorce, and remarriage, and to reveal recurrent patterns of behavior.

gentrification: The social phenomenon in which homes in formerly poor, overcrowded, ghetto neighborhoods are purchased and privately rehabilitated by more affluent families for their personal dwellings or for investment. This has the effect of raising the property values, rents, and property tax rates of all the homes in the neighborhood, forcing the removal of the remaining less affluent people and their replacement by those who can afford to live there. The gentrified neighborhood may seem more desirable, but the people who are displaced have to crowd into other neighborhoods, and the resulting population pressure causes those neighborhoods to decline.

genuineness: Sincerity and honesty; one of the important qualities in developing an effective therapeutic relationship. Genuineness includes being unpretentious with clients, speaking honestly rather than only for effect, acknowledging one's limitations, and providing only sincere reassurances.

geriatrics: A branch of the medical profession that specializes in the treatment of diseases of old age.

gerontological social work: An orientation and specialization in social work concerned with the psychosocial treatment of the elderly—the development and management of needed social services and programs for the aged population and for elderly individuals.

gerontology: The scientific study of aging.

gerrymandering: The creation of political boundaries of unusual or unnatural shape so that some groups are politically under- or overrepresented. For example, a city might divide its legislative districts so that residents of a central city ghetto are divided among five other districts, making them minorities in each new district.

gestalt psychology: A group of theories that emphasizes the whole of an organism or environment rather than its parts and focuses on the interrelationships in mental perceptions. It is a school of psychology influenced by Kurt Lewin and Wolfgang Kohler that has influenced but is not synonymous with *gestalt therapy.*

gestalt therapy: A form of psychotherapeutic intervention developed and popularized by Frederick S. Perls and others. The approach seeks to help individuals integrate their thoughts, emotions, and behaviors and orient themselves more realistically toward their current perceptions and experiences. Emphasis is placed on becoming aware of and taking responsibility for one's own actions, on spontaneity of emotional expression and perception, and on recognizing the existence of gaps and distortions in one's own thinking.

gestation: The period from conception to birth. In humans, the gestation period averages 266 days.

ghetto: A geographic and usually poor section of a city, inhabited predominantly by ethnic groups or *minorities of color.* Usually those who reside in such areas do not do so by choice. Ghettos originated in late-fourteenth-century Spain to segregate Jews, often behind guarded walls, to minimize their influence on Christians. Ghettos for Jews continued to exist in various European cities until after World War II.

GI Bill: The common name for the group of laws and programs, starting in 1944, that provide educational, housing, insurance, medical, and vocational training opportunities for U.S. military veterans. These programs originated to help integrate into society the veterans returning from World War II and to upgrade the American *work force.*

Gideon v. Wainwright: The 1963 U.S. Supreme Court ruling that all indigent defendants in criminal cases have the right to free legal counsel.

Gilbert Act: The 1782 English welfare reform laws. The legislation abolished many *workhouses* and reorganized others so that they were managed by municipal employees rather than private entrepreneurs. Children under 6 who resided in these workhouses were placed in foster homes, and many recipients became eligible for *outdoor relief.*

Ginnie Mae: See *Government National Mortgage Association (GNMA).*

Girls Clubs of America: See *youth service organizations.*

glaucoma: An eye disease in which fluid builds up between the cornea and the iris and the resulting pressure on the eyeball injures certain nerve cells.

goal-directed behavior: Any activity that is directed toward conscious or explicitly defined objectives.

goal-setting: A strategy used by social workers and other professionals to help clients clarify and define the objectives they hope to achieve in the helping relationship and then to establish the steps that must be taken and the time needed to reach those objectives. The community organizer–social worker uses goal-setting by helping key members of the target population or client community define their objectives and spell out the goals they want their people to achieve.

go-between role: The process of mediation that occurs when a social worker or other professional intervenes between conflicting parties (such as husband and wife, parent and child, buyer and seller, landlord and tenant, or two members of a therapy group) and seeks to enhance mutual understanding and reduce tensions.

goldbricking: A pejorative term indicating that an individual is only appearing to be working on a job but is actually loafing.

gonorrhea: An infectious disease transmitted primarily by sexual contact. It causes inflammation of the genital organs and may eventually lead to sterility. The gonococcus organisms are highly vulnerable to most antibiotics. The disease was once a major cause of blindness among newborn children whose mothers were infected, but the routine use of silver nitrate solution in babies' eyes at birth has largely overcome the problem.

good-faith bargaining: The requirement that both parties in a dispute, such as a couple or members of a family or community, discuss issues with open minds and make the possibility of discussion equal for all participants.

goodness of fit: The degree to which a person or other element in a system is able to adapt to or modify the environment so that mutual stability is the result. See also *adaptation, ecological perspective,* and *life model.*

good works: A term formerly used to describe activities to help the disadvantaged through *philanthropy, charity,* volunteer work, and personal examples of moral behavior. These activities were viewed by religious and political leaders and social philosophers as moral obligations to God and society—a view that motivated many of the social welfare activities that preceded government-funded welfare programs.

Government National Mortgage Association (GNMA): An agency of the U.S. *Department of Housing and Urban Development (HUD)* that finances or insures financing for the purchase of low-cost housing or of homes in areas where conventional loans are difficult to obtain. Mortgages issued by the association are informally known as *Ginnie Maes.*

graduated tax: See *progressive tax.*

graft: Misappropriation of public money by one or more public officials.

Gramm-Rudman-Hollings Act: The informal title of the Public Debt Limitation–Balanced Budget and Emergency Deficit Control Act (P.L. 99-177), budget reduction legislation enacted in 1985 requiring progressively lower deficits in the federal budget in each fiscal year from 1986 through 1991. The legislation called for cuts in both domestic and defense spending but excluded *social security, the Food Stamp program,* debt interest, and some long-term defense contract expenditures. The deficits were to be limited to $171.9 billion in 1986, $144 billion in 1987, $108 billion in 1988, $72 billion in 1989, and $36 billion in 1990, and the budget was to be balanced in 1991. The legislation specified automatic spending cuts whenever these targets were not met.

grandfather clause: Also known as a "grandparent clause"; an exemption to a new agreement, rule, or requirement so those who were already engaged in the relevant activity before a certain time need not fulfill the new requirements. For example, social workers who were members of the *National Association of Social Workers (NASW)* and who met certain practice and supervision requirements before 1973 could become members of the *Academy of Certified Social Workers (ACSW)* without having to pass the qualifying examination that was required of later applicants.

grandiosity: An exaggerated sense of self-importance, in its more extreme forms equivalent to a *delusion of grandeur.*

grants-in-aid: Payments made by one organization, such as a government agency, to another to achieve a specified purpose. For example, the federal government might grant payments to states, or states might make such payments to cities, to help fund and ensure the existence of the local organization's *public assistance* programs. See also *block grants.*

grantsmanship: In social administration, the ability to develop proposals for special project funding. The ability includes skills in research design, verbal communication, salesmanship, writing, assessing needs, innovation of new techniques for problem solving, coordination of plans, and political and administrative activity as well as knowledge about the appropriate sources of project funds.

grass-roots organizing: The *community organization* strategy of helping the members of a neighborhood or geographic region at the local level to develop stronger relationships, common goals, and an organization that will help them achieve those goals. The focus of attention is on organizing the people who will be affected by changes, rather than on organizing only the community leaders. This involves educating and mobilizing people for action toward agreed-upon goals.

gray ghettos: Neighborhoods or housing projects, often in older, decaying areas of inner cities, whose residents are primarily poor and elderly. The term has also been used to refer to private retirement villages and communities zoned for the exclusive use of people over a certain age.

gray market adoption: The adoption of dependent children outside the legitimate social agencies and legal institutions. Such adoptions are often arranged by physicians, lawyers, or other professionals who personally know couples who seek to adopt and parents who feel obliged to give up their children for adoption. These arrangements are questionable because they involve little of the systematic evaluation and home study that go on in the legitimized adoption process. However, in many jurisdictions the practice is not strictly illegal, as in the case of *black market adoptions.*

Gray Panthers: The advocacy group founded in 1970 to work on behalf of the social and economic needs of the aged. The group's major focus is on state and national legislation affecting the elderly and on acting as watchdog in the implementation of the legislation.

Great Depression: The severe and extended economic crisis that occurred in the United States and many other nations during the 1930s, ending with reindustrialization in preparation for World War II. In 1933, 16 million people were unemployed (nearly one-third of the U.S. *work force*). Largely in response to the resulting hardships, President Franklin D. Roosevelt's Administration established the *New Deal* program, which redefined the federal role in helping individuals and assuring the general welfare.

Great Society: President Lyndon B. Johnson's name for the social welfare goals and programs established as a *War on Poverty* during his Administration. Some of these efforts included the *Model Cities program*, the *Head Start program*, the *Office of Economic Opportunity (OEO)*, *Medicaid*, and *Medicare*.

green card: The name commonly used for the U.S. government's registration card that identifies the holder as being a permanent U.S. resident who is a citizen of another nation. The card (which is no longer green) is officially U.S. Government Form I-551, "Alien Registration Recipient."

greenhouse effect: The heating of the environment due to the burning of fossil fuels (such as coal and oil). Burning these fuels results in an atmospheric gain in carbon dioxide molecules. The excess carbon dioxide in the atmosphere does not prevent the sun's rays from reaching the earth's surface but prevents the escape of heat radiating from the ground. Some scientists believe that, unless there is a drastic reduction in the use of fossil fuels, the earth's weather and heat level is likely to increase by five degrees in the next 30 to 100 years, an increase that could significantly change the earth's climatic patterns.

greenlining: A tactic used by community organizers in which residents of a neighborhood are mobilized to withdraw their funds from banks that are not equal opportunity lenders or that practice *redlining* (excluding certain neighborhoods from receiving loans).

grief reaction: Experiencing deep sadness as the result of an important loss. This emotional response is normal and in healthy people will gradually subside in a limited time.

grief work: A series of emotional stages or phases following an important loss, which gradually permit adjustment and recovery. The individual typically reminisces, expresses emotions, accepts, adjusts to the new situation, and forms new relationships.

grievance: A formal complaint about some procedure or regulation that is not being followed, resulting in some harm to the complainant.

gross national product (GNP): The total value of a nation's annual output of services and goods.

group: A collection of people, brought together by mutual interests, who are capable of consistent and uniform action. Major types of groups include the *primary group*, whose members are in face-to-face association and share a wide range of traits and interactions, and the *secondary group*, whose members infrequently or never have face-to-face contact, are impersonally associated, and share only one or a few traits and common interests. Other types of groups are *single session groups, theme groups,* and *marathon groups.*

group cohesiveness: The degree of mutual attraction or reciprocal benefit experienced or anticipated by individuals in relation to a social collective with which they identify.

group dynamics: The flow of information and exchanges of influence between members of a social collective. These exchanges can be modified by group leaders or helping professionals and used to achieve certain predetermined objectives that may benefit the members.

group eligibility: Being qualified for a benefit or obligation as the result of membership in some association or occupation of a defined social status. For example, everyone who reaches a certain age may become qualified for specified *social insurance* benefits.

Group for the Advancement of Doctoral Education in Social Work (GADE): The association of social work educators in the nation's doctoral social work programs. Doctoral educators began meeting in 1974 to synchronize their efforts to coordinate and standardize doctoral requirements. The organization became official in 1977, and its members now have annual meetings, conduct workshops, and prepare materials to assist doctoral programs in schools of social work.

group health insurance: A plan for insuring all members of an established group who want to join (for example, all employees of a company, all government workers, all members of NASW) and their dependents against the cost of illness.

group identity: The degree to which an individual affiliates with, feels part of, and emulates the characteristics of a social collective.

group psychotherapy: A form of *psychotherapy* that treats individuals simultaneously for emotional disorders by emphasizing interactions and mutuality, Most professionals consider the term to be synonymous with *group therapy*. Some writers, however, make a distinction between group psychotherapy, group therapy, and *social group work*. They consider group psychotherapy to be only one type of group therapy. The former uses group treatment techniques to help individuals resolve emotional problems, whereas the latter uses a wider range of intervention strategies to help individuals deal with problems of social maladjustment as well as emotional disorders. *Social group work,* although it shares some of these objectives and techniques, is not limited to treating disorders and problems but includes education and positive group experiences for helping healthy individuals achieve greater personal fulfillment.

group therapy: An intervention strategy for helping individuals who have emotional disorders or social maladjustment problems by bringing together two or more individuals under the direction of a social worker or other professional therapist. The individuals are asked to share their problems with other members of the group, discuss ways to resolve their problems, exchange information and views about resources and techniques for solving the problem, and share emotional experiences in a controlled (by the professional) setting that enables the members to work through their difficulties. A typical format in group therapy is to have six to eight members meet with a professional therapist in a facility provided by the therapist for 90 minutes once each week. Among the many variations of group therapy are "closed groups" (no new members are added once the group has begun, usually with a termination date established in advance) and "open groups" (a new member is added whenever a member of the group terminates, and the group continues indefinitely). Group therapy is a format used by practitioners of many different orientations, including *behaviorism, transactional analysis, family therapy, gestalt therapy,* and *psychoanalysis.* See also *sensitivity group* and *marathon group.*

group work: See *social group work.*

GS civil service ranks: The designations of salary level and rank within the federal civil service, according to the "General Schedule." The GS levels range from 1 to 18. Clerical and subprofessional ranks are usually GS 1 through 6. College graduates and skilled technical personnel usually hold grades between 6 and 12. Agency management personnel tend to hold grades 12 to 15. Top-level civil servants in planning and management positions hold the "supergrade" ranks 16 to 18. See also *Office of Personnel Management (OPM).*

guaranteed annual income: A proposal made by some social policy experts to eliminate the *means test* (which determines on a case-by-case basis whether individuals have sufficient economic resources to meet a given standard of living). Rather than evaluate each person's resources and needs as the basis for assistance, every individual or family would receive a specified amount of money or service each year from the relevant government agency, regardless of need. See also *negative income tax.*

guardian: A person (or entity) who has the legal responsibility for the care and management of another person, usually a child or an adult who has been declared in court to be incapable of acting for himself or herself. This

guardian ad litem: A court-appointed representative designated to preserve and manage the affairs and property of another person who is considered incapable of managing his or her own affairs in the course of litigation. The guardian ad litem has no permanent control over the person's property and is considered an officer of the court.

guidance counselor: A professional person who is knowledgeable and skilled in delineating alternatives, helping to articulate goals, providing information and advice, and facilitating client self-awareness. Guidance counselors are frequently employed in educational institutions and personnel offices of business organizations to give clients direction in vocational opportunities, work and study habits, and problem resolution.

guilt: An emotional reaction to the perception of having done something wrong, having failed to do something, or violating an important social norm. The reaction is often a loss of self-esteem and a desire to make restitution. In *psychodynamic* theory, this reaction can be *unconscious* and based not on any actual wrongdoing but on concealed drives and motives that are contrary to the prohibitions established by the *superego.*

H

habeas corpus: A court requirement that the custodian of a prisoner or otherwise institutionalized individual bring the person before the judge. The court may then determine whether the party is being held in violation of his or her constitutional rights to due process.

habituation: A type of adaptation in which an individual has learned to eliminate responses to repeated and distracting stimuli. For example, an abused child might appear to become indifferent to continued physical punishment. Some social workers and other professionals also use the term to refer to a form of *drug dependence* in which the individual has more of a psychological craving than a physical addiction (manifested by *withdrawal symptoms*).

halfway houses: Transitional residences for individuals who require some professional supervision, support, or protection but not full-time institutionalization. Such facilities are used mostly by formerly hospitalized mental patients, parolees, and those with alcohol and *drug dependence.* (There are other transitional residences, called quarterway and three-quarter-way houses, which offer more or fewer services according to need.)

hallucination: An imagined perception of some object or phenomenon that is not really present. Often a symptom of a *psychosis,* it may involve hearing nonexistent voices (auditory hallucination), seeing objects that aren't there (visual hallucination), smelling (olfactory hallucination), tasting (gustatory hallucination) and touching (haptic hallucination).

hallucinogen: A drug or chemical that, when ingested, results in *hallucinations.* Examples are *LSD* and mescaline.

halo effect: The tendency to evaluate individuals either too favorably or too negatively on the basis of one or a few notable traits.

handicap: Any physical or mental disadvantage that prevents or limits an individual's ability to function as others do.

Handicapped Children Act of 1975: See *Education for All Handicapped Children Act.*

hard-to-reach clients: Individuals, families, and communities who need and are eligible for professional assistance and social work intervention but who are unaware of, unmotivated for, or fearful of the service offered.

hardware: In computers, the physical machinery—including the computer, keyboard, monitor, modem, and other equipment—designed for the storing, processing, analyzing, and transmitting of data.

hashish: A resin produced in the tops of marijuana plants, which contain the most powerful concentration of tetrahydrocannabinol (THC)—the active ingredient in marijuana.

Hawthorne effect: The phenomenon that often occurs in social research in which subjects behave differently from their norm because of their awareness of being observed. For example, a social worker who observes the interactions of the members of a psychiatric hospital ward may not be seeing the same behaviors that occur when the ward is not being observed.

head injury: A trauma that temporarily or permanently damages tissue in or near the cranium, possibly resulting in brain or nerve damage. Internal head injury may affect some cognitive or motor functions or result in some *functional impairment,* even though there may be no overt symptoms of damage. Many victims of even severe head injuries can be treated by physicians and health care and social service personnel, and can achieve virtually full return to healthy functions.

"headshrinker": A slang expression applied to psychiatrists, psychologists, and clinical social workers who seek to develop insight and to bring about behavioral changes in their clients.

Head Start: The *Great Society* federal program established in 1965 to provide preschool children of disadvantaged minority families with compensatory education to offset some of the effects of their social deprivation. A related program known as Project Follow Through was established in 1967 to help children from low-income families receive additional compensatory education through the elementary years.

health: The state of complete physical, mental and social well-being and, according to the *World Health Organization (WHO)*, not merely the absence of disease or infirmity.

Health and Human Services, U.S. Department of: See *Department of Health and Human Services, U.S. (HHS).*

health care: A term pertaining to activities designed to treat, prevent, and detect physical and mental disorders and to enhance people's physical and psychosocial well-being. The health care system includes personnel who provide the needed services (physicians, nurses, hospital attendants, health care social workers, and so on); facilities where such services are rendered (hospitals, medical centers, nursing homes, *hospices, outpatient* clinics); laboratories and institutions for detection, research, and planning; educational and environmental facilities that help people prevent disease; and a myriad of other organizations and people involved in helping people to become more healthy, stay healthy, return to health, or minimize the consequences of ill health.

Health Care Financing Administration: The organization within the U.S. *Department of Health and Human Services* that assesses the nation's health care programs and their financing and oversees *Medicare* in cooperation with the *Social Security Administration (SSA)* and *Medicaid* in cooperation with state departments of public assistance.

Health, Education, and Welfare, U.S. Department of: See *Department of Health, Education, and Welfare, U.S. (HEW).*

health maintenance organization (HMO):   A comprehensive health care program and medical group that offers services for a fixed annual fee. In this alternative to the fee-for-service model, enrollees voluntarily prepay for their medical and health care, including treatment and prevention of physical and mental illness. HMOs usually have their own medical care facilities, staffed by physicians of all specialties as well as social workers and other health care providers.

health planning: Rational efforts to assure that people's physical and mental health care needs are being met and that available health care resources are used as effectively as possible toward this end. Health planning is conducted in government organizations, private medical and research organizations, and educational institutions. It includes prevention and early detection activities as well as treatment and follow-up care. Health planning also involves decision making about such things as how many health care personnel will be needed in the future, how to finance and control health care costs, where to locate medical facilities, and what methods are most effective and cost-effective. Health planning also involves environmental considerations such as proper sewage treatment, air quality, and the provision of nutritious food.

Health Resources Administration (HRA):   The organization within the U.S. *Public Health Service* whose mission is to maintain and improve the utilization, quality, and cost effectiveness of the nation's health care system. HRA helps fund the training of health care personnel, facilitates the appropriate distribution of health resources and personnel, stimulates the construction of needed health care facilities, and identifies anticipated health resource problems so as to be prepared for future needs.

Health Services Administration (HSA):   The organization within the U.S. *Public Health Service* that helps local communities find effective ways of meeting their present and future health needs. HSA provides health professionals to areas designated as having critical shortages of such personnel.

heart attack: An event in which the blood vessels that feed the heart become blocked and the heart muscle does not receive enough blood. Symptoms usually include severe chest pains, sweating, hot flashes, and nausea, and permanent damage to the heart may occur.

heart disease: A term for any of a variety of different disorders affecting the heart muscle and adjacent tissue, involving the circulatory system. Heart disease is the leading cause of death among men over 40. Those with increased risk include diabetics, smokers, and people with high blood pressure and high serum cholesterol.

hebephrenic schizophrenia: A type of *psychosis* characterized by wild excitement, giggling, silly behavior, and rapid mood shifts. This disorder is also known as "schizophrenia, disorganized type."

helplessness, learned: A pattern of behavior, frequently seen in victims of spouse and child abuse, in which the individual responds passively to risks of harm. The person may behave without obvious symptoms in every other way but has come to believe there is nothing that can be done and that no effective help is available.

hemodialysis: The medical process of purifying the blood of patients who are suffering renal (kidney) failure. This process involves a machine through which the blood is circulated on one side of a semipermeable membrane while a special *dialysis* fluid is on the other side. Blood waste products diffuse through the membrane and are discarded with the dialysis fluid.

Henrician Poor Law: The English legislation, enacted in 1536 during the reign of King Henry VIII, whose primary purpose was to organize the ways the nation would deal with its "able-bodied" poor. Officially named "The Act for the Punishment of Sturdy Vagabonds and Beggars," it placed responsibility for the care of the poor with local officials who could collect taxes for the purpose. The officials furnished work for the unemployed and restricted begging to handicapped persons. Penalties for begging by the able bodied included branding, enslavement, removal of their children, and, for repeated offenses, execution.

hepatitis: A viral disease resulting in swelling and inflammation of the liver. Symptoms include nausea, fever, weakness, loss of appetite, and often jaundice. Treatment centers around extensive bed rest and controlled diet. The virus is spread by contact with contaminated food or water (infectious hepatitis) or by injections of contaminated blood or using contaminated needles (serum hepatitis). It also sometimes occurs as a complication of other diseases, such as cirrhosis of the liver, mononucleosis, and dysentery.

heredity: The transmission of characteristics from parents to offspring through chromosomes that bear the genes; also, the tendency of an individual to manifest the traits of his or her progenitors.

heroin: A potent narcotic drug synthesized from morphine, the principle active ingredient in opium poppies. It is taken by sniffing, injecting under the skin, or by injection into a vein (*mainlining*). Its effect on the user is euphoria or apathy and, for some, a "rush," a sensation that has been described as similar to an orgasm throughout the entire body. Once addicted, the user also seeks further doses to avoid the intensely discomforting experience of *withdrawal symptoms*. Heroin is highly addictive and, partly because of its high cost and nonexistent quality control, contributes to an increased death rate and to higher incidence of organized and street crime. Heroin use is illegal in the United States.

herpes: A viral infection resulting in blisterlike eruptions. Herpes simplex takes the form of recurring blisters filled with clear fluid, known as cold sores when they appear around the lips and a canker sores when in the mouth. Herpes genitalis is a viral infection in the genital area. Herpes zoster, also called shingles, is a painful viral infection of the nerves, most commonly appearing on the chest-abdomen area and sometimes following other nerve pathways.

heterogeneous: Possessing diverse traits.

heterosexuality: Association with and orientation toward sexual activity with members of the opposite sex.

heterostasis: The tendency of a system or organism to become unstable.

HEW (U.S. Department of): See *Department of Health, Education, and Welfare, U.S. (HEW)*.

HHS (U.S. Department of): See *Department of Health and Human Services, U.S. (HHS)*.

hidden agenda: One set of goals and purposes concealed in another.

hierarchy of needs: The view of Abraham Maslow and professionals of the *humanistic orientation* that people's needs occur in ascending order. One fulfills physiological needs first, followed by needs for safety, belongingness, self-respect and self-worth, and finally self-actualization, or achieving one's full potential. See also *motivation* and *self-actualization*.

Hispanic: Pertaining to the culture of Spanish- and Portuguese-speaking people. In the United States, the term is often applied to people of Latin American ethnic background and to aspects of the culture of Spanish-speaking people.

high blood pressure: See *hypertension*.

histrionic personality disorder: A type of *personality disorder* that has all or many of the following characteristics: overly dramatic behavior, overreaction to minor events, craving for attention and excitement, tantrums, appearance to others of shallowness and lack of genuineness, apparent helplessness and dependence, proneness to manipulative gestures, and suicide threats. A person who has this disorder is commonly referred to as a "hysterical personality" or a hysteric.

holistic: Oriented toward the understanding and treatment of the whole person or phenomenon. In this view, an individual is seen as being more than the sum of separate parts, and problems are seen in a broader context rather than as specific symptoms. One who maintains a holistic philosophy seeks to integrate all the social, cultural, psychological, and physical influences on an individual.

Hollis-Taylor Report: A 1951 study of social work education, conducted by Ernest Hollis and Alice Taylor, demonstrating the profession's increasing specialization, fragmentation, and growing orientation toward the case-by-case treatment of problems. The report recommended social work education that emphasized a more generic orientation and a greater concern for social issues and social action. Many of the recommendations were accepted by the profession and became a foundation for the current objectives of social work education.

Holocaust: Great destruction of the lives and property of a people. Today the term is most often applied to the planned efforts of the Nazis during World War II to eliminate the Jewish population of Europe. See also *genocide.*

homebound: A term referring to a shut-in or one who, because of illness or disability, must remain bedridden or within the confines of the home, institution, or immediate neighborhood.

home care: The provision of health, homemaker, and social services to clients in their homes.

home health services: Programs that provide for medical, nursing, and follow-up care of patients in their homes. Many of these services are provided in the private sector by for-fee health care personnel or by private nursing service care, financed in part by *third-party payment.* Public health care services in the patient's home are also available. This provides a system that often is more comfortable for the patient and more economical than hospitalization or nursing home care.

homelessness: The condition of being without a home. Generally, the homeless man or woman is impoverished and transient and often lacks the social skills or emotional stability needed to improve the situation unless help is provided. See also *bag lady.*

homemaker: A person whose primary role and activity is to maintain a comfortable and secure living environment for his or her family.

homemaker services: A health or social service program to help clients remain in their own homes. Usually, one or more helpers visit the clients' homes on predetermined schedules, performing such activities as preparation of meals, doing laundry, cleaning house, and providing transportation and some nursing. These homemakers are usually public employees, and their services often help keep clients out of more expensive hospitals or nursing home facilities.

homeostasis: The tendency of a system or organism to maintain stability and, when disrupted, to adapt and strive to restore the stability previously achieved.

Homestead Act: The 1862 federal legislation designed to redistribute the population, provide opportunities, and settle the open lands in the West. The law authorized any U.S. citizen to receive free 160 acres of unoccupied government land by agreeing to live on it for five years.

home visits: In social work, the act of going to clients' homes in order to provide professional social services. Home visits have been part of the social work repertoire since the days of *friendly visitors,* and they occur for many reasons. Some social workers make home visits because their clients are handicapped or otherwise unable to come to the agency. Some do so because they believe the helping process can be more effective and efficient if conducted in an environment familiar to the client. Other home visits occur because the worker seeks to mobilize a neighborhood or county toward a social cause. In some instances, social workers are required to make such visits unexpectedly to investigate the client's normal living conditions. This is frequently done in order to ascertain if the client is as poor or as incapable of providing child care as has been claimed.

homicide: The killing of one human being by another.

homogeneous: Possessing the same or similar traits. See also *heterogeneous.*

homophobia: The irrational fear of homosexuals or of *homosexuality.* The term is often applied to people who have strong negative feelings about homosexuals and to people who support antigay activities. Some psychoanalytic theorists suggest that homophobia may often be the result of an individual's latent homosexuality accompanied by efforts to conceal the tendency from oneself or others.

homosexuality: The erotic or sexual interest in and preference for members of the same sex. According to *DSM-III,* this orientation is not considered to be a mental disorder unless it is *ego dystonic* (that is, the sexual preference is not accepted by the individual, is a source of anxiety, and is resisted by efforts to have a heterosexual orientation). The term is used for both men and women. See also *gay* and *lesbian.*

homosexuality, latent: In *psychodynamic* theory, the presence of erotic impulses, outside the individual's conscious awareness, toward one or more members of the same sex. The individual might give behavioral clues about this orientation but does not engage in overt homosexual activity. See also *latent homosexual.*

homosexual panic: Severe distress related to an individual's *fear* or *delusion* of being thought to be homosexual by others or of being raped or seduced by someone of the same sex. It sometimes appears as an initial symptom of *schizophrenia* (especially paranoid type), or as a manifestation of latent homosexuality.

Horatio Alger story: An expression referring to an individual's development from impoverishment to affluence supposedly because of hard work, thrift, and honest character; based on the nineteenth-century "rags to riches" novels of Rev. Horatio Alger, Jr.

hospice: Originally, a lodging house for travelers; most social workers and health care professionals now use the term to describe programs, services, and settings for the terminally ill. Hospice services are usually offered in nonhospital facilities in homelike atmospheres where families, friends, and significant others can be with the dying person.

hospice care: The provision of health, homemaker, and social services in nonhospital homelike facilities for the terminally ill.

hospital social work: The provision of social services in hospitals and similar health care centers, most often within a facility's department of social services or social work. The services provided include preventive, rehabilitative, and follow-up activities, as well as discharge planning and information gathering and providing. Other services include assisting patients with the financial and social aspects of their care and counseling patients and their families.

hot line: A communications system that provides for immediate and direct telephone contact between certain people in times of emergency. Many communities have established such systems so that trained listeners are on hand to receive calls from people who experience emotional or social problems. There are also special-purpose hot lines such as those for runaways, whistle-blowers, suicide prevention, family violence, and other problems.

household: The U.S. *Census Bureau* term referring to all persons, whether related or not, who live in the same dwelling unit. This includes individuals (single-person households) as well as groups of persons.

housing programs: Publicly funded and monitored programs designed to provide suitable homes, especially for those unable to find or pay for them themselves. In the United States most of these programs are administered by the *Department of Housing and Urban Development (HUD)*. These programs include Low-Rent Public Housing, the Rent-Subsidy Program, Lower-Income Housing Assistance, Home Ownership Assistance for Low-Income Families, Rural Rental Housing Loans, Farm Labor Housing Loans, Indian Housing Improvement Programs, and Housing Repair Assistance for Low-Income Families. In addition, the government sponsors a guaranteed mortgage loan program and housing assistance for veterans.

HTLV-III: Human T-Cell Lymphotropic Virus, the *AIDS* virus.

HUD (U.S. Department of):   See *Department of Housing and Urban Development, U.S. (HUD)*.

Hull House: The most famous *settlement house*, founded in Chicago in 1889 by Jane Addams and Ellen Gates Starr. Among the first of its kind, it was a community center for the poor and disadvantaged of the area and was the setting for initiating various social reform activities.

human capital: (1) Expenditures to enhance the quality of a people, which increases their productivity; (2) investment in the citizens of a nation through public education, health and security programs, and job training, which ultimately contributes to a more economically healthy society; (3) an individual's overall skills, abilities, educational experience, and intellectual potential, which are brought to the labor market.

human development: The physical, mental, social, and experiential changes that take place over a person's life cycle. These changes are continuous, occur in fairly consistent sequences, and are cumulative with other changes. Human development occurs in a predictable manner, but the rate of change is unique to each individual.

humanistic orientation: A group of concepts, values, and techniques that emphasize people's potential rather than their dysfunctions. Social workers and other therapists with this orientation tend to help clients by developing the therapeutic *relationship* and by concentrating on the "here and now." See also *self-actualization*.

human rights: The opportunity to be accorded the same privileges and obligations in social fulfillment as are accorded to all others without distinction as to race, sex, language, or religion. In 1948, the U.N. Commission on Human Rights spelled out these opportunities. They included the basic *civil rights* recognized in democratic constitutions, such as life, liberty, and personal security; freedom from arbitrary arrest, detention, or exile; the right to fair and public hearings by impartial tribunals; freedom of thought, conscience, and religion; and freedom of peaceful association. They also included economic, social, and cultural rights, such as the right to work, education, and social security; to participate in the cultural life of the community; and to share in the benefits of scientific advancement and the arts.

human services: Programs and activities designed to enhance people's development and well-being. This includes providing economic and social assistance for those unable to provide for their own needs. The term "human services" is roughly synonymous with "social services" or "welfare services" and includes planning, organizing, developing, and administering programs for and providing direct social services to people. The term came into wider use in 1979 when the U.S. *Department of Health and Human Services (HHS)* was established to replace the U.S. *Department of Health, Education, and Welfare.* It was felt that the term "welfare" had a negative connotation and the organization would have more influence with the new name. Use of the term "human services" (and "human resources") instead of "social welfare services" is also part of the trend toward including other professionals in addition to social workers as appropriate for employment in the services arena.

hunger strike: Refusal to eat, as a protest against conditions considered unjust or unacceptable. Social workers and other activists have called attention to existing conditions by going on such fasts themselves or by organizing groups to refuse food.

Huntington's chorea: A genetic disorder, also known as Huntington's disease. It is transmitted by a dominant gene and affects half the offspring of those who carry the genes. The symptoms—which include mental deterioration, such as *hallucinations,* and profound mood swings, dementia, and choreiform movements (stiffness and jerky, involuntary gestures)—do not appear until about age 30. *Genetic counseling* is important for those who have the disease and their offspring.

hyperactive child syndrome: See *attention deficit disorder.*

hyperactivity: Excessive muscular activity, usually with rapid movements, restlessness, and almost constant motion. Its causes may be symptomatic of anxiety, neurosis, organic brain damage, or physiological or neurological disorders. This term is still used informally but has been replaced diagnostically by *attention deficit disorder* with hyperactivity.

hyperkinesis: A childhood disorder characterized by excessive motor activity, reduced attention span, and accompanying difficulties in learning and perceiving accurately. Roughly synonymous with *hyperactivity,* the term now preferred by professionals is *attention deficit disorder* with hyperactivity. The syndrome has also been known as "hyperkinetic child syndrome," "hyperkinetic reaction of childhood," "minimal brain damage," "minimal brain dysfunction," and "minimal cerebral dysfunction."

hypertension: High pressure of blood pulsing against the walls of the blood vessels. This is a chronic disorder of the cardiovascular system that affects over 30 million people in the United States and is a predominant risk factor in *stroke, heart attack, renal disease,* and eye diseases. A person with high blood pressure generally cannot feel any symptoms, so it can only be detected reliably by using a blood pressure cuff (sphygmomanometer). Physicians are especially concerned when the systolic pressure (caused when the heart contracts) exceeds 140 or the diastolic pressure (caused when the heart relaxes) exceeds 90.

hyperventilation: Taking in more air than can be processed by the body, which results in lowered levels of carbon dioxide in the blood stream. Usually the behavior is the result of anxiety and often leads the individual to feel dizzy, lightheaded, and faint.

hypnosis: The phenomenon of being in a mental state of aroused concentration so intense that everything else in the subject's consciousness is ignored. The hypnotic state is similar to becoming completely absorbed in a movie or book. All hypnosis is self-hypnosis, and the role of the hypnotist is to offer suggestions for deepening the level of concentration. Generally, hypnotized subjects will not do anything contrary to their moral or ethical codes and can come out of trances at will. Forms of hypnosis are used successfully in therapeutic interventions, such as hypnotherapy. Subjects can be taught to use self-hypnosis to achieve specific goals such as weight loss, cessation of smoking, pain relief, and overcoming *phobias.*

hypochondria: Preoccupation with the details of one's bodily functions and overconcern about the possibility of having a disease; also called hypochondriasis. It is generally believed to be caused by neurotic anxiety. Hypochondriac individuals typically present physical symptoms but no actual disturbance in bodily function. They often seek help from various medical specialists but are reluctant to accept reassurance of well-being. See also *somatization disorder.*

hypoglycemia: Low level of sugar in the blood. Left untreated, it may cause the appearance of *psychogenic* symptoms that can lead to inappropriate treatment for emotional disorders. Because of the possibility of hypoglycemia, prudent social workers advise clients about to enter psychotherapy to get a physical exam first.

hypomania: Behavior that is similar to, but less severe than, that observed in individuals with *bipolar disorder,* manic type. The individual in this state seems euphoric, energetic, and creative but may also be impatient and grandiose and use poor judgment.

hypothesis: A tentative proposition that describes a possible relationship among facts that can be observed and measured. The proposition is often stated in negative fashion as a *null hypothesis* (for example, "There is no difference between the work of MSWs and BSWs as measured by. . ."). Social workers and other professionals also use the term informally to indicate a theory believed to account for what is not entirely understood.

hysteria: A term originally used by Freud to describe patients with symptoms he believed to be the result of suppressed sexual and oedipal conflicts. See also *conversion disorder* and *anxiety hysteria*.

hysteric: A historical term still used informally by social workers and other professionals to describe a person with some or all of the following characteristics: overly dramatic behavior, overreaction to minor events, craving for attention and excitement, tantrums, appearance to others of shallowness and lack of genuineness, apparent helplessness and dependence, proneness to manipulative gestures, and suicide threats. In treatment such a person would be likely to be diagnosed as having a *histrionic personality disorder*.

hysterical neurosis, conversion type: A disorder caused by *anxiety* and resulting in the appearance of some physical dysfunction that has no physical cause. The individual is said to use the symptoms unconsciously to avoid some undesired activities or to get some support from others that might not otherwise be available; a synonym for *conversion disorder*.

I

IASSW: See *International Association of Schools of Social Work (IASSW).*

iatrogenic: A term relating to a physical or psychological illness originating in the treatment or intervention process. Technically, the term refers to the action of a physician or to medicine that results in the patient's developing a new disease. However, the term has been broadened and now also includes the illnesses that individuals or groups develop as a result of intervention by helping professionals, including social workers. For example, some clients develop extreme dependency on their social workers and may become afraid to act independently, a syndrome that may be iatrogenic.

id: In *psychoanalytic theory,* the part of the mind or psyche that harbors the individual's instinctive or biological *drives, libido,* or psychic energy. In the healthy individual the id is completely *unconscious* and not in contact with the social environment. Its demands are centered on the body, and it is governed solely by the *pleasure principle.* It attempts to force the *ego,* which is generally governed by the *reality principle,* to meet its demands without regard to the long-term consequences.

idealization: The overestimation of another person or of specific attributes of that other person.

ideas of reference: An inaccurate belief that the behaviors of others or environmental phenomena take place in order to have some effect on the individual. For example, a man encounters two strangers who are conversing and assumes they are talking about him. This is a form of *delusion* and sometimes appears as a symptom in *paranoid disorders, schizophrenia, histrionic personality disorder,* and in people who have profound feelings of inadequacy.

ideation: The process of developing a belief. For example, a person with *suicidal ideation* is one who starts thinking about death, about want-ing to die, and about specific actions that will help to reach that goal.

identification: A mental process in which a person forms a mental image of another person who is important and then thinks, acts, and feels in a way that resembles the other person's behavior. Identification often promotes ego integration and personal growth.

identified patient (or client): The member of a family or social group for whom therapy, help, or social services are ostensibly sought. This person has typically been viewed by the relevant others as "sick" or "crazy," even though they may have just as many, or more, problems and may implicitly need and receive just as much help from the perceptive therapist or social worker.

identity: An individual's sense of self and of uniqueness as well as the basic integration and continuity of values, behavior, and thoughts that are maintained in varied circumstances.

identity crisis: Confusion about one's roles in life. The individual enters a period of doubt about being willing or capable of living up to the expectations of others and is uncertain about what kind of person to be if those expectations are not met.

identity versus role confusion: The fifth stage of human psychosocial development, according to Erikson, occurring approximately between ages 12 and 18. The conflict facing youngsters is to establish clear ideas about their values, vocational objectives, and place in life, or there may be a lack of clarity about how to fit into the social environment. This is the period in which there is greatest likelihood of an *identity crisis.*

ideology: A system of ideas that is the product of one's values, experiences, political persuasion, level of moral development, and aspirations for humanity. For example, a social worker's ideology is likely to include a concern for *equal rights* for all people and an interest in providing greater opportunities for the less privileged.

idiosyncratic: A term applied to a trait or characteristic that is unique to the subject or phenomenon being observed and not representative of others of the same class.

idiot: An obsolete term once used to refer to a mentally retarded person with an IQ score of 25 or less.

IFSW: See *International Federation of Social Workers (IFSW)*.

illegitimate: A term for activity that is against laws, norms, or values; the term is also commonly applied to people born to parents who are not legally married to each other.

illicit drugs: Chemical substances whose use is unlawful.

illiteracy: Not knowing how to read or write.

illiterate, functional: A person who possesses some reading and writing skills but not of sufficient quality to permit their use in normal socioeconomic relationships.

image: (1) A consciously experienced mental picture arising from one's memory; (2) the overall judgmental reaction of relevant others to an individual, institution, organization, or nation.

imagery relaxation technique: A self-help and therapeutic procedure to reduce anxiety, in which the subject concentrates on being in an environment that is his or her ideal place for relaxation. Thinking about the place and re-creating its sounds, colors, smells, and pleasures for about 5 to 10 minutes helps the person become more relaxed.

image, social work: The way people typically judge the profession and occupation of social work and its practitioners, whether or not this is an accurate view.

imbecile: An obsolete term once used to refer to a mentally retarded person with an IQ score below 50 and above 25.

immigrant: One who has moved to and intends to reside permanently in another country. See also *green card*.

immigration: Moving to a new country or region, usually for the purpose of permanent settlement.

Immigration and Naturalization Service, U.S.: The federal government organization within the U.S. Justice Department responsible for regulating and enforcing the laws pertaining to the entry into and residence in the United States of people from other nations. The McCarran-Walter Act of 1952 (P.L. 82-414), and its 1965 amendments (P.L. 89-326) have been the nation's major codification of procedures for *immigration* and *naturaliza-*

tion. In 1986 these procedures were changed, permitting *undocumented aliens* who entered the United States before that time to remain, but making it more difficult for others to enter the country.

immunization: Preventive medical procedures that reduce susceptibility to certain diseases. This occurs most frequently through inoculation or vaccination—the injection into the body of certain viruses or bacteria to cause a mild and controllable form of the disease so that the body develops resistance to its more serious forms.

impact analysis: The assessment used by social policymakers in determining the effect of a new law or policy on the relevant community.

implied consent: An agreement to participate expressed by gestures, signs, actions, or statements that are interpreted as agreement, or by nonresisting silence or inaction. This is often used as a defense in rape trials in which the defendant claims to have acted in the belief that the victim consented to his advances.

implosive therapy: In *behavior therapy*, the technique in which the client is presented with images of anxiety-producing stimuli and is encouraged to experience as much anxiety as possible. Because the anxiety-producing images do not result in any harm, the anxiety responses are not reinforced and the symptoms are more likely to be extinguished.

impotence: A male sexual disorder, also known as erectile dysfunction, characterized by an inability to achieve or maintain an erection. See also *sexual dysfunction*.

impounding: The legal action of taking into the custody of a court or law officer any item of a person's possessions, including automobiles, funds, bookkeeping records, and so on. This is done for the safekeeping of the item pending the outcome of a legal action.

impulsiveness: The inclination to act suddenly, in response to inner urges, without thought and with little regard to the consequences of the action.

inadequacy: An individual's perception of being inferior or of being incapable of fulfilling certain social expectations.

incapacitation: Lack of ability to provide sufficient care or judgment for oneself, due to diminished physical or mental functioning.

incarceration: Confinement in an institution, such as a prison or mental hospital. Usually this occurs for the purpose of punishment or protection of society from the individual or to impose treatment or protective custody on the individual.

incentive: A reward or object of value that produces in an individual the motivation to act in a way that will lead to its acquisition.

incentive contracting: A systematic method often used by public organizations to improve delivery and quality of goods or services. The provider (contractor) is guaranteed more compensation if the goods or services meet predetermined time and quality standards.

incest: Sexual intercourse between close relatives—that is, people who are too closely related to be permitted by law to marry.

incestuous desire: An individual's urge, whether consciously recognized or not, to engage in erotic activity with a close relative.

incidence rate: In population and demographic reports, the number of new cases of a physical or mental disorder, crime, or social problem that develops in an identified population group within a specific period of time. See also *prevalence rate* and *epidemiology.*

income distribution: The division of moneys and other resources among individuals or family units in an economy. Economists also apply this term to the division of income among functions in the economy, such as labor, capital, and real estate. Income distribution is a primary indicator of the economic well-being of various demographic groups in society (such as women, the elderly, blacks, people who live in the South, and divorced people). The U.S. *Census Bureau,* and the U.S. *Departments of Labor* and *Health and Human Services (HHS)* compile income distribution statistics to determine the extent and location of poverty and affluence and to help in economic and social welfare planning. See also *Lorenz curve.*

income maintenance: Social welfare programs designed to provide individuals with enough money or goods and services to maintain a predetermined standard of living.

income strategy: A social welfare policy of providing direct monetary aid, based on predetermined objective criteria, to those in need. This is distinguished from a *service strategy* policy, in which social workers evaluate each person's situation and provide counseling and in-kind *benefits.* For example, an income strategy would be to pay each needy family a certain amount for housing so that they can make their own choices. The service strategy, in this example, would be to provide public housing or advice about living more frugally.

income transfer payments: See *transfer payments.*

incompetent: Without the ability to fulfill obligations. This is also a legal term that has several connotations, depending on the circumstances. These include inability to consent legally to make or execute a contract; insufficiency in knowledge needed to carry out some legal obli-gation; inability to stand trial because the person is unable to assist rationally in his or her own defense; or inability to understand the nature of the charge or the consequences of conviction.

incorporation: In psychosocial theory, a primitive *defense mechanism* in which the individual seeks symbolically to ingest a person, part of a person, or an object to whom or which there is great attachment. In the first months of life this may be a literal goal, but later it is done figuratively or in the *unconscious* imagination.

incrementalism: In social planning, the effort to take into account a variety of political and pluralistic influences by striving not only for the best possible rational decision but the most acceptable steps that result from compromise and mutual agreement. Thus, the planner explores various paths and makes progress toward desired goals through bargaining, compromising, and taking steps that are *satisficing* (good enough to make progress but not necessarily the best from the viewpoint of some of the participants).

incremental social change: Gradual adaptation and adjustment made by social institutions to reflect changes in the values, needs, and priorities of the people. Institutions retain their existence and basic character but modify their goals and means to accommodate to the demands of those served. This is the opposite of *structural social change.*

indenture: An obligation in which one person is required to serve or work for another for a specified length of time. In colonial America, indentured servitude was a common practice by which immigrants would receive transportation to their new homes in exchange for working for several years. Later, the practice was frequently applied to parentless children who were compelled to become indentured to a caretaker. From this practice, and that of *apprenticing,* originated many of the principles of *foster care.* Indenture is still practiced, illegally or covertly, by some people who exploit the circumstances of immigrants or *undocumented aliens.*

independent living: The capability of an individual to be self-governing and not dependent on others for care, well-being, or livelihood. To be capable of independent living is seen as being able to handle one's own financial affairs and to perform the necessary tasks of daily living without the necessity of continued reliance on others. Programs that help people achieve independent living promote the provision of social and medical services and also the modification of homes that permit people access to all rooms and facilities.

independent practice associations (IPAs): Alliances of professionals in private practice who work together with *third-party payment* organizations to provide services for members of a designated group. See also *preferred provider organizations (PPOs).*

independent social work: The practice of social work outside the auspices of traditional social agencies or government organizations. In addition to private practitioners, those engaged in such social work include self-employed proprietary social workers who have autonomous consultation firms, or who organize and manage private for-profit institutional facilities or educational institutions.

independent variable: In systematic research, the factors that are thought to influence or cause a certain behavior or phenomenon. The factor that is being influenced is the *dependent variable.*

indeterminant sentence: In the corrections and justice systems, the *incarceration* of an individual for an unspecified amount of time. The decision to release is thus based on the prisoner's demonstrated ability and willingness to satisfy certain standards. Variations of this system have been tried in many nations. The juvenile courts in many United States jurisdictions once used some elements of this system.

indictment: A written accusation submitted by a prosecutor to a grand jury charging an individual with a crime.

indigenous worker: A member of a community who becomes active in helping professionals achieve some service goals for that community. Indigenous workers may be volunteers or paid, and their role often includes identifying sources of problems, educating residents as to the services being offered, linking clients with professional service providers, and *counseling.*

indirect cost: Consequences, outcomes, or expenditures that are not immediately anticipated, apparent, or paid for by those who initiated an action. For example, although most of the direct cost of the U.S. drug problem is the funding that goes for law enforcement and treatment, an indirect cost is the lack of productivity in many of the victims.

indirect practice: Those professional social work activities, such as administration, research, policy development, and education, that do not involve immediate or personal contact with the clients being served. Indirect practice makes *direct practice* possible and more efficient and as such is considered essential and of equal importance to the mission of the profession.

indirect treatment: The term used by some social caseworkers to describe work in the environment on behalf of the client. Such work includes *mediation*, education, *advocacy*, and locating resources. These activities are said to require virtually the same skills and techniques as are needed in direct casework treatment.

individualism: The sociopolitical and philosophical concept that emphasizes the pursuit of people's own interests rather than the common or collective good. See also *rugged individualism.*

individualization: The ethical value in social work and other helping professions for understanding the client as a unique person or group rather than as one whose characteristics are simply typical of a class. For example, a social worker adhering to this principle would treat a young unwed mother as though her background, needs, and values were hers alone and not necessarily the same as those of others in similar circumstances.

individuation: The process by which individuals come to understand themselves as differentiated from others and the whole social system of which they are a part. The term is frequently used to describe the process by which toddlers and young children grow progressively independent from their mothers or other caregivers. See also *separation-individuation.*

indoor relief: A historically important form of social welfare benefit in which the recipient was required to reside in an institution in order to remain eligible. *Almshouses* or poorhouses were the most common types of indoor relief; they have been mostly discontinued in the United States in the twentieth century.

inductive reasoning: The process by which theories and generalizations are evolved from a set of particular observations. Specific observations may be chosen in order to create explanations about a larger set of phenomena. See also *deductive reasoning.*

industrial social work: Professional social work practice, usually conducted under the auspices of employing organizations or trade unions, or both, for the purpose of enhancing the employees' overall quality of life within and beyond the work setting. Many social workers use the term synonymously with *occupational social work.*

industry versus inferiority: The fourth stage of psychosocial development, according to Erikson, occurring approximately between ages 6 and 12. The child may seek to acquire the basic social skills and competencies required for effective survival in the adult world or may come to feel unworthy and less able than peers to accomplish these tasks.

inequality: Social disparity in power, opportunity, privilege, and justice.

inequity: A disparity of power or opportunity to receive just treatment or equal privilege. Social workers often apply this term to social conditions in which people face institutional obstacles or social barriers in their efforts to achieve the same social goals available to others. The term usually differs from the term *inequality*, in that it implies lack of opportunity for justice or privilege (such as fair court trials or opportunities to elect representative officials). Inequality, on the other hand, more often implies the actual disparity of possessions, education, health care, and so on, that exists between different groups.

infanticide: The killing of a baby.

infantile autism: See *autism.*

infantilization: Overtly or covertly encouraging a person to behave in a manner more appropriate to an infant or small child. This pattern is often seen in parents or spouses who use *overprotection.* Examples are speaking to the person in baby talk or not requiring the person to behave with appropriate maturity. The term is also used to indicate behavioral regression or to indicate that a person's behavior is appropriate to a much younger person.

infant mortality rate: The demographic measure of the number of neonatal deaths that occur in proportion to the population as a whole or to the population of potential mothers (*fecundity rate*). The infant mortality rate is often used as a key factor in assessing a nation's or a community's health and health care programs.

inferiority complex: Alfred Adler's concept of an individual's persistent and extensive feelings of inadequacy and of being at a lower order than is expected.

inflation: Increases in the cost of living in an economy that create a decrease in purchasing power.

influence tactics: See *tactics of influence.*

information and referral service: A social agency or office established within an agency to inform people about existing benefits and programs and the procedures for obtaining or using them and to help people find other appropriate resources and sources of help.

information theory: See *communication theory.*

informed consent: The client's granting of permission to the social worker and agency or other professional person to use specific intervention procedures, including diagnosis, treatment, follow-up, and research. This permission must be based on full disclosure of the facts needed to make the decision intelligently. Informed consent must be based on knowledge of the risks and alternatives. One of the greatest risks in professional malpractice suits is failure to achieve informed consent.

infrastructure: The foundation facilities, buildings, and systems of a society, such as its highways, parks, public spaces, railroads, bridges, telephone lines, power plants, and water and sewage lines.

inhibition: Hesitancy or restraint in action or behavior. In *psychoanalytic theory* the term also refers to the *superego's* restraining of some instinctual impulse. In behavioral terms, it is any process in which a response is restrained.

initiative versus guilt: The third of the eight stages in psychosocial development, according to Erikson, occurring approximately between ages 3 and 6. The child may be encouraged for actively seeking to learn, discover, and experiment. On the other hand, the child may develop a pattern of passivity because rejection, punishment, and restrictiveness lead to a sense of wrongdoing or "badness."

injunction: A court process and legal order by which a party is forbidden to take a particular action or is made to refrain from taking a particular action (for example, entering another party's home, selling a contested property, or visiting an unwilling ex-spouse). The order may be of temporary, permanent, or indefinite duration.

inkblot test: See *Rorschach test.*

in-kind benefits: See *benefits.*

in loco parentis: The legal expression referring to the circumstances in which an organization assumes the obligations of parenting a child or other person without a formal adoption. Most commonly, such relationships exist when a child is in a residential institution such as a *reformatory* or boarding school.

inmate: One who is confined in a prison, hospital, or other institution; a prisoner or patient.

innate: Present at birth.

inner city: A term used in *urbanology* and other social sciences to describe an area within a city that is usually characterized by high population density, racial ghettoization, and a decaying *infrastructure.*

input-output analysis: A tool used by economists and planners to chart the linkages between organizations. In social welfare the chart is constructed by listing all the social agencies in a column and then listing them in the same order in a row across the top. Numbers are written in the resulting columns to indicate the frequency with which any two agencies are linked according to some criteria. This method graphically reveals which organizations are isolated, which are sharing responsibilities and resources, and so on.

inracial adoption: *Adoption* of a child of one racial background by adoptive parents of that same racial background (for example, a black child being adopted by black parents).

insanity: A legal and lay term used to indicate the presence of a severe mental disorder in an individual. Used as a legal term, the mental disorder is considered to be so serious as to negate the individual's responsibility for certain acts such as criminal conduct. The person declared legally insane is thought to lack substantial capacity either to appreciate the wrongfulness of a criminal act or to act in conformity with the requirements of the law. Used as a lay term, insanity is roughly synonymous with "crazy" or "psychotic." It is not used by mental health professionals in their diagnostic nomenclature. See also *McNaughten rule.*

insecurity: A feeling of being unprotected or helpless due to economic or social realities or to emotional conflicts.

in-service training: An educational program provided by an employer and usually carried out by a supervisor or specialist to help an employee become more productive and effective in accomplishing a specific task or the overall objectives of the organization. Usually, but not always, such training occurs on the job and for short time periods.

insight: Self-understanding and awareness of one's feelings, motivations, and problems. In several forms of psychotherapy and clinical social work, it refers to raising awareness of or illuminating the client's inner conflicts and their origins, areas that had previously not been well understood.

insolvency: An individual's or business's inability to pay debts when they come due, even if the party has assets that are sufficient but inaccessible.

instincts: Patterns of behavior that are characteristic of a given species and seem to derive from inherited rather than learned processes.

institution: A fundamental custom or behavior pattern of a culture, such as marriage, justice, welfare, and religion. Also, an organization established for some public purpose and the physical facility in which its work takes place, such as a prison.

institutional network: The aggregate of human service agencies in a community that make up the service system.

institutional versus residual model: See *residual versus institutional model.*

institutional welfare provision: A society's permanent set of programs to provide for the overall *social security* and well-being of its people. These provisions usually include a society's *universal programs,* such as public education, medical care for the aged, and *social insurance,* but exclude *means-tested* programs or those that are temporarily in effect to deal with supposedly extraordinary circumstances.

instrumental conditioning: See *operant conditioning.*

instrumental means: The tools and facilities necessary to complete a task or fulfill a *role* successfully.

intake: Procedures used by social agencies to make the initial contacts with the client productive and helpful. Generally, these procedures include informing the client about the services the agency does and does not offer, providing information about the conditions of service, such as fees and appointment times; obtaining pertinent data about the client; interviewing to get a preliminary impression of the nature of the problem; arriving at an agreement with the client about willingness to be served by the agency; and assigning the client to the worker or workers who are best suited to provide the needed services.

integrated method: Social work practice that involves a high degree of professional knowledge and skill in bringing together the concepts and techniques used in serving individuals, families, groups, and communities. The social worker using the integrated method is considered to be more than a *generalist,* or one who simply combines some basic casework, group work, and community organization knowledge and skills.

integration: The process of bringing together components into a unified whole. Psychologically, an individual's internal connection of values, ideas, ideals, knowledge, motor responses, and relevant social norms. Sociologically, the process of bringing together diverse social or ethnic groups and achieving harmonious relations.

integrity versus despair: The last of the eight stages in human psychosocial development, according to Erikson, occurring from about age 54 to death. The individual may develop a sense of integration with humanity and of the unique meaning of his or her own life, or there may be a sense of regret about how that life has been lived and a fear of death.

intellectualization: A *defense mechanism* and personality tendency in which the individual ignores feelings and emotions and analyzes problems or conflicts as objectively as possible, but usually in a stylized or overly rational manner.

intelligence quotient (IQ): An index of a person's relative level of "intelligence," as determined by performance on a specialized test. The tests are designed to determine a person's abilities to use abstract concepts effectively, to grasp relationships, to acquire information about the relevant environment, and to meet and adapt to novel situations. The resulting IQ scores are said to indicate the individual's mental potential, and test subscores are sometimes used in psychiatric assessments. The mean IQ score is 100, and those with scores between 90 and 110 are considered "normal." Those whose scores are below 70 are often considered to need special educational help. Major intelligence tests include the WAIS (Wechsler Adult Intelligence Scale) and the WISC (Wechsler Intelligence Scale for Children).

interdisciplinary activity: Team *intervention*, or *collaboration*, on behalf of a specific *client* or *client system*, which involves members of different professions or disciplines. For example, a social agency might call on a social worker, psychologist, clergyman, nurse, and physician to coordinate their respective specialties in order to help a *multiproblem family*. See also *social work team* and *interprofessional team*.

interest group: A segment of the population or members of a formal or informal association who have common interests, goals, concerns, or desires that often lead to purposeful and united action; also known as a *special interest group*.

intergenerational relations: The degree to which members of different age groups engage with one another. See also *age segregation*.

intergroup relations: Societal institutions and activities that involve and seek to enhance cooperation and mutual respect between various identifiable sectors in the population—especially ethnic, racial, religious, geographic, socioeconomic, and other kinds of groups. These activities are also known as "race relations," "interreligious relations," and "intercultural education." Social work specialists often engage in intergroup relations activities in which they seek to remove or reduce the barriers, different priorities, and misunderstandings that exist between groups. Among the national organizations involved in intergroup relations are the National Conference of Christians and Jews, American Friends Service Committee, and the *Southern Christian Leadership Conference (SCLC)*.

intermarriage: Legal wedlock between couples of different races, ethnic groups, religions, and social classes.

intermittent reinforcement: In *behavior modification*, a schedule of *reinforcement* in which one type of response is reinforced at some times but not at others.

internalization: The process of incorporating the norms of one's culture; taking in and accepting as one's own the values, attitudes, style, and social responses of one's primary group or other reference groups.

International Association of Schools of Social Work (IASSW): An international organization of social work educators and social work schools throughout the world, whose mission is to improve training and ensure consistent standards for social work education.

International Classification of Diseases (ICD): A statistical classification of all human diseases, including mental disorders, that is compiled by the *World Health Organization (WHO)*. The publication, generally referred to as the *ICD* and followed by an edition number, is issued approximately every ten years. The first edition, called the *International List of Causes of Death,* was completed in 1900.

International Council on Social Welfare (ICSW): An international organization headquartered in Vienna, Austria, that fosters cooperation between nations in the development and maintenance of social welfare programs. ICSW coordinates welfare activities between nations, facilitates research, disseminates information, and sponsors conferences among social welfare leaders of different nations.

International Federation of Social Workers (IFSW): The professional association of social workers from nations in every geographical area of the world. Its purpose is to establish policy and actions designed to meet more of the human and welfare needs of the world's people and to establish better standards of service and related activities of interest to the membership. IFSW cosponsors, with other international organizations, various meetings and symposia that foster opportunities for social workers from various countries to meet together and exchange knowledge.

international social work: The practice of social work in nations throughout the world and the use of social work knowledge, values, and skills to help meet the human and welfare needs of all peoples. Virtually every country has a national department responsible for some phase of social services and personnel to carry out the functions of those departments. International social work organizations emphasize efforts to educate workers to ensure that social service needs are met. Also emphasized are efforts to exchange knowledge and effective methods between nations. Organizations that have been active in international social work include *UNICEF,* the Organization of American States (OAS), the International Labor Organization, the International Social Security Association, and *UNESCO.* Many voluntary organizations also have international social work aspects, including the *Red Cross* and Red Crescent, *YMCAs* and *YWCAs,* the International Union for Child Welfare, the International Conference of Catholic Charities, and many others. A major forum for international social work is the *International Council on Social Welfare (ICSW).*

International Union for Child Welfare (IUCW): An international organization, with headquarters in Geneva, Switzerland, comprising government, public, and private organizations of many nations that are concerned about the well-being of the world's children. The union facilitates research, provides training, and disseminates information that can benefit children.

interpersonal skills: See *social skills.*

interpretation: Explanations, offered to the client by a social worker or psychotherapist, to enhance understanding, make connections, and facilitate the development of *insight.*

interprofessional team: A small, organized group of persons, each trained in different professional disciplines and possessing their own skills and orientations, working together to resolve a common problem or achieve a common goal. The team members contribute their special talents through continuous intercommunication, reexamination, and evaluation of individual efforts toward team objectives and with group responsibility for the final outcome. The interprofessional team may include the members of a *mental health team* (such as psychiatrists, psychologists, social workers, and psychiatric nurses) but is not limited to them. For example, such a team—which might be brought together to help a community cope with a disaster—could consist of social workers of various specializations as well as physicians, nurses, economists, architects, engineers, sanitation specialists, and political scientists. See also *social work team, interdisciplinary activity,* and *collaboration.*

interrater reliability: In systematic research, the degree to which different people give similar scores for the same observation. For example, a researcher might give all the social workers in an agency identical lists of a client's problems and then ask them to rank those problems as to which must be dealt with first. If the workers identify the same problems for immediate attention, this would be described as a "high interrater reliability."

intersectoral planning: The attempt by social planners to look at problems or groups of people in a comprehensive fashion. This makes possible the coordination and integration of the efforts of single-issue organizations, which focus

their efforts on one problem *(sectoral planning).* Intersectoral planning occurs, for example, in welfare councils and community action agencies and on human resources commissions.

interval measurement: In research, a level of measurement that includes the properties of *nominal measurement* and *ordinal measurement* but also requires that there are equal intervals between the units of measurement. Most of the well-standardized psychological tests use interval measurement.

intervention: Interceding in or coming between groups of people, events, planning activities, or an individual's internal conflicts. In social work, the term is analogous to the physician's term "treatment." Many social workers prefer using "intervention" because it includes "treatment" and also encompasses the other activities social workers use to solve or prevent problems or achieve goals for social betterment. Thus it refers to *psychotherapy, advocacy, mediation, social planning, community organization,* finding and developing resources, and many other activities.

interview: A meeting between people in which communication occurs for a specific and usually predetermined purpose. When the interview is between a social worker and client, the most typical purpose is some form of problem solving. To achieve that purpose there are many types of social work interviews, including *directive, nondirective, fact-gathering,* and *intake.* Interviews may be of individuals, groups, families, and communities. Most interviews often combine different types in the same sequence of contacts.

interview schedule: A tool used especially in fact-gathering conferences or surveys to guide the interviewer toward the information that is sought. For example, schedules can consist of lists of specific yes-no or *closed-ended questions* that are to be read to the respondent, or they may consist of *open-ended questions* that serve as reminders for the questioner.

intestate: Not having a valid will. When a person dies intestate the estate is generally settled by court-appointed administrators.

intimacy versus isolation: The sixth of the eight stages of psychosocial development, according to Erikson, occurring approximately from age 18 to 24. The individual faces the challenge of developing one or more close and warm relationships or facing life alone.

intoxication: The state of being inebriated as a result of ingesting an exogenous substance. These substances include alcohol and drugs, and the resulting behavior ranges from temporary euphoria, slurred speech, and impaired motor functioning to such maladaptive behaviors as ineffective job performance, impaired judgment, and deteriorating social functioning.

intrapsychic: Occurring within one's personality or psyche.

introjection: In *psychoanalytic theory*, a mental mechanism in which the individual withdraws feelings from a person or object and directs them internally to an imagined form of the person or object. For example, an individual may introject parental criticism, turning it into some type of self-criticism.

introspection: Self-examination of thoughts, values, and feelings.

introvert: One whose psychic energy, interests, thoughts, and feelings tend to be directed inward rather then toward the social and physical environment; the opposite of an *extrovert.*

inventory: In social research, a type of *interview schedule* used to guide the researcher in assessing the presence or absence of specific phenomena, behavior, or attitudes.

inverse relationship: An association between two phenomena in which a higher frequency in one variable accompanies a lower frequency in another. In social research it is sometimes called *negative correlation.*

investment-versus-consumption concept: A controversy about the ultimate objectives of social services, often faced in social planning. One view (consumption) holds that social programs should provide goods and services to disadvantaged people to improve their living conditions and that this is a worthwhile goal in itself. The other view (investment) holds that social programs exist as an economic investment by enabling recipients to become more economically productive and that social service priorities should be those programs that serve this purpose.

invisible loyalties: Alliances between family members that occur outside the conscious awareness of any of them. Most commonly this *family therapy* term refers to unconscious commitments that children acquire to support one or both parents or other family members.

in vitro fertilization: Human conception by removing the woman's ovum surgically, placing it in a medium that preserves and nourishes it, introducing live sperm cells, maintaining the joined cells until some growth and divisions occur, and then inserting the embryo in the woman's uterus.

in vivo desensitization: A *behavior therapy* procedure in which the subject gradually approaches a feared stimulus while in a relaxed state. The subject and worker make a list of situations that elicit fear and rank these items from least to most anxiety producing. The subject then enters a state of relaxation through meditation, imagery relaxation, muscle relaxation, deep breathing relaxation, and so on. In this state the subject is gradually desensitized to the feared stimuli.

involuntary client: One who is compelled to partake of a social worker's or other professional person's services. For example, an individual may be required to seek a social worker's services by a court decision, by the fact of *incarceration,* or by family or employer pressure.

IPAs: See *independent practice associations (IPAs).*

irritation response theory: The view, held by some economists and social planners, that people will strive harder to improve their circumstances if social welfare is punitive and minimal.

isolation: The condition of being separated and kept apart from others. Psychologically, aversion to or fear of contact with others. In *psychodynamic* theory it is a *defense mechanism* in which memories are separated from the emotions that once accompanied them. For example, a client may have been terrified when subjected to child abuse but when relating the incident to the social worker 20 years later seems to feel indifferent to it.

IQ test: See *intelligence quotient (IQ).*

J

Jewish social agencies: Private organizations originally established in larger cities to serve the unique social welfare needs of Jewish families and individuals. The organizations included Jewish Family Service Agencies, Hebrew Benevolent Associations, and Jewish Welfare Societies. Most of these agencies now provide services to members of all faiths and ethnic groups.

Job Corps: The federal program established in 1964 as part of the *Economic Opportunity Act,* designed to provide employment and work skills to school dropouts. Jobless youth between ages 16 and 21 work and study at training centers or in conservation camps. The Job Corps is managed by the U.S. *Department of Labor,* which contracts with local public and private agencies to establish the training centers. The program was partially modeled after the *Civilian Conservation Corps (CCC)* and similar *New Deal* programs.

job description: Explicit obligations and specific tasks required of an employee as conditions of employment. Some job descriptions also state certain educational, experiential, and skill requirements expected of the incumbent.

JOBS program: Job Opportunities in the Business Sector, one of the federally supported employment programs established in 1964 as part of the *Economic Opportunity Act.* Aimed at able-bodied but long-term unemployed individuals, the program was meant to encourage the private sector employer, through tax incentives and direct wage subsidies, to hire unskilled workers. *CETA* largely supplanted the JOBS program in 1973.

Job Training Partnership Act: The 1982 federal law (P.L. 97-300, P.L. 97-404) designed to replace some of the functions of the *CETA* program and encourage more private sector, local, and state involvement in employment training programs.

joining: The *family therapy* process, described by Salvador Minuchin and others, in which the

therapist becomes a part of the family's interactional system so as to help change those parts of the system that are dysfunctional.

joint budgeting: A form of interagency *linkage* in which two or more service providers share decisions about the financing of existing or new social services. For example, two organizations could decide to reduce their respective expenses by eliminating some of their duplicated services. See also *joint funding.*

Joint Commission on Mental Illness and Health: The organization of health and welfare agencies that, in 1961, completed a five-year study of the nation's need for mental health services. The findings led to federal funding for *community mental health centers* and improvements in state mental hospital programs.

joint custody: A legal decision involving a divorcing husband and wife and the respective responsibilities each of them will have for the care of their children. Typically, both parents maintain permanent homes for the children, and the children live with each for relatively equal amounts of time.

Joint Economic Committee: A U.S. Senate and House of Representatives combined committee, established in 1946, to obtain information and make recommendations to Congress on possible legislative action pertaining to the economy of the United States and the economic welfare of its citizens.

joint funding: A form of interagency *linkage* in which two or more service providers or two or more funding services help to finance a project or ongoing service collaboratively. For example, agencies or foundations that might be unable to afford to establish their own *outreach* programs could establish one together. See also *joint budgeting.*

joint interview: Variations of the *interview* format in which more than a single interviewer and single interviewee meet. In one form the social worker or other professional meets with the client and others who are relevant to the client (for example, teachers, guidance counselors, and classmates). In another form the worker meets simultaneously with several different clients who may have no relationship with one another. In a third form, the client meets with two or more workers simultaneously.

justice system: The social institutions, facilities, and people, including police, the prison and parole systems, the legal profession, the judiciary, and investigative organizations, that provide the means for enforcing and interpreting the laws of the land. In the United States, this system is coordinated and influenced, to a major extent, by the U.S. Department of Justice, which is headed by the attorney general. This department oversees the Federal Bureau of Investigation (FBI), the Bureau of Prisons, the Drug Enforcement Administration, the Law Enforcement Assistance Administration, the *Immigration and Naturalization Service,* the Parole Commission, and other agencies. The system also includes the judicial and court system, from the Supreme Court to local justices of the peace. See also *criminal justice system* and *juvenile justice system.*

juvenile: For purposes of criminal law, a young person who has not yet attained the age at which he or she would be treated as an adult. The term is distinguished from "minor," which is used to refer to legal capacity. The age differs from state to state, although the *Juvenile Justice and Delinquency Prevention Act* of 1974 defines a "juvenile" as one who has not yet reached 18.

juvenile court: A court of law that has jurisdiction over delinquent, dependent, or neglected children. Generally the court is responsible for determining whether the alleged offense was committed by the accused juvenile and for overseeing the resulting rehabilitation or penalty process. See also *Gault.*

juvenile delinquency: In a particular jurisdiction, a pattern of antisocial actions by juveniles that would be regarded as criminal in nature if committed by adults.

Juvenile Justice and Delinquency Prevention Act: The 1974 federal law (P.L. 93-415) whose purpose is to discourage the institutionalization of juveniles. It provides federal *block grants* to states in order to achieve community-based alternatives to *reformatories* and to juvenile correctional institutions.

juvenile justice policy: A component of *criminal justice policy* involving society's guidelines and established procedures to be considered when deciding how to cope with the illegal conduct of minors. Elements of current U.S. juvenile justice policy include giving the juvenile the same legal rights to trial and counsel granted to adults, incarceration in facilities that are segregated from adult institutions, shorter sentences, clearing the record after a specified period of good behavior, and an orientation that tries to be more therapeutic than punitive. See also *Gault.*

juvenile justice system: That part of the *criminal justice system* that is oriented toward the control and prevention of illegal behavior by young people (those under 22 in some jurisdictions and under 16 or 18 in others) and toward the treatment of minors engaged in such behavior. See also *Borstal system.*

juvenile offenders: Young people, usually under the age of legal responsibility (18 in most states) who have been convicted of law violations, including felonies, misdemeanors, and any other form of *delinquency.*

K

Kerner Commission: The National Advisory Commission on Civil Disorders, a fact-finding group appointed by President Johnson in 1967 and headed by Governor Otto Kerner of Illinois to determine the causes of and make recommendations on solutions to the civil rights protests and riots of that period. The commission report, issued in 1968, blamed white racism and the limited opportunities available to ghetto-dwelling blacks. Few of its proposals were implemented.

Keynesian economics: The theories of British economist John Maynard Keynes (1883–1946), including the recommendation that during economic slumps, government should increase public spending to provide employment and stimulate commerce.

kinesics: Communication through nonverbal body motions. See also *communication theory.*

kleptomania: Pathological stealing. Explanations for this phenomenon vary, but most jurisdictions do not accept it by itself as justification or as a defense against punishment or other legal action.

knowledge base: In social work, the aggregate of accumulated information, scientific findings, values, and skills and the methodology for acquiring, using, and evaluating what is known. Social work's knowledge base is derived from the social worker's own research, theory building, and systematic study of relevant phenomena and from the direct and reported experiences of other social work practitioners. It is also derived from information made available by clients and members of other disciplines and professions and from the general knowledge of society as a whole.

Kohlberg moral development theory: A set of related concepts proposed by Lawrence Kohlberg to explain the way an individual's moral thought and ideas about "right and wrong" change with age. Six stages or levels of development are delineated: (1) rules are obeyed to avoid punishment; (2) rules are obeyed to obtain rewards; (3) the individual obeys rules mostly to avoid being disliked and to be seen as being "good"; (4) the individual develops an appreciation for society's need for rules and a conscience or sense of guilt at wrongdoing; (5) the individual understands that there are competing and contradictory values and that some impartial judgments are necessary; and (6) the individual appreciates the validity of universal moral principles and develops a commitment to them. Most individuals are believed to have completed the first two stages (preconventional level of moral development) by age 9. The next two stages (conventional level) are usually completed during early adolescence. Most people do not reach the last two (postconventional level) until after age 20, and many people never reach this level at all, according to Kohlberg.

Kübler-Ross death stages: The psychological reactions to impending death described by Elisabeth Kübler-Ross, based on her interviews with terminally ill patients. The five stages identified are (1) denial and isolation, (2) anger, (3) bargaining, (4) depression, and (5) acceptance. Some patients go through these stages in a different order, some go back and forth between some or all of the stages, and still other patients never go through any of them.

kurtosis: In statistics, the degree of flatness or pointedness around the mode of a frequency curve. For example, a social agency plots on a graph the times during a one-year period that new clients are accepted and finds that most come during the summer. A frequency curve would show a peak during that period.

L

labeling: The application of a name to a person or a person's problem based on observed traits or patterns of behavior. Some social workers view labels (for example, such psychiatric diagnostic terms as *passive-aggressive*) as a form of name-calling or generalization about people that leads toward stereotyping and away from *individualization*. Other social workers consider it a necessity to facilitate research and communication about a person's problem without having to include prolonged detailed descriptions.

labeling theory: The hypothesis that when people are assigned a label, such as "paranoid schizophrenic," to indicate some kind of disorder or deviance, others tend to react to the subjects as though they were deviant. Also, the subjects may begin to act in a way that meets the others' expectations. This may be a type of *self-fulfilling prophecy* and an example of the *Hawthorne effect*.

labile: Having the tendency toward emotional flexibility, freedom of movement, and abrupt changes in mood or affect. See also *emotional lability*.

labor force: The segments of a society that can or do produce all its marketable goods and services. The U.S. *Census Bureau* includes in this definition both employed and unemployed persons. Those not in the labor force include some people who are retired, in school, engaged in family housework, disabled, "voluntarily idle," and others. The labor force participation rate (LFPR) is the number of people who produce marketable goods and services divided by the number who are eligible for employment.

labor intensive: Pertaining to those organizations in which the greatest outlay is for personnel; also, pertaining to corporations and agencies that require many workers to provide the service or manufacture the product and that do not or cannot replace personnel through automation. Social agencies and most other service provider organizations tend to be labor intensive.

labor mobility: The degree to which a society permits or encourages its workers to move from one job to another within the same employment organization, between organizations, and from one location to another. Economists generally believe that those societies with a relatively high level of labor mobility are likely to become more economically productive than are those that are less flexible.

labor theory of value: The concept suggested by Karl Marx and other socialist theoreticians stating that the value of each product or service should be determined by the amount of labor required to produce it.

labor union: An association, primarily of wage or salary earners and employees in a particular industry (such as government employees or automobile workers) or craft (plumbers or teachers), whose purpose is to advance the economic interests and working conditions of its members. Many social workers belong to such labor unions as the *American Federation of State, County, and Municipal Employees (AFSCME)* and the *American Federation of Government Employees (AFGE)*.

"lady bountiful": A term once frequently applied, somewhat derisively, to social workers and volunteer workers who provide goods and services to those in need. The term originated in the U.S. Civil War when upper-class women donated and personally delivered food, clothing, and advice to those in need. Many of these women subsequently began working as *friendly visitors*, the precursors to professional *social workers*.

laissez-faire: In social policy, the idea that government should not interfere with any aspect of the economy and that individuals will provide all needs and services because of financial incentives. This is a relative concept, but in its pure form it is the classic capitalistic model of society. In social administration, the term refers to the management practice of minimal involvement.

Lane Report: The study, conducted in 1939 by Robert P. Lane, analyzing the field of *community organization* and describing it as a professional entity. The report influenced the social work profession to incorporate community organization as one of its three major practice methods, along with *social group work* and *social casework*. The report drew on earlier conceptualizations, especially those of Eduard C. Lindeman and Jesse F. Steiner.

language disorder: A *developmental disorder* involving difficulty in comprehending or expressing language. In language disorders of the "expressive type," the individual has an age-appropriate understanding of language but fails in some way to verbalize accurately. For example, a child may have trouble articulating certain sounds or remembering more than a few words at a time. In language disorders of the "receptive type," the individual fails to develop comprehension of language. With some children this is related to sensory deficits, and with others it may be due to problems of recall, integration, or sequencing.

larceny: Stealing, theft; the unlawful taking of property that belongs to another person.

last hired–first fired principle: Seniority as the criterion in employment retention. This principle has been criticized, especially by women and *minorities of color,* as being discriminatory because it works against those who have more recently entered the labor force.

latchkey child: A youngster who comes home from school to spend part of the day unsupervised because the parents are still at work.

latency-age child: Approximately, a child who has passed the age of 6 but has not yet reached puberty. Common in social work usage, the term refers to the *latency stage* in the *Freudian theory* of psychosexual development. The term was used originally to suggest that the individual's sexuality is latent or dormant, though this premise is now questioned.

latency stage: In the Freudian theory of psychosexual development, the stage of personality development in the child that follows the *phallic (oedipal) stage* and precedes the *genital stage* (adolescence). Freud viewed this as a time in which no new conflicts are introduced but the child consolidates previous progress. Other analytic theorists, such as Harry Stack Sullivan and Erik Erikson, saw this stage as important for the child's developing social skills and sexual identity.

latent homosexual: A term sometimes applied to an individual who believes him- or herself to have a *heterosexual* orientation but who has unconscious desires for erotic gratification with members of the same sex. Latent homosexuals may be in deep conflict about sexual orientation and expend great psychic energy in denying to themselves and others that such conflicts exist. Such denial might take the form of overt hostility toward homosexuals, avoidance of them, or avoidance of any behaviors that seem more appropriate to members of the opposite sex. See also *homosexuality, latent.*

latent schizophrenic: One who appears to have some symptoms of *schizophrenia* (sometimes including *flat affect,* some *paranoid ideation,* and thought disorder) but has no clear-cut psychotic episodes or gross breaking with reality. In DSM-II (1968), psychiatrists also referred to individuals with such symptoms as "borderline" or "pre-psychotic" or as having "incipient" psychosis, but in *DSM-III* (1980) the diagnostic label for such conditions is "schizotypal personality disorder."

law: The body of rules and legislative pronouncements established and recognized by a state, nation, tribe, society, or community as binding on its members.

Law Enforcement Assistance Administration (LEAA): The federal program created in 1968 by the Omnibus Crime Control and Safe Streets Act that provides funds, often in matching arrangements with state governments, for rehabilitation of offenders, recruitment and training of corrections personnel, and improvement of correctional facilities.

Law of Settlement and Removal: The historically significant English statute, enacted in 1662, that led to the widespread use of *residency laws* in determining eligibility for *public assistance*. Under this law, municipal employees were authorized to help only poor citizens and to expel from their jurisdictions anyone who might become dependent on assistance.

lay analysis: Psychoanalysis as practiced by one who does not have a medical degree but who has acquired special training in its theory and technique. Social workers and others with this training and experience may be considered lay analysts.

layoff: A temporary but indefinite separation from employment, not because of dissatisfaction with the employee but because of the employer's economic situation, supply shortages, or market declines.

LCSW: See *Licensed Clinical Social Worker (LCSW).*

LDS Social Services: The organization of social agencies affiliated with the Mormon (Latter Day Saints) Church, with branches in major communities throughout the United States, that provide family services, child welfare services, services for the aged, and other social services for all families and individuals in need. See also *sectarian services*.

lead poisoning: The absorption of quantities of lead, sometimes resulting in brain damage, respiratory illness, other health problems, or death in the affected individual. The lead may come from such sources as lead-based paint or the exhaust of automobiles that burn leaded gas. The population at greatest risk for lead poisoning is young children who live in older buildings in which lead-based paints were used. They may ingest paint chips or breathe lead residue. Other *at-risk populations* include people in highly congested cities where automobile exhaust may contain high levels of lead.

League of Women Voters: A voluntary organization established in 1920 to educate people about the political process and to scrutinize and conduct research on the electoral process and government structure at the national, state, and local levels. An outgrowth of the Woman Suffrage Association, the league originally sought to educate women in the rational use of their newly acquired right to vote. The league, which opened its membership to men in 1974, has chapters in most cities in the United States.

learned helplessness: See *helplessness, learned*.

learning disabled: A descriptive term for children of normal or above-average intelligence who experience a specific difficulty in school, such as *dyslexia* (reading difficulty), dysgraphia (writing difficulty), or dyscalculia (math or calculation difficulty).

learning theory: *Behaviorism* and *social learning theory*, the concepts that underlie *behavior therapy* and *behavior modification*; the concept that human behaviors result from finding success or failure with certain responses to various environmental stimuli.

leftist: A person with liberal or radically liberal political views or affiliations. The designation derives from the tendency, in European legislatures, to seat members of the more liberal parties on the left side of the aisle or presiding officer.

legal defense fund: Moneys collected and held to pay the expenses of individuals or groups who are, or who may become, involved in *litigation*. Those for whom such funds are established are usually unable to meet these expenses themselves.

legal regulation: The control of certain activities, such as professional conduct, by government rule and enforcement. In social work, legal regulation occurs through *licensing, certification,* or *registration of social workers*. In each of these,

the public is assured by the relevant legal jurisdiction that the social worker possesses the traits or qualifications required by law in order to receive that designation.

legal separation: An agreement between a husband and wife, enforced by law, that permits them to live apart without being divorced.

Legal Services Corporation: The federal agency, established in 1974, that provides funding for local programs that furnish legal services to eligible clients, especially poor people.

legitimation: The acquisition of rights or authority to fulfill specified functions or pursue specified goals.

lesbian: A woman whose erotic or sexual preference is for other women. See also *gay* and *homosexuality*.

less-eligibility principle: The premise that poor people should not be given financial assistance that raises them to a level exceeding that of the lowest-paid employed person in the community.

leukemia: *Cancer* of the blood-producing tissues—including bone marrow, lymphatics, liver, and spleen—resulting in increased production of white cells and a commensurate reduction of red cells and other blood elements. The onset of leukemia can occur at any age.

libido: In *psychoanalytic theory*, sexual instinct (energy toward expression of pleasure and seeking a love-object as well as erotic gratification); a basic psychic drive.

Licensed Clinical Social Worker (LCSW): A professional social worker who has been legally accredited by a state government to engage in clinical social work practice in that state. The initials LCSW after a professional's name indicate possession of the license and the relevant qualifications. Qualifications for the license vary from state to state. Many states require an MSW degree from an accredited graduate school, several years of supervised professional experience, and successfully passing the state's social work licensing exam. Information about these requirements can usually be obtained from the relevant state's Bureau of Professional Licensing or the state Department of Mental Health.

Licensed Independent Clinical Social Worker (LICSW): A designation used by some state professional *licensing* bodies, and by some third-party financing institutions, to indicate that the practitioner is qualified for independent practice. The designation is sometimes used for social workers who have been granted the status of an independent *vendor*, requiring neither physician's referral nor supervision as a condition of *third-party payment*.

licensing: Granting a formal governmental authorization to do something that cannot be done legally without that authorization—for example, to practice clinical social work.

life cycle: The age-related sequence of changes and systematic development undergone by an individual from birth to death. Although most people are said to go through similar changes in a fairly predictable order, the life cycle concept also includes idiosyncratic options.

life model: The social work practice approach that uses the *ecological perspective* as a metaphor for focusing on the interface between the client and the environment. The worker who uses this approach views stressful problems in living (life transitions, interpersonal processes, environmental obstacles) as consequences of person-environment transactions. According to Carel B. Germain and Alex Gitterman (*The Life Model of Social Work Practice,* New York: Columbia University Press, 1980, p. 5), the approach uses an integrated method of practice with individuals and collectivities to release potential capacities, reduce environmental stressors, and restore growth-promoting transactions.

life-space interview: The interview procedure, developed by Fritz Redl and others, designed to take place in close proximity to the time and place of important symbolic events in the interviewee's life. The premise is that the impact of the meeting at such times and places is so powerful that it more than makes up for the time taken by the interviewer to be available at such times.

life-space social work: Professional social work intervention, based on the concepts of the *life-space interview,* that takes place outside the agency's walls and in the client's environment at times that are important to the client.

lifestyle-associated disorder: A health problem brought about by an individual's manner of living rather than a specific disease. Examples of such disorders may include obesity and physical weakness due to lack of exercise.

linear causality: The idea that one event is the cause and another is the result or response. This notion has been questioned by many family systems theorists who suggest that it is too simplistic, at least where families are concerned. They say *circular causality* is a more accurate depiction of the way people, especially families, influence one another—not in a cause-effect relationship but through a series of repeating cycles and interacting loops.

linear perspective: The term used by family therapists who have a *systems theories* perspective to describe people who think in cause-effect terms. To have a linear perspective is to view behavior and events as resulting directly from specific causes rather than as being part of an endless cycle in a system. The linear perspective is said to be narrow and rigid in not considering the myriad of influences and circularity of patterns that exist in social and environmental systems.

line item budgeting: A financial statement listing each of the objects of expected expenditures for the forthcoming year, often presenting them by comparing the expenditures for each item with those of the previous year.

linkage: In social work, the function of bringing together the resources of different agencies, personnel, voluntary groups, and relevant individuals and brokering or coordinating their efforts in behalf of a client or social objective. See also *collaboration.*

literacy: Knowing how to read and write.

lithium carbonate: The chemical compound that, in carbonated form (Li_2CO_3), is used by physicians in the treatment of serious *affective disorders* such as the manic phase of *manic-depressive illness.*

litigation: Civil and other disputes contested in courts of law; also, involved in legal action.

litigious client: A recipient of social work services who indicates a predisposition to initiate a lawsuit against the worker or the agency.

live supervision: A technique for enhancing clinical social work skills whereby the supervisor sits in on sessions or observes them in progress through one-way mirrors or closed-circuit TV monitors and periodically points out various client dynamics and suggests different approaches or techniques.

living will: A formal statement specifying an individual's wishes about the management of his or her own death. The statement is made particularly in relation to the possibility of maintaining life, when viability and cognitive functions are impaired, only through medical life support systems. The prototype living will has been prepared by Concern for the Dying, an organization headquartered in New York City.

loan shark: A moneylender who exploits poor people by charging excessive interest for instant cash and sometimes recovers the money through threats, taking the client's property, or actual violence.

lobbyists: The term used for special interest groups and individuals who seek direct access to lawmakers in order to influence legislation and public policy. The term originated in the tendency of some of these people to frequent the lobbies of legislative houses in order to meet lawmakers.

logotherapy: The meaning-oriented philosophy and treatment application developed by Victor Frankl and others and used by members of many disciplines to help people search for the humanistic and spiritual significance of their lives.

longevity: The length or duration of life.

longitudinal study: Repeated testing of the same phenomenon or group of subjects over a significant period of time.

long-term care: A set of health, personal, and social services delivered over a sustained period to persons who have lost some measure of functional ability. According to Rosalie A. Kane, this type of care may be delivered in nursing homes or in the community, provided by agencies or paid personnel or by friends and neighbors. Although the elderly constitute the population most frequently needing long-term care, it is also used with developmentally disabled adults, mentally ill adults, chronically physically impaired persons, and, most recently, victims of *AIDS.*

long-range planning: Efforts to assess objectives and examine proposed programs, services, and resources to establish priorities for an extended period of time in the future. The long-range planner supplements the normal year-by-year decision-making process with a comprehensive overview of goals and the means needed to achieve them over periods of time often exceeding 5 or 10 years.

loose association: A term pertaining to the tendency to shift abruptly from one thought to another, with little, if any, apparent direct connection between the thoughts. Loose association is sometimes symptomatic of severe *anxiety* or *depression* and in its more severe forms can be symptomatic of psychotic processes or *primary process thinking.*

Lorenz curve: A graphic representation, developed by economist M. O. Lorenz, of a nation's existing degree of income inequality. The vertical axis of the graph represents the percentage of the nation's total family income. The horizontal axis indicates the percentage of families. Thus, a nation with perfect income equality would be represented by a 45-degree line, because 10 percent of the nation's families receive 10 percent of total income, and so on. The amount of deviation from that line indicates the degree of inequality.

loss: The state of being deprived of something that was once possessed, as through death, divorce, disasters, or crime victimization. Social workers and other professionals consider loss to be the crucial element in *crisis* and a major precipitator of many forms of *depression.* Many social workers spend most of their professional time helping individuals, families, and communities adjust to loss by helping them to compensate or substitute for loss in the short and long term.

lower class: According to sociologists, the *socioeconomic class* in which people tend to have the least amount of income and financial security, the poorest job prospects, minimal educational attainments, and orientations that often include apathy and hopelessness.

Low Income Home Energy Assistance program: The federal program, within the *Family Services Administration (FSA)* of the U.S. *Department of Health and Human Services (HHS),* that helps poor families to pay their heating bills.

LSD: Lysergic acid diethylamide—also known simply as "acid"—a synthetic hallucinogenic drug that produces changes in sensation and perception, sometimes resulting in *hallucinations,* changes in the thought process, and *depression.* Prolonged heavy use of the drug may result in recurrences (known as flashbacks) of the effects of prior use of the drug weeks or even months after the last dose.

Lutheran Social Services: The organization of social agencies affiliated with the Lutheran Church, with branches in major communities throughout the United States, that provides family services, child welfare services, services for the aged, and other social services for all families and individuals in need. See also *sectarian services.*

M

macro orientation: In social work, an emphasis on the sociopolitical, historical, economic, and environmental forces that influence the overall human condition, causing problems for individuals or providing opportunities for their fulfillment and equality. This perspective is contrasted with social work's *micro orientation.*

macro practice: *Social work practice* geared toward bringing about improvements and changes in the general society. Such activities include some types of *political action, community organization,* public education campaigning, and administration of broad-based social service agencies or public welfare departments.

MADD: Mothers Against Drunk Driving, a national organization established in 1980 to influence legislation, police activity, judicial decisions, punishment, prevention, and education pertaining to the operation of motor vehicles while under the influence of alcohol or drugs.

magical thinking: The idea that one's thoughts or desires influence the environment or cause events to occur. It is normal in children under the age of 5 and is also commonly seen among some uneducated people and in certain relatively isolated societies. Among mature people in modern society it may be symptomatic of certain mental disturbances such as *paranoia.* See also *ideas of reference.*

mainlining: A slang expression to describe the injection of a narcotic drug, usually *heroin,* directly into the bloodstream through a vein.

mainstreaming: Bringing people who have some exceptional characteristics into the living, working, or educational environments to which all others have access. In education, for example, a child with certain learning or physical disabilities is permitted to attend classes and activities available to "normal" children. Mainstreaming permits individuals to have greater opportunity for socialization and integration. However, it also subjects them to greater risks of social rejection and reduction of special care.

major affective disorder: One type of *affective disorder* in which the degree of mood changes tends to be more extreme and incapacitating. The major affective disorders include *major depression* and *bipolar disorder.* The less extreme mood disorders, such as *cyclothymic* and *dysthymic disorders,* are not listed in *DSM-III* as "Major Affective Disorders" but as "Other Specific Affective Disorders."

major depression: One of the *major affective disorders,* characterized by such symptoms as loss of interest in one's usual activities, irritability, poor appetite, sleeplessness or excessive sleeping, decreased sexual drive, fatigue, psychomotor agitation, feelings of hopelessness, inability to concentrate, and *suicidal ideation.* Major depression can be subdivided into two groups, the "single episode" (at least four symptoms present almost daily for more than two weeks) and the "recurrent episode" in which the symptoms come and go. Someone with major depression may be distinguished from someone with a *bipolar disorder* by the fact that he or she has not had a *manic episode.* Major depression may be distinguished from *dysthymic disorder* (or *depressive neurosis*) by its duration and severity, although individuals can be diagnosed as suffering both disorders at the same time.

maladaptive: Pertaining to behaviors or characteristics that prevent people from meeting the demands of the environment or achieving personal goals.

maladjustment: The inability to develop or maintain the values, thoughts, and behaviors needed to succeed in the environment.

malingering: The act of feigning disability or illness, usually to avoid some undesired obligations or to achieve some real or imagined personal benefit. See also *factitious disorder.*

malnutrition: A physical condition, usually but not necessarily evidenced by emaciation, due to an insufficiency of needed food elements. Primary malnutrition is caused by a deficiency in the quantity or quality of foods containing such essentials as protein, vitamins, and minerals. This may result from an overall scarcity of food, from the individual's economic inability to purchase food, or from poor eating habits. Secondary malnutrition is caused by the body's inability to use or absorb certain nutrients, as sometimes happens in diseases of the pancreas, liver, thyroid, kidneys, and gastrointestinal system. Some of the diseases of malnutrition are rickets, scurvy, beriberi, pellagra, and some forms of anemia.

malpractice: Behavior by a social worker or other professional person that violates the relevant *code of ethics* and that proves harmful to the client. Among a social worker's actions most likely to result in malpractice are inappropriately divulging confidential information; premature, unnecessarily prolonged, or otherwise improper termination of needed services to the client; misrepresentation of one's knowledge or skills; providing social work treatment as a replacement for needed medical treatment; providing information to others that is libelous or that results in improper *incarceration;* financial exploitation of the client; sexual activity with a client; and physical injury to the client that may occur in the course of certain treatments (such as group encounters).

Malthusian theory: The theory proposed in the nineteenth century by English economist Thomas R. Malthus, stating that populations will increase in geometric ratio (2–4–8–16–32, and so on), whereas food supplies and other necessities can only increase in arithmetic ratios (2–3–4–5, and so on). According to the theory, this will lead to overpopulation problems unless populations are controlled by war, natural disasters, or sexual restraint. This theory was used, in part, to justify the sufferings of the poor, especially at the beginning of the Industrial Revolution.

management: See *administration in social work.*

management by objectives (MBO): The administrative procedure in which an organization's members achieve consensus about group results to be achieved, the resources to be devoted to each result and the deadline for reaching specific objectives. Inherent in this managerial approach is a clear and accessible budget, specified performance criteria, managers to assess the criteria, and monitoring procedures that encourage individual group members to assess progress.

management information systems (MISs): An administrative method often used in social agencies to acquire, process, analyze, and disseminate data that are useful for carrying out the goals of the organization efficiently. MISs may be used to keep track of staff activity and the services that are provided to clients.

management tasks: The principal activities of a social welfare administrator or manager. According to Rino Patti (*Social Welfare Administration,* Englewood Cliffs, N.J.: Prentice-Hall, 1983, pp. 34–35), there are six basic tasks: (1) planning and developing the program; (2) acquiring financial resources and support; (3) designing organizational structures and processes; (4) developing and maintaining staff capability; (5) assessing agency programs; and (6) changing agency programs.

mania: A term used in three different ways to describe certain mental and behavioral states: (1) an intense preoccupation with some kind of idea or activity, as in *kleptomania* (stealing), nymphomania (abnormal and excessive desire for sexual intercourse), and pyromania (preoccupation with setting fires); (2) a state of agitation, accelerated thinking, hyperactivity, and excessive elation seen in some *major affective disorders* (such as the *manic episode* in *manic depressive illness*) and certain organic mental disorders; (3) a lay term used in describing "insanity" or "mental breakdowns" in which the individual seems violent or highly agitated.

manic-depressive illness: A disorder characterized by profound mood swings ranging from deep, prolonged *depression* to excited, euphoric, agitated behavior. The term has been replaced in the diagnostic nomenclature of psychiatrists by the label *bipolar disorder.*

manic episode: A period of time during which a person behaves in an agitated, excited, hurried, impatient manner and seems euphoric, assertive, verbal, and hyperactive. During this phase the person's judgment and appropriate precautions are minimal, often leading to conflicts with others.

"man in the house" rule: A provision, once common in many state welfare departments, in which the presence of a man—whether or not related to the family—was considered sufficient evidence that financial dependency did not exist, leading to curtailment of public assistance eligibility. Most states ended the practice in the 1960s through legislation and court rulings.

Mann Act: The federal law (36 Stat. 263, 36 Stat. 825) that prohibits taking a person, usually a woman, across state lines for "immoral purposes" such as prostitution.

Manpower Development and Training Act: The 1962 federal legislation (P.L. 87-415) that funded state employment agencies and private enterprise for on-the-job training to help workers acquire needed employment skills. In 1973 these programs were incorporated into *CETA*. See also *Economic Opportunity Act* and *Job Corps*.

manpower planning: The systematic process of defining the problems and personnel needs of a social organization, such as a social agency, establishing a system of objectives relevant to those problems and needs, determining activities required to meet objectives, identifying and analyzing tasks, creating jobs and career ladders, and designing *in-service training.*

manslaughter: The unlawful, but unpremeditated, killing of another person. Laws in most jurisdictions distinguish between voluntary and involuntary manslaughter. The involuntary type refers to causing death through such criminally negligent acts as reckless driving. Voluntary manslaughter is an intentional *homicide* under mitigating but not justifiable circumstances, such as killing someone who has provoked uncontrollable rage or terror.

marasmus: A gradual deterioration and emaciation found in some infants and young children, particularly those who are cared for in institutional settings. Often, the child appears to have the symptoms of *malnutrition.* Many investigators believe marasmus is caused by child not being touched, held, fondled, and parented.

marathon group: A form of *group psychotherapy* or *sensitivity group* training in which participants remain together for extended periods of time, usually 18 to 24 hours or more.

marijuana: Cannabis, a plant whose active ingredient, tetrahydrocannabinol (THC), induces mild euphoria, certain intensified sensory impressions, and drowsiness when taken into the system either by smoking or ingesting it. It is considered to be psychologically addictive but it is debatable whether or not it is physically addictive. Some research indicates that its harmful effects include increased risk of heart and lung diseases, increased likelihood of accidents, loss of motivation, and possibly a greater risk of genetic problems for succeeding generations.

marital contracts: The term used by family therapists to indicate the expectations and motives that each partner brings to the marriage. These expectations and motives may be conscious or unconscious in the person who holds them and may or may not be known to the partner. In healthy marriages, each person's contracts become known to both, and agreements are reached so that the husband's and wife's individual contracts become jointly shared. In those marriages where the contracts remain concealed and separate, the couple is prone to confusion, suspicion, and disappointment with one another. The term "marital contracts" is also used to

indicate formal, written, and legally enforced agreements made between marrying couples, usually to specify the financial terms and obligations each partner is to assume. See also *prenuptial agreement.*

marital skew: A *family therapy* term indicating that a husband or wife dominates the other and controls the relationship or takes the lead in maintaining its healthy or unhealthy aspects.

marital therapy: Intervention procedures used by social workers, family therapists, and other professionals to help couples resolve their relationship, communications, sexual, economic, and other family problems. There are many different theoretical orientations, treatment models, and therapy techniques. The major theoretical approaches currently used by social workers include the psychosocial, behavioral, and systems orientations. According to Robert L. Barker (*Treating Couples in Crisis,* New York: Free Press, 1984, pp. 64–78), treatment models include *conjoint therapy, concurrent therapy, collaborative therapy,* and *couples group therapy.*

market strategy: In *social welfare* policy development, the premise that the nation's free economic institutions can provide needed social services without distracting from the work ethic, without the need for extensive public service delivery systems, and without centralized planning. Critics of this strategy contend that this method of delivery of benefits will favor those with the most resources and deprive those who have the greatest disadvantages.

marriage counseling: A form of *marital therapy.* Many professionals consider the term "marriage counseling" to be synonymous with "marital therapy." Others believe that "counseling" is less intense and more directive and deals with couples who may be less troubled. Existing empirical research has not yet clearly demonstrated that there are significant differences between the two. Nevertheless, many social workers and other professionals who treat couples prefer the term "marital therapy" because they believe it conveys a more technical and sophisticated repertoire of techniques and has a more theoretical and professional orientation.

Marsh Report: The 1943 recommendations by Canadian social workers and others that were a major factor in the development of Canada's present *social welfare* system.

masochism: The conscious or unconscious tendency to seek opportunities to be physically or emotionally hurt; also, a sexual disorder of the *paraphilia* class, in which the individual becomes sexually excited through being harmed, threatened, or humiliated. See also *sadomasochism.*

matching grants: A procedure for raising funds and motivating organizations to allocate funds for certain programs. To raise funds, a contributor promises to give the organization an amount of money that is equal to or a percentage of the amount received from other sources during a specified period. Federal and state governments also use the procedure to motivate localities to develop certain programs by promising to give a specified amount of money for every dollar the locality contributes.

maternity benefits: The provision of cash and social and health services to new mothers. Many nations, not including the United States, provide such benefits to all new mothers regardless of their economic status. See also *demogrant.*

maternity homes: Temporary residential facilities for unwed mothers that often provide counseling, social services, health care, and education as well as shelter away from the expectant mother's usual environment during the pregnancy. Some maternity home personnel help facilitate *adoption, abortion,* reintegration into the community, and financial assistance.

maternity leave: Time off from employment for a mother or mother-to-be to assure healthy prenatal or postnatal development. Various employer organizations have widely divergent policies about maternity leave. Some grant several months off, before and after the birth, with full pay and restoration of the job upon return. Others permit virtually no paid time off or grant only a few days' "sick leave." Most social workers have long argued for more generous maternity leave policies, saying that their absence discriminates against women or does not recognize that the nation's future well-being depends on encouraging healthy reproduction. A recent Supreme Court ruling upholding a California law requiring employers to grant maternity leave may encourage other states to review their policies in this area.

MBO: See *management by objectives (MBO).*

McCarran-Walter Act: See *Immigration and Naturalization Service.*

McNaughten rule: A set of legal principles for the guidance of courts in helping to determine whether or not a defendant may be declared innocent by reason of *insanity.* Based on the 1843 British case of Daniel McNaughten, the accused is considered not responsible for the crime if "laboring under such a defect of reason from disease of the mind as not to know the nature or quality of the act; or, if he did know it, that he did not know that what he was doing was wrong." Some jurisdictions use different criteria for judgments in insanity pleas. For exam-

ple, the American Law Institute's formulation states that "a person is not responsible for criminal conduct if at the time of such conduct as a result of mental disease or defect he lacks substantial capacity either to appreciate the wrongfulness of his conduct or to conform his conduct to the requirements of law."

mean: A *measure of central tendency,* also known as the arithmetic average, it is found by adding scores and dividing this sum by the number of scores. For example, if an agency wanted to know the mean, or average, amount of time each client was seen during a week, it would add the total amount of minutes the agency workers spent with clients that week and divide this sum by the number of clients seen.

means test: Evaluating the client's financial resources and using the result as the criterion to determine eligibility to receive a benefit. The client applying for certain economic, social, or health services will be turned down if the investigator determines that the person has the "means" to pay for them. Programs and services that use the means test to determine client eligibility include *Medicaid, Aid to Families with Dependent Children (AFDC),* the *Food Stamp* program, and *general assistance.* To make means test evaluations the worker usually considers the client's income, assets, debts and other obligations, number of dependents, and health factors.

measure of central tendency: A way of summarizing data about frequency distributions in statistics and research. The three types are the *mean,* the *median,* and the *mode.*

media campaigning: A strategy to raise public awareness about a problem or goal and mobilize social action toward its elimination or achievement by getting the relevant newspapers and radio and TV stations to run stories about it. This is done through such activities as issuing press releases, arranging "photo opportunities" and interviews with reporters, writing letters to the editor, paying for advertising, and preparing free public service messages.

median: A *measure of central tendency,* the point in a distribution that has the same number of scores above and below it. Its advantage over the *mean* in reporting statistical data is that it is not affected by a few extreme scores.

mediation: Intervention in disputes between parties to help them reconcile differences, find compromises, or reach mutually satisfactory agreements. Social workers have used their unique skills and value orientations in many forms of mediation between opposing groups (for example, landlord-tenant organizations, neighborhood residents—halfway house personnel; labor-management representatives, or divorcing spouses). See also *conciliation* and *mediation, divorce.*

mediation, divorce: A procedure used by social workers, lawyers, and other professionals to help settle disputes between divorcing couples outside the courtroom adversarial process. In some states, mediation occurs under the auspices of the courts, but in other localities it is done as a private service. The goals include helping the couple make mutually acceptable compromises, understand the nature of their marital difficulties, agree on equitable distribution of possessions, make custody arrangements for the children, and disengage emotionally from the unhealthy parts of the relationship.

mediator role: The activity of the family therapist who sometimes acts as a go-between in getting various members of the family to communicate more clearly and fairly with one another. This role is not the same as in divorce mediation. See also *conciliation.*

Medicaid: The *means-tested* program, established in 1965, that provides payment for hospital and medical services to people who cannot afford them. Funding comes from federal and state governments under the auspices of the U.S. *Health Care Financing Administration.* In most areas administration of the program is handled through local *public assistance* offices. *Supplemental Security Income (SSI)* recipients may also be helped with Medicaid applications in their local social security offices.

Medic Alert: The privately funded national organization that maintains medical records on people who are registered with it and provides emergency medical information about them to health care providers. Medic Alert provides its registrants with special bracelets or other identification so that health care providers are informed about the patient's special needs during crises. For example, a registrant may become unable to communicate that he or she is allergic to certain medications or has other physical conditions that are not readily evident. A 24-hour-a-day telephone switchboard is maintained and accepts collect calls.

medical model: A social work approach to helping people that is patterned after the orientation used by many physicians. This includes looking at the client as an individual with an illness to be treated, giving relatively less attention to factors in the client's environment, diagnosing the condition with fairly specific labels, and treating the problem through regular clinical appointments.

medical social work: The social work practice that occurs in hospitals and other health care settings to facilitate good health, prevent

illness, and aid physically ill patients and their families to resolve the social and psychological problems related to the illness.

Medicare: The national health care program for the aged, established in 1965 and administered through the *Social Security Administration,* the U.S. *Health Care Financing Administration,* and to some extent, in certain localities, with the assistance of some commercial and nonprofit health insurance companies. Funding comes from employer-employee contributions as part of the individual's *social security,* from *earmarked taxes,* and from general federal revenues. Eligibility is not based on need but on reaching the age of 65.

Medi-Credit: A proposed health care financing program in which the costs of premiums paid to private health insurance companies could be credited directly against personal income taxes.

meditation: A state of concentrated relaxation, the systematic practice of which reportedly leads to feelings of heightened well-being and reduced anxiety. According to Charles Zastrow (*The Practice of Social Work,* Homewood, Ill.: Dorsey Press, 1985, p. 474), meditators typically concentrate on and repeat a word, phrase, or sound (for example, a mantra) for about 20 minutes while remaining in a passive attitude, in one comfortable position, and in an environment free of distractions.

melting pot theory: The idea that immigrants to a new nation become socialized and take on the values, norms, and personality characteristics of the majority culture while losing some of their unique cultural traits.

membership model in social work: The social work orientation that synthesizes physiological functioning, social interaction, object-relations theory, and symbolization and views the professional role as rendering aid in the management of human membership. Humanness, according to this view, does not rest on individualism but is only possible through membership in the community and social structures that are derived from it. The orientation, which was first delineated by Hans S. Falck, emphasizes the common membership of clients and social worker, the mutuality of giving and receiving, the social (rather than individualistic) nature of self-determination, and reciprocity among members, institutions, community, and society.

menarche: The biological process that occurs in young women as menstruation begins.

meningitis: Bacterially or virally caused inflammation of the membranes that surround the brain or spinal cord or both. Antibiotic drugs have greatly reduced mortality and the effects of the disease, such as paralysis, arthritis, deafness, and blindness. Symptoms of meningitis may include fever, headache, vomiting, delirium, severe rigidity in the neck and back, and convulsions.

menopause: The biological process that occurs in middle-aged women as menstruation ceases. In some women the hormonal changes result temporarily in certain accompanying physiological and psychological symptoms.

mental cruelty: A legal ground for divorce in many jurisdictions, in which the behavior of one spouse imperils the mental health of the other to the extent that continuing the relationship is considered unbearable.

mental disorder: A synonym for *mental illness.*

mental health: The relative state of emotional well-being, freedom from incapacitating conflicts, and the consistent ability to make and carry out rational decisions and cope with environmental stresses and internal pressures.

Mental Health Association: The voluntary citizen's organization, founded in 1909 by Clifford Beers and others, whose purpose is to promote social conditions that enhance the potential for good mental health and to improve the methods and facilities for treating mental illness.

mental health professional: One who has specialized training and skills in the nature and treatment of mental illness and uses them to provide clinical, preventive, and social services for people who have, or may be vulnerable to, mental disorders. Mental health professionals include psychiatrists, psychologists, psychiatric nurses, social workers, and members of some other disciplines that provide special expertise and help for emotionally disturbed people.

mental health team: Professionals and ancillary personnel from several different disciplines who work together to provide a wide range of services for clients (and the families of clients) who are affected by mental disorders. Members of such teams include psychiatrists (who usually head them), social workers, psychologists, and nurses. In some psychiatric facilities the team members may also include physical and occupational therapists, recreation specialists, educators, personnel and guidance counselors, psychiatric aides, volunteers, and *indigenous workers.*

mental health workers: Mental health professionals, paraprofessionals, volunteers, and aides who work in facilities or organizations concerned with meeting the needs of the mentally ill or those vulnerable to mental illness. Mental health workers are distinguished from mental health team members only in that their efforts are not necessarily coordinated with those of other workers to achieve specified, focused goals.

mental hospitals: Institutions that specialize in the care and treatment of people suffering from *mental illness.* These institutions may be publicly or privately financed and may provide a full range of health care services or be limited in type of care provided. Many of the existing public mental hospitals in the United States were established as a result of the influence of social reformer Dorothea Dix (1802–1887).

mental hygiene: A synonym for *mental health.* The term often implies efforts to develop facilities and procedures for the treatment of the mentally ill and to educate people to live in ways that foster emotional stability and psychological well-being.

mental illness: Impaired psychosocial or cognitive functioning due to disturbances in any one or more of the following processes: biological, chemical, physiological, genetic, psychological, social, or environmental. Mental illness is extremely variable in duration, severity, and prognosis, depending on the specific type of affliction. The major forms of mental illness include *psychosis, neurosis, affective disorders, personality disorders, organic mental disorders,* and *psychosexual disorders.*

mental retardation: The condition of below-average intellectual potential and slow intellectual development, which may be the result of genetic factors, trauma, organ damage, or social deprivation.

mental status exam: A systematic evaluation, made primarily by psychiatrists and other physicians, to determine a patient's level of psychosocial, intellectual, and emotional functioning and orientation as to time and place. During the interview the doctor observes the patient's *affect,* thought content, perceptive and cognitive functions, and need and motivation for treatment. This may be done, in part, by asking such questions of the patient as "What day is today?" and "Where are you now?" The patient may also be asked to repeat a series of numbers forward and backward and to interpret several aphorisms, such as "People who live in glass houses shouldn't throw stones."

mercy killing: See *euthanasia.*

merit system: An organization's set of rules, regulations, and policies used in personnel management to assure employees that their opportunities for promotion and retention on the job will be fairly based on performance. Federal government workers are protected in this system by the *Merit Systems Protection Board.*

Merit Systems Protection Board: An independent organization in the U.S. federal government designed to protect the integrity of the federal *merit system.* Appeals by federal workers who charge unfair treatment and other violations of federal regulations are evaluated by the board, and violators may be prosecuted.

metamessage: A person's communication that comments on the verbal statement he or she is making. For example, a client might say, "I'm not angry!" (primary statement) while banging a fist (metamessage). The metamessage may be verbal or nonverbal, conscious or unconscious, and consistent with or contradictory to the primary statement.

metaphor: A type of analogy or figure of speech used to describe something to which it is not literally applicable. Metaphors are used by social workers and their clients to connote feeling and imagination as well as objective reality. For example, a worker could describe a client as a "hurricane" to convey a variety of behavioral and personality characteristics.

metastasis: The spreading of a disease, such as *cancer,* from one part of the body to others.

methadone treatment: The use of the synthetic narcotic methadone to help wean addicts from heroin. Methadone blocks the euphoric action of heroin and acts as a painkiller to reduce the discomfort of heroin withdrawal. However, methadone itself is addictive, even though it has less severe withdrawal symptoms. Methadone clinics give methadone to patients and supervise their use of it. For such treatment to be truly effective, it must be accompanied by psychosocial therapy.

methods in social work: The term used by social workers, especially those in education, to identify specific types of intervention. Social work activities that have been identified as methods include *social casework, social group work, community organization, administration in social work, research, policy,* and *planning,* direct clinical practice, family and marital treatment, other micro practice, and what is called "generic social work practice, combined micro-macro."

Mexican American: A resident of the United States whose parents or ancestors are from Mexico. See also *Chicano.*

mezzo practice: *Social work practice* primarily with families and small groups. Important activities at this level include facilitating communication, *mediation,* negotiating, educating, and bringing people together. This is one of the three levels of social work practice, along with *macro practice* and *micro practice.* All social workers engage, to some extent, in all three, even though they may give major attention to only one or two of the levels.

micro orientation: In social work, an emphasis on the individual client's psychosocial conflicts and on the enhancement of technical skills for use in efficient treatment of these problems. This perspective is contrasted with social work's *macro orientation.*

micro practice: The term used by social workers to identify professional activities that are designed to help solve the problems faced primarily by individuals, families, and small groups. Usually micro practice focuses on direct intervention on a case-by-case basis or in a clinical setting. See also *macro practice* and *mezzo practice.*

midlife crisis: The inner conflict and, often, the changed behavior patterns that occur in some middle-aged individuals who are reassessing the meaning and direction of life, questioning their future goals, examining their relative progress toward achieving their goals, and coping with different social demands made on them.

midwife: A nonphysician who assists a mother through the process of childbirth.

migrant laborer: A worker who travels from place to place to take short-term or seasonal jobs, such as those in agriculture and construction. Often such workers travel in groups, typically with their families, and are vulnerable to exploitation by employers. They and their children have limited or minimal opportunities to obtain education, social skills, and health care.

Milford Conference: The study group, comprising social workers, agency executives, and board members, set up to determine whether social work was a disparate group of specialties or a unified profession with integrated knowledge and skills. The group published its conclusions in the 1929 book *Social Case Work: Generic and Specific* and emphasized that social casework in all settings used basically the same skills and knowledge. The conference is considered by social workers to be one of the most important milestones in the history of the professsion because it led to the still-existing principle that social work, despite its service in a variety of settings, is one profession. See also *generic-specific controversy.*

milieu therapy: A form of treatment and rehabilitation for socially and mentally disordered people who usually live in institutional settings. Treatment is not restricted to individual hours with a professional therapist but also occurs in the total environment of this closed setting, which is also referred to as the "therapeutic community." Those being treated attend group sessions for everyone in the facility, elect their own leaders, and provide one another with social and emotional support throughout the day. The entire environment is considered vital to the treatment process.

military social work: Professional social work intervention on behalf of active-duty military personnel and their families. This form of practice is accomplished by social work officers in the U.S. Army and U.S. Air Force. Civilian professional social workers also provide services in Navy, Army, and Air Force settings. Military social workers provide such services as evaluating and treating emotionally disturbed military personnel or members of their families, finding and developing social resources, and facilitating communications not only between military personnel but also between individuals in the military and their relatives who live in other locations.

mimesis: Imitation of the behaviors of another person. This is often seen among family members who tend to assume the same verbal and physical gestures, expressions, or postures. Social workers and other therapists sometimes imitate the movements and posture of clients, especially when working with families or groups, to facilitate *joining* or alliance building.

mind reading: The alleged ability of a person to know the thoughts and feelings of another person without direct communication. This term is used by social workers as a figure of speech in *marital therapy* and *family therapy* to describe the tendency of one family member to interpret or describe to the worker what he or she believes are the views or the feelings of another family member.

minimal brain dysfunction: See *attention deficit disorder.*

minimum market basket: A concept used by economists and social welfare planners to indicate the least quantity of food required for survival; a form of *minimum needs estimation.*

minimum needs estimation: The delineation by social welfare planners of the least quantities of food, clothing, housing, and goods that an individual requires for survival. This concept is used as a basis in establishing income poverty lines.

minimum wage: A payment made to employees that, by law or contract, is the lowest amount the employer is permitted to pay for specified work. United States labor policy establishes that employers may not hire workers unless they guarantee to pay at least the amount established by government regulations.

minorities of color: People who have *minority* status because their skin color differs from that of the community's predominant group. In the United States the term usually refers to *blacks, Orientals, American Indians,* and certain other groups.

minority: A group, or a member of a group, of people of a distinct racial, religious, ethnic, or political identity that is smaller or less powerful than the community's controlling group.

Minority Business Development Agency: The U.S. federal agency, within the Department of Commerce, designed to help minorities establish and maintain businesses. The agency administers laws requiring that a percentage of moneys spent on government projects be set aside for minority-owned businesses.

Miranda: The 1966 U.S. Supreme Court ruling, in *Miranda v. Arizona,* requiring police to inform suspects of their constitutional rights before questioning them.

MISs: See *management information systems (MISs).*

miscegenation: Marriage or sexual relations between a man and woman of different races in violation of a law. Antimiscegenation laws were common in the United States but were generally abolished by legislation or court decrees in the 1960s.

misdemeanor: A minor criminal offense. Such acts as breaking street lights, defacing property, and littering are usually misdemeanors. See also *felony.*

missing person: An individual whose whereabouts remain unknown to his or her *significant others.* If the missing person is a minor, the appropriate term is usually *runaway.*

mixed economy: A society or environment in which services and transfers of funds occur through the participation of public, nonprofit, and proprietary organizations.

mobility: The ability to move with relative ease or flexibility. See also *social mobility.*

Mobilization for Youth: A multifaceted social service *demonstration program,* established in New York City in the early 1960s, designed to test the theory that poor urban youth will enter mainstream society if social barriers to opportunities are removed. Funded at first by the Ford Foundation and later by the federal government, the program provided some direct counseling services but was more oriented toward training; facilitating communication; legal, political, and consumer education; developing purposeful and positive group experiences; and changing the neighborhood social structure. The successful results of the program were largely incorporated on a national scale into the *War on Poverty* programs of the Johnson Administration.

mobilizer role: In social work, the responsibility to help people and organizations combine their resources to achieve goals of mutual importance. This is accomplished by bringing clients together, enhancing lines of communication, clarifying goals and steps to achieve them, and devising plans for gaining greater support. Other roles are the *facilitator role,* the *enabler role,* and the *educator role.*

mode: A *measure of central tendency* in statistics and research, it is the number that occurs most often in a given series. For example, an agency wants to know how many clients are seen by most of its workers in a given day. A few of the 20 agency workers typically see about 12 clients daily, and a few others see only about 5. But most of the workers see 8 clients per day, which is the modal number.

model: A representation of reality. For example, social workers use the *life model* to represent the interplay of forces found in the client's environment that influence and are influenced by the client.

Model Cities program: A federal program established in 1966 to coordinate and integrate the various government efforts in housing; urban renewal; community development facilities, transportation, and education; and economic opportunities in participating cities. Federal officials would coordinate government programs and resources with local efforts. The federal *block grant* approach, in which funds are supplied to the cities without requiring specific allocations, has largely supplanted the Model Cities program.

modeling: In behavioral therapy and *social learning theory,* a form of learning in which an individual acquires behaviors by imitating the actions of one or more other persons.

Model Licensing Act: Legislative guidelines developed by the *National Association of Social Workers (NASW)* that specify recommended conditions and qualifications for states to use in *licensing* social work practice. Social workers and lobbyists with various state legislatures offer the Model Licensing Act to assist legislators in writing their own laws pertaining to social work licenses. The act specifies what social work practice is and is not, outlines the recommended qualifications for doing it, and indicates the procedures to be taken to enforce compliance.

mongolism: See *Down's syndrome.*

monogamy: The state of being married to one person.

mononucleosis: A viral infection that most commonly affects adolescents and young adults with such symptoms as sore throat, fever, and chills; feelings of weakness and tiredness; and enlarged lymph nodes.

moral development: Acquiring the values, feelings, and thoughts that lead to behaviors that are consistent with standards of right or wrong. Many theorists have proposed models about how this is accomplished, including Gilligan,

Kohlberg, Piaget, Mischel, Erikson, and others. See also *Kohlberg moral development theory* and *values clarification.*

morbid: Diseased or disordered.

morbidity rate: The proportion of people in a specific population who are known to have a specific disease or disorder during a certain time period.

mores: Social customs that are accepted, traditional, and enforced by others in the social group.

moron: An obsolete term, once used to refer to a mildly mentally retarded person with an IQ score below 70 and above 50.

morpheme: In *communication theory,* a basic unit of meaningful language. Morphemes include words, prefixes, and suffixes.

morphogenesis: The concept used in *systems theories* to depict the tendency of a living system to change its structure and to evolve into a system that has a different structure. The tendency of a system toward morphogenesis is balanced by the system's equally powerful tendency toward *morphostasis.*

morphostasis: The concept used in *systems theories* to depict the tendency of a living system to retain its structure and to resist change. The tendency of a system toward morphostasis is balanced by the system's equally powerful tendency toward *morphogenesis.*

mortality rate: The number or proportion of deaths in a specified population during a certain time period. The mortality rate is also known as the *death rate.*

Mothers Without Custody: A national *self-help organization,* with chapters in many larger communities, whose members are mothers living separately from one or more of their minor children because of court decisions, intervention by child protection agencies, or *child snatching* by ex-spouses. Mothers Without Custody members meet regularly to exchange information and provide mutual support and encouragement.

motivation: A set of physical drives, desires, attitudes, and values that arouse and direct behavior toward the achievement of some goal.

motivation-capacity-opportunity theory: The assessment model used by social workers to predict the likelihood that a client will make effective use of the help offered. Charlotte Towle first formulated the triad, and social work researchers Lillian Ripple, Ernestina Alexander, and Bernice W. Polemis studied its relevance. Their findings concluded that when clients have adequate motivation and the capacity to partake of services provided in an appropriate manner, they will make use of the services, unless there are restrictive or unmodifiable forces outside the agency or influences on the client.

mourning: Expressions of sorrow or grief, typically accompanying the death of a loved one.

MSW: The master's degree in social work, awarded to students who have completed the requirements of accredited schools of social work. Requirements for the MSW typically include successful completion of 60 academic hours, including about 24 hours of field placement, spread over the equivalent of two full-time years. The student is also required to complete a thesis or research project. In some schools the degree is known as the MSSW (master of science in social work, master of social service work), MSSA (master of social service administration), or MA in social work. All are essentially the same in terms of educational requirements and standards.

muckrakers: The name first used by President Theodore Roosevelt to describe a group of journalists, speakers, agitators, and social activists who sought to make the public aware of specific abuses, unethical practices, and corrupt business and political activities that exploited and endangered people. The muckraking movement was especially prominent in the United States from 1900 to 1915 and resulted in many of the social reforms of the Progressive Era. The term is still used and often applied to social workers, writers, investigative reporters, and other reform-minded people who call attention to current examples of abuse and corruption.

multiaxial classification: The system for assessing mental disorders used by the American Psychiatric Association's *DSM-III.* Five levels, or "Axes," are used in looking at each subject. They are Axis I, clinical syndromes and related conditions; Axis II, specific developmental and personality disorders; Axis III, related physical conditions; Axis IV, degree of contributing stressors; and Axis V, highest level of functioning during the past year. By evaluating the subject on these five levels, the diagnostician is able to consider many of the factors relevant to the client rather than only the more obvious symptoms of mental disorder.

multiple causation theory: The view that a given disorder or social phenomenon is the result of many different factors operating simultaneously and in many cases somewhat independently of one another. This is a view particularly emphasized by those who use *systems theories* as their orientation and by those who question the concept of *linear causality.*

multiple impact therapy: A team form of treatment used by social workers and other professionals, especially with *multiproblem families.* It is typically intensive and relatively short term, with members of the professional team meeting with various subgroups or individuals from the family. Then different subgroups meet with the professionals, and so on, in a variety of combinations.

multiple personality: A form of *dissociative disorder* in which an individual has two or more distinct personalities. The individual may not be aware of the existence of these other personalities. Nonprofessionals often inappropriately confuse this term with *schizophrenia.*

multiple sclerosis: A slowly progressive disease of the central nervous system that usually affects its victims during their twenties. The symptoms may include some of the following: paralysis or numbness of various parts of the body, convulsions, visual and speech disorders, emotional problems, bladder control disturbances, and muscular weakness. The symptoms have a tendency to increase and decrease in severity at varying intervals.

multiple tic disorder: See *Tourette's disorder.*

multiproblem family: A kinship group whose members are seen by the social worker and treated for a variety of different social, economic, and personality difficulties at the same time. Viewing some family clients as "multiproblem" enables the social worker to use many intervention techniques to address more than one problem at a time.

multivariate analysis: In research, a group of statistical techniques, including analysis of covariance and factor analysis, that tests the results of two or more variables acting simultaneously.

mumps: A contagious viral disease that results in painful swelling of the salivary glands, especially under the jawbone.

muscle relaxation technique: A therapeutic and self-help approach to reducing stress and anxiety; it is accomplished when the subject first tightens and then relaxes a set of muscles while concentrating on those muscles. The procedure has many variations but basically consists of sitting in a quiet, private place and then flexing, holding for a few seconds, and relaxing different muscle groups in a predetermined sequence (such as right hand, right forearm, right shoulder, and so on) until all the muscle groups have been relaxed. The technique is also used in conjunction with other therapy approaches, such as *systematic desensitization.*

muscular dystrophy: A progressive disease of the skeletal muscles that usually begins in early childhood. In some forms, patients are confined to wheelchairs by the time they reach adolescence, and the likelihood that they will live to middle age, although increasing, is still low. Early manifestations of the disease include progressive muscular weakness, waddling gait, coordination problems, and sometimes learning disorders and mental retardation. Causes are not well established for all types, but in many male victims it is an inherited disease, passed on through the mother.

mutism: A refusal or inability to speak.

mutual aid groups: Formal or informal associations of people who share certain problems and may meet regularly in small groups to provide one another with advice, emotional support, information, and other help. The term "mutual aid group" is roughly synonymous with *self-help group*, except that it implies the exchange of more tangible services and resources, such as pools for baby-sitting, transportation, purchasing power, home repairs, and similar activities.

mutual help: The efforts of people who face similar problems to provide assistance for one another. Social workers often encourage and facilitate such efforts among client groups. For example, *networks* of senior citizens may provide

mutual help by calling one another periodically throughout the day to assure that all is well. See also *mutual aid groups*.

mutuality: The efforts of two or more people to act together in ultimate harmony in order to achieve benefits for each. In *systems theories* it is the concept of interdependence between various subsystems, such as social worker and client, landlord and tenant, or parents and children. See also *pseudomutuality*.

mutual withdrawal: The condition of indifference, boredom, noncommunication, and nonmotivation to resolve problems that sometimes occurs among troubled couples and family members.

myocardial infarction: A circulatory system disease in which a blood vessel that carries blood to the heart muscles (for example, a coronary artery) becomes blocked due to a blood clot or hemorrhage. Often this occurs because the artery wall has become hardened or narrowed by *arteriosclerosis*. The resulting interruption of blood flow to the heart muscle often results in the death of some tissue in the heart and sometimes in heart failure.

ll

x

f

N

NAACP: See *National Association for the Advancement of Colored People (NAACP)*.

NAACSW: See *North American Association of Christians in Social Work (NAACSW)*.

narcissism: Excessive self-preoccupation and self-love; an extreme form of *egocentrism*.

narcotic: A natural or synthetic drug that has a depressant effect on the nervous system, relieves pain and anxiety, and alters moods. The major narcotic is opium (and its constituents *codeine* and morphine), from which *heroin* is derived. Narcotics tend to be addictive, and their side effects can often endanger the life of the user.

NASW Code of Ethics: The explication of the values, rules, and principles of ethical conduct that apply to all social workers who are members of the *National Association of Social Workers (NASW)*. The original *Code of Ethics* for social workers was implicit in the 1951 Standards for Professional Practice of the *American Association of Social Workers (AASW)*. NASW developed a formal code in 1960 and has made subsequent revisions. The current Code of Ethics was adopted by the 1979 Delegate Assembly and has applied to social workers since 1980. See the complete NASW Code of Ethics in this volume.

National Academy of Practice (NAP): A professional, scientific, and educational organization, established in 1981, and modeled in part on the National Academy of Sciences, that comprises bodies of distinguished practitioners from each of the major health professions, including social work. NAP's goals are to promote excellence in professional practice for the benefit of all people and to provide a forum to which government and society can direct public policy concerns in health care. The National Academy of Practice in Social Work was the second section to be activated.

National Advisory Commission on Civil Disorders: See *Kerner Commission*.

National Association for the Advancement of Colored People (NAACP): The largest and oldest of the U.S. civil rights organizations. It was established in 1909 when social workers Mary White Ovington and Henry Moskowitz and others helped organize blacks and whites who were outraged about a series of lynchings. The NAACP now has over 1,500 local chapters throughout all 50 states and works to achieve its goals primarily through legal actions to protect the rights of black citizens, nonpartisan political action to enact civil rights laws, and education and public information.

National Association of Black Social Workers (NABSW): The professional association, formed in 1968, comprising black social workers or social workers who are interested in the goals of the organization. These goals are to deal with problems pertinent to the black community on all levels, including working with clients, promoting programs serving blacks, and assisting black social workers. NABSW holds annual conventions, performs research and educational functions, and publishes the journal *Black Caucus*.

National Association of Puerto Rican Social Service Workers (NAPSSW): The professional association of social workers of Puerto Rican and other Hispanic heritages whose members work primarily toward the improvement of social conditions for Puerto Ricans and other Hispanics and for the professional goals of Puerto Rican social workers.

National Association of Social Workers (NASW): The organization of social workers established in 1955 through the consolidation of the *American Association of Social Workers (AASW)*, the *American Association of Psychiatric Social Workers (AAPSW)*, the *American Association of Group Workers (AAGW)*, the *Association for the Study of Community Organization (ASCO)*, the American Association of Medical Social Workers (AAMSW), the National Association of School Social Workers (NASSW), and the Social Work Research

Group (SWRG). With some 100,000 members in 55 chapters, NASW's primary functions include promoting the professional development of its members, establishing and maintaining professional standards of practice, advancing sound social policies, and providing other services that protect its members and enhance their professional status. The organization has developed and adopted the *NASW Code of Ethics* and other generic and specialized practice standards. Certification and quality assurance are promoted through the *Academy of Certified Social Workers (ACSW)*; the *NASW Register of Clinical Social Workers;* and the Diplomate in Clinical Social Work. Among NASW's political action programs are *PACE* and *ELAN.* NASW also sponsors professional conferences, continuing education programs, and produces journals, books, and major reference works such as the *Encyclopedia of Social Work* and this dictionary. See also *National Center on Social Work Policy and Practice.*

National Center for Health Statistics Research (NCHSR): The federal agency of the *Department of Health and Human Services* that provides for the collection, interpretation, and dissemination of data pertaining to the nation's health. Data include *incidence rates* and *prevalence rates* of various diseases and manpower resources for health and medical care and social services.

National Center on Child Abuse and Neglect: The federal organization, within the *Administration for Children, Youth, and Families (ACYF)* of the U.S. *Department of Health and Human Services (HHS),* whose mission is to mobilize national efforts to prevent, control, and treat the problem of child abuse and neglect. The organization, headquartered in Washington, D.C., has centers in cities throughout the nation. It facilitates research, maintains databases, and accumulates and disseminates information to health care providers, educators, researchers, and others.

National Center on Social Work Policy and Practice: The social work organization established by NASW in 1986 to collect, analyze, and disseminate information about U.S. social welfare needs. The information comes from the direct experiences of social work practitioners and, after analysis, is used to inform legislators and the public about social problems and proposed solutions. The information is also used to enhance social work practice effectiveness. The center coordinates fundraising to be used in policy formulation, research, and social work education.

National Conference on Catholic Charities: See *Catholic Charities USA.*

National Conference of Charities and Corrections: See *National Conference on Social Welfare (NCSW).*

National Conference on Social Welfare (NCSW): A federation of social welfare agencies in the public and private sectors, including secular and religious agencies, as well as individuals concerned about the social welfare of Americans. Established in 1879 as the Conference of Charities, it changed its name to the National Conference on Charities and Corrections in 1884, to the National Conference of Social Work in 1917, and to its present name in 1957.

National Consumers League (NCL): The advocacy and educational organization founded in 1899 to protect those who make and purchase products. In its early years it was led by social worker–lawyer Florence Kelley and successfully fought for improved working conditions, child labor laws, minimum wages, shorter working hours, and safe and effective consumer products.

National Council of Senior Citizens (NCSC): A federation of more than 4,000 senior citizens' clubs around the nation, founded in 1961 to coordinate the activities of senior citizens in educating the public, lobbying, and developing services and programs.

National Council on Aging: A national organization comprising individuals and agencies that provide services for the elderly. The council coordinates conferences and procedures for exchanging information between organizations and helps disseminate information to researchers, academicians, health care providers, family members of elderly persons, and others interested in services to the elderly. Through its National Institute on Aging, Work, and Retirement (NIAWR), it strives to promote opportunities for middle-aged or older people to obtain employment or prepare for retirement.

National Education Association (NEA): A professional membership association of teachers, school administrators, and related personnel. Its major objectives are improved educational practices, facilities, standards, and conditions for teachers and students.

National Federation of Societies for Clinical Social Work (NFSCSW): The organization, established in 1971, comprising social workers who have at least MSW degrees and are interested in clinical social work in social agencies or private practice. NFSCSW publishes the *Clinical Social Work* journal.

national health insurance: A proposed program to help every citizen pay for health care costs in the existing medical marketplace. There are many variations in the proposal, but basically it would use and supplement existing health insurance procedures and extend coverage to everyone. Payrolls would contain an *earmarked tax* for this insurance, and individuals would, if able, pay a percentage of the health care provider's bill, with the remainder to be paid by the government. This proposal is not to be confused with a *national health service.*

national health service: Direct governmental provision of medical personnel and facilities for citizens to receive complete health care; also known as "socialized medicine." This system is common in many countries, excluding the United States. However, a form of national health service is provided to certain groups in the United States, including needy veterans, members of the armed forces and their families, tuberculosis victims, and American Indians. This system is not to be confused with *national health insurance.*

National Indian Social Workers Association (NISWA): The national professional association established in 1970 for social workers of American Indian or Alaska Native descent. Goals of NISWA include promoting the welfare of American Indians through influencing legislation, educating and sensitizing other social workers and social work educators about the needs of American Indians, and conducting research about Indian populations.

National Institute of Mental Health (NIMH): A federal organization, part of the U.S. *Department of Health and Human Services (HHS),* that supports research and training and oversees plans for the care and treatment of the mentally ill and facilitates programs to enhance the nation's mental health.

National Institutes of Health (NIH): The U.S. *Public Health Service* organization that supports, coordinates, and conducts research into the causes, prevention, treatment, and cure of diseases. NIH has many component institutes, each of which specializes in a particular type of disease or health concern. NIH components include the National Cancer Institute; National Institute of Child Health and Human Development; National Institute of Allergy and Infectious Diseases; National Institute of Arthritis, Diabetes, and Digestive and Kidney Diseases; National Institute of Environmental Health Sciences; National Eye Institute; National Institute on Aging; National Institute of Neurological and Communicative Disorders and Stroke; National Institute of General Medical Sciences; National Institute of Dental Research; National Heart, Lung, and Blood Institute; and National Library of Medicine.

National Organization for Women (NOW): A volunteer organization, with local chapters throughout the United States, established in 1966 to enhance the economic and social opportunities for women through public education, lobbying,

legal actions against discriminatory procedures, and helping candidates sympathetic to NOW's goals get elected.

National Recovery Administration (NRA): The federal organization established in 1933, early in President Roosevelt's first term, to take immediate action to solve problems arising from the economic crisis. Mostly involved with establishing new codes regulating businesses and labor, NRA was absorbed into other agencies by 1936.

National Urban League: See *Urban League, National.*

National Welfare Rights Organization (NWRO): An association of public relief clients formed in 1966. The goals of NWRO are to help people fight bureaucratic policies without having to rely on social workers and to facilitate improvements in welfare legislation and programs.

National Youth Administration (NYA): The *New Deal* federal program that sought to provide part-time jobs for high school and college students so they could complete their educations.

Native Americans: See *American Indians.*

nativism: The idea that certain personality factors are not learned but are genetically transmitted or present at birth.

natural helping network: Informal, flexible linkages and relationships between *nonprofessionals* who voluntarily provide important services and supports to people in need and those to whom they provide the services. Most natural helping networks develop among members of the needy person's family or neighbors, fellow employees, members of the person's church, members of associations or social classes to which the person belongs, or altruistic people in the community.

naturalization: Officially becoming a citizen or national of a country.

NCSW: See *National Conference on Social Welfare (NCSW).*

"near poor" population: Families and individuals who are employed but earn only slightly more than is received by those who benefit from *public assistance* or *social security.*

needs: Physical, psychological, economic, and social requirements for survival, well-being, and fulfillment.

needs assessments (NA): Systematic appraisals, made by social workers and other professionals in evaluating their clients, of problems, existing resources, potential solutions, and obstacles to problem solving. In social agencies, needs assessments are made on behalf of the clients who receive clinical services; in communities, on behalf of all the residents. The purpose of needs assessments is to document needs and establish priorities for service. The data come from existing records such as census and local government statistics as well as from interviews and research on the relevant population.

needs group: People who know a problem through personal experience. In social policy development and community organization, representative victims of a problem are often included in planning committees to discuss and decide how to assist others who have the problem.

negative feedback: In *systems theories* and in *communication theory*, a signal or message that stops or retards further output.

negative income tax: A program designed to standardize procedures for assisting poor families while eliminating a *means test* through use of the federal income tax system. Taxpayers whose incomes fall below a specified minimum are reimbursed up to that amount from the federal treasury. A form of negative income tax was instituted in 1975 in the United States through the *Earned Income Tax Credit* program.

negative reinforcement: In *behavior modification*, the strengthening of a response through escape or avoidance conditioning.

neglect: Failure to meet one's legal and moral obligations or duties, especially to dependent family members. When such conduct results in potential harm to others, legal proceedings may be taken to compel the person to meet the relevant obligations or face punishment.

negligence: Failure to exercise reasonable care or caution, resulting in others' being subjected to harm or unwarranted risk of harm; also, failure to fulfill responsibility that is necessary to protect or help another. Contributory negligence may occur when a person's failure to exercise prudent caution, combined with the negligence of another, results in harm to a third individual. For example, if a social worker does not report knowledge about a person's neglect of a child who has been harmed, the worker could be charged with contributory negligence. Criminal (or culpable) negligence may occur when one is so reckless, careless, or indifferent to others' safety that injury or death results.

negotiation: In community organization and other forms of social work, the process of bringing together those who are opposed on some issues and arranging for them to communicate clearly and fairly, to bargain and compromise, and to arrive at mutually acceptable agreements.

neighborhood: A region or locality whose inhabitants share certain characteristics, values, mutual interests, or styles of living.

neighborhood information center: A social program proposed by Alfred J. Kahn and other social welfare planners in which highly accessible and geographically convenient organizations are used as entry points to the total social service system. They would provide information, advice, and referrals but would not replace the intake evaluation function of social agencies. The centers could be *freestanding* or located in post offices, libraries, municipal buildings, and shopping centers.

Neighborhood Youth Corps: The federal program to assure local jobs for unemployed teenagers, established as part of the Economic Opportunity Act of 1964. In 1974 it became part of the *CETA* program.

negative transference: *Transference* that results in expressions of hostility or distrust or feelings of ill will that a client may have for a psychotherapist or other person.

neoconservatism: A revision of certain aspects of traditional conservative philosophies and views that retains most other aspects of these views. Thus, there are many different neoconservative philosophies rather than a single one. The term is often applied to an attitude that favors more controls on morality and financial incentives and subsidies to businesses to encourage their growth, rejecting the traditional conservative view that government should be unobtrusive and minimal. See also *conservatism*.

neo-Freudian: A theoretical orientation that basically follows *Freudian theory* but puts greater emphasis on sociocultural factors, interpersonal relationships, and psychosocial development into and through adulthood. There is no single neo-Freudian school, as those who have been given this designation also diverge from one another. However, leading neo-Freudians include Harry Stack Sullivan, Karen Horney, Alfred Adler, Erich Fromm, and others.

neoliberal: One who has revised certain aspects of traditional liberal philosophies and views while retaining most other aspects of these views. Thus, there are many different neoliberal philosophies rather than a single one. The term is most commonly applied to those who change their traditional liberal views and espouse fewer direct welfare benefits and similar programs.

neonatal: Pertaining to newborn infants.

nervous breakdown: An imprecise lay term that carries many different meanings, usually having to do with any kind of emotional condition that has resulted in hospitalization or severe emotional disability interfering with normal functioning. Social workers or other professionals do not use this term in professional communications.

net present value analysis: See *NPV analysis*.

network: A formal or informal linkage of people or organizations that may share resources, skills, contacts, and knowledge with one another.

networking: The social worker's therapeutic efforts to enhance and develop the social linkages that might exist between the client and those relevant to the client, such as family members, friends, neighbors, and associates. Within the network are people who can be effective resources in helping to achieve the client's goals. The term "networking" is also used by professionals to indicate the relationships they cultivate with other professionals in order to expedite action through the social system.

network therapy: The family treatment procedure in which a large number of people who are important to an individual or to a nuclear family are brought together with that family to discuss how everyone can help resolve the existing problems. Included in such meetings can be members of the extended family, neighbors, classmates, fellow employees, other professionals, and clergy.

neurolinguistic programming (NLP): A communications model of human behavior developed by Richard Bandler and John Grinder and others and used by social workers and other psychosocial therapists, educators, and business personnel to assess, build rapport with, and help clients. Major components of the model are "neuro" (the processing of information perceived through the five senses by the nervous system), "linguistic" (the systems of verbal and nonverbal communication that organize the neural representations into meaningful data), and "programming" (the ability to organize the neurolinguistic systems to achieve specific outcomes). To assess someone's behavior, the NLP counselor must identify the client's representational system and join with that system (that is, the counselor must sense the information in the same way as the client).

neuromuscular disorders: A group of neurological diseases that results in progressive weakness or uncontrolled ability of the muscles and in atrophy. Major diseases of this type include *muscular dystrophy, Huntington's chorea, Tourette's disorder, Parkinson's disease,* and other disorders.

neurosis: A term pertaining to a group of mental disorders that are characterized by persistent and disturbing symptoms of anxiety, such as nervousness, irritability, and somatic complaints. The anxiety is said to be a maladaptive way of dealing with internal conflict. The symptoms can range from mild to severe but are relatively amenable to psychotherapy. The specific disorders of this type include *generalized anxiety disorder, dysthymic disorder, depersonalization disorder,* *dysthymic disorder, depersonalization disorder, hysterical neurosis, obsessive-compulsive neurosis,* and *phobic disorder.*

Newburgh welfare plan: The controversial and much-debated system of providing public assistance services in Newburgh, New York, beginning in 1960. Designed primarily to reduce welfare costs, the system gave applicants minimal help, often with payments in kind rather than in cash, and subjected them to stringent residency requirements. The program was terminated as state and federal funds became increasingly important in financing welfare costs, but the idea of the Newburgh policy continues to be controversial.

New Deal: President Franklin D. Roosevelt's name for the plans, programs, and legislation enacted during his first administration in response to the *Great Depression.* New Deal programs included the *Social Security Act, Federal Emergency Relief Administration (FERA), Civilian Conservation Corps (CCC), Works Progress Administration (WPA),* rural electrification, and legislation that regulated banking and securities practices, farm management, and unemployment exchanges.

new property: The guaranteed assets, services, and resources that are available to a resident of a jurisdiction. Also known as the "social wage," the "new income," and as *entitlement* programs, these assets are seen by social planners and economists as being as important in considering an individual's standard of living as income from work or assets from unearned income.

NIMH: See *National Institute of Mental Health (NIMH).*

no-fault divorce: Legal dissolution of a marriage that occurs without the necessity of declaring that one or the other spouse is guilty of marital misconduct. Prior to the enactment of no-fault divorce laws in several states, most marriages could be legally terminated only when one party proved that the other was guilty of behavior that was grounds for divorce. The most common basis for no-fault divorce is voluntary separation for a specified amount of time.

nomadism: The regular shifting of habitation by an individual or group, usually in search of a more suitable environment or better economic opportunities.

nominal group technique: A tool used by social planners in *organization development (OD)* to assess existing problems, needs, interests, or objectives. Participants in a meeting write these factors on small cards. The leader collects and categorizes the cards and posts them on a board for all to see. Then the group members consider each issue and decide how to proceed. Alternatives are considered as to cost, readiness, motivation, acceptability, and availability of other resources.

nominal measurement: The lowest level of measurement used by researchers, consisting simply of classifying observations into categories (for example, gender, race, religion, and so on) that must be mutually exclusive and collectively exhaustive. Appropriate statistics for nominal-level variables include chi-square, phi lambda, and contingency coefficients.

noncategorical grants: Disbursements of funds from one organization to another without any specified objective or requirement for spending. An example is the federal government's *revenue sharing* with state governments.

nondirective: A term applied to an approach in counseling or therapy that emphasizes a warm, permissive, accepting atmosphere to encourage the client to discuss problems freely. In the nondirective approach to therapy, called *client-centered therapy* by some professionals, the worker or therapist asks very few questions and offers few, if any, suggestions or advice. This helps create the environment in which the client can reach his or her potential.

nonjudgmental: A term pertaining to a fundamental element in the social worker–client *relationship,* in which the worker demonstrates an attitude of tolerance and an unwillingness to censor the client for any actions. The worker does not suspend judgment but conveys to the client that the working relationship takes precedence over any possible feelings of disapproval.

nonprofessional: One who is not a *professional.* Generally, the term is applied to *paraprofessionals,* support staff, ancillary personnel, and volunteers who work with professionals in service organizations, such as social agencies and hospitals, and assist the professionals in accomplishing less technical tasks. Nonprofessionals usually have specific training or experience in the jobs they carry out. The term should not be confused with the term *unprofessional.*

nonprofit agencies: Organizations established to fulfill some specified social purpose other than monetary reward to financial backers. Technically the term includes government or tax-supported agencies, but it is usually reserved for private, voluntary social agencies and excludes for-profit *proprietary social agencies.* Nonprofit agencies have explicit policies and established boards of directors. They are funded from a variety of sources, including revenue coming directly from clients, third parties, public contributions, philanthropic contributions, and government grants-in-aid, and are usually tax-exempt. Most of the traditional social agencies, professional associations, and social change organizations are nonprofit—for example, *Family Service*

America (FSA), Catholic Charities, Child Welfare League of America (CWLA), National Association of Social Workers (NASW), National Association for the Advancement of Colored People (NAACP), American Civil Liberties Union (ACLU), and the *Red Cross.*

nonverbal communication: Exchanges of information between people through gestures, facial expressions, posture, tone of voice, and vocal sounds other than words. See also *communication theory, kinesics, paralinguistics,* and *proxemics.*

nonwhite: The U.S. *Census Bureau* term for population groups that are not Caucasian, including blacks, American Indians, Chinese, Japanese, and other people of color.

normal: A term denoting a culturally defined concept of behaviors or phenomena that are not markedly different from the average, usual, or expected.

normal distribution: An expected frequency distribution within which cases or scores occur. In presenting research findings that show a normal distribution, the results may be plotted on a graph that appears to be symmetrical and bell shaped. Most scores fall near the *mean,* forming the highest point of the bell, and fewer cases are located on either side of the slope as distance from the mean increases.

normative: Pertaining to the average or expected behavior patterns of a group or community.

norms: The rules of behavior, both formal and informal, and expectations held collectively by a culture, group, organization, or society.

North American Association of Christians in Social Work (NAACSW): An organization of professional social workers who profess belief in Christian thought and values. The organization began in 1950 at Wheaton College with a series of meetings known as the Evangelical Social Work Conference. The conference was incorporated as the National Association of Christians in Social Work in 1953, adopting its present name in 1984.

nosology: The science of classification, particularly of diseases and disorders.

NPV analysis: Net present value analysis, a method used in program planning and budgeting to help determine what benefits are available in relation to costs when measured over time. NPV rates programs according to the difference between the present value of the benefits and the costs required over time to achieve those benefits. It is an alternative to *cost-benefit analysis.*

nuclear complex: Freud's original name for the *Oedipus complex.*

nuclear family: The kinship group consisting of a father, a mother, and their children.

null hypothesis: A negative statement about proposed relationships in research data so that the facts obtained can fail to confirm the expected results. Thus, a typical hypothesis stated in null fashion would be, "There is no difference between the results of A and B." The null hypothesis permits statistical tests of significance and demands more rigorous testing procedures than when attempting to prove an affirmative statement.

nurse practitioner: A professional nurse who completes additional training, such as a master's degree certificate program, and acquires skills and performs tasks that were traditionally performed only by physicians, including routine physical examinations, taking complete medical histories, providing independent psychotherapy, and coordinating health and social services resources.

nursing home: A residential facility that provides extended health care for people who are ill or unable to take care of themselves.

nurturance: Behaviors and activities that further the growth and development of another person, family, group, or community.

nutrition: The process by which living organisms assimilate materials that are necessary for sustenance, energy, and growth. Human nutrition involves the use of food substances (nutrients)—including the proper balance of proteins, carbohydrates, and fats—as well as vitamins, minerals, and water. Good human nutrition requires a well-balanced diet containing an adequate but not excessive amount of food and calories. Failure to achieve this balance can result in various diseases, dysfunctions, deficiencies, or death. See also *malnutrition.*

O

OASDHI: Old Age, Survivors, Disability, and Health Insurance, the current name for the federal government's *social insurance* program under the *Social Security Act*. Under the provisions of the *Federal Insurance Contributions Act (FICA)*, the government collects payroll and employer taxes from most adult Americans and uses the funds to partially finance the payments made to retired, surviving, and disabled beneficiaries and *Medicare* recipients.

OASI: Old Age and Survivors Insurance, the original name for a central part of the *Social Security Act* of 1935 under which certain people over 65 or their surviving dependents were covered by the new federal insurance program. With subsequent revisions in the Social Security Act, the insurance coverage was expanded to include workers who became disabled and sick *(OASDHI)*.

objectivity: The ability to evaluate a situation, social phenomenon, or person without prejudice or subjective distortion.

object permanence: The understanding that something exists independently of oneself and continues to exist even when it can no longer be seen or otherwise perceived.

object relations theory: A psychoanalytic concept about an individual's relationship with others, based on early parent-child interactions and internalized self-images that are focused on these interactions; the *neo-Freudian* view that *libido* and aggressive drives toward self-pleasure are no more important than are the child's object-seeking drives.

obsession: A repetitive and persistent thought, action, or ritual that is believed to occur as a mechanism for controlling or relieving anxiety. Psychoanalytic theorists say this may be a way for individuals to deal with unconscious conflicts.

obsessive-compulsive disorder: A type of *anxiety disorder* in which the individual experiences unwanted recurrent and persistent ideas, im-

pulses, or images *(obsessions)*, or engages in seemingly intentional behaviors that are performed ritualistically *(compulsions)*.

OBRA: See *Omnibus Budget Reconciliation Act (OBRA)*.

occupancy rate: The number of persons per room, per dwelling, or per household; a figure for determining actual housing density and housing needs.

occupational health: The preservation of physical and mental well-being in the workplace through the maintenance of sanitary and safe facilities and conditions.

Occupational Safety and Health Administration (OSHA): The organization within the U.S. *Department of Labor* that assures that conditions in the workplace are safe. OSHA administers training programs on occupational safety and health standards, conducts inspections, and issues citations to noncomplying employers.

occupational social work: The provision of professional human services in the workplace through such employer-funded programs as *employee assistance programs (EAPs)* and occupational *alcoholism* programs. The goal is to help employees meet their human and social needs by providing services (including marital and family therapy) and dealing with emotional problems, social relationship conflicts, and other personal problems. Occupational social work can be involved in *macro practice* (such as organizational interventions on behalf of employee groups) as well as individual clinical activities. Many social workers use the term synonymously with *industrial social work*.

Oedipus complex: In the *Freudian theory* of psychosexual development, the erotic interest and attachment developed by a young child (usually between ages 3 and 7) for the parent of the opposite sex and the concomitant feelings of rivalry with and envy of the parent of the same sex. The child's feelings are repressed and unconscious but are often manifested in flirtatious behavior with one parent and hostile behavior with the other.

Office of Child Support Enforcement: See *Child Enforcement Office, U.S.*

Office of Economic Development (OED): The federal organization, within the U.S. *Department of Health and Human Services (HHS)*, established in 1969 to stimulate the growth of private profit-making businesses in neighborhoods where there is high unemployment. OED finances the establishment of urban and rural community development corporations. See also *Community Services program.*

Office of Economic Opportunity (OEO): The organization created by the *Economic Opportunity Act* of 1964 to implement President Johnson's *War on Poverty.* Various programs originally within the organization included *Head Start, VISTA,* and the *Job Corps.* By 1969 much of the OEO had been dismantled and many of its programs transferred to other federal departments. The remaining part of the office became the *Community Services Program.*

Office of Human Development Services (OHDS): The organization within the U.S. *Department of Health and Human Services (HHS)* that oversees federally sponsored programs for delivering *personal social services.* Within this office are the *Administration for Children, Youth, and Families (ACYF)*, the *Administration for Native Americans,* and the *Administration on Aging.*

Office of Management and Budget (OMB): The office within the executive branch of the U.S. government that assists the president in preparing the federal budget and formulating the nation's fiscal program. OMB also helps the president administer the budget and determine if allocated funds are capable of achieving their goals. OMB keeps the president informed about how various government agencies' funds are being spent and helps in proposing legislation for congressional action.

Office of Personnel Management (OPM): The organization that administers most of the federal employment system. Its functions include recruiting, training, testing, promoting, firing, and laying off federal workers as well as maintaining criteria for employment, pay grades, and benefits. OPM was established by the Civil Service Reform Act of 1978, which transferred the functions of the Civil Service Commission to OPM and the *Merit Systems Protection Board.*

Office of Technology Assessment (OTA): The organization within the legislative branch of the U.S. government that provides Congress with information about both the beneficial and the adverse effects of technological change and helps Congress anticipate and plan for the uses of technology and policy alternatives. OTA compiles and publishes data on such subjects as the effectiveness of psychotherapy and professional interventions.

Office of Voluntary Action: See *ACTION.*

Old Age Assistance (OAA): The *public assistance* program for the needy elderly. Once the major form of *outdoor relief* in the United States, it was administered and mostly financed by the states, leading to a wide variation in benefits and in stringent residency and relatives' responsibility requirements. The *Social Security Act* of 1935 and its mandatory insurance program to protect retired workers reduced but did not eliminate the need for OAA. In 1972, the state OAA programs were consolidated, along with the *Aid to the Blind (AB)* and the *Aid to the Permanently and Totally Disabled (APTD)* programs, into the federal *Supplemental Security Income (SSI)* program for the needy aged, blind, and disabled.

Old Age, Survivors, Disability, and Health Insurance: See *OASDHI.*

Older Americans Act: The federal legislation (P.L. 89-73) enacted in 1965, with several subsequent amendments, that defined U.S. policy toward the aging and created the *Administration on Aging* to carry it out. The administration oversees state and city agencies that contract with private providers as well as directly offering homemaker services, transportation, socialization programs in senior citizens' centers, and legal aid services for the elderly.

Older Women's League (OWL): A national organization, founded in 1980, that provides a united voice on behalf of middle-aged and older women. Of particular concern are such issues as pension equity and social security provisions for women.

ombudsman: An individual appointed by a government or private agency to investigate reports and charges of illegal, unethical, or unfair practices by the people employed by that organization.

Omnibus Budget Reconciliation Act (OBRA): The 1981 federal legislation (P.L. 97-35) that amended *Title XX* of the *Social Security Act* and decentralized many social service programs, funding activities, and responsibility from the federal to the state governments, primarily through *block grants.*

oncology: The medical specialty that studies and treats cancer and tumors.

open adoption: Exchange of information and contact between birth parents and adoptive parents before, during, and after the adoption process and later through the adopted person's life. The degree of openness has many variations and can include the exchange of names, biographies, and medical records, or it can include face-to-face meetings and ongoing contacts. There is considerable controversy about the ultimate value or harm of this procedure.

open-ended group: In *social group work* and *group psychotherapy*, the type of group that permits the inclusion of new members to replace those who have left the group. Some social workers also use this term for group meetings that have no predetermined ending time.

open-ended questions: In social work interviews, as well as systematic opinion research, a form of questioning that permits the respondent to answer in any way he or she wants. This is in contrast to closed-ended questions (such as yes-no or multiple choice), which require the client simply to choose among the alternatives offered. For example, the social worker asks, "Why do you think it is difficult to get a job?" instead of "Is it difficult for you to get a job?" Both types of question are useful in social work interviews, depending on the goals of the working relationship. See also *questioning*.

open system: In *systems theories*, a system that accepts input from outside and is amenable to change based on different conditions in the environment. For example, an open family system is structured so that its members can become involved with outsiders, bringing them and their ideas into the family unit to effect some changes in the way the family interrelates.

operant conditioning: A type of learning, defined by B. F. Skinner, in which behaviors are strengthened or weakened by altering the consequences that follow them. Operant conditioning differs from Pavlovian or *respondent conditioning*, which has the effect of controlling antecedent rather than consequent conditions.

operant therapy: The use of operant conditioning as a form of treatment.

operational definition: In research, the specific delineation of the phenomenon to be studied in terms of how it will be measured.

Operation PUSH: People United to Save Humanity, the voluntary social activist and *civil rights* organization founded by the Reverend Jesse Jackson in 1976. Among its goals is helping the nation's schoolchildren be motivated toward academic excellence and against the use of drugs and nonproductive behaviors.

opinion survey: A systematic data-gathering technique used to determine what people at a given time in a given area think about a certain subject. A representative sample of the population being investigated is interviewed verbally or by means of structured and sometimes self-administered questionnaires. Opinion surveys of certain communities are often made by social activists, planners, and community organizers to understand and later influence the concerns, problems, and goals of the people.

opportunity costs: A social planning concept in which the value of the resources that must be expended to achieve a certain objective is weighed against the cost of alternatives that would have to be forgone to achieve that objective.

opportunity programs: Social welfare programs and organizations whose orientation is toward preparing client groups for greater access to the opportunities that exist for others. The goal of such programs is not necessarily to help clients "adjust" or gain insight but to acquire skills and resources. For example, the *Mobilization for Youth* program was oriented toward helping young people who were vulnerable to juvenile delinquency to learn social, economic, and vocational skills so they would have a better chance of entering the economic mainstream.

opportunity theory: The hypothesis that deviant behavior is more likely to occur among specific groups (for example, youths who are at risk for *juvenile delinquency*) when the opportunities to achieve socially acceptable goals are restricted and opportunities to behave in socially unacceptable ways are more available. The theory has been tested in such programs as New York's *Mobilization for Youth.*

oppression: The social act of placing severe restrictions on a group or institution. Typically, a government or political organization that is in power places these restrictions formally or covertly on oppressed groups so that they may be exploited and less able to compete with other social groups.

oral character: Also known as "oral personality," a descriptive term from *psychoanalytic theory* referring to an individual who tends to be overly dependent or greedy and demanding to be "filled up." This individual's satisfactions come largely through such activities as eating, smoking, drinking, and talking. Such a person is thought to be fixed at an early stage of personality development.

oral phase: The first stage in the *psychosexual development* of the personality, which occurs at ages up to 2. During this phase the infant seeks pleasure by stimulating the mouth and oral cavity and experiences the world through literal and psychic incorporation. According to *Freudian theory*, during this age the zone of sexual pleasure is the oral cavity, which explains the intense satisfaction the infant derives from nursing. Self-concept and feelings of personal worth are usually said to develop during this stage.

ordinal measurement: In research, a level of measurement that entails classifying observations into mutually exclusive categories that can also be ordered along some dimension, such as socio-economic status.

ordinal position: See *birth order theories.*

organic: Pertaining to the biological aspects of an individual. The term is used most commonly by social workers and other mental health professionals to distinguish diseases that are caused by physiological disorders from psycho-social (functional) problems.

organic mental disorders: Mental disturbances that are caused by permanent or temporary damage to the brain. The disorders may be related to the aging process, to the ingestion of toxic substances such as alcohol and other drugs, or to certain physiological dysfunctions. Among these disorders are the "organic brain syndromes," which include *delirium, dementia, amnesia,* organic delusions, organic hallucinations, organic affective syndrome, organic personality syndrome, and atypical or mixed organic brain syndrome.

organization: In social work and community development, the process of helping individuals and groups arrange their efforts, communication, and structure so that they will work together in a coordinated whole to achieve mutually beneficial goals.

organization development (OD): The administrative technique that draws on *systems theories* and human relations orientations to enhance the group members' ability to solve problems together, communicate more effectively, and achieve greater efficiencies in production by encouraging innovation and coordination. OD is both a long-term process and a management style. It uses a variety of techniques including *sensitivity groups, T-groups, feedback* systems, process consultation, and team building.

orgasmic impairment: The *sexual dysfunction* manifested by a woman's inability or difficulty in achieving orgasm. Primary orgasmic impairment occurs in those who never have orgasms. Secondary orgasmic impairment occurs in women who have been orgasmic in the past. The cause may be *psychogenic, organic,* or combinations of both. Psychiatrists no longer use this as a diagnostic label. See also *psychosexual disorders.*

orphanage: A term once used to refer to residential institutions for parentless or poor children. Such facilities have been and are being reduced or dismantled in favor of various *foster care* programs.

orthopsychiatry: An interdisciplinary field that emphasizes the development of mental health from early childhood on, prevention of mental illness, and the early (childhood) treatment of those who have mental disorders.

osteomyelitis: An infection of the bone marrow.

osteoporosis: A disorder of the bones associated with calcium deficiency and characterized by increasing porosity and brittleness and decreased density in the bone matter. The major *at-risk groups* are middle-aged and older women.

outcome evaluation: A process aimed at determining if a program is achieving its objectives and whether the results are due to the interventions provided. Outcome evaluations range from subjective judgments made by clients and staff to those that are rigorous experimental investigations.

outcome variables: In research, phenomena that are seen as the consequence of experimental manipulations or interventions.

outdoor relief: The form of welfare assistance that takes place outside *almshouses, orphanages,* and other residential facilities. Most forms of *public assistance* are of this type. See also *indoor relief.*

outpatient: One who receives treatment at a health care facility without being admitted for overnight stays or assigned a bed for continuous care.

outreach: The activities of social workers, especially in neighborhood-based agencies, to bring services and information about the availability of services to people in their homes or usual environments.

overbedding: The practice of building more hospital facilities than are needed in a given community. This contributes to increased charges for inpatient care costs, because the full beds have to carry the costs of the empty ones.

overcompensation: An individual's extreme efforts to counterbalance a real or imagined deficiency. When it originates in the *unconscious,* psychoanalytic theorists consider this to be a *defense mechanism.*

overloving: Intense emotional investment in another person, including the wish to control that person "for his or her own good." The term was coined by Sophie Freud, who pointed out that it is a feeling or state experienced as love, but because of its "runaway nature" it is also narcissistically motivated.

overprotectiveness: The tendency of some parents or parent surrogates to shelter their children excessively, through avoidance of situations they believe have potentials for psychological or physical harm. The result is that these children often do not learn to become sufficiently independent. Overprotection may also occur between marital partners or other family members.

overseers of the poor: People who in sixteenth- and seventeenth-century England and colonial America were appointed as public officials to help collect local taxes and use these funds to provide relief for the destitute and, primarily, jobs for the able-bodied unemployed. Overseers of the poor were established in the *Henrician Poor Law* of 1536 and served as local officials for the government and for churches. Some social welfare historians trace the evolution of the modern social work profession to the overseers of the poor.

overt behaviors: An individual's actions that are observable to others. Such actions are now described by behaviorists as "overt" to distinguish them from behaviors that are not observable but that can be recorded or registered by various instruments (electroencephalographs, blood pressure gauges, "lie detectors," and so forth).

overutilization: See *utilization review.*

ovulation: Release of a female reproductive cell, that is, the ovum or egg, into one of the two fallopian tubes. This takes place in women about 14 days, on the average, after *menstruation.*

P

PA: See *professional association.*

PACE: Political Action for Candidate Election, the political action committee of the *National Association of Social Workers (NASW).* The organization helps coordinate personnel and financial resources of interested membership to elect political officials. See also *ELAN.*

Pacific Islanders: Indigenous residents of and immigrants from the islands and islets in the Pacific Ocean, including those in the areas known as Polynesia, Melanesia, and Micronesia. In the United States, the term is most often applied to people from the U.S. Trust Territory of the Pacific Islands, including the Marshall and Marianas Islands, and from Guam and American Samoa.

palimony: An award, granted in a court of law, that is similar to *alimony,* and requires support payments to one partner in a couple that formerly lived together in a nonmarital relationship.

pandemic: A term applied to a social problem, disease, or mental disorder that is appearing on a broad scale throughout a specific large area (such as a city, a nation, a continent, the entire world).

paradoxical directive: In certain types of *family therapy,* an approach in which the social worker or other therapist tells the family members to continue their symptomatic behavior and sometimes to "improve on it." This makes them more aware of the existence of the behavior and the gains they derive from it and finally gives them more control over it.

paralinguistics: Nonverbal vocalizations accompanying speech that give additional meaning to communications and convey the speakers' emotions and cultural stances. Paralinguistics include tone of voice, tempo, pauses, loudness, sighs, laughs, clearing the throat, and so on. See also *communication theory.*

paranoia: A mental disorder whose most prominent characteristics are permanent and un-

shakable suspiciousness and persecutory *delusions,* but in which the individual is otherwise clear thinking. This disorder is classed as one of the *paranoid disorders* and is not to be confused with *schizophrenia* (paranoid type) or *paranoid personality disorder.*

paranoid disorders: A classification of mental disorders characterized by persistent persecutory *delusions* or delusional jealousy that are not the result of *schizophrenia* (paranoid type), *organic mental disorder,* or *personality disorder.* According to *DSM-III,* the types of paranoid disorder are *paranoia,* "Shared Paranoid Disorder" (delusions developed through a relationship with another person who has such delusions), "Acute Personality Disorder" (persecutory delusions that have occurred for less than six months), and "Atypical Paranoid Disorder."

paranoid ideation: An unfounded suspicion that one is under surveillance or is being followed, talked about, or persecuted. This behavior may be, but is not necessarily, symptomatic of several mental disorders, including *schizophrenia* (paranoid type), *paranoid disorders,* and paranoid *personality disorder.*

paranoid personality disorder: See *personality disorder.*

paranoid schizophrenia: See *schizophrenia.*

paraphilia: A *psychosexual disorder* in which unusual fantasies, bizarre acts, or the use of non-human objects are necessary for sexual arousal. The acts or fantasies may include repeated or fantasized sexual activity involving suffering, humiliation, and nonconsenting partners. Also referred to as "sexual deviations" and "perversions," paraphilias include fetishism (arousal through such objects as shoes, female undergarments, fur, or parts of the human body), transvestism (dressing in clothes of the opposite sex), zoophilia (sexual activity with animals), *pedophilia* (sexual activity with prepubertal children), exhibitionism (exposing the genitals to strangers), *voyeurism* ("Peeping Tomism"), sexual masochism (sexual arousal through being humiliated, beaten, or made to suffer), and sexual sadism (sexual arousal through inflicting psychological or physical suffering on another).

paraphilic coercive disorder: A *paraphilia* in which an individual derives erotic gratification primarily from imposing brute force or threats of violence on another or from watching them imposed. When the victim is compelled to participate in sexual activity, the term used is "paraphilic rapism"—that is, a sexual perversity in men who are aroused only when forcing others sexually.

paraphrasing: A technique used in social work interviews in which the worker expresses the idea of what the client has just said so that the relevant points are pulled together and emphasized. This helps clients clarify their own thoughts and assures them that the worker understood the message.

paraplegic: One who suffers motor or sensory paralysis of half the body, usually the lower half.

parapraxis: Informally known as a Freudian slip; an error in verbalization that, according to Freud, reveals what is in the subject's *unconscious.* For example, a client who fears that a social work investigator is going to reduce some welfare benefit refers to him or her as the "social worrier."

paraprofessional: An individual with specialized knowledge and technical training who works closely with and is supervised by a professional and who performs many of the tasks formerly carried out by the professional. Such people include paralegals, physician's assistants, and *social work associates.*

parens patriae: A legal doctrine that refers to the role of the state as guardian of people who are unable to care for themselves. The concept is most often used in courts in deciding to intervene in family matters, such as *custody of children,* divorce disputes, and removal of children to foster homes. Using this authority, the public at large is saying that a child is not the absolute property of a parent but a trust given to a parent by the state.

Parent Effectiveness Training (PET): An educational program designed by William Gordon to help parents learn to interact with their children more effectively.

Parents Anonymous (PA): A national *self-help organization,* with chapters in larger U.S. communities, whose members help one another restrain themselves from abusing their children. PA maintains hot lines and "buddy systems" and holds regular meetings, patterned partly on the *Alcoholics Anonymous (AA)* program.

Parents Without Partners (PWP): A national *self-help organization,* with chapters in most U.S. communities, most of whose members are divorced or widowed people raising children. PWP provides opportunities for its members to share their mutual concerns about child rearing and maintaining healthy social relationships. It sponsors discussion groups and educational and social activities that are comfortable and useful for the parents and the children.

Parish Poor Rate: An early system of national taxation to help pay for the needs of eligible poor people, which started in England in 1572. The system included a register of persons needing assistance and efforts to create jobs and social conditions to help reduce the incidence of poverty.

Parkinson's disease: A disease characterized by progressive motor disability and manifested by tremors or shaking, muscle stiffness, and poor coordination. The initial onset occurs most frequently among people between ages 50 and 65. Some patients become severely incapacitated but live long lives, and others may die within a few years as a result of complications.

parole: The release of a prisoner before completion of full sentence because of good conduct in prison, promised good conduct, and continued supervision by an officer of the legal system (often a social worker) once out of prison.

partialization: The social work process of temporarily considering a client's interconnected problems as separate entities so that work toward their solution can be more manageable. The process includes the development of priorities or distinguishing those problems or needs that demand immediate attention from those that can be postponed for a time.

participant modeling: A technique used in *behavior therapy* and *behavior modification,* in which the client directly observes the social worker or some other person interacting with a feared stimulus without being harmed. The client is then gradually encouraged to interact with the same stimulus without fear of harm.

participant observation: A technique in social science research in which the investigator systematically becomes as much as possible a member of the group being studied.

participative management: A decision-making strategy used by some social agency administrators involving all those who are likely to be affected by desired organizational change. This strategy includes building voluntary *consensus* and commitment among the organization's personnel, clientele, sponsors, and other interested groups in order to achieve organizational goals.

passive-aggressive: A term pertaining to the behavior of an individual who uses covert actions to fight another person or organization. The individual may feel angry but powerless in direct confrontations, so he or she becomes obstructionistic, obstinate, and inefficient and tends to pout and procrastinate. Because the anger is often unconscious, the reaction is also usually unconscious. When this behavior is deeply ingrained and persists through many different situations and life phases, it may indicate the presence of a *personality disorder.*

passive-dependent: A term pertaining to the behavior of an individual who tries to get others or one other person to assume all the relevant responsibilities in the individual's life. When deeply ingrained and persistent in many situations, the behavior may indicate the presence of *dependent personality disorder.*

passive resistance: A nonviolent form of social activism in which individuals or groups stop using or cooperating with the institutions to which they object. For example, in the late 1950s, when blacks in the South objected to the rule requiring them to sit in the back of buses, they banded together in refusing to ride the buses. Without direct confrontation, the movement passively but effectively resisted the objectionable policy.

passivity: A behavior pattern in which the individual seldom initiates action but submissively responds to forces in the environment.

paternalism: A principle of authority in which one person or institution manages the affairs of another. The term is often used disparagingly against social workers and social welfare organizations that try to help people solve their problems without the direct involvement of those being helped.

paternity suit: A legal proceeding to determine who is the father of a child born out of wedlock and to require him to contribute to the child's support.

path analysis: In social research, a statistical technique for analyzing the direct and indirect relationships between variables and representing them in a diagram.

pathology: The study of the nature of physical or mental diseases, including causes, symptoms, effects on the subject, and the circumstances in which the disease occurs. The term is also used more broadly in referring to physical or behavioral deviations from the norm that can or do result in disease or dysfunction. See also *psychopathology.*

patients: Those who are receiving the care and treatment of physicians and health care personnel. Social workers generally use the term *client* when referring to the individuals they are serving. However, the term "patient" is more commonly used by social workers who are employed in health care settings (for example, hospital and medical social workers).

patients' rights: The care and treatment that is legally, morally, and ethically due to *patients.* These rights include knowing what the health care alternatives are, who is providing the professional service, what the relevant research is, and the right to have visitors and communication outside the facility. The *American Civil Liberties Union (ACLU)* has delineated patients' legal rights. They include the right to (1) informed participation in all decisions involving one's health care; (2) privacy respecting the source of payment for treatment and care; (3) prompt attention, especially in emergency situations; (4) clear, concise explanation of all proposed procedures in understandable terms, including the risk of death or serious side effects, and not to be subjected to any procedure without voluntary, competent, and understanding consent; (5) clear, complete, and accurate evaluation of one's condition and prognosis before being asked to agree to any test or procedure; (6) access to all information contained in one's medical record while in the health care facility, and ability to examine the record on request; (7) refuse any particular drug, test, procedure, or treatment; and (8) leave the health care facility at will regardless of physical condition or financial status, although the patient may be requested to sign a release stating that he or she is leaving against the medical judgment of the doctor.

pauper: A term formerly used to refer to a poor person.

pay equity: The principle that people who do the same jobs should receive the same wages or salaries, regardless of sex, age, ethnic or racial backgrounds, or need. See also *comparable worth.*

payroll tax: A tax, levied on wages or salaries, that is paid by employers and usually designated for such programs as *unemployment compensation;* some economists also refer to this as an income tax. See also *earmarked taxes.*

PC: See *professional corporation.*

PCP: Phencyclidine, an illegal drug (except as an animal tranquilizer) that in low doses produces euphoria and numbness but in higher doses may produce delirium, convulsions, violent behavior, and changes in the users' perceptions of their bodies. Also known as *angel dust,* "lovely," and "loveboat," the drug can have severe and permanent effects.

Peace Corps: The federal program, established by President John F. Kennedy in 1961, that sends

American volunteers to underdeveloped countries for two years to provide training in over 300 skills, particularly in agriculture, natural resource development, science, and public administration. In 1971 the Peace Corps was placed under the new umbrella agency, *Action,* along with *Vista, Foster Grandparents,* and the Office of Voluntary Action.

Pearson's r correlation: Also known as the Pearson product moment correlation coefficient; a statistical measure of the strength of relationships between two variables (such as weight and height) that are measured at intervals.

pedophilia: A *paraphilia* involving the act or fantasy of sexual activity with a prepubertal child as the preferred way to achieve sexual excitement or gratification.

peer group: An association of people who have the same social status (for example, profession, occupation, age group, or sex).

peer pairing: A therapeutic technique used especially for socially isolated children and adults who might have difficulty relating to the social worker on a one-to-one basis or who cannot tolerate small groups. The therapist sees the client and another person who has similar characteristics (such as age, gender, or type of personality) together and treats both simultaneously. This model has been used most frequently in schools, residential facilities, hospitals, and clinics.

peer review: A formal evaluation by a relevant *peer group* of an individual's general competence or specific actions. In social work and other professions, the term refers to a formal process in which professional standards of intervention have been spelled out and practices are monitored by colleagues. For example, if a client or someone making a *third-party payment* (such as an insurance company) suspected some wrongdoing by a social worker and complained to the person's professional association or state licensing authority, a panel of fellow social workers could review the case to determine appropriate action.

peer review organization (PRO):   A formal and sometimes legally mandated association of people who are members of one profession, brought together to evaluate the work of other members of that profession in accomplishing a specific set of tasks or objectives. This is commonly done by reviewing the professional's case records to determine if the type of treatment plan, methods, and outcome are commensurate with the organization's objectives and the client's needs. The U.S. federal government has required the establishment of PROs in hospitals and nursing homes that receive federal funds to oversee the administration of the *DRG* (diagnostic related groups) system.

pellagra: A disease that results from a dietary deficiency of niacin; its symptoms include inflammation of the skin and mucous membranes and gastrointestinal disturbances.

penology: The study of prison and reformatory management, crime prevention, and the rehabilitation of criminals and *delinquents.*

pension: A payment made regularly to an individual because of retirement, age, loss, or incapacitating injury or to dependents in the event of the beneficiary's death. *Social security* benefits as well as retirement income provided by employers are generally considered to be forms of pensions.

People-to-People Committee for the Handicapped: A voluntary organization that provides information to families of handicapped people about available services and self-help activities. The committee publishes the *Directory of Organizations Interested in the Handicapped,* which contains an extensive listing of organizations that give information about treatments, training, equipment, and techniques used to help the handicapped.

perception: The psychic impressions made by the five senses (seeing, hearing, smelling, tasting, and touch) and the way these impressions are interpreted cognitively and emotionally, based on one's life experiences.

perceptual distortion: Incongruity between a physical reality and the way it is perceived, understood, or interpreted cognitively by the individual.

performance budgeting: A plan used by administrators to allocate resources based on predicted or observed results rather than on costs of maintaining existing structures.

period prevalence: See *epidemiology.*

permanency planning: In *child welfare* work, a systematic effort to provide long-term continuity in dependent children's care as an alternative to temporary foster placements. This might be done by facilitating adoptions, by establishing clear guidelines for remaining in foster care, or by helping the children's natural families become capable of meeting the children's needs.

permissiveness: A high degree of tolerance by those in control for the behavior of an individual or group. Permissiveness is seen in parents who allow their children to behave in ways that others might not find acceptable. It is also seen in *laissez-faire* societies, in which the government authorities exercise relatively little control or enforcement of laws or norms regulating public behavior.

personality disorders: Patterns of relating to and understanding others that are so maladaptive, inflexible, and deeply ingrained that they produce significant social impairment. Personality disorders are usually recognizable in one's adolescence. In *DSM-III* they are *Axis II disorders.* There are 12 major types of personality disorder: They are *paranoid, schizoid, schizotypal, histrionic, narcissistic, antisocial, borderline, avoidant, dependent, compulsive, passive-aggressive,* and the atypical personality disorders.

personal social services: Those social services whose basic purpose is to enhance the relationships between people and between people and their environments and to provide opportunities for social fulfillment. Personal social services are distinguished from institutional services (*income maintenance* programs, *health care,* education, employment, and housing) and include counseling and guidance, developing mutual aid and *self-help groups, family planning,* and services for the aging and for children. Sheila Kamerman (*Social Work,* 28 [Jan.–Feb., 1983], p. 9) describes them as helping services that do not involve the provision of money, health care, education, or housing.

person-in-environment perspective: Among social workers and other professionals, an orientation that views the client as part of an environmental system. This perspective encompasses the reciprocal relationships and other influences between an individual, relevant others, and the physical and social environment.

person-situation configuration: The concept used in *social casework* pertaining to the threefold interrelationship consisting of the person with the problem, the situation in which the problem exists, and the interaction between them. The interaction is influenced by internal conflicts or reactions (stress) and environmental pressures (press).

person-oriented record: A format used by some social workers and some social agencies to keep specific, accountable, and goal-directed records of the intervention process with each client. An adaptation of the physician's *problem-oriented record (POR),* the person-oriented record contains an initial database, treatment plan, assessment, progress notes, and the progress review (to evaluate a client's progress over a specified time such as every 6 or 12 weeks).

persons in need of supervision (PINS): The legal designation used in some states for *status offenders,* such as runaway children, truants, or juveniles whose parents are unable to manage them properly. In some jurisdictions these same people are known as CHINS (children in need of supervision) or JINS (juveniles in need of supervision).

PERT: Program Evaluation Review Technique, a procedure commonly used in organiza-

tional management to relate goals to means in a rational and systematic way. It looks at program objectives and indicates all the activities that need to be performed, the time required for each, the sequence in which they should take place, and the resources required. This may be charted and posted so that all personnel are informed.

pertussis: A highly communicable infectious disease, popularly known as whooping cough, occurring predominantly in young children. The victim develops respiratory difficulty and eventually begins coughing rapidly. This causes the child to gasp for air, during which a high-pitched, whooping sound occurs. In the United States, pertussis has been controlled to a great extent by immunization during infancy.

perversion: See *paraphilia.*

petit mal seizures: See *seizure disorders.*

phallic stage: The third stage in the psychosexual development of the personality, according to *Freudian theory,* which occurs approximately between 3 and 6. During this phase the child's zone of pleasure centers in the genitalia. The *Oedipus complex* is a culmination of this phase, during which the healthy child works through rivalry with the parent of the opposite sex so that a loving relationship can exist with both parents and self-esteem can develop in the child.

phenylketonuria (PKU): A genetically transmitted metabolic disorder in which the victim's body fails to produce enzymes needed to break down certain natural amino acids. PKU may be characterized by mental retardation and neurological and skin disturbances.

philanthropy: A term derived from the Greek meaning "love of mankind"; it has come to refer to practical efforts to promote the public welfare by donating funds or resources to worthy causes. Philanthropic activity, especially in the secular community, was rather spontaneous and haphazard until the late nineteenth century. The field of social work was born, in part, as an effort to make these activities more systematic and effective in their raising and distribution of funds.

phobia: An intense and persistent fear, not based on actual danger or threat, of an object or situation. Psychosocial theorists think this is caused by *displacement* of an *unconscious* conflict onto an external object, where it will be presumably more tolerable and avoidable. Behavioral theorists think it is a consequence of a chain of associations of various negative stimuli. Phobias are the main symptom of *phobic disorders* (phobic neuroses). There are theoretically an infinite number of identifiable phobias. Some common ones are *agoraphobia* (fear of leaving familiar environments), acrophobia (fear of heights), claustrophobia (enclosed areas), nyctophobia (darkness), xenophobia (strangers), and zoophobia (animals).

phobic disorder: Also called phobic neurosis, an *anxiety disorder* in which anxiety is the predominant disturbance. The essential feature is a persistent and irrational fear of a specific object or situation resulting in serious attempts to avoid it. The three types of phobic disorder are *agoraphobia* (fear of leaving familiar environments), *social phobia* (fear of situations involving public scrutiny), and *simple phobia* (fear of some specific object or situation, such as animals or heights).

Piagetian theory: A theory of *cognitive development* proposed by the Swiss psychologist Jean Piaget (1896–1980) to explain the processes by which humans come to perceive, organize knowledge, solve problems, and understand the world. According to this theory, human cognitive development is the product of consistent, reliable patterns or plans of interaction with the environment, known as *schemes*. Schemes are goal-oriented strategies that help the person achieve some intended result. These schemes are sensorimotor (occurring in infancy and early childhood, in which reflexes and motor responses are prevalent) and cognitive (based on experience and on mental images, reflecting the person's ability to develop the use of abstract reasoning and symbolism). Two processes in cognitive development are *assimilation* (the way new information, events, and methods of problem solving are integrated into existing schemes) and *accommodation* (changes in existing schemes that occur through interaction with the environment and learning from experience). Piaget delineated four stages of cognitive development: the *sensorimotor, preoperational, concrete operations,* and *formal operations stages.*

PINS: See *persons in need of supervision (PINS).*

placater role: A recurrent pattern of communication one assumes in relating to others, characterized by talking in an ingratiating way, apologizing, avoiding disagreements, and by attempting repeatedly to gain the approval of the relevant other person. This role was delineated by Virginia Satir (*Peoplemaking,* Palo Alto, Calif.: Science and Behavior Books, 1972, p. 63), who described this person as a "yes-man" who feels worthless without the approval of others. Other roles are the *blamer role,* the *computer role,* and the *distracter role.*

placebo: An inert preparation that is made to appear identical to or presented to patients as an active drug. When used in *double-blind* research, the investigator tests the effectiveness of a drug by giving it to half the subjects and the placebo to the others. Sometimes placebos are also given to patients who apparently do not need an active drug but do seek the attention or *secondary gain* that comes from using one. A physical effect based on an individual's belief that the inactive substance is working is referred to as a "placebo effect."

placement: The assignment to or location of an individual in a setting that is suitable to achieve a specified purpose. Social workers use the term mostly to indicate the assignment of a child or dependent adult to a facility or persons who can provide for their needs. The term also refers to the social work student's assignment to a social agency for practice in field work.

planned parenthood: A social movement advocating population control and reproductive restraint. The term is also used as a synonym for contraception or *birth control.* See also *family planning.*

planning: The process of specifying future objectives, evaluating the means for achieving them, and making deliberate choices about appropriate courses of action. Neil Gilbert and Harry Specht (*Planning for Social Welfare,* Englewood Cliffs, N.J.: Prentice-Hall, 1977) indicate that this process of choice involves two aspects. There is rational decision making, which seeks to examine all relevant alternatives and select from among them, and there is incremental decision making, which encompasses a more limited range of alternatives and practical considerations. See also *social planning* and *social policy.*

play therapy: A form of psychotherapy used by social workers and other professionals to facilitate communication. The client uses toys to act out conflicts or to demonstrate situations that cannot be verbalized. Play therapy is most commonly used in work with children but is also effective and useful with adults in certain circumstances.

plea bargaining: Negotiation between a prosecuting attorney and a person accused of a crime (and his or her defense counsel), resulting in a disposition of the case. Typically, the accused agrees to plead guilty to a lesser charge and forgoes a jury trial. The advantage to the accused is that the case is resolved sooner and at less risk of serious penalty. The advantages to the public are that court dockets are less backlogged and cases can be resolved with less cost.

pleasure principle: A principle in *Freudian theory* stating that the individual begins life seeking only gratification and pleasure and the avoidance of pain and discomfort. The developing child eventually learns that immediate gratification sometimes has to be subordinated, so the *reality principle* starts to emerge. Thereafter the person faces a lifelong conflict between both. The healthy *ego* tries to adhere to the reality principle while allowing some room for the pleasure principle.

Plessy v. Ferguson: The 1896 Supreme Court decision upholding a state law permitting segregation of the races in public transportation. The ruling, which was extended to segregation in other public places, held that segregation was permissible under the Constitution as long as "separate but equal" facilities existed. The ruling was not reversed until the 1954 Supreme Court decision in *Brown v. Board of Education.*

pluralism: The view that there is more than one type of reality; also, the acceptance of the divergent cultural, racial, ethnic, and religious styles and identities of various groups in a society.

pluralistic society: A society composed of people of many different racial, ethnic, religious, and cultural characteristics.

PMS: See *premenstrual syndrome (PMS).*

point prevalence: See *epidemiology.*

polarization: A phenomenon in which two or more objects, individuals, or groups develop opposing or contrasting tendencies. In social activism and *community organization,* the term is used to indicate the process by which an organization's members split into opposing camps over an issue or policy, possibly leading to a stalemate in the organization's decision-making capacity. However, polarization can also lead to the revitalization of an organization. A skilled social worker can point out or emphasize differences among the factions to encourage the formation of more intense rivalries, greater involvement, and stronger coalitions. Each of the rival groups often achieves better coordination and in-group loyalties and thus is better equipped to achieve the original goals. Using this phenomenon requires intense effort and highly skilled professional intervention.

police social work: Professional social work practice within police precinct houses, courthouses, and jail settings to provide a variety of social services to victims of crimes, people accused of crimes, and their families. Some of these workers counsel police officers and members of their families under job-related stresses. They sometimes act as advocates and public relations specialists for police departments and help in *mediation* with various community groups. A major activity is helping resolve domestic troubles in which the police are called. Some police social workers are civilians, and others are police officers as well as professional social workers.

policy: The explicit or implicit standing plan that an organization or government uses as a context for making its decisions. This plan is the totality of the principles, positions, legislation, regulations, political platforms, social norms, and guidelines that are relevant to the organization and the people it serves. See also *social welfare policy.*

policy analysis: Systematic evaluations of a policy and the process by which it was formulated. Those who conduct such analyses consider whether the process and result were rational, clear, explicit, equitable, legal, politically feasible, compatible with social values, cost-effective, and superior to all the alternatives, in the short term and in the long run.

policy decision-making theories: Explanations for the sociopolitical influences and considerations that are translated into specific policies and laws. L. D. Mann and others have identified five models that are used to explain how policy decisions are made. They are the "traditional model" (public-spirited citizens form planning groups, hire a planner, make rational decisions, and propose fair plans); "power pyramid model" (a few business leaders influence politicians and impose decisions on those lower in the social structure); "Yale polyarchic power model" (different issues each have different leadership patterns); "qualified diffused influence model" (influence is spread among many interest groups that change in size and importance over time); "decision process model" (the systems approach that sees decision making as a flow in which final decisions are the result of a series of interactions between various systems that have an interest in the decision. (C. S. Prigmore and C. R. Atherton, *Social Welfare Policy,* Lexington, Mass.: D. C. Heath & Co., 1979, pp. 193–194.)

policy statement: A formal and accessible explication of the policies that guide an organization or any of its relevant aspects.

poliomyelitis: A contagious viral disease that can cause nerve damage resulting in permanent paralysis of affected muscles; formerly known as infantile paralysis. Polio, as it is more commonly called, has been largely controlled in the United States by preventive vaccines administered to young children.

political action: Coordinated efforts to influence legislation, election of candidates, and social causes. Social workers engage in political action by running for elective office, organizing campaigns in support of other candidates or issues, fundraising, and mobilizing voters and public opinion. According to Maryann Mahaffey and John W. Hanks, eds. (*Practical Politics: Social Work and Political Responsibility,* Silver Spring, Md.: National Association of Social Workers, 1982), political action also includes lobbying, testifying before legislative committees, and monitoring the work of officeholders and government workers. Social workers are also involved in political action through their professional association's two political action units, *PACE* and *ELAN*.

political activism: Engaging in activities that influence the decisions and viewpoints of elected officials or their appointees, civil servants, and the electorate. Such activities include *voter registration drives,* social *consciousness-raising,* fundraising to help finance legislators' campaigns, lobbying, running for political office, engaging in *media campaigning,* and helping to monitor elections to assure their fairness.

polygamy: Plural marriage; a social custom that permits having more than one wife or husband at the same time. If the marriage involves one husband with more than one wife, it is also referred to as "polygyny." If it involves one woman with more than one husband, the term is "polyandry." "Polygamy" is not synonymous with "bigamy." "Bigamy" refers to an illegal act of marriage without having obtained a divorce from the previous spouse. Polygamy is legal in some societies.

poorhouse: A form of *indoor relief* funded by government organizations or by private charities in which needy people are provided with temporary or permanent residential care; an *almshouse.*

poor law: A generic term technically referring to any government statute pertaining to the economic and social care of and control of the poor or measures to reduce the extent of poverty. However, the term is primarily used to refer to a group of repressive statutes in colonial America and in England before the twentieth century. These laws established *almshouses, indoor relief,* and concepts about the *unworthy poor* and were generally conceived to discourage people from seeking relief. See also *Elizabethan Poor Law, Henrician Poor Law, Statute of Labourers,* and *Poor Law of 1834.*

Poor Law of 1834:   The English legislation enacted in 1834 to revise the *Elizabethan Poor Laws* of 1601. The new law was punitive and based on the premise that the poor lacked strong or moral character. The laws discontinued *public assistance* for all able-bodied citizens except those in public institutions and imposed the *less-eligibility principle* so that no beneficiary would receive as much as the lowest wage earner. The program was taken from local authorities and administered nationally. The principles of the Poor Law of 1834 had a significant influence on public welfare policy in the United States for over a century.

population: The total number of persons in a nation or other specified geographic region; also, the number of people of a specified class or group (such as women, Catholics, blacks, the handicapped, and so on) in a specified place or geographic region. In social research, the term refers to all people or cases that could theoretically be available for an investigation. It is from the population that a *sample* is taken for research. See also *universe.*

populism: A political orientation in which the interests of wage earners, farmers, and less affluent families take precedence over those of business and professional groups.

POR: See *problem-oriented record (POR).*

positive connotation: A therapy technique, used especially in family systems orientations, in which the social worker ascribes positive motives to a client's behavior in order to promote family cohesion and greater willingness to work together.

positive reinforcement: Strengthening a desired behavior or response by presenting a reinforcing stimulus contingent on performance of the response. The reinforcer may be a desired object, a privilege, verbal approval, or any other stimulus that strengthens the response.

positive transference: *Transference* that results in expressions of affection, love, erotic desire, or feelings of warmth and closeness that a client may have for a psychotherapist or other person.

postpartum depression: Feelings of sadness experienced by some new mothers in the first few weeks or months after giving birth. The symptoms are thought to be related to hormonal changes and other physiological and psychological adjustments.

postplacement contact: Follow-up activity by a social worker who, or social agency that, has facilitated a new *placement* for a client to ensure that the needs of the placed individual and the new caregiver are being met. The activity normally includes telephoning or personally visiting the client and the caregiver in the new setting. Usually such contacts are prearranged, but in certain circumstances they take place without prior notice. Postplacement contact is most often done in *foster care* for children, *nursing home* care for the elderly, and *halfway houses* for people who were incarcerated or institutionalized because of illness, handicap, or criminal behavior.

posttraumatic stress disorder: A psychological reaction to experiencing an event that is outside the range of usual human experience. Stressful events of this type include accidents, natural disasters, military combat, rape, and assault. Stresses that are not unusual to people, such as marital problems, bereavement, and illness, are excluded from this class of disorders. Individuals may react to these events by having difficulty concentrating, feeling emotionally blunted or numb, being hyperalert and jumpy, and having painful memories, nightmares, and sleep disturbances.

poverty: The state of being poor or deficient in money or means of subsistence.

poverty line: A measure of the amount of money a government or a society believes is necessary for a person to live at a minimum level of subsistence or standard of living. The first measure of this type was issued by the United States in 1968. It has since been revised regularly in proportion to changes in the *cost-of-living index.* The original poverty line was calculated by a formula that multiplied the cost of a subsistence food budget by a factor of three.

power group: Members of a community who, because of their social status and positions, influence the decisions made on behalf of the community and who have greatest access to resources. Power group members usually include political leaders, financial and industrial executives, clergy, and local indigenous leaders.

power of attorney: A written notarized statement in which one person appoints another as his or her agent and grants that person the authority to act in specified situations. The power of attorney is used to establish the agent's authority to another party. It is most commonly used to authorize the agent to sell property or handle other legal matters when the principal is unable to do so.

PPBS: Program Planning and Budgeting Systems, an administrative analysis procedure used in federal government agencies and departments as well as other large organizations. PPBS relates costs to outputs (goods, services, and other products) rather than to inputs (labor, capital, and interest on debt). The procedure specifies objectives and measures progress in achieved end products, including amounts and distributions.

PPOs: See *preferred provider organizations (PPOs).*

practical nurse (PN): A *paraprofessional* specialist in the care of people who are ill. Practical nurses complete training programs that last one year or more, after which they carry out important but less technical nursing duties such as administering medication, monitoring tests, and feeding and cleaning the patients. Those who are licensed in the state to provide such services are known as LPNs (licensed practical nurses). See also *registered nurse (RN).*

practice theory: A grouping of concepts that systematically pulls together what is known about physical and psychological behavior and social systems and their interaction, the relevant values and goals to be achieved, and the specific techniques and skills available to permit purposeful action.

"practice wisdom": A term often used by social workers to describe the accumulation of information, assumptions, ideologies, and judgments that have seemed practically useful in fulfilling the expectations of the job. Practice wisdom is often equated with "common sense" and may or may not be validated when subjected to empirical or systematic analysis.

practicum: Part of the professional education of students, in which they apply the knowledge and skills acquired primarily through classroom assignments to direct practice with clients. In social work education this occurs primarily in *field placement* assignments in which students work, under close professional supervision, with clients in actual social agencies or other social service settings.

precipitating cause: An event or change that seems to result in an individual's disorder or problem; the "last straw" that led the person to seek the social worker's help.

preconscious: A term pertaining to thoughts, images, and perceptions that are not in one's immediate awareness but that can be recalled with relative ease.

predictor variable: In social research, a systematically measured performance, rating, or score that is used to estimate the likelihood that an individual can accomplish a subsequent objective. For example, many schools of social work require student applicants to take academic aptitude tests. The resulting scores are predictor variables to indicate the likelihood of a student's success in the program.

preferred provider organizations (PPOs): Affiliations of professionals, often in private practice, who fulfill contracts to receive *third-party payments.* PPO members agree to provide professional services to members of a designated group at a favorable fee-for-service rate, and the third party agrees to channel members of its group to the PPO. See also *independent practice associations (IPAs).*

pregenital: In *psychoanalytic* concepts, the *oral* and *anal phases* of personality development and the manifestations of those stages that recur in later life.

pregnancy: The reproductive state of carrying a fetus within the body; that is, the time between *conception* and birth. Human pregnancy is normally a process lasting about 280 days, during which rapid changes in the development of the fetus occur in the mother's uterus. Determining the existence of pregnancy may be based on observation of certain symptoms. Physicians use three distinct categories of pregnancy criteria. The presumptive symptoms of pregnancy include failure to experience the anticipated menstrual period, nausea or vomiting (often called morning sickness), fatigue and need for excessive sleep, frequent urination, alteration of skin pigmentation around the nipples, and softening of the cervix. Probable symptoms of pregnancy include positive results of laboratory tests for pregnancy (urine sampling for the presence of a specific level of the hormone called chorionic gonadotropin), abdominal enlargement, and uterine changes. Positive signs of pregnancy include fetal heartbeat, fetal movements within the uterus, and the presence of a fetal skeleton as shown by x ray. It is important to determine the existence of pregnancy fairly soon after conception and to determine the relative health of the fetus. See also *amniocentesis* and *chorionic villi sampling (CVS)*.

prejudice: An opinion about an individual, group, or phenomenon that is developed without proof or systematic evidence. This prejudgment may be favorable but is more often unfavorable and may become institutionalized in the form of a society's laws or customs.

premature birth: The birth of a baby significantly before completion of the normal *gestation* period or a baby with very low body weight (usually under 4 pounds).

premenstrual dysphoric disorder: The term some psychiatrists use in their diagnostic nomenclature to refer to *premenstrual syndrome (PMS)*.

premenstrual syndrome (PMS): Feelings of discomfort and related personality fluctuations that affect some women during the several days of their menstrual cycles immediately prior to *menstruation*. Some medical researchers indicate that hormone secretions peak during these days and hypothesize that this may influence the feelings and behaviors of some, but not all, women. Other professionals discount this hypothesis, and some discount the existence of PMS entirely.

prenatal: Prior to birth.

prenuptial agreement: A contract entered into by two people who plan to marry, delineating the rights and obligations of each in the event of divorce, annulment, or death.

preoperational stage: The second stage of development described in *Piagetian theory*, lasting from about age 2 to 7. During this time the child begins to use symbols and some reasoning ability but still cannot group objects and must deal with each thing individually.

prescribing the symptom: A technique, used by social workers and other professionals engaged in family therapy, in which the therapist uses

paradoxical directive to tell one or more members of a family to continue their symptomatic behavior under specified circumstances. For example, the therapist might tell certain family members to pout every Tuesday. This helps them realize the existence of the symptom and that it is under their voluntary control.

prescription, medical: A physician's written order to a pharmacist or patient describing the type and amount of drug or other treatment to be used, the duration of use, and other special directions. Physicians often use some of the following abbreviations in writing prescriptions: ad lib. (as needed); a.c. (before meals); b.i.d. (twice a day); dieb. alt. (every other day); o.d. (every day); p.c. (after meals); q.h. (every hour); q.2h (every two hours); q.3h (every three hours); t.i.d. (three times a day); q.i.d. (four times a day); q.s. (as much as needed); stat. (immediately); and p.r.n. (when needed).

presenting problem: The perceived symptoms, overt issues, or difficulties the client believes to constitute the problem and for which help is sought. Because the social worker recognizes that the problem may be due to underlying causes or that there can be inaccuracies in the way the problem is understood by the client, consideration of the presenting problem is only the beginning of the assessment phase.

pretest: A preliminary test, such as a *questionnaire*, administered to a few people similar to those who will be evaluated. A research procedure, its purpose is to identify any problems, confusing questions, or other errors before going through the entire research process.

prevalence rate: A measure of the number of cases of some problem or disease that exists in a given population during a specified time period. See also *incidence rate* and *epidemiology*.

prevention: Actions taken by social workers and others to minimize and eliminate those social, psychological, or other conditions known to cause or contribute to physical and emotional illness and sometimes socioeconomic problems. This includes establishing those conditions in society that enhance the opportunities for individuals, families, and communities to achieve positive fulfillment. See also *primary prevention, secondary prevention*, and *tertiary prevention*.

preventive health programs: Activities in the public and private sectors to ensure that people remain in good health and are protected from disease. The U.S. *Public Health Service*, state and local health departments, as well as private health and welfare organizations and *foundations* are the primary coordinators of these programs in the United States. The activities include *vaccination* against disease, instruction in hygiene, enforcing standards of sanitation, and research into the causes and cures of diseases.

price controls: Government regulations that limit the amount of increase or decrease in the prices consumers are charged for goods and services. The purpose is to control inflation and increase employment. This policy is often accompanied by *wage controls.*

price discrimination: Charging different people different prices for the same goods or services. See also *means test* and *sliding fee scale.*

price supports: *Price controls* in which a government maintains prices at a specified level regardless of the costs of production or the amount people would pay on the open market. Governments usually do this by giving direct financial assistance to producers of the goods or services or by purchasing them at a set price. See also *subsidy.*

primal therapy: A form of psychotherapy based on intense *catharsis.* The therapist may encourage *regression* in clients by focusing on early childhood experiences to the extent that the client expresses primitive (primal) emotions through such dramatic means as loud, prolonged screaming.

primary gain: Direct relief from *anxiety* achieved by using a *defense mechanism.* See also *secondary gain.*

primary group: People who are in intimate and frequent face-to-face contact with one another, have norms in common, and share mutually enduring and extensive influences.

primary prevention: Actions taken to keep conditions known to result in disease or social problems from occurring. For example, a community's development of sanitation facilities, recreation centers, and parks helps prevent stress-related disorders and diseases. Social welfare efforts in primary prevention include the development of social insurance programs and settlement house activities that help socialize and educate people so they can avoid problems and enhance their opportunities. See also *prevention, secondary prevention,* and *tertiary prevention.*

primary process thinking: Disorganized and irrational thoughts expressed without reference to the individual's external world. Psychoanalytic theorists believe that such expressions represent thoughts from the deepest parts of the psyche and include unconscious thoughts that haven't been screened or "processed" by the *ego.* Such expressions are sometimes seen in psychotic patients and in some people who speak while asleep.

private practice: In social work, the process in which the values, knowledge, and skills of social work, acquired through sufficient education and experience, are used to deliver social services autonomously to clients in exchange for mutually agreed payment. According to Robert L. Barker (*Social Work in Private Practice,* New York: National Association of Social Workers, 1984, pp. 20–31), ten norms apply to private social work practitioners: the private practitioner (1) has the client (rather than an agency or organization) as the primary obligation; (2) determines who the client will be; (3) determines the techniques to be used; (4) determines practice professionally rather than bureaucratically; (5) receives a fee for service directly from or on behalf of the client; (6) has sufficient education as a social worker; (7) is sufficiently experienced; (8) adheres to social work values and standards; (9) is licensed or certified to engage in private practice if the jurisdiction has such regulations; and (10) is professionally responsible.

private social agencies: *Nonprofit organizations* that provide *personal social services,* mostly to members of targeted population groups (such as residents of a certain neighborhood or those of a certain religious affiliation, ethnic group, age category, or interest group), and are funded by voluntary and philanthropic contributions and money from government grants. Those organizations are generally incorporated and have elected board members who represent the community and establish policy. Organizations that provide such services for profit are called *proprietary agencies.*

privatization: The tendency in some societies to rely on or encourage the private sector to meet the social needs of the people. In the United States this tendency is seen in the reliance on private health, educational, and social institutions and entrepreneurs to provide services. In social work this tendency is seen in the growth of social service provision through private, for-profit corporations, partnerships, *private practice,* and *proprietary social services.*

privileged communication: The premise and understanding between a professional person and client that the information revealed by the client will not be divulged to others without express permission. In fact, the laws and judicial interpretations in each state are not always consistent or clear about this premise. Courts in most states have honored privileged communication for social workers and other professional groups, except when there is a risk of public danger or a threat to the public good.

PRO: See *peer review organization (PRO).*

probability sampling: In social research, the systematic selection of cases in a way that allows the researcher to calculate the likelihood, or level of probability, that any given case would be selected from the population. This makes it possible to estimate the degree to which the sample is likely to represent the population. See also *random sample.*

probation: A specified time during which an individual is to demonstrate possession of certain abilities or qualifications. In the *corrections* field, probation is a status in which *incarceration* is suspended on the condition that the subject fulfills certain requirements. These requirements often include periodic visits to a court-designated probation officer, who may be a social worker.

problem-oriented record (POR): A format used by physicians, social workers, nurses, and other professionals to develop and maintain efficient case records. Developed by Dr. Lawrence Weed, originally as the problem-oriented medical record, it has been applied in multidisciplinary contexts and adapted for the needs of many different professions. The record contains four components: the database (face-sheet information; *presenting problem;* relevant demographic, cultural, and medical data; addresses and mailing lists, and so on); the problem list (each problem has a number, so that when it is resolved it is convenient to see and check off); the plan (different possible steps to take in resolving each of the numbered problems); and the follow-up action (what has actually been done to implement the plan). The POR is highly focused on specific problems and their progress and resolution and thus makes the professional more easily accountable than do less focused, chronological summaries. See also *process recording* and *SOAP charting method.*

problem-solving casework: A form of *social casework,* developed primarily by Helen Harris Perlman, that draws on concepts in *ego psychology, role theory,* and, implicitly, on a consolidation of the *diagnostic school in social work* and the *functional school in social work* (Perlman, *Casework: A Problem-Solving Process,* Chicago: University of Chicago Press, 1957). Among the most important practice methods this model stresses are clear delineation of the goals of the casework intervention, focused and time-limited intervention, and concern for the environmental and social forces that influence and are influenced by the client.

process recording: A method of writing about the worker-client interactions during the intervention process. The case record using this format begins with *face sheet* factual data about the client and relevant social, environmental, economic, and physical factors. Then it briefly describes the *presenting problem* and includes documenting data about the problem. The worker then includes a statement of goals, obstacles to reaching the goals, means to reaching them, and —where applicable—a written contract signed by both worker and client. The record then contains entries for each contact the client makes with the worker or agency, including telephone calls and messages from other family members. The entry is headed by the date and time of the visit or contact and a summary of the factual information obtained as well as any subjective impressions the worker has developed. These entries are not as elaborate as in verbatim records but are more chronologically stated than in *problem-oriented records (POR)* or *person-oriented records.* Because of recent legislation, court rulings, and ethical principles, workers are often advised to prepare their records so they are accessible to other workers, clients, peer reviewers, or providers of *third-party payments.* This is in order to protect the clients' rights during emergencies, when the worker is inaccessible, or in cases of *quality assurance* evaluations and *peer review.*

prochoice movement: Organized efforts to influence public opinion, legislation, judicial interpretations, and legal enforcement and to gain financial support and medical access that are considered necessary for permitting *abortion.* The name of this movement came about primarily as a response to the name used by those who were fighting against abortion, known as the "prolife movement." The prochoice movement advocates education and opportunities for pregnant women to choose abortion, *adoption,* or keeping their babies.

prodromal phase: See *schizophrenia.*

profession: A system of values, skills, techniques, knowledge, and beliefs a group of people holds in common and uses to meet a specific social need. The public comes to identify this group as being suited to fulfill the specific need and often gives it formal and legal recognition, through licensing or other sanctions, as the legitimate source for providing the relevant service. The group enhances its public credibility by expanding its body of knowledge, making the knowledge accessible to its members, refining its skills and values, ensuring that its members comply with its established standards, and making public the actions it takes to reach these goals.

professional association (PA): The designation used after their names by some individuals and groups who provide professional services to indicate their legal status as corporations (for example, "Jane Doe, MSW, PA"). See also *professional corporation* (PC).

professional corporation (PC): A corporation or legal association formed to practice a profession. The professional or professional group that is incorporated has the letters PC or PA after the names and degrees. Members of the corporation are shareholders, and all are members of the profession being practiced. Professional corporations have allowed professionals certain tax advantages not available to individuals and permits professionals to join together without assuming personal liability for the practices of other members.

professionalism: The degree to which an individual possesses and utilizes the knowledge, skills, and qualifications of a profession and adheres to its values and ethics when serving the client.

Professional Standards Review Organizations: See *PSROs.*

Program Evaluation and Review Technique: See *PERT.*

Program Planning Budgeting System: See *PPBS.*

Progressive Era: The name given by historians to the period (roughly from 1890 to 1915) in the United States when social reformers and advocates for socioeconomic justice were effectively demanding changes. The reformers and *muckrakers* sought and achieved changes in corrupt political practices at the local and national levels, established *settlement houses* in many poor neighborhoods, enacted laws for occupational and consumer safety, and influenced enactment of social welfare laws and programs for children, women, and the disadvantaged.

progressive tax: A government's revenue collecting system in which those in a higher income bracket pay a higher percentage (as well as a higher amount of money) in taxes than do those in lower income brackets. For example, a person with a taxable income of $20,000 would pay 10 percent of that amount in taxes, and a person with a taxable income of $100,000 would pay 30 percent of that amount in taxes. See also *regressive tax.*

prognosis: The social worker's or other professional's prediction of the likely course, direction, and outcome of the problem that is being addressed.

projection: A *defense mechanism* in which unacceptable aspects of one's own personality are rejected or attributed to another person or entity, for example, the corporation, the state, the school, or a parent.

projective identification: A process whereby an individual uses *projection* onto another member of his or her family, group, or organization and then induces that person or the others to behave in accordance with the projected attitudes.

projective test: A procedure that uses systematic but unstructured *stimulus* objects or situations designed to elicit the subject's way of perceiving and understanding the world. The premise is that the subject will project unconscious thoughts onto the stimulus object and reveal possible psychopathology. Major projective tests are the *Rorschach test* and the Thematic Apperception Test (in which the subject is shown a series of vague pictures and tells a story for each). Certain forms of *play therapy* are also considered to be types of projective tests.

prolife movement: See *right to life movement.*

proprietary practice: In social work, the delivery of social services for profit, generally in nonclinical settings by self-employed professionals. The term "proprietary practice" is essentially synonymous with *private practice,* except that the latter is usually used for clinical practice. Proprietary practice social workers typically provide their own facilities and offer these facilities and their own professional skills in such capacities as private consultants, organizers of special interest groups, and caretakers for specific client groups. Some develop private profit-making institutions for clients who require physical care along with special social services (for example, a private facility for adolescent substance abusers).

proprietary social agencies: Organizations or facilities that are usually owned or staffed by social workers and other professionals and that are intended to make a profit by providing a specified type of social service. These agencies provide essentially the same services as traditional nonprofit agencies, except that the charges to the recipient or recipient's agent may be higher. Examples of such organizations are private *halfway houses,* residential and educational facilities, camps, inpatient mental health facilities, training centers, research institutes, consultation services, and social action and community organization programs.

proprietary social services: The use of the knowledge, training, skills, values, ethics, and methods of professional social work in order to make a profit for providing social services. See also *privatization.*

prosocial behavior: Actions an individual, organization, or society takes to benefit society without the anticipation of external reward. What is considered to be of social benefit is relative and based on one's cultural values.

prostitution: The illegal act of offering oneself for sexual contact with another in exchange for money or other benefits.

protective custody: The *placement* of an individual by the legal authorities in a facility to keep him or her from the danger of harm by others or from self-inflicted injury.

protective services: Interventions by social workers and other professionals on behalf of individuals—such as children, the handicapped, the aged, and retarded people—who may be in danger of harm from others or who are unable to take care of their own physical needs. The workers are usually employed by the local department of social services or a similar agency or may work with the courts or law enforcement agencies. The primary job is to investigate situations in which a person may be at risk (as in child abuse or neglect of a handicapped person), to help ameliorate the situation, to minimize further risk, and to find and facilitate alternative placements and resources for the person at risk.

Protestant ethic: A value and behavioral orientation that is generally associated with hard work, self-discipline, deferred gratification, and the belief that such efforts will result in rewards, possibly including more money, higher social status, greater freedom, and eventual entry into heaven. This orientation derives its name from the moral teachings of such Protestant leaders as Calvin, Luther, and Wesley and has guided the conduct of many middle-class American families since colonial times.

provider: The term used by *third-party payment* organizations (health insurers, government agencies, and so on) in referring to the professionals and institutions that have served the client and to which reimbursement is made. See also *vendor.*

provision systems: The interacting social organizations that supply the products and services that people need, want, and demand; also, the network of social relationships that, together or individually, identify the kinds of products and services needed and demanded, develop the necessary natural and social resources, distribute those resources, and evaluate the effects. In different societies these systems may have a competitive, self-interested orientation or an egalitarian, cooperative orientation.

proxemics: Spatial behavior; the study of the way humans influence one another through the use of space. This includes such factors as the distance people need between one another for various types of communication and the arrangement of their furniture, homes, and streets to facilitate certain kinds of communications. See also *communication theory, sociofugal arrangements,* and *sociopetal arrangements.*

pseudomutuality: A facade of harmony among members of a family, group, or organization when the members are actually antagonistic. According to the *family therapy* approach, pseudomutuality may result in serious internal conflict within individual members.

PSROs: Professional Standards Review Organizations; a federally mandated program that requires those professions and service-providing organizations such as hospitals, nursing homes, and residential care facilities, which receive *third-party payments* from federal and state treasuries, to have their work evaluated by objective overseers. The program permits local review organizations to be set up by professional groups and associations of provider organizations if they follow specified federal guidelines. These organizations periodically review case records, medical charts, and other documents to determine if procedures are being carried out competently, efficiently, and cost-effectively.

psychiatric emergency: Sudden or unexpected behavior in a person that indicates symptoms of mental disorder requiring immediate action by a *psychiatrist* or members of a *mental health team.* The most common behaviors that result in psychiatric emergencies include *suicide* attempts or threats, active *hallucinations* that seem threatening, *fugue states,* drug-induced harmful behavior, and precipitous deterioration of the mental faculties. Sometimes this deterioration is related to the misuse or discontinuance of prescribed *psychotropic drugs.*

psychiatric labels: Descriptive or diagnostic terms applied to people by *psychiatrists,* physicians, or mental health professionals to characterize a person's psychiatric processes. They may be formal diagnostic terms such as those used in *DSM-III* (such as *bipolar disorder* or *conversion disorder*) or less formal characterizations (such as *hysteric,* "phobic," or "drug addict"). Critics of psychiatric labels say their use is inaccurate and dehumanizes people, precludes the principle of *individualization,* oversimplifies problems, and minimizes the impact of the psychosocial and environmental systems in which they take place. Proponents of psychiatric labeling say it is necessary for efficient communication between helping professionals and important for the conduct of research.

psychiatric social work: Social work in a mental health setting. The psychiatric social worker provides *psychotherapy* and other social services for those with mental disorders and, in collaboration with the psychiatrist and other members of the *mental health team,* works with the patient's family members. The worker usually has an MSW or higher degree and additional experience in working with psychiatric problems. Because the social work profession is emphasizing the common elements of its various specialties, psychiatric social work is not so distinct an entity as it formerly was. See also *American Association of Psychiatric Social Workers (AAPSW).*

psychiatrist: A physician who specializes in the treatment of mental disorders. The psychiatrist makes specific diagnoses of the mental disorder and prescribes, supervises, or directly provides the necessary treatment, which may include *psychotherapy, psychotropic drugs,* hospitalization with *milieu therapy,* and other medical treatments. Qualifications to be a psychiatrist include four years of medical school and four or more years of approved residency training, usually in mental hospitals or hospital psychiatric wards.

psychoactive drugs: Drugs that induce changes in the user's mood, cognitive ability, or perceptions. They include both *psychotropic drugs* (those prescribed by physicians to help their patients achieve psychological or emotional changes) and many *illicit drugs* or *controlled substances* (those used illegally by abusers to induce perceptual distortions, mood and activity level changes, euphoria, and similar mental experiences).

psychoanalyst: A professional person who uses the theories of *psychosexual development* and personality structure as well as the special *psychotherapy* techniques originated by Sigmund Freud (1856–1939) and his followers. Most psychoanalysts in the United States are psychiatrists, but the specialty also includes social workers and other mental health professionals who have qualified through advanced psychoanalytic training and personal psychoanalysis. Typically, psychoanalysts see their patients for 45 or 50 minutes, four or five times weekly, for an indefinite period, sometimes lasting several years. The client often reclines on a couch and verbalizes through *free association.* The psychoanalyst interprets the patient's dreams and the expressions of emotions related to *drives, unconscious* motives, and unhealthy use of *defense mechanisms.*

psychoanalytic theory: The hypotheses and treatment applications about human personality and its development as proposed by Sigmund Freud, with later elaborations and modifications by many theorists and analysts such as Carl Jung, Alfred Adler, Otto Rank, Wilhelm Stekl, Melanie Klein, Ernest Jones, and others. Most of the concepts now recognized as psychoanalytical are from *Freudian theory* (that is, the *pleasure principle,* the *reality principle,* the *libido,* the *unconscious,* the *id,* the *ego,* the *superego,* and *psychosexual development theory*). Concepts that were emphasized by other analysts include *defense mechanisms* (Anna Freud), *object relations* (H. V. Dicks), *inferiority complex* (Adler), collective unconscious and archetypes (Jung), will theory (Rank), *psychosocial development* (Erikson), *separation-individuation* (Mahler), and parataxic distortion (Harry Stack Sullivan). Psychoanalytic theory, and especially its progeny *ego psychology* and *neo-Freudian theory,* has been very influential in the theories of *clinical social work* and *social casework,* particularly in the *diagnostic school in social work,* and especially between 1940 and 1965.

psychodrama: A technique used primarily in certain forms of *group therapy* in which clients perform roles, often playing the parts of themselves in various socially stressful situations and sometimes playing the parts of their antagonists. This gives them the opportunity to act out their inner feelings to relieve anxiety, to practice handling situations better, and to experience the situation from another person's viewpoint. The other group members or psychodrama participants play roles, too, which gives everyone a chance to relate to one another from different perspectives.

psychodynamic: Pertaining to the cognitive, emotional, and volitional mental processes that consciously and unconsciously motivate one's behavior. These processes are the product of the interplay between one's genetic and biological heritage, the sociocultural milieu, past and current realities, perceptual abilities and distortions, and one's unique experiences and memories.

psychogenic: A term pertaining to a disorder or condition that originates in an individual's mind or psyche rather than in the body's physiological mechanisms. The term is generally used as the antonym for *organic.*

psycholinguistics: The study of language, communication, and metacommunication as they are affected by psychosocial factors. See also *communication theory.*

psychologist: One who studies behavior and mental processes and may apply that knowledge to the evaluation and treatment of mental disorders. Psychologists have many specialties, including experimental, educational, counseling, industrial, and clinical orientations. Clinical psychologists are those who apply the knowledge about human behavior to the treatment of various psychosocial disorders, usually in offices, hospitals, or mental health settings. To become a clinical psychologist a person must obtain an academic degree in psychology, either a master's degree or a Ph.D. or Psy.D. degree from an accredited academic institution. This is usually followed by a requirement of two years' supervised work experience.

psychoneurosis: A synonym for neurosis or *anxiety disorder.* In the nineteenth century, Freud and other neurological researchers needed to distinguish between disorders that were apparently caused by physical problems and those that seemed to come from the psyche. The term "psychoneurosis" was coined to refer to nervous symptoms of a psychological origin, whereas "neurosis" was used for somatic neurological problems. See also *neurosis.*

psychopath: An imprecise lay term for one who has a mental disease. The word is derived from the word "psychopathology," the study of psychological pathology or disease, and was once used by mental health professionals to refer to a person with a diagnosis of *antisocial personality* disorder.

psychopathic personality: See *antisocial personality.*

psychopathology: The study of the nature of mental, cognitive, or behavioral disorders, including causes, symptoms, effects on the subject and the psychosocial circumstances in which the dysfunction occurs. The term is also used in referring to personality or behavioral traits that may lead to problems or underachievement for the individual or for those in contact with the individual. Virtually every mental or behavioral disorder that is diagnosable by psychiatrists or any social relationship problem that prevents an individual from reaching his or her potential for well-being can be considered pathological.

psychopharmacology: The study and use of drugs to bring about changes in behavior and personality. See also *psychotropic drugs.*

psychosexual development theory: The concepts derived from *psychoanalytic theory* and *Freudian theory,* which describe the process by which much of the individual's personality is formed. According to this theory, the individual is motivated by innate drives and instincts toward pleasure and immediate gratification. As the individual matures, there is a transformation through various stages of development. These stages are the *oral phase* (up to age 2), *anal phase* (ages 2–3), and the *phallic* or oedipal (ages 3–7). These are followed by a *latency phase* (from age 7 to puberty) and the *genital phase* (adolescence). If the individual resolves the conflicts inherent in each of these stages, the mature adult is relatively free of psychic pathology. If not, then adult *intrapsychic* conflict, *fixation,* and potentially serious emotional problems may result.

psychosexual disorder: Disturbances of human sexuality that are partly or totally *psychogenic.* The specific types of disorder include *gender identity* disorders (including *transsexualism*), *paraphilia* (including *pedophilia* and *exhibitionism*), and *psychosexual dysfunctions.* The degree to which these disorders are *psychogenic* or *biogenic (organic)* is still being debated. See also *sexual disorder.*

psychosexual dysfunction: One type of *psychosexual disorder,* whose most prominent feature is inhibition in one or more parts of the complete sexual response cycle. Specific psychosexual dys-

functions include inhibited sexual desire, inhibited sexual excitement, inhibited female orgasm, inhibited male orgasm, premature ejaculation, functional *dyspareunia, functional vaginismus,* and *ego dystonic* homosexuality.

psychosis: A group of serious and frequently incapacitating mental disorders that may be of *organic* or psychological origin and are characterized by some or all of the following symptoms: impaired thinking and reasoning ability, perceptual distortions, inappropriate emotional responses, inappropriate affect, regressive behavior, reduced impulse control, impaired reality testing, *ideas of reference, hallucinations,* and *delusions.* See also *schizophrenia* and *organic mental disorders.*

psychosocial assessment: The social worker's summary judgment as to the problem to be solved; also referred to as the "psychosocial diagnosis." This description may include diagnostic labels (such as *DSM-III* terms and codes), *International Classification of Diseases (ICD)* terms, results derived from psychological tests and legal status, brief descriptive expressions of the problem configuration, a description of existing assets and resources, the prognosis or prediction of the outcome, and the plan designed to resolve the problem. Throughout the intervention process the psychosocial assessment is a "work in progress," in that it is revised continually as new information is acquired, as circumstances and goals change, and as progress toward goals is made.

psychosocial crisis: The concept that individuals go through predictable phases or stages of development both mentally and socially throughout their lives and that each stage presents unique circumstances and challenges that the person must meet in order to make healthy developmental progress. The crisis occurs when the individual has had little prior experience in meeting the demands of the new stage and may become conflicted and less effective until the necessary social and psychological adjustments are made.

psychosocial development theory: The concepts delineated by Erik Erikson and others to describe the various stages, life tasks, and challenges that every person experiences throughout the life cycle. The phases and life tasks, defined elsewhere in this dictionary, are *trust versus mistrust, autonomy versus shame and doubt, initiative versus guilt, industry versus inferiority, identity versus role confusion, intimacy versus isolation, generativity versus stagnation,* and *integrity versus despair.* Some other psychosocial theorists describe different ages and life tasks.

psychosocial diagnosis: See *diagnosis* and *psychosocial assessment.*

psychosocial study: The social worker's process of acquiring the relevant information needed to decide on and develop a rational plan for helping the *client* (an individual, family, group, or community). This information may include the client's description of the problem, corroboration from other sources (such as medical records, school and personnel files, letters, telephone communication, and direct meetings with the client's family members and others who know the client), psychosocial history taking, information about the client's cultural and subcultural groups, information about the specific environment in which the client lives, and information about the various resources that might be used to help the client. The information obtained in the psychosocial study is used in arriving at the *psychosocial assessment.*

psychosocial therapy: A *relationship* that occurs between a professional and an individual, family, group, or community for the purpose of helping the *client* overcome specific emotional or social problems and achieve specified goals for well-being. Psychosocial therapy is a form of *psychotherapy* that emphasizes the interface between the client and the client's environment. The psychosocial therapist tends to focus on interpersonal and social relationship problems in addition to intrapsychic concerns. According to Francis J. Turner (*Psychosocial Therapy: A Social Work Perspective,* New York: Free Press, 1978, p. 5), psychosocial therapy also seeks to mobilize available resources or create needed ones and combine them with individual, group, and familial relationships to help persons modify their behaviors, personalities, or situations. This is done in order to help attain satisfying, fulfilling functioning within the framework of one's values and goals and the available resources of society.

psychosomatic: Pertaining to the interrelationship of the mind and body; usually the term refers to an individual's symptoms that appear to be physical but are partly or fully the result of psychological factors.

psychotherapist: A mental health professional who practices *psychotherapy.* The major disciplines whose members practice psychotherapy include *social work,* psychiatry, and clinical psychology. Some members of other professions are also psychotherapists, including *nurse practitioners,* physicians, *family therapy* specialists, clergy, guidance counselors, and educators. The legal qualifications for use of this title vary from state to state.

psychotherapy: A specialized, formal interaction between a social worker or other mental health professional and a *client* (an individual, couple, family, or group) in which a therapeutic relationship is established to help resolve symptoms of mental disorder, psychosocial stress, relationship problems, and difficulties in coping in the social environment. Some specific types of psychotherapy are *psychoanalysis, family therapy, group psychotherapy, supportive treatment, gestalt therapy, experiential therapy, primal therapy, transactional analysis (TA), psychosocial therapy, psychodrama,* and *cognitive therapy.* Recent surveys show more than 200 identifiable and distinct types of intervention and theoretical schools in mental health.

psychotic: Characteristic of a *psychosis.*

psychotropic drugs: Drugs used by psychiatrists and other physicians to help their patients achieve psychological or emotional changes. These drugs include the antidepressants (such as Elavil, Norpramin, Pertofrane, Sinequan, Aventyl, Vivactil, and others), the antianxiety drugs (such as Valium, Librium, Tranxene, Ativan, Serax, and various barbiturates), antipsychotic drugs (such as Thorazine, Haldol, Compazine, Selazine, Navane, Mellaril, Serentil, Trilafon, Prolixin, and others) and drugs that control manic behavior (lithium carbonate—that is, Eskalith, Lithane, or Lithonate).

PTP: *Procedural Terminology for Psychiatrists,* a systematic listing and coding of procedures and services performed by psychiatrists on behalf of their patients. PTP is a part of the physician's *CPT (Current Procedural Terminology).* Services of nonphysicians are not included in the PTP codes and should not be used to report services of nonphysicians.

puberty: The period of biological development in which the reproductive capacity of the male or female is established.

puberty rites: Formal or informal socially institutionalized behaviors applied to or required of youngsters to mark their newly established biological reproductive capability. In some cultures these behaviors are formal and ceremonial, such as requiring the youngster to start wearing "adult" clothing or to spend the night alone in the forest. Many puberty rites exist in the United States today, but they are informal and vary greatly among subcultural groups. Examples include beginning to wear makeup, smoke, drink, drive, or have sexual intercourse.

public assistance: A government's provision of minimum financial aid to persons who have no other means of supporting themselves. Funds come from the general revenues of the federal and state governments and not from any social insurance funds such as OASDHI. Some public assistance programs are administered at the federal level, including *Supplemental Security Income (SSI)* payments, which cover the *Old Age Assistance (OAA), Aid to the Blind (AB),* and *Aid to the Permanently and Totally Disabled (APTD)* programs. Other public assistance programs are administered by states and localities with the help of federal funding. These include *Aid to Families with Dependent Children (AFDC)* and *general assistance* for those ineligible for any other *categorical assistance* programs.

public defender: An attorney for persons who are accused of crimes or require legal services but are unable to pay for their own counsel. Public defender systems exist in most states largely as a result of the Supreme Court's ruling in *Gideon v. Wainwright* that indigent defendants must be furnished with legal representation.

public health: A system of programs, policies, and health care personnel whose goal is to prevent disease, prolong life, and promote better health. Efforts to achieve these goals are made through such public health measures as sanitation, control of communicable diseases, educating people about personal hygiene, organizing medical and nursing services for early diagnosis and prevention of disease, and developing health care facilities and access to these facilities. Public health programs are administered by many different federal, state, and local agencies.

Public Health Service: The federal organization, established in 1870 and now within the U.S. *Department of Health and Human Services (HHS)*, to initiate and coordinate the nation's effort to maintain and improve the health and health care of its people. The service is involved in sanitation and education, *primary prevention,* setting and enforcing standards for food and drug processing and handling, investigating imported organic products, controlling epidemics, and overseeing and conducting health research. Within the Public Health Service are the *Centers for Disease Control,* the *Food and Drug Administration (FDA),* the *Health Resources Administration (HRA),* the *Health Services Administration (HSA),* the *National Institutes of Health (NIH), and the Alcohol, Drug Abuse and Mental Health Administration (ADAMHA).*

public housing: Residential facilities that are built, maintained, and administered by a local or federal government to provide low-rent or no-rent homes for needy people. Most of these programs are under the authority of the U.S. *Department of Housing and Urban Development (HUD)* and local housing authorities. "Public housing" is a term that could theoretically apply to many additional federally subsidized programs designed to help people obtain residences, such as the Rent Supplement Program, Lower Income Housing Assistance, Rural Housing Loans, Farm Labor Housing Loans and Grants, and the Indian Housing Improvement Program, as well as the FHA (Federal Housing Administration) homeowners' loans and the *Veterans Administration (VA)* home loan programs.

public welfare: The relative well-being of a society and its people as manifested by a nation's policy of providing for the protection and fulfillment of its citizens. To most people this term is now also a synonym for *social welfare* and *public assistance.*

Public Works Administration (PWA): The *New Deal* program, established in 1935, to stimulate depressed industries and cope with the unemployment of their former workers by contracting with private organizations to build public facilities such as parks, recreation centers, post offices, and government buildings.

pulmonary disorders: A group of diseases associated with decreased ability to inhale oxygen into the lungs and expel carbon dioxide. Such disorders include bronchial asthma, emphysema, pneumonia, chronic obstructive pulmonary disease (COPD), and acute respiratory distress syndrome. These conditions have varying causes, including smoking, injury to the respiratory system, and obstructions of the airways.

punishment: (1) A penalty imposed for misbehavior (for example, a parent spanking, isolating, or withdrawing privileges from a child) or illegal acts (for example, *incarceration*); (2) in *behavior modification,* the presentation of an unpleasant or undesired event following a behavior, the consequence of which is that there is decreased probability that the behavior will be repeated.

purchase-of-service agreements: A fiscal arrangement between two or more social agencies or between an agency and a government body, usually involving a contract between an agency with funds and another that can provide needed services. Purchaser agencies are thus able to extend services to their clientele, and provider agencies can increase their budgets, extend their services, and in many cases increase their profits.

Puritanism: The system of values and beliefs that was prominent in the seventeenth century, characterized by severe penalties for nonconforming behavior, strict discipline, and controls on what was considered immoral. Much of the Puritan philosophy was implicit in the English *Poor Laws* and was imported into colonial America.

purposeful expression of feelings: One of the fundamental elements of the social worker–client *relationship,* in which the worker encourages the client to communicate certain emotions. The client is helped to express those emotions that may be debilitating when not communicated. The worker encourages purposeful expression of feelings by listening, asking relevant questions, listening intently to answers, and avoiding any behavior that seems intolerant or judgmental.

Q

q-sort technique: A tool used in social research, in which subjects are given a series of statements, each of which is written on a separate card, and asked to sort them into various piles to indicate the degree to which they apply to the subject.

quadriplegic: One who suffers paralysis of the body's four limbs or paralysis from the neck down.

qualitative research: Systematic investigations that include inductive, in-depth, nonquantitative studies of individuals, groups, organizations, or communities.

quality assurance: The measures an organization takes to determine that its products or services measure up to the standards established for them. This may be done by having supervisors, peers, consumer advocates, or legally designated overseers inspect the work, review the description of the work, or evaluate the system for producing the work. Products or services that fail to meet standards may be rejected, procedures for their completion may be revised, and sanctions can be brought against the provider. The quality assurance measures used for social workers include the following: sufficient education from accredited schools of social work, entry-level work experience under qualified supervision, licensing and certification, competency examinations, and continuing education requirements; for the professions measures include a professional *code of ethics* that is accessible to the public, *peer review,* utilization review, program evaluations, professional sanctions, civil malpractice suits, and criminal negligence charges. This term is synonymous with "quality control."

quality assurance programs in social work: Those measures taken by the social work profession to determine and demonstrate that its practitioners meet the standards that have been made explicit. According to Claudia J. Coulton (*Social Work Quality Assurance Programs: A Comparative Analysis,* New York: National Association of Social Workers, 1979, pp. 2–3), these programs contain one or more of the following components: a patient or client information system (which tends to record physical and social characteristics of the client, problems or goals, and services received and outcomes); a *peer review* system (which evaluates the worker's initial contact, assessment, formulation of goals, actual intervention, and termination and outcomes); and various systems for assuring that social work coverage is available.

quality circles: In organizational management, a procedure in which a small number of employee volunteers, usually 6 to 12 people from the same work area, meet regularly to discuss positive ways to solve problems. The organization usually provides advance training in decision making for these volunteers, but they have no direct decision-making power. Quality circles are considered effective alternatives to the anonymous "suggestion box" method of gaining new insights from the employees' perspective. This approach has been developed and used more in Japan and other nations than in the United States and in large industries more than in human service agencies.

quality control: See *quality assurance.*

quantitative research: Systematic investigations that include descriptive or inferential statistical analysis. Examples are experiments, survey research, and investigations that make use of numerical comparisons.

questioning: A primary tool in the social work interview, the procedure in which the worker systematically requests from the *client* information, feedback, and emotional expression. The worker's questioning process gives focus and direction to the client and to the *working relationship* and is a medium through which the client develops self-understanding and learns new skills and insights. Questioning takes many forms, depending on the immediate and long-term goals of the interview.

questions, closed-ended: *Questioning* designed to encourage the client to reveal specific information concisely and factually, without opinion, embellishment, or detail. Such questions are usually posed by the social worker to keep the client from digressing, evading, or providing irrelevant information when interview time is limited. Such questions are frequently answered yes or no or with one-word responses. Examples of closed-ended questions are: "Did you go to school every day this week?" and "When did you lose your job?"

questions, direct: *Questioning* that compels the client to address a certain topic, often one that the client may wish to avoid or minimize. Direct questions may be closed-ended ("Did you drink any liquor this week?") or open-ended ("How do you think you are affected by alcohol?").

questions, indirect: *Questioning* that helps the client feel less pressured and bombarded and permits him or her not to respond if desired and to have more flexibility about how to respond. An example is when a worker comments to a client, "It must be difficult to have to work all day and then take care of the kids all night."

questions, open-ended: *Questioning* designed to encourage the client to provide subjective impressions and more detailed factual data in whatever manner the client wishes to express them. An example of an open-ended question is: "What are your thoughts about that?"

questionnaire: A set of written questions seeking specific facts or subjective opinions on a given subject, used by social work interviewers and researchers to guide and systematize the information being gathered. Questionnaires may be so highly structured that they can be self-administered by the client, who merely gives yes-no responses. Or they can be relatively unstructured, consisting of a list of subjects that remind the investigator to ask relevant questions.

quorum: The minimum number of members required to be at a meeting before it can conduct its official business.

quota system: An organizational plan, social policy, or legal doctrine that specifies how many, or what proportion of, people of an identified status will be included in an identified group. The system may be designed to exclude people (as in some past U.S. immigration laws that permitted a higher number of Europeans than Africans or Asians to enter the country) or include people (as in some *affirmative action programs*). For example, a city may decide that half its police officers should be black to reflect the population and overcome past discriminatory policies, so it mandates that efforts will be made to reach the 50-50 quota).

R

racism: Stereotyping and generalizing about people, usually negatively, because of their race; commonly a basis of *discrimination* against members of racial minority groups.

radical social work: The ideology among some social workers that the most effective way to achieve goals of *equality* and solutions to social problems is to eliminate or make major changes in existing institutions. Radical social work includes techniques for peaceably bringing about these changes, including *passive resistance, demonstrations,* strikes, and political and social activism.

random sample: A group of subjects or cases systematically taken from a *population* so that each one is as likely to have been selected as every other one. In this way the resulting sample will be a valid representation of the population from which the cases were selected.

randomization: In social research, the assignment of subjects to groups on a nondirected basis.

rape: The criminal act of forcing a nonconsenting person to engage in some form of sexual contact. The force may take the form of violent assault or real or implied threat. The victim may be a man or boy but much more frequently is a woman or girl, and the perpetrator is almost always a man.

rapport: In social work interviews, the state of harmony, compatibility, and empathy that permits mutual understanding and a working *relationship* between the client and the worker.

rapprochement: The fourth subphase in the *separation-individuation* process of human development proposed by Margaret Mahler, which lasts from about the age of 18 months to 2 years. If *fixation* or deviation occurs during this phase, according to Mahler, it is likely to lead to *borderline* or narcissistic disturbances in later life.

ratio: A mathematical relationship of one number to another, found by dividing one of the numbers into the other. For example, if an agency has 10 social workers and 500 clients, there are 50 clients for every social worker, or a 50 to 1 ratio. In social agency management, ratios are frequently used, as in the ratio of assets to liabilities, revenue to expenses, and salaries to total budget. When the base number (for example, the total agency budget) is expressed as 100, the ratio is expressed as a percentage (for example, 80 percent of the total agency budget goes for salaries).

measurement: In research, a level of measurement that includes the properties of *nominal, ordinal,* and *interval measurement* but also has the property of true zero.

rational casework: A type of *clinical social work* intervention, based on the concepts of *cognitive theory* and delineated especially by Harold D. Werner. This approach concentrates on the client's rational thinking processes.

rational-emotive therapy: A psychotherapeutic method based on *cognitive theory* and the ideas of psychologist Albert Ellis, in which the client is encouraged to make distinctions between what is objective fact in the environment and the inaccurate, negative, and self-limiting interpretations made of one's own behavior and life.

rationalization: Presenting in logical terms, or interpreting the reasons for, some action or event; also, a *defense mechanism* in which a person explains or justifies an action or thought to make it acceptable when it is unacceptable at a deeper psychological level.

reaching out: Activities by the social worker to gain the trust or motivation of fearful, unmotivated, or *hard-to-reach clients.* Such activities might include tangible gifts (a cup of coffee or a piece of candy), a concrete service (cutting through some red tape with another agency), or special favors (extending the length of a session, telephoning the client between meetings, and so on).

reaction formation: A *defense mechanism,* deriving from *psychodynamic* theory, in which the person behaves or thinks in ways, or assumes values, that are the opposite of the original unconscious trait. Thus, a social worker who has an unconscious dislike for children might specialize in working with them, advocating more stringent legal measures against child abuse.

reality principle: A principle in *Freudian theory* stating that the young child soon comes to learn that the satisfaction of immediate impulses must be reconciled with the often competing demands of the environment. Thus, the *ego* finds ways to compromise between the demands of the environment and the internal drives that are related to the *pleasure principle.*

reality testing: One's relative ability to judge and evaluate the external world and to distinguish between it and the ideas and values that exist in one's mind.

reality therapy: A form of psychosocial and behavioral intervention, developed by Dr. William Glasser, in which the client is helped to develop a success-identity based on love and worth. Reality therapists focus on the client's behavior rather than feelings and on the present and future rather than the past. They encourage responsible behavior and the working out of alternative solutions to problems. They don't accept client excuses, don't offer sympathy, rarely ask "why," and place little emphasis on taking case histories. Positive results have been reported with the use of reality therapy in institutional settings in particular, and it has also been used extensively in individual and group work with people labeled as chronic schizophrenics and with delinquents.

reapportionment: The political process of changing the boundaries of a legislative district or the number of representatives to which a district is entitled. See also *gerrymandering.*

reassurance: In social work interviews, the expression by the worker of positive belief in the client and in the client's activities and motivations to improve the situation.

recertification: The *quality assurance* measure in which experienced professionals are required to demonstrate that they have maintained their ability to provide competent services. Once the professional shows that the ability remains, a formal declaration that the requirements have been fulfilled is used. This is often done by compelling professionals to pass examinations at designated times during their careers, to take a specified number of qualified training and retraining programs or units of continuing education, or to demonstrate continued practice competence to peers.

recession: A socioeconomic condition characterized by lowered business activity, higher un-

employment, and reduced purchasing power. Recession is considered a milder or shorter version of economic *depression.* See also *stagflation.*

recidivism rate: The number of people, in a specified time period, who return to an institution relative to the population of that institution. For example, a mental hospital with a 50 percent annual recidivism rate would see half its discharged patients return within a year.

recidivist: An individual who relapses or returns to a former condition or tendency; also, one who returns to an institution because of a recurrence of the behaviors or conditions that led to the original placement.

reciprocal inhibition: A technique used in *behavior modification* in which suppression of an undesired *response* or behavior is accomplished by associating it with a dominant antagonistic response. For example, in *systematic desensitization,* relaxation responses are paired with anxiety responses until the anxiety is inhibited. The technique was developed by Joseph Wolpe.

reciprocal interactions: Mutual responsiveness. For example, the behavior of one person to another leads to a behavior by the other, leading to a behavior of the first, and so on.

reciprocity: A mutual exchange or interchangeability in which privileges granted to one are returned by the other. The term is used by many professions that have state licensing to regulate their practice. For them, reciprocity refers to agreements made between certain states to permit the professional license holder in one state to practice in the other and vice versa without having to undergo that state's examinations or meet its other requirements.

reclassification: Formal and official changes made by an employer organization in the job descriptions, educational requirements, and personnel standards of its current and potential employees. Social workers in public agencies have been particularly affected by such actions, which have included reducing educational requirements for entry-level jobs, equating formal education with experience, and using non-BSWs and non-MSWs to perform tasks once reserved for them. Organization leaders sometimes say they use reclassification to streamline their operations and reduce expenditures. See also *declassification.*

reconstituted family: Also referred to as a "remarried family," a family unit comprising a legally married husband and wife, one or both of whom has a child or children from a previous marriage or relationship. See also *stepfamily.*

recording: In social work, the process of putting in writing and keeping on file relevant information about the client; the problem; the prognosis; the intervention plan; the progress of treatment; the social, economic, and health factors that contribute to the situation; and the procedures for termination or referral. There are many different types of recording, depending on the agency's requirements, the worker's style, and the type of intervention. These may include the narrative summary, the *psychosocial assessment,* the *behavioral assessment,* the *problem-oriented record (POR),* and the *SOAP charting method.*

Recovery, Inc.: The national *self-help organization,* with chapters in most larger communities, whose members meet regularly to help one another recover from emotional problems or the effects of mental illness.

recurrent expenditures: The amount an organization, such as a social agency, must pay out on a regular basis, including salaries, costs of expendable supplies, interest on loans, and so on.

Red Cross: The international organization and federation of over 100 autonomous national societies concerned with the alleviation of human suffering and the promotion of public health and civil rights. The emblem of the organization, which was founded in Switzerland in 1863 by Jean Henri Dunant, is based on the Swiss flag. The International Red Cross often acts as a neutral intermediary between nations at war or in conflict and works to assure humane treatment of prisoners of war. The American Red Cross, founded in 1881 by Clara Barton, emphasizes disaster relief, social services to military personnel and veterans, health and safety programs, and the coordination of blood and organ donations to hospitals.

red-light district: In many cities, an area where there is a concentration of prostitutes, sexually oriented shops and clubs, and drug-related crime.

redlining: The practice by certain financial institutions of designating an area of a city as being too risky and unprofitable to lend money to those who want to rebuild or refurbish buildings there. The term came from the red line that various institutions drew on maps around *ghetto* areas to identify those locales that would not be funded. See also *greenlining.*

redneck: A disparaging term used to describe unsophisticated, dogmatic, racially prejudiced, and often hostile people with rural or small-town orientations.

reductionism: A method of explaining a theory, a methodology, or data by reducing their more complex aspects to less complex ones. Often, the effect of doing this is to oversimplify the phenomenon and give it an inaccurate interpretation.

reference group: A social *status,* culture, subculture, or association of any type whose behav-

iors, values, and lifestyles are emulated by an individual. The person may or may not be a member of the group with which he or she is identifying.

referral: The social work process of directing a client to an agency, resource, or professional known to be able to provide a needed service. This process may include knowing what the available resources are, knowing what the client's needs are, facilitating the client's opportunity to partake of the service, and following up to be certain that the contact was fulfilled.

reflection of feeling: The technique used in social work interviews in which the worker clarifies and shows the client what his or her feelings are at the moment and encourages further expression and understanding of those feelings. Often the worker reflects the client's feelings by *paraphrasing,* pointing out revealing *parapraxis,* body language, and *paralinguistic* expressions of concealed feelings.

reflex: An involuntary response to some stimulus.

reformatory: An institution where young people who have been convicted of delinquent or criminal activity are confined and given special training, therapy, and education in order to help them overcome antisocial behavior tendencies; also known as "reform school."

reformer: A *social activist* who seeks to bring about changes in institutional structures or human behavior.

reform school: See *reformatory.*

reframing: A technique used by family therapists to help families understand a symptom or pattern of behavior in a different context. For example, a child diagnosed as depressed could be seen by the family as being disrespectful and detached from them. This changes the understanding of the problem from an individual's illness to a family problem.

refugee: One who seeks safety or protection from previously experienced dangers, such as immigrants to the United States who have sought to escape religious, ethnic, or political persecution in their native lands. Such people often become the clients of social workers, and the workers are often called upon to find the resources to help in their protection.

Refugee Assistance Program: The federal program, administered by the *Family Services Administration (FSA)* of the U.S. *Department of Health and Human Services (HHS)* to provide funds and assistance to immigrants to the United States.

registered nurse (RN): A professional who practices the science of providing continuous care for people who are ill. Nurses have successfully completed extensive training in professional schools of nursing and are registered as being skilled in the performance of specific health care services. Many nurses become specialists, working with psychiatric patients, newborn infants, and maternity patients; specializing in emergency room care; or providing skilled assistance to surgeons. There are several routes to becoming a registered nurse: (1) a four-year baccalaureate program in a university; (2) a two-year associate degree program in a community college; and (3) a two- or three-year diploma from a degree-granting hospital program. Increasingly, as the need for greater knowledge and skills becomes essential, more RNs come from the four-year baccalaureate route. See also *practical nurse.*

registration of social workers: An organization's or government's listing (or registry) of people who identify themselves or are identified as social workers. This is a form of *quality assurance* and sometimes public regulation that has a minimal degree of regulatory power (compared to *licensing* and *certification*). The organization usually specifies some qualification criteria to permit a worker to be included in the registration. For example, in the *NASW Register of Clinical Social Workers* (5th ed., Silver Spring, Md.: National Association of Social Workers, 1987) the applicant for registration must pay a fee, have a master's or doctoral degree from an accredited school of social work, have two years or 3,000 hours of post-master's professionally supervised clinical social work practice, have at least two years or 3,000 hours of direct practice in the past 10 years, and be a member of ACSW or be licensed or certified in a state at a level at least equivalent to ACSW standards. Some exceptions to these criteria exist under certain circumstances for field or agency supervisors or social work school faculty.

regression: Behaviors and thought patterns that indicate a return to earlier or more primitive levels of development. This is often seen in people who are exposed to severe stress, trauma, or conflicts that cannot be resolved.

regression analysis: In social research, a statistical technique for predicting the outcome of one variable that is paired with another variable.

regressive tax: A government's revenue-collecting system in which less affluent people pay an equal or higher percentage of their taxable incomes than do more affluent people. For example, a person with a taxable income of $20,000 pays 20 percent of that amount for taxes, and someone earning $100,000 pays 15 percent tax on his or her income. See also *progressive tax.*

rehabilitation: Restoring to a healthy and useful capacity or to as satisfactory a condition as possible. Social workers usually use this term in the context of helping people who have been impaired through injury, disease, or dysfunction. This process of helping occurs in hospitals, social agencies, clinics, schools, prisons, and many other settings and may include physical therapy, psychotherapy, exercise, training, and lifestyle changes.

reinforcement: In *behavior modification,* a procedure that strengthens the tendency of a response to recur. According to Martin Sundel and Sandra Stone Sundel (*Behavior Modification in the Human Services,* 2nd ed., Englewood Cliffs, N.J.: Prentice-Hall, 1982), if a reinforcer is arranged to follow a behavior, there is increased probability that the behavior will be repeated. Similarly, if performance of a response removes an aversive event, there is increased probability that the behavior will be repeated.

rejection: Refusal to grant, acknowledge, or recognize something or someone. An individual may experience rejection when his or her ideas, requests, or presence are not accepted by relevant others. Social workers find that some of their clients with low self-esteem or poor self-confidence believe they are experiencing rejection when being ignored or not being given what they want.

relabeling: A technique used by family therapists to make a family problem more amenable to treatment by defining a symptom. The family members change the way they understand the symptom or behavior and begin to respond to it differently, often in a more healthy way.

relationship: In social work, the mutual emotional exchange; dynamic interaction; and affective, cognitive, and behavioral connection that exists between the worker and the client to create the working and helping atmosphere. Social workers such as Felix Biestek (*The Casework Relationship,* Chicago: Loyola University Press, 1957) have found that it is created through adherence to certain ethical behaviors, including *acceptance, confidentiality, individualization,* and *nonjudgmentality* of the client, as well as permitting the client ultimate *self-determination, purposeful expression of feelings,* and *controlled emotional involvement.* The term "relationship" was first described for social workers by Virginia Robinson (*A Changing Psychology in Social Casework,* Chapel Hill: University of North Carolina Press, 1930).

relative's responsibility: A term pertaining to laws and moral codes that compel specified members of the family to care for or pay for the care of another family member who is in need. The legal requirements in this area vary widely from state to state. All states have such laws pertaining to the care of minor children. Most states have eliminated or relaxed their laws requiring a person to care for parents, siblings, or more distant relatives.

reliability: In *psychosocial assessments,* the individual's degree of dependability and consistency; in social research, the dependability and consistency of scores on a test that is repeated over time with the same group. Researchers use three types of reliability: test-retest reliability is the correlation between the first and second test of the group being measured after some time has elapsed; split-half reliability is the correlation between the scores achieved by a group of subjects in one part of a test and the group's scores on another similar part of the same test; interrater reliability is the correlation between the scores of different subjects evaluating the same procedures or phenomena.

remarried family: See *reconstituted family.*

remission: Cessation or abatement of the symptoms of a physical or mental disease.

renal disease: Malfunction of the kidneys.

rent control: A government's regulation of the amount of money tenants are required to pay landlords and of the conditions under which evictions may occur, and the general overseeing of relationships between landlords and tenants.

rent strike: A strategy, often used in *community organization,* in which tenants withhold rent payments in order to pressure their landlords into improving the conditions of their housing.

replication: In research, the process of duplicating an experiment—in which the same hypothesis, variables, sampling procedure, testing instruments, and techniques for analysis are used—with a different sample of the same population.

representativeness: A concept in social research pertaining to the extent to which the information gathered is idiosyncratic and biased or typical of the entity from which the information was extracted.

repression: A *defense mechanism,* derived from *psychodynamic* theory, in which the individual unconsciously pushes out of the consciousness certain memories, ideas, or desires that are unacceptable or cause a high level of anxiety. Once these ideas or desires are contained in the unconscious, they cannot be recalled directly. However, they may emerge in one's behavior in disguised forms, and their effects are sometimes seen in slips of the tongue (*parapraxis*) or dreams. Because repression is, by definition, a mechanism of the *unconscious,* it should not be confused with *suppression,* which is the *conscious* act of putting unpleasant thoughts out of one's mind.

research: Systematic procedures used in seeking facts or principles.

resettlement: Moving and establishing a new, permanent residence in another area.

residency laws: Statutes that specify what qualifications must be fulfilled in order for an individual to be considered eligible for the privileges and obligations of that jurisdiction. For example, a person must live in a state for a specified time before becoming eligible to receive lower public college tuition rates or being able to get a divorce in that state. Residency laws that restricted eligibility for certain types of social services have been relaxed in recent years. For example, the U.S. Supreme Court ruled in 1969 (in *Shapiro v. Thompson*) that under usual circumstances, residency laws eliminating public assistance were unconstitutional.

residential facilities: Structures that house people who are without homes or who, for a variety of reasons, cannot stay in their homes. These facilities include boarding schools, shelters for abused women, orphanages, homes for juvenile delinquents, and centers where *residential treatment* takes place.

residential treatment: Therapeutic intervention processes for people who cannot or do not function satisfactorily in their own homes. Such treatment typically occurs in certain environments such as private schools, medical centers, penal institutions, and *shelters.* It usually includes a variety of professionally led assistance, such as individual or group psychotherapy, formal schooling, social skills training, recreation, and fulfillment of the needs usually met in one's home.

residual versus institutional model: The dichotomy described by H. L. Wilensky and C. N. Lebeaux (*Industrial Society and Social Welfare,* New York: Free Press, 1958), comprising two conceptions of social welfare. The residual model views social welfare as being primarily a *safety net* function in which programs are temporary substitutes for the failures of individuals and institutions. The institutional model views social welfare as having a "main line" function (equal to the other social institutions, such as family, religion, economics, and politics), in which programs are permanent and provide for the overall security and emotional support of human beings.

residual welfare provision: The idea that the public should provide social services and public assistance only to those people who, because of unusual circumstances, are not able to receive needed help through the family or the normal social structure and marketplace. See also *safety net.*

resistance: Avoidance behavior used by a client to defend against the influences of the social worker; also, in *psychoanalytic theory,* the mental process of preventing one's *unconscious* thoughts from being brought into the consciousness.

resocialization group: A type of *group therapy* or *self-help group* that helps people adapt to unfamiliar roles and statuses. Such groups exist for such people as *displaced homemakers,* recently widowed or divorced people, people who become physically handicapped, and adults who must care for their elderly parents.

resource allocation: The distribution of goods and services based on systematic decision making and predetermined criteria.

resources: Any existing service or commodity that can be called upon to help take care of a need. A primary skill of social workers is their ability to know of and utilize the existing resources of a community that can help their clients. Resources used by social workers typically include other social agencies, governmental programs, volunteer and *self-help groups,* natural helpers, and individuals in the community who possess the qualities and motivations that can help the client.

resource systems: The biopsychosocial and environmental sources of the material, emotional, and spiritual needs required for a person to survive, to realize aspirations, and to cope with life tasks. The three types of resource systems are the informal type (family, friends, and neighbors), formal type (membership organizations, such as the *National Association of Social Workers [NASW],* and labor unions), and the societal type (social security programs and educational and health care systems). A basic purpose of social work practice is to enhance the functioning of these resource systems and their linkages with people. See also *networking.*

respondent behavior: Behavior that is elicited by specific stimuli and subject to the principles of *respondent conditioning.*

respondent conditioning: The procedure in *behavior modification* in which a *stimulus* (such as food) that automatically results in a response (such as salivation) is presented repeatedly along with a neutral stimulus (such as a ringing bell) in order to elicit essentially the same response from the previously neutral stimulus. A synonym for *classical conditioning* (or Pavlovian conditioning).

response: A behavior. Usually the term is used to indicate a discrete form of behavior such as a knee jerk, salivation, or a pressing of a key, but the term also applies to broadly defined behaviors such as bringing home flowers for one's spouse or expressing anger to the social worker after being turned down in a request for assistance.

response repertoire: The accumulation of knowledge and skills that a person has learned and can perform effectively, comfortably, and without trial-and-error behavior.

restitution: The restoration of property or rights that had previously been taken away. People who have committed theft or property destruction are sometimes compelled to provide restitution to those they victimized. See also *victim compensation.*

restricted funds: Monetary or other gifts or grants and the income generated by them, which may be expended only for purposes specified by the donor or granter.

retardation: The slowing of an individual's physical or mental development or social progress; also, a significantly lower-than-average capacity for intellectual functioning (*mental retardation*) or a slowing of physical and emotional reactions (psychomotor retardation).

retirement: A state of withdrawal from regular employment or certain forms of work activity. Some employers encourage older or disabled workers to retire by providing pensions or lump-sum retirement compensation if they leave by a certain time. Many workers who have inadequate retirement benefits find they cannot retire or, if required to do so, find they need financial assistance. See also *social security.*

retribution: The dispensing of punishment for wrongdoing. The term can also refer to future rewards for good works.

retrograde amnesia: See *amnesia.*

revenue sharing: The governmental process of dividing a proportion of its income, which comes from taxes, and contributing those funds to another level or sector of government that provides needed services to the people. For example, the federal government contributes money to state governments so that they can provide *Aid to Families with Dependent Children (AFDC)* benefits.

reverse discrimination: The term sometimes used to describe the preferential treatment of a previously victimized minority group or person to the disadvantage of the majority. Generally, the practice has been used to withhold opportunities from whites and men to give more opportunities to blacks and women. See also *affirmative action.*

rheumatic fever: An infectious disease; symptoms often include inflammation of the joints, fever, nosebleeds, and skin rash. In its more serious forms, there is inflammation of the heart valves, which may become scarred and deformed (rheumatic heart disease). Penicillin and extended rest are used in treating rheumatic fever.

Maintenance doses of penicillin, often for several years, are sometimes given to children to prevent a recurrence of the fever, especially to prevent rheumatic heart disease.

rickets: A bone disease caused by vitamin D deficiency. In children, the disease symptoms include softening of the bones, enlargement of the cartilage, bowleggedness, and deformities in the chest and pelvis. With the addition of vitamin D to milk and the use of vitamin supplements, prevention of rickets has been effective in the United States.

rights: The obligations of society to each of its members; that which is legally or morally due to an individual by just claim. These are more specifically identified as *civil rights, equal rights,* and *human rights.*

right to life movement: A loosely coordinated body of groups, institutions, and individuals working to change laws and norms that permit and facilitate *abortion.* The movement is also referred to as the "prolife movement." See also *prochoice movement.*

right to refuse treatment: The legal principle, upheld in numerous court cases or contained in explicit statutes in several states, that an individual may not be compelled to undergo any form of treatment, including social work intervention, unless there is a life-threatening emergency or the person exhibits seriously destructive behavior. This principle has been applied to people who are involuntarily committed to mental hospitals, prisons, and other institutions. It has also influenced the way social work services are integrated with *income maintenance* programs in *public assistance* programs. Thus, a public assistance recipient is no longer compelled to receive counseling to obtain financial aid.

right to treatment: The legal principle, established in the *Wyatt v. Stickney* decision, that an individual who is confined in an institution has the right to receive the treatment necessary to offer a reasonable chance for improvement so that the person can function independently and be released from that institution. This right has led many facilities that lack the resources for individual treatment to discharge their clients. See also *deinstitutionalization.*

rite of passage: A formal or informal activity, ceremony, or behavior that a group uses to recognize the movement of one of its members into another role or set of expectations. Examples include graduation ceremonies, bar mitzvahs, retirement parties, and mothers helping their daughters apply makeup for the first time. See also *puberty rites.*

Roe v. Wade: The 1973 decision by the U.S. Supreme Court that state laws forbidding abortions were unconstitutional under specified circumstances. The Court held that, in the first trimester, abortion must be left to medical judgment. In the second trimester, the state may, if it chooses, regulate abortion to protect maternal health but may not prohibit abortion. In the third trimester, the state may regulate or prohibit abortion except when necessary to preserve the mother's life. The decision has been the source of considerable controversy to many people in recent years.

role: A culturally determined pattern of behavior that is prescribed for an individual who occupies a specific *status;* also, a social norm that is attached to a given social position that dictates reciprocal action. For example, a person who occupies the status of "social worker" is expected by others—that is, clients, supervisors, the profession, the general public, and so on—to behave in the manner generally prescribed for all social workers.

role ambiguity: A condition or state in which roles carry few clear or consistent expectations. For example, a new client goes to a social worker but is not sure what social workers do to help and thus does not know quite what to expect from the meeting.

role complementarity: See *complementarity.*

role conflict: The experience of one who occupies two or more social positions that carry incompatible expectations. For example, a social worker may be expected by the client to be immediately available during times of crisis but is expected by the supervisor to see clients only according to a predetermined schedule.

role discomplementarity: The condition that exists when an individual's various roles are not consistent with one another or with the expectations held by relevant others. For example, the client and the supervisor have certain expectations of the worker but have not made clear what those expectations are, so that they cannot be fulfilled. Social scientists identify five conditions in which role discomplementarity occurs. They are (1) cognitive discrepancy, which is based on a lack of knowledge of what the appropriate expectations are (for example, the worker or client does not know what the other expects and thus cannot fulfill those expectations); (2) status discrepancy, in which one person expects another to fulfill expectations that are not appropriate to that person's social position (for example, the client expects the worker to provide medical information); (3) allocative discrepancy, in which one person does not choose to accept responsibility for fulfilling the other's expectations even though capable of doing so (for example, the client wants the worker to treat the whole family, and the worker wants to work only with the individual); (4) discrepancy of value orientations, in which those who have expectations of one another have incompatible values (for example, the client expects the worker to help her end her marriage, and the worker expects to help save the marriage); and (5) absence of instrumental means, in which the reciprocal expectations are compatible but the people lack the tools necessary to carry them out (for example, the client and worker both want the worker to increase the financial supports to the family, but there is not enough money to do this).

role playing: A rehearsal of behaviors that will be useful in a subsequent situation to fulfill some expectation or achieve some goal; also, a reexperiencing of the past as one imagines being another person (a parent, a sibling, and so on); a technique to elicit self-awareness and understanding of others. Social workers often help their clients rehearse for real situations. For example, a worker asks a client to pretend she is going to ask her boss for a raise in order to make it easier for the client actually to confront her boss. Role playing is a technique developed by J. L. Moreno in his *psychodrama* method of therapy and is now used in various *group therapy* systems, *game analysis,* and leadership training programs to help individuals test certain behaviors and receive immediate feedback about approaches to the situation.

role reequilibration: The process that takes place between two or more people to end *role conflicts* or *role discomplementarity* by clarifying mutual expectations.

role reversal: A situation in which one person changes behaviors and begins to act in a way that is expected of another person. For example, a father might begin to act childishly around his son, who in turn acts with more maturity around his father.

role strain: Any form of *role conflict* or *role discomplementarity.*

role theory: A group of concepts, based on sociocultural and anthropological investigations, which pertain to the way people are influenced in their behaviors by the variety of social positions they hold and the different expectations that accompany those positions. See also the related terms used in this dictionary, including all those beginning with *role,* as well as the terms *status, norms,* and *sanctions.*

role vigor: The relative degree of deviation from a role's expectations permitted by the culture. For example, more role vigor is permitted

for women in large, pluralistic urban areas than in small towns.

Rorschach test: A *projective* psychological test, designed by Swiss psychiatrist Hermann Rorschach, in which clients are given a series of ten standardized inkblots and asked to report what they see. Responses can indicate personality traits, interests, thought processes, and so forth.

rubber fence concept: A metaphor used in *family therapy* to describe how some families maintain boundaries between themselves and others. A boundary may seem to stretch to incorporate what is seen as positive and to contract when apparently threatened. For example, if a social worker makes suggestions to such a family, the members might appear to expand in incorporating the new ideas into the family dynamics but would later contract to their original configuration.

rubella: A short-term, mild form of measles, also called German or three-day measles. Though rarely fatal to children or adults, this disease is particularly dangerous to the *fetus* of an infected pregnant woman and can result in miscarriage or a variety of *congenital* conditions.

rugged individualism: The ideology, espoused by certain economists, politicians, and others, that people should be left to their own initiatives in providing for their needs. According to this view, even though difficulties might be experienced, it strengthens people's character and capacity to cope more effectively with any other problems that might be faced in the future.

rumination disorder of infancy: An *eating disorder* in some infants, characterized by repeated regurgitation, in which the infant loses weight or fails to gain weight and may develop nutritional deficiencies. The cause of this condition is not understood, but it is not due to gastrointestinal illness or nausea.

runaway: A minor who has departed the home of his or her parents or legal guardians contrary to their wishes and who intends to remain independent of their control. The federal government maintains a National Runaway Hotline to help these youngsters and possibly reunite them with their parents.

rural social work: Social work practice oriented to helping people who have unique problems and needs arising out of living in agricultural or sparsely populated areas or small towns. These people face most of the same problems and needs as do urban clients; in addition, however, they often encounter difficulties because of limited services and *resource systems,* less acceptance of any variations from the social norms prevalent in the area, and fewer educational and economic opportunities.

rural social work: Social work practice oriented to helping people who have unique problems and needs arising out of living in agricultural or sparsely populated areas or small towns. These people face most of the same problems and needs as do urban clients; in addition, however, they often encounter difficulties because of limited services and *resource systems,* less acceptance of any variations from the social norms prevalent in the area, and fewer educational and economic opportunities.

rural social workers: Professional social workers whose predominant clientele and practice activities are in sparsely populated regions. According to O. William Farley et al. (*Rural Social Work,* New York: Free Press, 1982), the most successful workers in these settings are well-trained, creative professionals who can work in relative isolation with limited additional resources.

Russell Sage Foundation: A philanthropic organization, founded in 1907 by the widow of entrepreneur Russell Sage, for the improvement of social and living conditions in the United States. The foundation's financing of the social survey movement, of systematic research in social service programs, and of the development of social agencies contributed significantly to the professionalization of social work. Information made available through the foundation was used in the training of *friendly visitors.*

S

sadistic: Deriving pleasure from inflicting or causing pain to others.

sadistic personality disorder: A diagnostic term used by some psychiatrists and other mental health professionals to describe a type of *personality disorder* in which a person frequently seeks opportunities to impose mental or physical cruelty on one or more others.

sadomasochism: The presence, within an individual or between couples, of cruel, punishing behavior and behavior that is self-destructive. For example, in a sadomasochistic relationship, one person would persist in cruel behavior to the other, and the other would remain in the relationship and encourage more of the cruelty. See also *masochism* and *masochistic personality disorder.*

safety net: The idea that if some social service programs are eliminated through economic cutbacks, there will remain benefits and programs of last resort in case individuals or families cannot find needed resources on their own. See also *residual welfare provision.*

St. Vincent de Paul Society: An international Catholic lay group, established in France in 1833 by Antoine Frédéric Ozanam to provide financial relief, counseling, and social services for the poor. The organization has local centers in most nations with significant Catholic populations, including the United States.

Salvation Army: An international religious service organization involved in philanthropic and evangelical work. Founded in England in 1878 by William Booth, the army is patterned after military structures, including uniforms and military rank, because its goal is to wage war against evil and human suffering. The army has programs in nearly 100 nations, with its international headquarters in London. The army operates hospitals, community centers, social work agencies, alcohol and drug rehabilitation centers, emergency care facilities, disaster services, and well-known *soup kitchens.*

sample: In research, a part of the *universe* (the entire phenomenon being studied) from which a representative selection is made. See also *population.*

sanction: Permission to carry out, or official ratification of, some plan, granted by the established authority; also, a provision in law or a response by a *reference group* that penalizes an individual for not conforming. For example, social workers who are found to have violated their professional *code of ethics* may be subject to sanctions in the form of suspension from the organization or of the license to practice.

sanctuary: A place affording immunity or protection from arrest or harm. Social workers have been involved as private citizens in a sanctuary movement designed to help refugees from Central American nations establish new lives in the United States.

SASG: See *sexual assault survivor group (SASG).*

satisficing: A term used by social planners and community organizers to describe decision making among disparate groups in which the option chosen is a "good enough" compromise rather than the best possible choice. The compromise is made in order to keep the group progressing and moving incrementally toward the optimal goals.

Save the Children Federation: The voluntary agency founded in 1932 to provide social services and community development and financial assistance to communities, families, and especially children who live in impoverished nations or areas that have suffered disasters or are undergoing economic problems. Programs exist in many *Third World* nations as well as in such areas in the United States as Appalachia, *American Indian* reservations, poor neighborhoods in inner cities, and *Chicano* areas.

scapegoat: A member of a family or group who has become the object of displaced conflict or unfair criticism.

144

schedule of reinforcement: In *behavior modification*, a plan determining when the subject will be reinforced. This may occur at regular intervals or according to the number and type of responses the subject makes. See also *reinforcement*.

scheme: The mental structure, described in *Piagetian theory*, that allows information to be understood and processed if it fits the individual's cognitive processes.

schizoaffective disorder: A mental disorder in which the individual has symptoms of both *schizophrenia* and a major *affective disorder*. This term is infrequently used in diagnosis of mental illness because it is not very precise.

schizoid: A term applied to personality traits that include aloofness, social withdrawal, and indifference to the feelings of others. If such traits seem deeply ingrained and relatively permanent, the individual might be diagnosed as having schizoid personality disorder. If the person has these traits and is under the age of 18, the diagnosis might be "schizoid disorder of childhood or adolescence."

schizoid personality disorder: See *schizoid*.

schizophrenia: A form of psychosis, not apparently due to *organic mental disorder* or *affective disorder*, which lasts more than six months and whose active phase begins before the subject is 45. Its typical features include the following: thought disturbances (often including misinterpretation of reality, misperceptions, *loose associations, delusions,* or *hallucinations*), mood changes (inappropriate affect, blunted emotions, inability to empathize, and ambivalence), communication problems (incoherence or poverty of speech content), and behavior patterns that may be bizarre, regressive, or withdrawn. Depending on specific symptoms, many subtypes of schizophrenia have been identified, including *hebephrenic* (disorganized) *catatonic, paranoid,* and undifferentiated. The prognosis for complete recovery is extremely rare, although *psychotropic drugs, psychotherapy,* and help with social functioning enables most people to live fairly comfortable and somewhat independent lives. Many researchers believe schizophrenia is not a single disease but a group of disorders with similar overt features but differing etiologies. Laypersons often confuse schizophrenia with the rare and unrelated *dissociative disorder* known as *multiple personality*.

schizophreniform disorder: A disorder whose symptoms are identical with those of *schizophrenia* except that its duration is over two weeks but under six months.

schizophrenogenic parent: The concept used by some family therapists and psychoanalysts in describing a mother who is domineering and inconsistent or a father who is submissive and inconsistent in such ways as to precipitate *schizophrenia* in their offspring. There is little, if any, scientific evidence that verifies this theory.

School Lunch program: A national food program administered by the U.S. Department of Agriculture, with input from the U.S. Department of Education and from the *Department of Health and Human Services (HHS),* in which federal funds and farm commodities are given to states and local administrations to provide nutritious lunches for schoolchildren, including free lunches for eligible children from poor families.

school phobia: A young child's irrational fear of going to school, thought by some psychodynamically oriented therapists to be related to unresolved dependency needs or strong *separation anxiety*.

school social work: The specialty in social work oriented toward helping students make satisfactory school adjustments and coordinating the efforts of the school, the family, and the community to help achieve this goal. School social workers are often called upon to help students, families, and teachers deal with such problems as truancy, social withdrawal, overaggressive behavior, rebelliousness, and the effects of special physical, emotional, or economic problems. They also interpret the methods and philosophy of the school to the parents and community. See also *visiting teacher service*.

scientific method: A set of rigorous procedures used in social and physical research to obtain facts. The procedures include defining the problem, operationally stating in advance the method for measuring the problem, defining in advance the criteria to be used to reject hypotheses, using measuring instruments that have *validity* and *reliability*, observing and measuring all the cases or a representative sample of those cases, presenting for public scrutiny the findings and the methods used in accumulating them in such detail as to permit *replication*, and limiting any conclusions to those elements that are supported by the findings.

scripts: Characteristic patterns of behavior that tend to accompany specific social situations or relationships and that are often followed despite the fact that they can lead to outcomes that are inconsistent with the individual's overt objectives. The term was popularized through *transactional analysis (TA)* theory, which is partly built around an examination and analysis of these patterns, the circumstances in which they occur, and their consequences.

sculpting: An experiential technique, used especially by group and family therapists, in which one member of a group or family is asked to depict his or her understanding of the relationship with others. This is done by moving them into certain positions and asking them to hold certain gestures.

seasonal affective disorder (SAD): A *mood disorder,* characterized by many symptoms of *depression,* which affects some individuals during the colder, darker months of the year. Some researchers attribute SAD in some people to deficiencies in needed exposure to light for an extended period of time each day. Treatment for these people may involve moving to more sunny climates or regular exposure to special light-emitting equipment.

seasonal unemployment: One of the four types of unemployment (including *structural, cyclical,* and *frictional*). This type is related to regular changes in the weather or season. For example, farm workers, lifeguards, snow removal workers, and some construction workers cannot work at those jobs during certain predictable times of the year in certain localities.

secondary gain: The advantages or benefits one derives from a physical or mental illness, such as attention, freedom from responsibility, and disability benefits. See also *primary gain.*

secondary prevention: Efforts to limit the extent or severity of a problem through early identification of its existence, early case finding, isolation of the problem so that its effects on other people or situations are minimized, and early treatment. See also *primary prevention* and *tertiary prevention.*

second-order change: In *systems theory,* a fundamental and relatively permanent change in the structure of a system and the way it functions. See also *first-order change.*

sectarian services: Social welfare programs that began their existence under the auspices of or with the financial support of religious organizations or that are oriented toward providing social services primarily to members of a specified religious group. Examples are *Catholic Charities USA, Jewish social agencies, LDS Social Services, Lutheran Social Services,* the *Salvation Army,* and so on.

sectoral planning: Social planning within a special problem area, usually involving the interests of a specified target population or geographic area (for example, the elderly, undernourished mothers, delinquent youth, unemployed Hispanics, or inner-city residents). See also *intersectoral planning.*

sedatives: A term pertaining to drugs or procedures used to reduce anxiety or activity.

segregation: The separation or isolation of a group through social *sanctions,* laws, peer pressures, or personal preference. Voluntary segregation occurs when people choose to associate with others of their own kind. Involuntary segregation occurs when legal, political, or normative requirements, usually established by a dominant group, are imposed on the members of a less powerful group. See also *Plessy v. Ferguson.*

seizure disorders: Disorders associated with abnormal electrical activity in the brain, often resulting in distressing psychomotor activity. The causes of these disorders, once commonly called *epilepsy,* are thought to include lesions in the brain, endocrine abnormality, or neurological deficits. According to the manifestations that occur during attacks, the disorders may be classified into four major groups: (1) Grand mal seizures usually begin with an "aura," which may include feelings of numbness and dizziness, then loss of consciousness and jerking movements of the limbs, followed by a period of deep sleep and, just after awakening, muscular stiffness, fatigue, and headache. The attacks may last from less than a minute to more than 30 minutes, and their frequency can vary from several per day to one in several years. (2) Petit mal seizures are transient losses of contact with the environment. They may last only a second or up to two minutes, occurring infrequently or as often as 30 times per hour. Petit mal seizures usually occur in childhood and may disappear in adulthood. (3) Psychomotor seizures, more commonly known as "partial seizures" or "temporal lobe seizures," are usually not characterized by loss of consciousness, but by stereotyped movements and dramatic affective changes. (4) Jacksonian seizures tend to begin with convulsive twitching in one part of the body that may spread to others. For most victims of seizure disorders, medication can control or significantly reduce the symptoms.

selective eligibility: A policy by which social services are provided only to those people who meet predetermined criteria and the amount of benefit is related to the recipient's specific circumstances, economic status, or special needs, often determined by a *means test.* This policy may be contrasted with those of *universal eligibility* (in which everyone receives the same benefit) and *exceptional eligibility* (in which there are unique programs for special groups).

selective programs: Social welfare programs based on individualized assessments to determine eligibility. This occurs in programs using the *means test,* including *Aid to Families with Dependent Children (AFDC), Medicaid,* and *food stamps.* Selective programs are so named to distinguish them from *universal programs,* which are open to all people who fit specified categories without individualized assessments.

self-actualization: A relative term referring to the full development of one's potential. According to Abraham Maslow, this is a basic human motivation toward which one strives, especially after fulfilling the lower-order needs, which include physiological needs (food, air, water, and rest), safety needs (security, stability, and freedom from fear), belongingness needs (family, friends, affection, and intimacy), and esteem needs (self-respect and recognition of worth from others).

self-control: An individual's relative ability to restrict impulses or behaviors to appropriate circumstances in the environment.

self-defeating personality disorder: A *personality disorder* in which a person persists in behavior that does not allow him or her to reach his or her goals.

self-determination: An ethical principle in social work, which recognizes the rights and needs of clients to be free to make their own choices and decisions. Inherent in the principle is the social worker's helping the client to know what the resources and choices are and what the consequences of selecting any one of them will be. Usually it also includes helping the client implement the decision made. Self-determination is one of the major factors in the helping *relationship*.

self-disclosure: In social work interviews, the worker's revelation of personal information, values, and behaviors to the client. The profession does not declare that such revelations should or should not be made, and in certain limited circumstances it may be considered useful. However, there is some consensus that it should not occur unless it serves a therapeutic purpose or is designed to help achieve the client's goal.

self-esteem: An individual's sense of personal worth that is derived more from inner thoughts and values than from praise and recognition from others.

self-fulfilling prophecy: An expectation one has of another person, group, or social phenomenon that influences the way that person, group, or phenomenon is subsequently perceived. For example, a social worker may view all *Aid to Families with Dependent Children (AFDC)* recipients as too lazy to get jobs and ignore an AFDC client's request for advice about getting employment.

self-help groups: Voluntary associations of nonprofessional people who share common needs or problems and meet together for extended periods of time for the purpose of mutual support and exchange of information about activities and resources that have been found useful in problem solving.

self-help organizations: Formally structured organizations that provide mutual assistance for participants who share a common problem with which one or more of the participants have coped successfully. Some of the organizations of this type that have chapters throughout the United States include the following: *Alcoholics Anonymous (AA), Al-Anon, Batterers Anonymous,* Depressives Anonymous, *Gamblers Anonymous, Mothers Without Custody,* Narcotics Anonymous, Neurotics Anonymous, Overeaters Anonymous, Parents of Premature and High-Risk Infants, *Parents Without Partners (PWP), Recovery, Inc.,* Stroke Club International, and *Women for Sobriety.*

semiotics: Aspects of *communication theory* pertaining to signs and gestures used in language to clarify or obscure what is being communicated.

Seneca Falls Convention: The 1848 feminist meeting in Seneca Falls, N.Y., that outlined the right to equality for women. This delineation of feminist positions became a major part of the "platform" of the women's movement and helped lead to the passage in 1920 of the Nineteenth Amendment to the Constitution, giving women the right to vote.

senescence: The biological process of human aging as evidenced by the decline in functioning of various organs and senses. This term, which should be distinguished from "senility" or *senile dementia,* implies frailty, vulnerability to illness, and awareness of death.

senile dementia: A syndrome of old age that is associated with deterioration of brain tissues, often leading to such symptoms as loss of memory, confusion, stubbornness, perceptual distortions, and thought disorders. It is a syndrome characterized by generalized irreversible disturbance of the higher cortical functions. Senile dementia is not a disease itself but a syndrome associated with a number of diseases. The most common causes of senile dementia are *Alzheimer's disease* and multi-infarct dementia (a series of small strokes). Senile dementia is also referred to as "senility," "senile psychosis," and "primary degenerative dementia, senile onset."

senility: The condition of old age. Technically, the term pertains to all aspects of advanced age, but it usually suggests deterioration of physical or mental faculties, including loss of memory, increased rigidity of attitude, greater irritability, and narrowing of outlook. See also *senile dementia.*

sensitivity group: A training and consciousness-raising group rather than one that meets to resolve psychosocial or mental disorders. Such groups typically consist of 10–20 members and a leader, called a trainer or facilitator. The members participate in discussions and experiential activities to demonstrate how groups function, to show how each member tends to affect others, and to help them become more aware of other people's feelings and behaviors.

sensorimotor stage: The first phase of human development, according to *Piagetian theory,* which occurs from birth to approximately 18 months of age and is characterized by the formation of increasingly complex sensory refinements and motor skills that permit the child to better understand and control its environment.

sensorium: The *consciousness;* that part of the psyche that organizes the input from the senses into a fairly coherent understanding of the immediate environment. When a psychiatric report describes a patient as having a "clear sensorium," it indicates that the individual is oriented accurately as to time, place, person, and memory.

sentiment group: Individuals and groups that possess and express the predominant values, norms, and goals of the community. Sentiment groups often include civic and fraternal associations, labor unions, and ad hoc groups that have been brought together because of some problem or social cause.

separation: The breaking off of a tie or relationship. Social workers use this term in several different contexts, including marital separation (a husband and wife living in different residences), legal separation (agreement between spouses to live apart prior to divorce), separation anxiety (a child's fear of losing or being deprived of access to a parent or guardian), and *separation-individuation.*

separation agreement: An informal understanding or, more commonly, a written and witnessed agreement between spouses who intend to live apart, specifying the future conditions of their relationship. Usually the agreement describes how property is to be divided and covers child custody and support payments. Formal agreements may be entered in official records and become legally enforceable and not subject to modification unless both parties want a change. The terms of a separation agreement are frequently incorporated into a divorce decree.

separation anxiety: The fear that a young child experiences when threatened by the loss of the primary mother-figure. This fear is usually ended or minimized as the child gets older but often returns during acute *stress, crisis,* or life-stage transitions.

separation-individuation: According to Margaret Mahler, a psychosocial stage in human development in which the young child develops a sense of self-identity and a recognition that he or she is distinct from the mother. See also *individuation.*

service strategy: A social welfare policy designed to help clients obtain needed goods and services (such as food, housing, transportation, health care, or counseling) rather than direct monetary aid. For example, a service strategy would be to provide public housing for a needy client rather than providing the client with money for housing. See also *income strategy.*

settlement houses: Neighborhood-based facilities established in most urban centers to bring together people of different socioeconomic and cultural backgrounds to share knowledge, skills, and values for their mutual benefit. These centers are financed primarily through voluntary contributions and grants and staffed primarily by people indigenous to the neighborhood, educators, recreation specialists, and social workers whose primary orientation is *social group work, community organization,* and social planning. The social settlement movement began in London in 1884 at *Toynbee Hall,* where university students lived and met with their neighbors to exchange ideas. Soon hundreds of settlement houses were established in the United States with the same goals. Many of them have discontinued the residential aspect of the program, but many remain active in establishing neighborhood self-help programs and crime and delinquency abatement efforts and are involved in *political activism.*

sex discrimination: Treating people differently based on their sex. Usually the term refers to favorable treatment of males and relegation of females to subordinate positions. Sex discrimination is manifested in such activities as promoting men over equally capable women and paying male employees more than female employees for comparable work.

sexism: Individual attitudes and institutional arrangements that discriminate against people, usually women and girls, because of *sex role stereotypes* and generalizations.

sex therapy: Professional clinical treatment of the psychological and physiological dysfunctions of human sexuality. Such treatment is now typically provided to couples in *cotherapy* situations and provided by male-female teams of therapists. According to Robert Barker (*Treating Couples in Crisis,* New York: Free Press, 1984, pp. 219–221), there are four levels of such therapy: (1) "Providing permission," that is, conveying to couples that their behaviors and desires are normal; (2) "providing general information," that is, helping the couple know how to get the most out of sexual relationships; (3) "providing specific information," that is, advising the couple about how to correct some sexual disorders or improve some unsatisfactory behaviors; and (4) "providing intensive sex therapy." Intensive sex therapy begins with thorough physical exams to rule out or correct physiological problems. This is followed by intensive psychosocial and sexual history taking. If the sex therapists use *psychodynamic* perspectives, the subsequent treatment is likely to be more insight-oriented work toward resolving underlying conflicts that lead to the problem. If the sex therapists use behavioral perspectives, the subsequent treatment involves teaching the couple techniques for greater success, using *systematic desensitization* and other methods to achieve specified goals.

sexual abuse: The exploitation and mistreatment of children and adults in ways that provide erotic gratification for the perpetrator. Abusers tend to have such serious psychological problems as a *personality disorder, paraphilia* or other *psychosexual disorders,* and *psychosis.* Victims often cannot or are unwilling to understand or resist the advances of the perpetrator. Sexual abuse can include sexual intercourse without consent (or when the victim is beneath the age of consent), fondling genitalia, taking or showing pornographic pictures, and other forms of sexual *acting out.* Some social workers also include *rape,* seduction, sexual harassment, and sexual coercion as other forms of sexual abuse.

sexual assault survivor group (SASG): A form of time-limited group therapy for women who have been victims of sexual assault. SASGs typically consist of six to eight women, led by two female clinicians. The group meetings last 90 minutes per week for 12 weeks and focus on themes related specifically to sexual assault issues.

sexual development: Anatomical, hormonal, physiological, cognitive, emotional, and social changes in an individual that are related to the reproductive function of life. Sexual development begins at conception, when the egg is fertilized by a sperm cell that carries either an XX (female) or an XY (male) sex chromosome. Sexual development continues through puberty and menopause and ends only at death. See also *psychosexual development theory.*

sexual deviation: See *paraphilia.*

sexual dysfunction: The inability of an individual or couple to experience sexual intercourse in a satisfactory way. The cause of the dysfunction may be psychological or physiological or a combination of both. The most prevalent types of sexual disorders include the following: *orgasmic impairment,* vaginismus (involuntary contraction of vaginal muscles, which makes penetration impossible or painful), *dyspareunia,* erectile dysfunction (inability to achieve or maintain an erection of sufficient quality to permit or sustain penetration), premature ejaculation (the absence of voluntary control of ejaculation before

the partner reaches orgasm), ejaculatory inhibition (the man can become aroused and erect but has difficulty ejaculating intravaginally), and inhibited sexual desire.

sexual equality: Opportunities, benefits, and rights that are uniformly available to people, regardless of their sex.

sexual identity: The degree to which an individual takes on the behaviors, personality patterns, and attitudes that are usually associated with the male or female *sex role.* This is a synonym for *gender identity.*

sexuality: Characteristics of an individual that essentially pertain to the reproductive function, including anatomy and physiology, primary and secondary sexual traits, *sex role* patterns, and behavioral characteristics.

shame versus autonomy: According to Erikson, the basic conflict found in the second stage of human psychosocial development, occurring approximately between ages 2 and 4. During this time the toddler experiences social controls and discipline and is helped by the *socialization* process to achieve recognition of his or her uniqueness.

shantytowns: Densely populated settlements of impoverished people who have built homes out of scrap materials and on land they do not own. Because these people usually occupy the land illegally, they cannot demand public services and have little fire and police protection, water and sanitary facilities, or schools. Shantytowns are growing rapidly, especially in *Third World* nations, and are also found in more affluent nations that do not provide adequately for their poor.

shaping: Procedures used in *behavior modification,* in which new patterns of behavior are fashioned by reinforcing progressively closer approximations of the desired behaviors and not reinforcing others.

shared paranoid disorder: *Delusions* that develop as part of a close relationship with one or more others with *paranoid disorders.* This disorder is also called *folie à deux,* although more than two people may be involved.

shelters: Facilities that provide and maintain temporary residences and protection for people or animals in need. Shelters exist in most communities for battered and abused wives, homeless men and women, abandoned or abused children, victims of crimes and natural disasters, people experiencing a variety of other circumstances, and stray dogs and cats.

Sheppard-Towner Act: The U.S. federal child welfare and maternity health legislation enacted in 1921 and discontinued in 1929. Administered by the U.S. *Children's Bureau* under the leadership of social worker Grace Abbott, it established nearly 3,000 child and maternity health centers across the nation, mostly in rural areas. Despite great improvements in the nation's infant and maternal *mortality rates,* political pressure led to its abolition.

shock: A physical condition, often following a traumatic injury, in which the victim's blood circulation is impaired. Symptoms often include weak pulse, chills, nausea, irregular breathing, faintness, and weakness. The term "shock" is also used popularly to convey sudden surprise, fright, and the feeling that one's bodily systems have come temporarily to a halt.

shock therapy: See *electroshock therapy (EST).*

sibling rivalry: Competition between *siblings,* basically to gain parental favor or attention.

siblings: Brothers and sisters.

sibling therapy: The use of *family therapy* and other forms of helping interventions with *multiproblem families,* working only with children. This model is sometimes used when parents are uncooperative, resistant, or so inconsistent that their presence is more disruptive than productive. According to Karen Gail Lewis ("Sibling Therapy with Multiproblem Families," *Journal of Marriage and Family Therapy,* July 1986, pp. 291–300), the children are helped to develop and strengthen the bonds that exist between them so they can be more effective in providing one another with needed supports.

sickle-cell anemia: A genetically transmitted blood disorder in which a large proportion of red cells assume sicklelike shapes. The disorder affects primarily blacks of West African descent. In the United States, government grants have led to the establishment in health centers around the nation of free testing for the sickle-cell trait.

side-taking: A technique, used especially by family therapists, in which the worker actively and deliberately advocates for one family member over others in order to unbalance a dysfunctional system or break up a pattern in which both sides are stalemated.

SIDS: See *sudden infant death syndrome (SIDS).*

significance level: The degree to which a value that has been obtained through systematic data collection will not occur by chance. In research reporting this is expressed numerically to indicate the number of times out of a specified number of samplings that the result would probably occur by chance. In social science the significance levels are most often .01, .05, or .001, even though any other figure could be used as well. For example, if the .05 level is used, a specified outcome would occur by chance five times out of 100 samplings.

significant others: The most meaningful people in one's life.

single-parent family: A family unit and household comprising the children and the mother or father but not the other spouse. This family unit is not to be confused with the *reconstituted family,* in which the children and one parent are joined by a stepparent.

single-session group: A form of *group therapy* or *social group work* in which the members meet only once. Usually such groups are highly structured and focused on one type of problem. Some groups of this type are scheduled to last only an hour or two, but others may be scheduled for many hours, as in a *marathon group.*

single-subject design: A research procedure, often used in clinical situations to evaluate the effectiveness of an intervention. Behavior of a single subject, such as an individual client, is used as both a comparison and a control. Typically, the results of progress or change are plotted graphically. Single-subject design is also known as $N = 1$ design.

skew: A concept in research indicating that a distribution curve is not symmetrical.

skid row: A term once commonly used to describe areas, usually found in larger cities, frequented by homeless people and alcoholics, and containing many *tenement houses,* cramped deteriorating buildings, pawnshops, religious missions, and shelters.

skilled nursing facility: Health care structures and programs for patients who need relatively intensive and often long-term care, staffed primarily by more highly trained and experienced professional nurses and *nurse-practitioners* who may be specialists in certain types of health care. These facilities are sometimes described as hybrids between nursing homes and hospitals. The designation "skilled nursing home" has also been used in federal legislation, especially in Title XIX of the *Social Security Act (Medicaid).* This required Medicaid patients in need of nursing home care to be placed in skilled nursing homes, which were defined as being headed by a nonwaivered practical nurse. Facilities that Medicaid calls "skilled nursing homes" range from active treatment and rehabilitation programs to mere custodial care. See also *extended care facilities (ECF).*

Skinnerian theory: The learning theories developed by American psychologist B. F. Skinner. His concepts, especially that of *operant conditioning,* have greatly influenced the development of modern *behaviorism* and its use in treatment.

sliding fee scale: The practice, found among many social agencies and workers, in which clients are charged fees for service based on their ability to pay rather than on a fixed rate established in advance for everyone who receives the same service. See also *flat-rate fee*.

slum: A concentration of deteriorating buildings, many of which are inhabited by people who are economically and socially deprived.

SOAP charting method: A system used by social workers, physicians, nurses, and other professionals, especially in health and mental health care settings, to organize their notes on the medical charts. Part of the *problem-oriented record* originated by Dr. Lawrence Weed in 1968, such charting involves classifying information according to the acronym SOAP, which arranges records in four elements: (1) subjective information (such as symptoms reported by the client or family members), (2) objective information (such as sociodemographic information or data obtained from medical tests), (3) assessments and conclusions that the professional draws from the data, and (4) the plan (what the professional or agency is doing to resolve the problem).

social action: A coordinated effort to achieve institutional change in order to meet a need, solve a social problem, correct an injustice, or enhance the quality of human life. This effort may occur at the initiative and direction of professionals in social welfare, economics, politics, religion, or the military, or it may occur through the efforts of the people who are directly affected by the problem or change.

social activist: A professional organizer or indigenous layperson skilled at raising the public consciousness about a social problem or injustice and mobilizing available resources to change the conditions leading to these problems.

social agency: An organization and facility governed by a board of directors and usually staffed by human service personnel (including professional social workers, members of other professions, subprofessional specialists), clerical personnel, and sometimes *indigenous workers* to provide a specified range of social services for members of a population group that has or is vulnerable to a specific social problem. The agency may be funded by combinations of philanthropic contributions and privately solicited donations, by governments, or by fees paid by those served, or by *third-party payments*. Social agencies are accountable to their boards through accessible financial records, statements of purpose, and representatives from the community who serve on the boards of directors. The board members set overall policy, and administrators coordinate activities to carry out those policies. The organization has explicit bylaws that determine which clients to serve, what problems to combat, and what methods to use in providing service.

social casework: The orientation, value system, and type of practice used by professional social workers in which psychosocial, behavioral, and systems concepts are translated into skills designed to help individuals and families solve intrapsychic, interpersonal, socioeconomic, and environmental problems through direct face-to-face relationships. Many social workers consider "social casework" to be synonymous with *clinical social work*.

social causation theory: The idea that insecure and stressful economic and social conditions strongly increase the probability that a given individual experiencing them will develop social problems or mental disorders. This theory is often advanced to explain why there are higher rates of *incidence* and *prevalence* of mental illnesses, poverty, divorce, *spouse abuse*, and so on among people of certain *socioeconomic classes*, ethnic and racial backgrounds, and geographic areas of residence.

social change: Variations over time in a society's laws, norms, values, and institutional arrangements.

social class: A category of people in a society, ranked according to such criteria as relative wealth, power, prestige, educational level, or family background.

social control: The organized effort of a society or some of its members to maintain a stable social order and to manage the process of *social change*; also, efforts to constrain people, requiring them to adhere to established norms and laws.

social cost: The expenditures for certain programs or activities that are borne by society as a whole. For example, the rising unemployment rate among black youths is considered a social cost of racial discrimination and social and educational inequalities. The term "social cost" also refers to societal problems that do not easily lend themselves to financial calculations. An example is the social and emotional investment required for young couples to care for their disabled parents at home.

social Darwinism: The philosophy first articulated by English sociologist Herbert Spencer (1820–1903), who coined the phrase "survival of the fittest" and applied Darwin's theories of evolution to human economic conditions. The philosophy suggested that competition was normal and inevitable, that those who couldn't compete would be eliminated through natural selection, that only those who were inferior or inadequate to survive in society would be poor, and that the *laissez-faire* economic system was best because self-help was the only way out of poverty. This philosophy has had great influence in the development of social welfare policy in the United States.

social distance: The relative degrees of isolation, aloofness, intimacy, and *social mobility* between people that occur or are permitted within a society or part of that society (such as a family, a group of workers, or a socioeconomic class). For example, one culture might discourage and another encourage physical embraces between men.

social ecology: The study of the reciprocal and adaptive relationship between the natural environment and human society.

social functioning: Fulfilling one's responsibilities to society in general, to those in the immediate environment, and to oneself. These responsibilities include meeting one's own basic human needs and those of one's dependents and making positive contributions to society. Human needs include physical aspects (food, shelter, safety, health care, and protection), personal fulfillment (education, recreation, values, esthetics, religion, and accomplishment), emotional needs (a sense of belonging, mutual caring, and companionship), and an adequate self-concept (self-confidence, self-esteem, and identity). Social workers consider one of their major roles to be that of helping individuals, groups, or communities enhance or restore their capacity for social functioning.

social gerontology: The scientific study of the societal and psychological aspects of aging.

social group work: An orientation and method of social work intervention in which small numbers of people who share similar interests or common problems convene regularly and engage in activities designed to achieve their common goals. In contrast to *group psychotherapy*, the goals of group work are not necessarily the treatment of emotional problems. The objectives also include exchanging information, developing social and manual skills, changing value orientations, and diverting antisocial behaviors into productive channels. Intervention techniques include, but are not limited to, controlled therapeutic discussions. Some groups also include education and tutoring, sports, arts and crafts, recreational activities, and discussion about such topics as politics, religion, sexuality, values, and goals.

social history: An in-depth description and assessment of the current and past client-situation, often included in the case records and medical records of clients. It is a document that describes the person's family and socioeconomic background and relevant developmental experiences. Typically, this document is prepared by social workers and social work assistants based on interviews with the client and members of the client's family, reviews of records and reports, consultation with other professionals and agencies, and direct observation of the client and the client's environment. The social history often precedes and forms the basis for social work assessment and service planning. It may also be used by other professionals, such as physicians, lawyers, and teachers, in their own decision making to serve the client. Many social histories are written in a narrative, chronological fashion. Others are organized topically. They frequently include the information under specific headings similar to the following: (1) presenting problem; (2) symptoms of the problem; (3) history of the problem (including recurring situations or repetitious psychological events); (4) current situation (including family, job, economic status, and relevant environmental, social, and health factors); (5) family background (including parents, grandparents, and other close relatives and relevant health and psychological factors about them); (6) educational and vocational background; (7) client goals (including relevant goals of immediate members of the client's family); (8) worker's assessment; and (9) worker's recommendations (including social work treatment plans). The history may also include other information the worker deems to be relevant to the presenting problem, goal, or agency function. Social histories are also used by other professionals, including physicians, teachers, and attorneys, to gain information needed in providing their services to the client.

social indicators: Quantitative measures about demographic, environmental, and societal conditions that are used in establishing comprehensive and balanced planning.

social inequality: A condition in which some members of a society receive fewer opportunities or benefits than other members.

social insurance: Government programs to protect citizens from the full consequences of the risks and situations to which they are vulnerable, such as unemployment, disability, death of a breadwinner, catastrophic medical care needs, impoverishment, retirement, and financial problems of old age. Typically the government requires covered individuals to make regular contributions to a fund that, theoretically, is set aside and used to pay for those who encounter the covered risk. The major system of this type in the United States has been *OASDHI.*

socialism: A system of economic organization in which all or most of the planning is centralized and most of the means of production are controlled by the government or a collective institution.

socialization: The process by which the roles, values, skills, knowledge, and norms of a culture are transmitted to its individual members.

socialized medicine: See *national health service.*

social justice: An ideal condition in which all members of a society have the same basic rights, protection, opportunities, obligations, and social benefits.

social learning theory: The conceptual orientation and treatment application that builds on and modifies principles of *behaviorism,* taking into account some internal cognitive processes. The major developer of this theory, which emphasizes reciprocal relationships and the ability to learn new responses through observing and imitating others, has been Albert Bandura.

social minded: Having an active concern for the welfare of a society and its institutional services that enhance the well-being of people.

social ministry: Activities and *sectarian services* carried out by clergy, religious workers, and volunteers to help the poor and disadvantaged and to combat social injustice.

social mobility: The degree to which a society permits, encourages, or forces people to change statuses, geographic residence, socioeconomic level, or cultural value orientations.

social movement: An organized effort, usually involving many people representing a wide spectrum of the population, to change a law, public policy, or social norm. Examples of social movements include the *temperance movement,* the *Townsend plan,* and various equal rights movements.

social networks: See *network.*

social phobia: An intense, continuous, and unreasonable fear of being observed or evaluated. Victims of this *phobic disorder* are most commonly afraid of public speaking or performing before audiences, using public lavatories or bathing facilities, or eating in restaurants. Typically, they fear they will show anxiety and be humiliated, a condition that often leads to the outcome they fear (a *self-fulfilling prophecy*).

social planning: Systematic procedures to achieve predetermined types of socioeconomic structures and to manage *social change* rationally. These procedures usually include designating some individual or organization to collect the facts, delineating alternative courses of action, and making recommendations to those empowered to implement them.

social policy: The activities and principles of a society that guide the way it intervenes in and regulates relationships between individuals, groups, communities, and social institutions. These principles and activities are the result of the society's values and customs and largely determine the distribution of resources and level of well-being of its people. Thus, social policy includes a government's plans and programs in education, health care, crime and corrections, economic security, and social welfare. It also includes social perspectives that result in society's rewards and constraints.

social problems: Conditions between people, and between people and their environments, leading to social responses that violate some people's values and norms and cause emotional or economic suffering. Examples of social problems include crime, social deviance, *social inequality, poverty, racism, drug abuse,* family problems, and maldistribution of limited resources.

social reform: Activity designed to rearrange social institutions or the way they are managed in order to achieve greater *social justice* or other desired changes. The term is most often applied to efforts to eliminate corruption in government or structural inequities such as institutional *racism.*

social security: The provisions a society makes to protect its citizens against the normal risks of life, such as sickness, unemployment, death of a wage earner, old age, or disability dependency. This term is also used as a synonym for the specific federal programs in the United States covered by the *Social Security Act.*

Social Security Act: The federal legislation, enacted in 1935, with several subsequent amendments, designed to meet many of the economic needs of the aged, dependent survivors, disabled people, and needy families. In its original form it contained two major provisions, a mandatory insurance program for workers and a public assistance program financed jointly from the federal and state treasuries. The insurance program collected payroll taxes from certain groups of workers and matching contributions from their employers and, with those funds, established a pension fund that the workers could draw on when they were injured or retired. Their surviving dependents could also receive benefits. Benefits varied according to how much the worker had earned and contributed. Through grants to the states the act also established an *Unemployment Insurance* program and awarded funds to states to develop uniform programs to care for poor children (ADC), needy older people (OAA), and blind people (AB). The Social Security Act has been used as the framework for much of the subsequent national legislation that provides for people's economic and social welfare needs. See also *OASDHI, Medicare, Social Security Administration (SSA), Federal Insurance Contributions Act (FICA),* and *Title XX.*

Social Security Administration (SSA): The federal organization created in 1935 to implement the provisions of the *Social Security Act.* The SSA is part of the U.S. *Department of Health and Human Services (HHS).* It has over 1,200 local service offices in nearly every county in the United States and its central records are maintained in its Baltimore headquarters. The local offices are primarily oriented to helping people with its three largest programs, *OASDHI, Supplemental Security Income (SSI),* and *Medicare.*

social services: The activities of social workers and other professionals in helping people to become more self-sufficient, preventing dependency, strengthening family relationships, and restoring individuals, families, groups, or communities to successful *social functioning.* Specific kinds of social services include helping people obtain adequate financial resources for their needs, evaluating the capabilities of people to care for children or other dependents, counseling and psychotherapy, referring and channeling, mediating, advocating for social causes, informing organizations of their obligations to individuals, facilitating health care provisions, and linking clients to resources.

social skill: The ability to relate to and work with others in achieving specific social goals. Examples include speaking understandably, writing clearly, and empathizing with and influencing people.

social stratification: The division of society into classes (for example, upper class, middle class, working class, lower class, underclass, and so on) according to such criteria as economic level, educational level, or cultural value orientation.

social therapy: A term often applied to the activities of social workers. In contrast to *psychotherapy,* it refers to providing concrete services, facilitating environmental supports for clients, and helping people deal with social problems and conflicts.

social utility: A way of looking at social services as part of the normal system of needs most people may use at some time in their lives. It sees social services as inherently the same as any other public utility and part of the *infrastructure,* including the transportation system, the educational system, the postal system, the water and sewerage systems, libraries, and museums. People who use social utilities, and thus rely on others in society, are not considered deviant or helpless. In the social utility concept, the user of social services is seen as a citizen, not a patient or client. This idea has been developed by Alfred J. Kahn (*Social Policy and Social Services,* 2nd ed., New York: Random House, 1979, p. 75).

social value: The relative worth to society of a service or commodity. The term is used to differentiate between the cash or dollar value of some items that are measured objectively and the value of other items that enhance the social good but cannot be measured as to dollar value. For example, a library building and its contents may have the same dollar value as a liquor store and its contents, but their social values differ.

social wage: See *new property.*

social welfare: A nation's system of programs, benefits, and services that help people meet those social, economic, educational, and health needs that are fundamental to the maintenance of society; also, the state of collective well-being of a community or society.

Social Welfare History Archives: The repository for the significant records, documents, and memorabilia of the social work profession and epochal events in the history of social welfare in the United States. The archive is located at the University of Minnesota in Minneapolis, and includes taped oral histories by some leading figures in the development of social welfare as well as important written materials.

social work: According to the *National Association of Social Workers (NASW),* "social work is the professional activity of helping individuals, groups, or communities to enhance or restore their capacity for social functioning and creating societal conditions favorable to this goal. Social work practice consists of the professional application of social work values, principles, and techniques to one or more of the following ends: helping people obtain tangible services; providing counseling and psychotherapy with individuals, families, and groups; helping communities or groups provide or improve social and health services; and participating in relevant legislative processes. The practice of social work requires knowledge of human development and behavior; of social, economic, and cultural institutions; and of the interaction of all these factors" *(Standards for Social Service Manpower,* Washington, D.C.: National Association of Social Workers, 1973, pp. 4–5).

social work associates: Members of the *social work team* who perform specific tasks or *episodes of service (EOS)* when so assigned by the professional social worker–team leader. According to Thomas L. Briggs ("Social Work Teams in the U.S.A.," in *Teamwork in the Personal Social Services and Health Care,* Susan Lonsdale, Adrian Webb, & Thomas L. Briggs, Eds., Syracuse, N.Y.: Syracuse University Press, 1980, pp. 38–44), social work associates are similar to *case aides,* although the range of their activities can go beyond work on a specific case.

Social Work Curriculum Study: The landmark report published in 1959 by the *Council on Social Work Education (CSWE)*, under the direction of Werner Boehm, which delineated the components of graduate-level social work education. The 13-volume study was used as a guide by CSWE in establishing criteria for accrediting schools of social work and by the schools as a means of developing effective educational programs.

social work education: The formal training and subsequent experience that prepare social workers for their professional roles. The formal training takes place primarily in accredited colleges and universities at the undergraduate *(BSW)* level and in accredited professional schools of social work in *MSW, DSW,* and other *doctoral programs.* Social work education includes extensive classroom activity as well as direct supervised work with clients *(field placement).* Social workers do not consider their education to be completed only because they have acquired their degrees. Upon graduation, most social workers provide services under the *supervision* of more experienced colleagues and then take additional formal courses *(continuing education).* See also *Council on Social Work Education (CSWE), curriculum policy statement, GADE, Hollis-Taylor Report,* and *Social Work Curriculum Study.*

social workers: Graduates of schools of social work (with either bachelor's or master's degrees), who use their knowledge and skills to provide social services for *clients* (who may be individuals, families, groups, communities, organizations, or society in general). Social workers help people increase their capacities for problem solving and coping and help them obtain needed resources, facilitate interactions between individuals and between people and their environments, make organizations responsible to people, and influence social policies.

social work knowledge: According to the *Standards for the Classification of Social Work Practice* (Silver Spring, Md.: National Association of Social Workers, 1982, p. 17), social work requires knowledge in some or all of the following areas: casework and group work theory and techniques; community resources and services; federal and state social service programs and their purposes; community organization theory and the development of health and welfare services; basic socioeconomic and political theory; racial, ethnic, and other cultural groups in society—their values and lifestyles and the resultant issues in contemporary life; sources of professional and scientific research appropriate to practice; concepts and techniques of social planning; theories and concepts of supervision and the professional supervision of social work practice; theories and concepts of personnel management; common social, psychological, statistical, and other research methods and techniques; theories and concepts of social welfare administration; social and environmental factors affecting clients to be served; theories and methods of psychosocial assessment and intervention and of differential diagnosis; theory and behavior of organizational and social systems and of methods for encouraging change; community organization theory and techniques; advocacy theory and techniques; ethical standards and practices of professional social work; teaching and instructional theories and techniques; social welfare trends and policies; and local, state, and federal laws and regulations affecting social and health services.

social work practice: The use of *social work knowledge* and *social work skills* to implement society's mandate to provide *social services* in ways that are consistent with *social work values.* Practice includes remediation (eliminating existing personal or social problems), restoration (rehabilitating those whose *social functioning* has been impaired), and prevention (planning, organizing, and providing services before problems develop, thus enhancing the prospects for social well-being). Some of the most important social work practice roles are administrator, advocate, broker, caregiver, case manager, communicator, consultant, data manager, evaluator, mobilizer, outreacher, planner, protector, researcher, socializer, supervisor, teacher, and upholder of equitable social values. Social work practice may occur in *micro practice, mezzo practice,* or *macro practice.*

social work skills: The *Standards for the Classification of Social Work Practice* (Silver Spring, Md.: National Association of Social Workers, 1982, pp. 17–18) identifies 12 skills as being essential in social work. They are being able to (1) listen to others with understanding and purpose; (2) elicit information and assemble relevant facts to prepare a social history, assessment, and report; (3) create and maintain professional helping relationships; (4) observe and interpret verbal and nonverbal behavior and use knowledge of personality theory and diagnostic methods; (5) engage clients (including individuals, families, groups, and communities) in efforts to resolve their own problems and to gain trust; (6) discuss sensitive emotional subjects supportively and without being threatening; (7) create innovative solutions to clients' needs; (8) determine the need to terminate the therapeutic relationship; (9) conduct research or interpret the findings of research and professional literature; (10) mediate and negotiate between conflicting parties; (11) provide interorganizational liaison services; and (12) interpret and communicate social needs to funding sources, the public, or legislators. The same policy statement identified the abilities necessary for social work practice. Social workers should be able to speak and write clearly, teach others, respond supportively to emotion-laden or crisis situations, serve as role models in professional relationships, interpret complex psychosocial phenomena, organize a workload to meet designated responsibilities, identify and obtain resources needed to assist others, assess their own performances and feelings and use help or consultation, participate in and lead group activities, function under stress, deal with conflict situations or contentious personalities, relate social and psychological theory to practice situations, identify the information necessary to solve a problem, and conduct research studies of agency services or their own practices.

social work team: A system for delivering social services in which several professional social workers, *social work associates, case aides, indigenous workers, volunteers*, and various ad hoc specialists work in an integrated and coordinated way to achieve a specified goal or *episode of service (EOS)*. According to Robert L. Barker and Thomas L. Briggs *(Using Teams to Deliver Social Services,* Syracuse, N.Y.: Syracuse University Press, 1969, pp. 6–17), the team members discuss in advance all the activities that can be accomplished to achieve the goal efficiently, and then various assignments toward that end are made by the social worker–team leader. Social workers also participate in interdisciplinary teams in such fields as mental health, health care, and developmental care.

Societies for the Prevention of Cruelty to Children (SPCC): Independent organizations in many larger communities that advocate for the rights and protection of children. The first SPCC was established in 1874 in New York after it was found that there were more legal protections against the abuse of animals than children. The well-established SPCAs (Societies for the Prevention of Cruelty to Animals) began taking child abuse cases to court, holding that children were animals and deserved at least as much protection. Soon thereafter, SPCCs were developed in over 250 communities. They were instrumental in early efforts to provide legal protections for children and in developing child welfare legislation.

Society for Hospital Social Work Directors (SHSWD): The professional membership association, established in 1966 and affiliated with the *American Hospital Association (AHA)*, comprising social workers who are in charge of the social service departments of health care facilities.

sociobiology: The scientific discipline that investigates the genetic and physical bases for behavior and human personality traits. A major premise of sociobiology is that certain behavior may be largely programmed into human brains and that learning and other aspects of culture are of relatively less importance.

sociocultural dislocation: The movement of an individual or group into a sociocultural system that has unfamiliar or unacceptable norms. The move may be permanent and inclusive, as in migrating from a *Third World* nation to an economically developed one, or it may be temporary and partial, as experienced by some *minorities of color* who live in ghetto areas and have jobs in affluent offices dominated by whites.

socioeconomic class: Categorization of groups of people according to specified demographic variables, such as level of income or education, location of residence, and value orientation. Sociologists often categorize the classes as "upper," "middle," "lower," and *working class*. Other observers make further distinctions, such as "upper middle class" and *underclass*.

sociofugal arrangements: A term pertaining to the physical design, setting, and decor of offices and facilities that tend to keep people apart and inhibit their interaction. For example, a social worker's sociofugal office and waiting room might contain stiff chairs lined straight against walls that are too far apart for easy communication; long, dark hallways in which clients must wait before seeing the worker; and metal desks and filing cabinets that act as barricades and further isolate the worker from the client. See also *sociopetal arrangements*.

sociogram: A diagram or graphic presentation used by group workers and other professionals to display how members of the group feel about one another and how they tend to align themselves with some and against some members of the group or organization.

sociopath: See *dyssocial*.

sociopetal arrangements: A term pertaining to the physical design, setting, and decor of offices and facilities that tend to draw people together and encourage interaction. For example, a social worker's sociopetal office might place comfortable chairs close to one another at attractive angles; have good lighting and music in the waiting area; and use file cabinets to form conversation nooks rather than barricades. See also *sociofugal arrangements*.

software: In computers, the programs (or instructions) that make the physical equipment *(hardware)* execute the desired operations.

solvency: The ability of an individual or organization to pay debts.

somatization disorder: One of the *somatoform disorders*, characterized by a subject's long history of complaints about symptoms that are not caused by physical disease, injury, or drugs. To receive this diagnosis, a male client must have at least 12 symptoms and a female client at least 14 symptoms, which include the following: being sickly for much of one's life; gastrointestinal symptoms (such as abdominal pain, nausea, vomiting, or diarrhea); pseudoneurological symptoms (such as fainting, muscle weakness, blurred or double vision, or memory loss); psychosexual symptoms (indifference to or pain during intercourse); pain, palpitations, shortness of breath, and for women, symptoms of female reproductive disorders.

somatoform disorders: Mental disorders that have the appearance of physical illness but, lacking any known organic basis, are generally thought to be *psychogenic*. The specific disorders in this category are *somatization disorder, hypochondria, conversion disorder,* and "psychogenic pain disorder."

soup kitchen: A facility, usually operated by a private charitable or religious organization, that prepares and serves food to the poor at little or no cost to the recipients.

Southern Christian Leadership Conference (SCLC): The civil rights organization—founded in 1956 by the Reverend Dr. Martin Luther King, Jr., and others—whose goal is the peaceful combat of racially motivated injustice.

span of control: In administration, the number of persons or activities under one person's supervision, including the amount of time the manager takes to supervise them effectively.

special interest group: See *interest group*.

specialist: A social work practitioner whose orientation and knowledge are focused on a specific problem or goal or whose technical expertise and skill in specific activities are highly developed and refined. See also *generalist*.

specialization: A profession's focus of knowledge and skill on a specific type of problem, target population, or objective.

"speed": A slang term for *amphetamines* (stimulant drugs that have been prescribed by physicians to help some people keep awake and alert or to lose weight). When used illicitly, as in taking excessive dosages over extended periods or in intravenous injections, these drugs are very dangerous and physiologically and psychologically addictive.

Speenhamland: An income subsidy system that originated in the Speenhamland district of England in 1795 and was later widely imitated. Workers who earned less than a predetermined amount had the difference made up from public funds.

spending down: An individual's intentional attempt to reduce total assets and income in order to be eligible for certain means-tested social insurance benefits. For example, a person who has a substantial amount of money in the bank would be ineligible for Medicaid, so he or she would dispose of the funds in order to become eligible.

spina bifida: Failure of the spinal column to close properly during early fetal development. The disorder is frequently associated with other problems such as retardation and hydrocephalus and its complications. Those affiliated with this disorder often require orthopedic, neurological, hospital, and other medical care and social services throughout their lives.

split-half reliability: See *reliability*.

splitting: In *psychoanalytic theory*, a primitive defensive process in which the individual is thought to repress, dissociate, or disconnect important feelings that have become dangerous to his or her psychic well-being. This may cause the person to get out of touch with his or her feelings and to develop a "fragmented self."

spouse abuse: The infliction of physical or emotional harm on one's husband or, more often, wife.

squatter: One who settles on rural or urban land belonging to another without title or right. Squatters usually have no legal rights except those they can acquire eventually through political or social pressure.

SSI: See *Supplemental Security Income (SSI)*.

staff development: Activities and programs within an organization designed to enhance the abilities of personnel to fulfill the existing and changing requirements of their jobs. These activities often include short-term in-service training classes, distribution of relevant information, group conferences, employing consultants and speakers from outside to meet with personnel, and funding certain employees to participate in meetings or training programs outside the organization. Staff development, although usually related to the specific job requirements of the employing organization, has broader functions as well. It also seeks to help personnel improve their overall career objectives and opportunities. According to Carol H. Meyer (*Staff Development in Public Welfare Agencies,* New York: Columbia University Press, 1966, pp. 98–99), a latent function of staff development is for the organization to attract and keep competent personnel and clarify and "humanize" the organization. Staff development is distinguished from professional education in that it does not grant academic credit, and its participants may have different degree levels.

staffing: In social welfare administration, an organization's activities designed to maintain and improve personnel effectiveness. This activity includes recruiting and interviewing prospective employees and volunteers; assigning, promoting, transferring, and firing employees; and providing for in-service training and staff development.

stage theories: The concept that every period of life is characterized by some underlying challenges and orientations that modify one's behavior and priorities. Each stage has characteristics that make it unique, and each higher stage incorporates many of the gains made in earlier ones. The degree to which one reconciles the conflicts inherent in each stage largely determines the likelihood of coping successfully in subsequent life stages. Among the best known of these concepts are Erikson's *psychosocial theory*, Freud's *psychosexual theory*, Piaget's theory of *cognitive development*, and the concepts delineated by Roger Gould, Daniel Levinson, Bernice Neugarten, Talcott Parsons, and Robert Bales.

stagflation: A nation's economic condition in which there is *inflation* without accompanying economic growth. This is often an indicator of economic *recession* or *depression*.

standard deviation: A statistical measure to indicate the degree of dispersion of a distribution. It is the average difference between individual scores and the mean score in a distribution, obtained by squaring the deviation scores, adding them together, dividing by one less than the number of scores, and taking the square root of the result. In a normal (symmetrical, or bell-shaped) distribution, 68.2 percent of the cases will fall between +1 or −1 standard deviation from the *mean*; 95.4 percent will fall between +2 or −2 standard deviations; and 99.7 percent of the cases will fall between +3 or −3 standard deviations.

standardized tests: Measurement tools used by social researchers, educators, and clinicians. The tests have already been used on many subjects, permitting a high degree of confidence in their *validity* and *reliability*. Standardized tests provide instructions, scoring procedures and standards, time limits, norms, and statistical data to make possible comparisons of the sample group with a much larger segment of society.

standard of living: A concept comprising the necessities, luxuries, and comforts an individual, group, class, or society needs or uses to live in a particular circumstance. The concept is often confused with "standards of consumption." Consumption involves the availability of consumer goods to the individual or the society. "Standard of living" includes available consumer goods but adds choices and variety of these goods, normal working conditions, amount of leisure time, and opportunities for using that time.

statistics: In research, quantitative procedures (which may be descriptive or inferential) that are used to describe or assess variables or relationships between variables; also, characteristics of a sample or subset of a larger population.

statistical significance: See *significance level*.

status: A social position that carries culturally defined expectations or *roles*. Statuses may be "achieved" (such as social worker, AFDC recipient, or government bureaucrat) or "ascribed" (such as woman, Hispanic, or child). Laypersons also use this term as a synonym for "prestige."

status offender: One whose actions are not essentially criminal but are in violation of certain laws. For example, this designation applies to children who are runaways, truants, or unmanageable by their parents.

Statute of Labourers: One of the world's earliest "public welfare" programs, initiated in England in 1349. It forbade giving charity to able-bodied people, compelled unemployed people to work for anyone who would hire them, forbade the unemployed to leave their hometowns or villages (or allowed them to go only to areas where there was work), and fixed the maximum wages that could be paid to workers.

statutory rape: A consenting sexual relationship with someone who is under the legal age of consent in a given jurisdiction.

stepfamily: A primary kinship group whose members are joined as a result of second or subsequent marriages. Such a family may include a stepfather (the husband of one's mother), a stepmother (the wife of one's father), a stepchild (the offspring of one's spouse by a previous marriage or relationship), and stepbrothers and stepsisters (the children of one's stepparent). Owing to the increased divorce and remarriage rates, stepfamilies constitute a major type of family constellation. See also *reconstituted family*.

stereotypes: Preconceived and relatively fixed ideas about an individual, group, or social *status*. These ideas are usually based on superficial characteristics or overgeneralizations of traits observed in some members of the group.

stimulus: In *behaviorism*, any event in the environment. A stimulus may be discriminative, eliciting, reinforcing, punishing, or neutral. See also *response*.

stimulus generalization: The ability of a subject to respond to one stimulus in the same way he or she responded to another, similar stimulus; the opposite of stimulus *discrimination.*

stranger anxiety: Fear or apprehension in the presence of unfamiliar people, most common among very young children.

strategic family therapy: The orientation and procedure used by some family therapists to help families and their members discontinue reciprocal interactions in which recurring patterns of symptomatic behavior occur. The therapist designs interventions to resolve specific problems whose resolution will require the family system to modify all other interactions.

strategic marketing: The development of a product or service that serves the interests of specific publics. According to Armand Lauffer (*Social Planning at the Community Level*, Englewood Cliffs, N.J.: Prentice-Hall, 1978, pp. 81–83), these publics include (1) input (resource suppliers, funders, and so on), (2) output (clients and other beneficiaries), and (3) throughput publics (paid staff and volunteers who are charged with turning resources, funds, and concepts into products or services). Strategic marketing uses technical means to segment publics geographically, demographically, functionally, and psychologically in order to define an agency's or program's "niche" or market. It also involves pricing, placing, and promotions to regulate demand for a specific product or service.

strategic planning: The process of formally or implicitly defining long-term goals and the alternative means toward their accomplishment. The goals are defined by specifying the target of intervention, the auspices, value implications, feasibility, and the interrelationships between various components of the social system. The goals thus established provide guidelines for looking at alternative means of achieving desired ends, which can often result in major modifications of existing programs and services.

stress: Any influence that interferes with the normal functioning of an organism and produces some internal strain or tension. "Human psychological stress" refers to environmental demands or internal conflicts that produce anxiety. People tend to seek an escape from the sources of these influences (called "stressors") through such means as *defense mechanisms, avoidance* of certain situations, *phobias, somatization,* rituals, or constructive physical activity.

stroke: A sudden interruption or blockage of the flow of blood to the brain, usually caused by the formation of a blood clot in the blood vessel or by *hypertension.* The resulting manifestations may include paralysis of certain parts of the body, speech and language deficits, sensory loss, cognitive and communicative disturbances, convulsions, and coma. Stroke survivors vary in their recovery progress. About 50 percent retain some permanent disability, such as speech or motor coordination problems. Recurrence is frequent and often fatal.

structural family therapy: An orientation and procedure in *family therapy* based on identifying and changing maladaptive arrangements, interactions, and the internal organization of subsystems and boundaries of a family. Structural family therapy was developed primarily by Dr. Salvador Minuchin and emphasizes helping families understand how they have developed rules and roles for their members and between themselves as a unit and outsiders.

structural social change: Basic and relatively rapid changes in social institutions and social values, often brought about by revolution, great political upheaval, or natural disaster. This is the opposite of *incremental social change.*

structural social work: A practice model that assumes that inadequate social arrangements are mainly responsible for many clients' problems and aims to help persons modify the social situations that limit functioning—for example, by connecting them with needed resources, negotiating difficult situations, and changing certain existing limiting social structures.

structural unemployment: One of the four types of unemployment (including *cyclical, seasonal,* and *frictional*), caused by poor economic conditions in one industry or geographic area when employment elsewhere is good.

student aid programs: Financial assistance to people attending colleges or other educational institutions, mostly through grants or loans. Sources of funds are privately funded scholarship funds, foundation grants, and, most importantly, state and federal grant and loan programs. The major federal programs include Pell Grants (based on a formula of student need and expected family contribution), National Direct Student Loans (low-interest loans to needy students), Supplemental Educational Opportunity Grants (based on need), Guaranteed Student Loans (the government guarantees repayment to banks that lend money to students), and the College Work Study Program, which provides matching funds to colleges to hire students on campus.

subemployment: The condition of having a job that pays below subsistence level or a job that does not utilize much of the worker's education or previous experience. Social workers describe many of the *working poor* as being subemployed.

sublimation: In *psychodynamic* theory, a defense mechanism in which those desires and instinctive drives that are consciously intolerable and cannot be directly realized are diverted into activities that are acceptable to the individual and society.

subpoena: A legal document ordering an individual to appear in court at a certain time. Failure to comply may result in some penalty.

subsidy: Money or commodities granted by a government or other organization to another level of government, organization, industry, or individual. See also *grants-in-aid* and *block grant.*

subsidized adoption: The provision of public financial assistance to families who adopt dependent children. Recent federal and state legislation has established criteria for subsidizing adoption. The two prominent criteria are that the child is not likely to be returning to the natural parents or should not be returning to them and that adoptive placement without a subsidy has already been attempted for a specified amount of time by the proper authorities but has been unsuccessful because of the child's physical or emotional condition or racial or ethnic background.

subsistence level: The lowest amount of money or resources one needs in order to survive.

substance abuse: A disorder related to the unhealthy use of alcohol or drugs. For an individual to be considered a substance abuser, he or she must have used the substance for over a month; had social, legal, or vocational problems as a result of its use; and developed a pathological pattern of use (episodic binges) or psychological dependence (a desire for continued use and an inability to inhibit that desire). See also *alcohol abuse* and *drug abuse.*

substance dependence: A disorder related to the unhealthy use of alcohol or drugs, which includes *substance abuse* symptoms but also includes symptoms of *tolerance* or *withdrawal symptoms.*

substitution: In *psychodynamic theory,* the *defense mechanism* in which the individual replaces an unattainable or unacceptable goal with one that is attainable and acceptable.

subsystem: A part of a *system* that itself comprises interacting and reciprocally influencing elements. For example, in the family system there are such subsystems as the parents, the children, the females, the males, the *nuclear family* system, and the *extended family* system.

sudden infant death syndrome (SIDS): The unexplained death of a young child, most frequently occurring between the ages of 2 and 5 months, sometimes referred to as "crib death." The cause is not yet well understood, but speculation centers around the possibility that some babies have not established adequate defense responses to respiratory problems. See also *apnea.*

suicidal ideation: Serious contemplation of *suicide,* or thought patterns that lead to killing oneself. Helping professionals note specific clues and circumstances to judge the probability that a client is going to attempt suicide. Among those that suggest higher probability are *depression,* especially when accompanied by a sense of hopelessness or unconnectedness with others in the present or past; major changes in sleep patterns; clear or implied statements indicating a wish to die or an intention to commit suicide; *substance abuse*; a recent experience of irrevocable loss; absence of a support system; easy access to lethal means (weapons, drugs, and so on); previous suicide attempts; suicide or suicide attempts by role models; and feelings of failure and rejection.

suicide: The act of intentionally killing oneself.

sunk costs: In social agency administration and social planning, the investment of time and effort made by an organization's personnel to develop, maintain, and facilitate their relationship patterns, status and power arrangements, and traditional ways of doing things.

sunset laws: Statutes that require an organization to demonstrate periodically that it is achieving the goals it was established to achieve. If the organization cannot do this, according to these laws, it is automatically discontinued. For example, some states have required certain professions that sought licensing to show after several years that the granting of licenses provided some benefit to the public.

sunshine laws: Federal requirements, based on a law enacted in 1976, stating that the meetings and hearings of most federal agencies—especially those that directly affect people's economic, legal, and welfare rights—must be conducted in public. This term now applies to the requirements that other organizations and levels of government conduct their business open to the scrutiny of those affected.

superego: In *psychodynamic* theories, that part of the psyche or personality that regulates the individual's ethical standards, conscience, and sense of right and wrong. The superego is said to begin its development by identifying with the apparent values and rules established by parent-figures. See also *ego* and *id.*

supervision: An administrative and educational process used extensively in social agencies to help social workers further develop and refine their skills and to provide *quality assurance* for the clients. Administratively, supervisors often assign cases to the most appropriate worker, discuss the assessment and intervention plan, and review the worker's ongoing contact with the client. Educationally, supervision is geared toward helping the worker better understand social work philosophy and agency policy, become more self-aware, know the agency's and community's resources, establish activity priorities, and refine knowledge and skills. Another function of supervision, according to Alfred Kadushin (*Supervision in Social Work*, New York: Columbia University Press, 1976, pp. 33–41), is to enhance the morale of the staff while maintaining the system. Less experienced workers tend to be supervised according to a tutorial model, whereas those with more experience achieve similar purposes through case consultation, peer-group interactions, staff development programs, or *social work teams*. Carol H. Meyer (personal correspondence with the author) distinguishes educational supervision (oriented toward professional concerns and related to specific cases) from administrative supervision (oriented toward agency policy and public accountability).

Supplemental Security Income (SSI): The federal public assistance program, established in 1972, that provides a minimum cash income for poor people who are old, disabled, or blind. Funding comes from the federal treasury and is usually supplemented by state funds. It is administered primarily by the *Social Security Administration (SSA)*, although its funds do not come from the social security payroll taxes of workers. Eligibility for SSI is determined by a *means test* and not related to one's previous work record.

supply subsidy: The concept of providing funds to organizations, or allocating funds to establish new organizations, so that they can provide services to people in need. This is in contrast to the *demand subsidy* concept, in which funds or vouchers are provided to individuals and families in need so that they can purchase goods and services in the existing service-providing market. Public housing is an example of the supply subsidy concept, and food stamps are an example of demand subsidies.

support group: See *support system*.

supportive treatment: The helping interventions used by social workers and other professionals, designed primarily to help individuals maintain adaptive patterns. This is done in the interview through *reassurance*, advice giving, information providing, and pointing out client strengths and resources. Supportive treatment supposedly does not seek to reach or change deeply unconscious material. However, the boundaries between supportive therapy and "deeper" insight-therapy are unclear and overlapping.

support system: An interrelated group of people, resources, and organizations that provide individuals with emotional, informational, material, and affectional sustenance. Members of a support system may include an individual's closest friends, family members, key members of the peer group, fellow employees, membership organizations, and institutions that can be called upon for help in times of need. Support systems comprising a few individuals who have regular direct contacts are called support groups.

suppression: (1) In *psychoanalytic theory*, the conscious psychic mechanism of putting unpleasant thoughts out of one's mind. Suppression is similar to *repression*, except that the latter is a *defense mechanism* operating unconsciously to remove threatening ideas from one's awareness. (2) In social conflict theories, suppression refers to actions taken by one group or organization to prevent other groups or individuals from expressing their ideas, assembling, or developing political power.

survey: A systematic fact-gathering procedure in which a specific series of questions is asked, through written or oral questionnaires, of a representative sample of the group being studied.

survivor syndrome: The behavior patterns, traits, and symptoms that tend to occur in people who have experienced dangerous, life-threatening events or trauma. Such people often have prolonged periodic anxiety, guilt feelings, anger, and fears, especially in situations that seem similar to the traumatic event. The syndrome has been experienced especially by *Vietnam veterans,* former prisoners of war, *Holocaust* survivors, sexual assault victims, crime victims, and people who have lived through serious natural disasters.

sustaining procedures: Relationship-building activities used by the social worker to help the client feel more self-confident and confident of the worker's competence and good will. They include listening with sincere interest and sympathy and conveying a sense of mutual respect, rather than superiority over the client. *Acceptance, reassurance*, encouragement, and *reaching out* are other sustaining procedures identified by Florence Hollis and Mary E. Woods (*Casework: A Psychological Therapy*, 3rd ed., New York: Random House, 1981).

symbiosis: A relationship between two organisms in which there is mutual biological or psychological dependence. This may occur between different species (flowers depend on insects for cross-pollination and provide food necessary for the insects' survival) or within a species (termites help one another to survive). Symbiosis occurs between a parent and a child and to some extent between mature adults in certain mutually beneficial social relationships. The term also refers to a person's identification with others to such an extent that it blocks his or her differentiated identity.

SYMLOG: Systematic Multiple Level Observation of Groups, a method developed by social psychologist Robert F. Bales to assess client behavior graphically and to quantify systematically actions in the worker-client system.

symptom: An indicator of the possible presence of an underlying psychological or physical disorder or of a psychosocial problem. For example, *flat affect* is symptomatic of *schizophrenia* and depression; *ideas of reference* are symptoms of *paranoia*; abnormally high fever is symptomatic of an infection; dramatic weight loss (25 percent of body weight) is symptomatic of *anorexia nervosa*; and *inflation* is symptomatic of a supply-demand imbalance.

syndrome: A cluster of behavior patterns, personality traits, or physical *symptoms* that occur together to form a specific disorder or condition.

synergism: Cooperative effort by discrete organizations, social agencies, or *subsystems*, that produces a more effective result than the sum of the output that could be achieved if the organizations acted independently.

syphilis: A contagious *venereal disease* transmitted primarily by sexual contact and rarely by contact with an open wound or transmission of infected blood or plasma. Untreated, the disease causes lesions in subcutaneous tissue and internal organs and degeneration of the nerves, often causing blindness and psychosis. Treatment with penicillin in the early stages is very effective.

system: A combination of elements with mutual reciprocity and identifiable boundaries that form a complex or unitary whole. Systems may be physical and mechanical, living and social, or combinations of these. Examples of social systems include individual families, groups, a specific social welfare agency, or a nation's entire organizational process of education.

systematic desensitization: A *behavior modification* technique, designed by Joseph Wolpe, that gradually alleviates the fear and anxiety associated with an object or event. Using relaxation exercises and guided imagery, the client is exposed to *stimuli* from a gradation of anxiety-provoking situations. For example, if a client is afraid of heights over six feet, the social worker might encourage the client to stand on the lowest rung of a stepladder while thinking of some pleasant experiences long enough for anxiety to end at that level. This process would be repeated slowly until the client is comfortable at levels higher than six feet.

systemic requisites: In *community organization* and social policy development, the identification of existing as well as potential resources and programs and the collaborative effort to link and coordinate these resources so that duplication and competition is avoided and the range and quality of service are expanded. See also *functional requisites*.

systems theories: Those concepts that emphasize reciprocal relationships between the elements that constitute a whole. These concepts also emphasize the relationships between individuals, groups, organizations, or communities and mutually influencing factors in the environment. Systems theories focus on the interrelationships of elements in nature, encompassing physics, chemistry, biology, and social relationships. See also *general systems theory, ecological perspective,* and *life model.*

T

tactics of influence: Activities of community organizers, social activists, and other social workers to encourage adoption of one policy over another. Some of the specific actions include holding case conferences with individuals and organizations to determine needs and needs provision, gathering facts, taking advocacy positions, convening and participating in committees, petitioning, *media campaigning*, providing expert testimony, working as *lobbyists, bargaining,* organizing demonstrations, initiating or coordinating *class action suits*, and engaging in *disruptive tactics.*

Tarasoff: The 1976 ruling by the Supreme Court of California (in the case of *Tarasoff v. Regents of the University of California*) stating that, under certain circumstances, psychotherapists whose clients tell them that they intend to harm someone are obliged to warn the intended victim. Subsequently, this decision has been upheld in many other states. The effect of the ruling is to make it more difficult for therapists to assure their clients of confidentiality and for clients to express certain hostile feelings to their therapists.

tardive dyskinesia: Abnormal and uncontrollable physical movements, especially of the mouth, lips, and tongue, and sometimes repetitive movements of the head, hands, and feet. This is seen in many clients who have used antipsychotic drugs over a period of time.

target behavior: In *behavior modification*, the behavior or behaviors selected for analysis or modification. Identifying the target behaviors is the first step in the therapist's *behavioral assessment.* This includes delineating the specific behaviors and the time and conditions in which they occur. For example, a social worker would list a target behavior for a youngster who frequently skips school as follows: "Student was absent from school an average of two times per week during the past two months." See also *unit of attention.*

target segments of society: In social planning and policy development, a category of people who are deemed most vulnerable to a given social problem or who are given special attention in efforts to find solutions or enhanced well-being. For example, a target segment might be all American mothers, everyone who is "functionally illiterate," or all residents of Tacoma, Washington. See also *unit of attention.*

target system: The individual, group, or community to be changed or influenced to achieve the social work goals. According to Allen Pincus and Anne Minahan (*Social Work Practice: Model and Method,* Itasca, Ill., F. E. Peacock Publishers, 1973, pp. 58–60), this is one of the four basic systems in social work practice (the others being the *change agent system,* the *client system,* and the *action system*). Target systems and client systems are sometimes but not always identical. They are different when the client is not to be changed. For example, a client may be a poor family that is being evicted, and the social worker's target system might be the landlord. Target systems and client systems may be the same when the client wants to achieve some self-change, such as relief from symptoms of emotional distress. See also *unit of attention.*

task-centered treatment: A model of short-term social work intervention in which the worker and client (1) identify specific problems, (2) identify specific tasks needed to change these problems, (3) develop a contract in which various activities are to occur at specified times, (4) establish incentives for their accomplishment, and (5) analyze and resolve obstacles as they are identified. The client may also be helped to accomplish tasks by simulation and guided practice in the worker's office before performing them independently during the week.

tax: A mandatory charge, usually of money, imposed by a government to help pay for its operating costs.

Tay-Sachs disease: A genetically transmitted metabolic disorder that results in fatal brain damage. It occurs mostly in infants of East European Jewish ancestry.

teams in social work: See *social work team*.

TEFRA: The Tax Equity and Fiscal Responsibility Act (P.L. 97-248), the U.S. legislation passed in 1982 that resulted in changes in financing and cutbacks in service of such programs as *Supplemental Security Income (SSI), Aid to Families with Dependent Children (AFDC), Medicare, Medicaid,* and child support enforcement.

temperance movements: Organized efforts to influence people to abstain from or modify their consumption of alcohol. These movements were especially strong in the United States, Canada, and European nations in the years 1850–1930. The major groups in the United States were the Women's Christian Temperance Union (WCTU), the Prohibition Party, and the Anti-Saloon League, which helped influence passage of many antiliquor laws, culminating in the Eighteenth Amendment to the U.S. Constitution, or Prohibition. The influence of these groups declined when Prohibition was repealed by the Twenty-first Amendment in 1933.

tenant organization: A formal or informal association of people, most of whom live in the same apartment building or housing complex and share an interest in maintaining or improving the conditions of their residence. Tenant organizations often present unity in confrontations with landlords or public housing authorities.

tenement house: A multifamily residential structure, usually old, run down, and rented to poor people.

terminal illness: A disease that is expected to result in a person's death.

termination phase: The conclusion of the worker-client intervention process; a systematic procedure for disengaging the working *relationship*. It occurs when goals are reached, when the specified time for working has ended, or when the client is no longer interested in continuing. It often includes evaluating the progress toward goal achievement and *working through, resistance, denial,* and *flight into illness*. The termination phase also includes discussions about how to anticipate and resolve future problems and how to find additional resources to call on as future needs indicate.

tertiary prevention: Rehabilitative efforts by the social worker or other professional to assist a client who has already experienced a problem to recuperate from its effects and develop sufficient strengths to preclude its return. Most forms of clinical intervention can be considered forms of tertiary prevention. See also *primary prevention* and *secondary prevention*.

test bias: A tendency built into a test causing its results to be inaccurate. For example, some aptitude tests are said to be culturally biased against some minorities when those minorities tend to score lower than do other test takers.

test case: A lawsuit to determine whether a law or legal practice is valid. Often the case is brought intentionally by a cause-oriented group to test the validity of a newly passed law. For example, a state enacts a law stating that psychotherapy may be provided only by psychiatrists. A social work group might designate one of its members to provide psychotherapy and therefore be arrested. The resulting court case could test whether the law could be upheld.

test-retest reliability: In research, the degree to which a test or procedure achieves a similar outcome the second time it is administered to a group of subjects as the first. For example, a group of social work students might be asked to take an aptitude test and after a period of time to take it again. Reliability is considered low if the second scores are very different from the first.

T-group: A training group, often made up of people who work together in one organization, that emphasizes communication, self-development, and cooperative problem solving. Some T-groups are highly structured, whereas others are highly unstructured to encourage the members to learn by experience how to be more effective in interpersonal relationships.

theme group: A type of *group therapy* or *social group work* for which the range of discussion is highly focused around a single subject or theme that is of concern to all the participants.

theory: A group of related hypotheses, concepts, and constructs, based on facts and observations, that attempts to explain a particular phenomenon.

therapeutic community: See *milieu therapy*.

therapist: One who helps individuals to overcome or abate disease, disability, or problems. Usually a therapist has had extensive amounts of training and supervised experience and often uses specialized techniques, tools, medications, and resources to accomplish goals. Social workers often use this term as a synonym for *psychotherapist* and are more specific when discussing other kinds of therapists, such as physical therapists, marital therapists, occupational therapists, and so on.

therapy: A systematic process and activity designed to remedy, cure, or abate some disease, disability, or problem. Social workers often use this term as a synonym for *psychotherapy, psychosocial therapy,* or *group therapy*. When social workers discuss other types of therapy, such as occupational therapy, physical therapy, recreational therapy, medication therapy, or *chemotherapy*, they use these more specific terms.

think tanks: Organizations funded largely by federal government and foundation moneys to conduct research and systematic inquiries, primarily into existing sociopolitical and environmental conditions and future trends. Such organizations include the Rand Corporation, the Hudson Institute, the Brookings Institution, and the Institutes for the Study of Poverty.

third-party payment: Financial reimbursement made to the social worker, social agency, or other provider of services to a client by an insurance company or government funding agency. See also *fiscal intermediaries* and *fourth parties*.

Third World: Those nations that are technologically underdeveloped and have high rates of poverty, illiteracy, population growth, illness, and nutritional deficiency. The term is used to distinguish between those nations and the developed ones in the Western and Soviet blocs.

thought disorders: Disturbances in the process and content of one's thinking, including such patterns as *hallucinations, delusions, loose associations, paranoid ideation, flight of ideas,* and *ideas of reference*. Thought disorders may be symptomatic of *organic mental disorders* or of *schizophrenia*.

thrombosis: Clogging of a blood vessel as a result of a blood clot. In a coronary thrombosis, the coronary arteries that supply blood to the heart are clogged, resulting in damage to the heart muscle.

Title XX: The 1975 provision (P.L. 93-647) added to the *Social Security Act* to separate income transfer programs from *personal social service* programs and to encourage the states to take a larger part in developing funding for these programs. Funding comes through *block grants* from federal to state governments. The states then have greater discretion in deciding where to put those funds. The ultimate goal is to help low-income families achieve greater self-sufficiency and to provide for needy people in an economical way. Title XX encourages such programs as day care for low- to moderate-income mothers who work and services for abused children and homebound elderly people. It is the nation's largest single source of funds for personal social services.

token economy: The therapeutic procedure, used in *behavior modification, milieu therapy,* and various institutional settings, in which the clients are given tokens, slips of paper, or coupons whenever they fulfill specified tasks or behave according to some specified standard. These tokens may then be redeemed for the client's choice of certain goods or privileges.

tolerance: A term pertaining to an individual's capacity to endure or resist the effects of certain drugs. Because drug response tends to decrease with repeated doses, the user increases the amount taken to get the same effect.

total disability: As used in *workers' compensation* and insurance contracts, the term refers to an individual's inability—usually caused by work-related injury or health problems—to perform the occupational requirements of the job category once held.

Tourette's disorder: A syndrome manifested in the victim by facial grimacing, abrupt and jerky movements of the limbs, hyperactive behavior, explosive temper, and foul language. Although the disorder is usually lifelong and involuntary, its symptoms tend to begin in children from ages 2 to 13, worsen through childhood, and decline in later years. The symptoms may spontaneously remit or cease during adulthood or be controlled successfully with certain drugs. The disorder is also known as Gilles de la Tourette's disease and "multiple tic disorder."

Townsend Plan: A proposal, made by Dr. Francis Townsend in the early 1930s, advocating federal payments of $200 monthly to all persons over 60 who agree to retire from work and spend the money within a month. The plan spurred a strong *social movement*, especially among the aged of the United States, and contributed in part to the development of the *Social Security Act*.

toxin: A poison.

toxoids: The poisonous waste products of disease-causing microorganisms that are used to make certain vaccines to protect against those diseases.

Toynbee Hall: The British *settlement house* that was established in 1884 and became the prototype for the 400 American settlement houses that developed in the next 20 years. It was located in a poor section of London and served as something of a "missionary outpost," bringing the ideas, values, and social skills of the affluent to the less fortunate.

tranquilizer: A *psychotropic drug* used by physicians in the treatment of mental disorders and emotional discomfort. Major tranquilizers, such as Thorazine, Stelazine, and Mellaril, are frequently used to help with psychotic symptoms. Minor tranquilizers, such as Valium, Librium, and Tranxene, are frequently used to help with symptoms of anxiety.

transactional analysis (TA): A form of group and individual psychotherapy that explores the way clients tend to interact with others, play games, perform roles as though scripted to do so, and are influenced by the three parts of the mental-cultural apparatus, known as the "parent," "adult," and "child."

transactions: Reciprocal exchanges between two entities, influencing or changing both.

transsexualism: The changing of one's sex through surgery, hormone injections, psychotherapy, and special training; also, a *gender identity* problem in which an individual has a strong and persistent desire to be a member of the opposite sex.

transference: A concept, originating in *psychoanalytic theory*, that refers to emotional reactions that are assigned to current relationships but originated in earlier, often unresolved and unconscious experiences. For example, a client who, as a child, felt extremely hostile to a parent and never resolved the feeling develops extremely hostile feelings toward the social worker even though there is no overt reason for such feelings. Transference is used by psychodynamically oriented social workers and other therapists as a tool for understanding and *working through* past conflicts. The transfer of affectionate feelings to the worker is known as *positive transference,* and that of hostile feelings as *negative transference.* See also *countertransference.*

transfer payments: Cash benefits, theoretically taken from one population group and redirected to another. Typically, this is done indirectly with money withheld from one group and placed into the government treasury, which then disburses funds to the eligible other party. For example, money is transferred from the young to the old in *social security,* from the employed to the unemployed in *unemployment compensation,* from the more affluent to the poor in the *Aid to Families with Dependent Children (AFDC)* program. In the United States in the mid-1980s, some of the other major income transfer programs are government pensions, *Supplemental Security Income (SSI), Medicare,* and *Medicaid.*

transients: People who change places of residence frequently or maintain no fixed address. Although such people are often the most in need of health and social services and financial assistance, because they have no permanent homes they are frequently not eligible for existing welfare assistance, which tends to be contingent on fulfillment of certain residency requirements.

transracial adoption: *Adoption* of a child of one racial background by a family of another racial background (for example, a black child and white adoptive parents). This is the opposite of *inracial adoption.*

transvestism: The *psychosexual disorder* in which erotic pleasure is derived from wearing clothing designed for members of the opposite sex.

trauma: An injury to the body or psyche by some type of shock, violence, or unanticipated situation. Symptoms of psychological trauma include numbness of feeling, withdrawal, helplessness, depression, anxiety, and fear. See also *posttraumatic stress disorder.*

triage: A crisis intervention technique for prioritizing the help that will be available to disaster victims. For example, physically injured earthquake victims may be organized or placed in such a way that medical personnel can provide help first to those in the most critical condition rather than on a first-come, first-served basis. The term originated as a military battlefield procedure of dividing casualties into three categories —those who will die regardless of help; those who will live whether they get help or not; and those who will live only if they receive immediate care. Help is given to this last group first.

triangulation: The process in which one individual who feels pressured, distressed, or powerless in relating to another individual brings into the relationship a third person to act as an ally or a distracter. For example, a mother who feels she has too little control over the children brings the father or a grandparent onto the scene. Or a social worker will sometimes find that an individual client will bring in a spouse or call attention to another family member who is present whenever there is pressure or confrontation.

trickle-down theory: The view that federal funds flowing into corporations and private sectors of the economy will stimulate more job opportunities and economic growth than would direct federal payments to and programs for the unemployed and poor.

trimester: A period of three months during pregnancy.

truancy: Failure to fulfill one's duty. This term especially applies to a child who stays away from school without permission.

trust versus mistrust: The basic conflict found in the first stage of human development, according to Eriksonian *psychosocial development theory,* occurring from birth to approximately 2 years of age. The infant may develop feelings of security and confidence in those who provide care or possibly, because of inconsistent nurturing, may come to doubt that others are reliable.

Truth in Lending Act: The 1968 federal law (P.L. 90-321) requiring full and clear disclosure of the terms of loans for which individuals apply. Commercial lenders, including banks, credit card companies, retailers, and real estate organizations, are required to reveal the amount of interest charged, both as an annual percentage and a dollar amount.

tubal ligation: A surgical method of *birth control* in which the fallopian tubes are severed and tied off.

tuberculosis: An infectious disease that most commonly affects the lungs and is caused by the tubercle bacillus, which may enter the human body through contact with infected people, through inhalation, or through ingestion (contaminated food or dishes). The incidence of tuberculosis has been dramatically reduced by better sanitary conditions, pasteurization of milk, early case findings through sputum examinations and skin tests, and vaccines.

"turf issues":   Conflicts, usually between members of an organization or between different professional groups, about the allocation of responsibilities and benefits. For example, social workers are sometimes involved in such conflicts with psychologists, psychiatrists, or pastoral counselors in deciding who should be authorized to provide psychotherapy.

Type A personality: A pattern of thinking and behaving characterized by impatience, competitiveness, and excessive concern about time. People who have Type A personalities are said to be at high risk for heart disease and other disorders. See also *Type B personality*.

Type B personality: A pattern of thinking and behaving characterized by patience, noncompetitiveness and a relaxed attitude about time. People who have Type B personalities are said to be at low risk for heart disease and other disorders. See also *Type A personality*.

typhoid fever: An infectious disease, spread primarily through contaminated water or food, whose symptoms include high fever, diarrhea or constipation, red spots on body, enlargement of the spleen, and damage to various organs. Its incidence has been dramatically reduced through vaccination, sanitary laws pertaining especially to food handlers, and laws promoting a cleaner and safer environment.

typologies: Classification systems used by social workers and others to delineate the components of an entity under scrutiny. For example, many social workers use the *typology of casework treatment,* developed by Florence Hollis, to classify the various activities used in social work intervention.

typology of casework treatment: The classification of techniques used by social workers in direct work with individual clients, formulated by Florence Hollis and Mary E. Woods (*Casework: A Psychological Therapy,* 3rd ed., New York: Random House, 1981, pp. 93–103). The techniques consist of sustaining procedures, direct influence, ventilation, reflective consideration of the person-situation configuration, reflection about the dynamics of patterns or tendencies, and thinking about the historical development of those patterns. The typology permits examination of environmental as well as internal influences.

U

Uncle Tom: A term of contempt, based on the character in Harriet Beecher Stowe's antislavery novel, *Uncle Tom's Cabin,* referring to a black person whose behavior toward whites is considered servile or whose behavior is seen as antithetical to the interests of blacks as a group.

unconditioned response (UR): A response that occurs without the necessity of prior conditioning. In Pavlov's experiments, the dog's salivation when given food was the UR. Then, food was presented after a bell was rung; eventually the dog began to salivate at the sound of the bell, whether or not food was given. Salivation at the sound of the bell was the *conditioned response (CR).*

unconditioned stimulus (US): A *stimulus* that elicits a response without the necessity of conditioning or learning. For example, in Pavlov's experiments, the food was the US because it elicited salivation with no prior conditioning. When a bell was rung prior to the presentation of food, it became the *conditioned stimulus (CS)* when it began to elicit salivation from the dog even when no food was near.

unconscious: In *psychoanalytic theory,* that region of the mind or psychic structure that is not subject to an individual's immediate awareness and is the seat of all forgotten memories and thoughts, *primary process thinking,* repressed impulses, biological drives, and the *id.*

unconscious motivation: A compelling wish or drive that is out of an individual's immediate awareness but that influences him or her to act in a way that would seem contrary to his or her rational objectives. For example, a client who has had a difficult session with a social worker "forgets" to attend the next scheduled session.

underachiever: One whose overt performance is not as accomplished as would be expected from the person's past activities, school or work record, or scores on aptitude tests.

underclass: A term used by some journalists and economists in referring to people and families who have been long-term poor, unemployed, and lacking in the resources or opportunities to improve their situations in the future. See also *culture of poverty.*

underemployment: In individuals, the condition of working fewer than full-time hours or working in jobs that are beneath their levels of education or previous salary, usually because there are no more suitable available jobs; in societies, the economic condition in which workers have to limit their work hours or incomes so that others can also work and have some income.

underprivileged: A term pertaining to people who are deprived of the social, cultural, and economic benefits that are available to most others in their society.

underutilization: See *utilization review.*

undifferentiated ego mass: A *family therapy* concept describing the members of a family as lacking much separate identity or differentiation of self and being "stuck together."

undocumented alien: In the United States, an individual from another nation who has entered this country without legal status and is subject to deportation.

undoing: A *defense mechanism* in which an individual engages in a repetitious ritual in order to abolish the results of an action previously taken and found to be unacceptable. For example, an individual who injures a youngster through reckless driving begins driving slowly and carefully every day through the area where the accident occurred.

unearned income: Money received from sources unrelated to employment, such as interest on savings, dividends on investments, and capital gains.

Unemployed Parent Program of AFDC (AFDC-UP): The 1961 revision of the AFDC regulations, which, in many states, extended eligibility to families that included unemployed fathers. Prior to AFDC-UP, eligibility in most states was restricted to poor families that had no male head of household. See also *Aid to Families with Dependent Children (AFDC)*.

unemployment: The condition of being without a job and the resulting income that is necessary to meet economic needs independently. The term is usually applied by economists and government statisticians only to those people without jobs who want to and are able to work.

unemployment compensation: Financial assistance for eligible persons who have temporary loss of income due to unemployment. In the United States this assistance is provided primarily through the *Unemployment Insurance* program.

Unemployment Insurance: The program established in 1935 as part of the *Social Security Act* to protect workers temporarily from economic hardship due to involuntary job loss. The federal government levies a payroll tax on nearly all employers and credits most of these funds to each state's unemployment insurance fund. When an eligible worker becomes unemployed, compensation is paid for a specified time. Applications, eligibility determination, and processing of funds is, for the most part, handled through the states' public employment offices. The amount and duration of benefits vary from state to state.

unemployment rate: The economic and statistical measure of the proportion of people without jobs who are willing and able to work, relative to the number of employed persons in the population. The figure is often used by social and economic planners to help determine actual and potential economic circumstances of specific population groups, such as teenagers, blacks, college graduates, people over 50, women, blue-collar workers, and so on.

UNESCO: The United Nations Educational, Scientific, and Cultural Organization, an agency of the United Nations established in 1945 with headquarters in Paris. Its primary objectives include promoting the free interchange of ideas and of cultural and scientific accomplishments, fundamental education for all peoples, and preserving the cultural heritage of mankind.

UNICEF: The United Nations Children's Fund, an agency of the United Nations established in 1946 (as the U.N. International Children's Emergency Fund). Its primary goal is to provide health, education, and social services to children, especially in underdeveloped nations. It is financed by voluntary contributions from nations and individuals.

United Jewish Appeal (UJA): The organization founded in 1939 to systematize and coordinate fundraising efforts for programs in behalf of needy Jews. Contributions to the organiza-

tion help support domestic Jewish social service agencies and educational facilities and needy Jews worldwide. Funds are also designated for helping immigrants become established in Israel.

United Neighborhood Centers of America (UNCA): The organization whose aim is to improve the quality of life at the neighborhood level. Founded by Jane Addams and other social workers and pioneer leaders of the *settlement house* movement, the organization was formerly known as the National Federation of Settlements. In 1959 it became known as the National Federation of Settlement and Neighborhood Centers, taking its present name in 1979.

United Service Organizations (USO): The program established in 1941 to coordinate the recreational, social, and welfare services given by six private, voluntary agencies (*YMCA, YWCA*, Travelers Aid, the *Salvation Army*, Catholic Community Service, and the Jewish Welfare Board) to members of the U.S. armed services.

United Way: The national federation of local organizations established to systematize and coordinate voluntary fundraising efforts. The money raised through the United Way is used to fund social agencies, nonprofit human service organizations, and some health, education, and recreation programs in local communities. The organization was established in 1918 and has been known in some localities as the United Campaign, the United Fund, the Community Chest, and the Red Feather Organization.

unit of attention: The focal point of intervention to which the social worker directs efforts to provide help or effect change. For example, the unit of attention for the clinical social worker with a psychoanalytic orientation would be the intrapsychic processes of the individual, and that of a community organizer would be the interacting social forces that exist in a given community. Units of attention for group workers are the group process; for psychosocially oriented workers, the person-situation configuration. Specific behaviors may be considered the unit of attention for behaviorally oriented workers, and a proposed bill in Congress could be the unit of attention of a social activist. See also *target behavior, target segments of society,* and *target system.*

universal eligibility: A social service policy in which services or benefits are provided at the same rate to all citizens or residents of a nation without regard to their specific needs, economic status, or circumstances. When applied, this policy can take the form of such *universal programs* as the family allowance system in some nations. This concept is contrasted with the policy of *selective eligibility* (using a *means test* or other assessment to determine eligibility for a social service) and *exceptional* *eligibility* (social programs developed for selected groups, based primarily on political pressure or public sympathy). See also *demogrant*.

universal program: Social welfare programs that are open to everyone in a nation who falls into a certain category. These programs do not subject people to individualized tests of income or need. *Social security* and *Medicare* are examples of universal programs in the United States (*public assistance* and *Medicaid* are *selective programs*).

universe: A term used in social research to designate a group of people or objects that are identified as the whole from which a *sample* is taken. In voter preference polls, for example, the universe consists of all potential voters. See also *population*.

unprofessional: A term applied to behavior engaged in by a professional person in the course of practice that does not measure up to the standards of the profession. Usually it is conduct in violation of the profession's *code of ethics* or the laws pertaining to the licensing of the profession in the relevant jurisdiction. The term is not to be confused with the term *nonprofessional*.

unsocialized delinquent: The term referring to a youngster whose periodic trouble with the authorities and antisocial behavior stem from insufficient guidance, role models, or exposure to people who have more acceptable standards of behavior.

"unworthy poor": A pejorative term applied to poor people who were considered too lazy to work or too dishonest to be acceptable in polite society. This designation was used primarily before the twentieth century to distinguish people who did not "deserve" public assistance from the *worthy poor* (such as widows and handicapped people), who did. The term is no longer used officially but its underlying philosophy is still held by many. See also *victim blaming*.

"uppers": Slang for *amphetamines,* the *controlled substances* that have been used in weight control and to keep people awake and alert. When abused they are psychologically and physiologically addictive.

Upward Bound: The *War on Poverty* program, established in 1964, designed to provide special education and incentives to encourage students not to drop out of school.

urbanization: A social trend in which people adopt the lifestyles, residential patterns, and cultural values of those who live in or near cities; also, the physical development of a rural area so that it includes features found in cities.

Urban League, National: The community service and civil rights organization established in 1910 to help end racial discrimination and help socially disadvantaged people. Largely staffed by social workers and professionals from related fields, it provides direct services in such areas as unemployment, housing, education, social welfare, family counseling and planning, legal affairs, and minority business development.

urbanology: The study of cities and their problems.

urban renewal: A social philosophy and a set of programs designed to prevent urban blight in those areas where satisfactory housing exists, tear down slums and replace them with new buildings where suitable housing no longer exists, and rehabilitate neighborhoods that are beginning to decay. The U.S. Housing Act of 1949 and subsequent legislation provided for procedures by which cities could apply for federal urban renewal aid. In 1970 the Housing Act was revised to include new *community development,* which can result in new additions to cities and free-standing new communities. Most federal urban renewal funding now comes through *block grants.*

user charges: The social service policy of requiring the client or recipient of service to pay for part or all of the cost of providing the service. This is in contrast to programs that are provided at no cost or low cost to the recipient, with the funds coming from general government revenues, through public or privately supported agencies, or private insurance payments.

usury: The act of charging excessive or unlawfully high rates of interest on loaned money.

utilitarianism: The ethical philosophy that holds that the rightness or wrongness of an action is determined by whether its consequences are useful or not.

utility theory: In economics, the concept that a person obtains satisfaction (utility) through the consumption of goods and that the individual will attempt to establish priorities of consumption in order to achieve the highest possible level of satisfaction. The theory suggests that the higher the level of satisfaction for a given cost and unit of time, the more desirable a particular item.

utilization review: A formal process of evaluating the type and amount of service offered and delivered to organizations to determine if those services are justified. Organizations that receive funds from government bodies or other third-party groups are most likely to be subject to such evaluations, as the funders want to know if they are getting proper value for their costs. The review might determine the existence of overutilization (too many services delivered or too many demands made on available services) or underutilization (insufficient demand or delivery to justify the costs spent on services).

V

vaccine: A preparation used to increase the body's resistance to a specified disease.

vaginitis: An inflammation of the vagina, caused primarily by the presence of an excessive number of otherwise harmless microorganisms.

vagrancy: Wandering from place to place with no permanent home or job.

validity: In social research, the concept concerned with the extent to which a procedure is able to measure the quality it is intended to measure.

value added tax (VAT): An indirect sales tax that is levied on products at each stage of production in proportion to their increase in worth. These add-ons are finally passed on to the consumer. VAT is a *regressive tax* rather than a *progressive tax.* This form of taxation is common in many European nations.

value judgment: An assumption made about the worth of some person, group, place, or event.

value orientation: The characteristic way individuals or groups look at their own and others' standards of conduct, moral principles, and social customs.

values: The customs, standards of conduct, and principles considered desirable by a culture, a group of people, or an individual. Social workers, as one group, specified some of their overall values in the *NASW Standards for the Classification of Social Work Practice* (Silver Spring, Md.: National Association of Social Workers, 1982) as follows: (1) commitment to the primary importance of the individual in society; (2) respect for the confidentiality of relationships with clients; (3) commitment to social change to meet socially recognized needs; (4) willingness to keep personal feelings and needs separate from professional relationships; (5) willingness to transmit knowledge and skills to others; (6) respect and appreciation for individual and group differences; (7) commitment to develop clients' ability to help themselves; (8) willingness to persist in efforts on behalf of clients despite frustration;

(9) commitment to social justice and the economic, physical, and mental well-being of all in society; and (10) commitment to a high standard of personal and professional conduct.

values clarification: A method of education in morality and ethical principles that occurs by bringing together people to share their opinions and value perspectives. This exposes the participants to different ideals and permits them to appreciate the relative nature of values.

vandalism: Intentional and illegal destruction of public or private property.

variable: In social research, a characteristic that may vary or assume different quantified values. See also *dependent variable* and *independent variable.*

variance: In research, a measure of dispersion within the distribution of events; in statistics, the square of the *standard deviation;* in social administration, the difference between budgeted expectations and actual results; in urban development, a legal exemption from zoning and building codes.

V Codes: In the American Psychiatric Association's *DSM-III,* a list of conditions that are not specific mental disorders but are reasons for which individuals seek the services of mental health professionals. Each of these conditions is given a number, as in the mental disorders, but these numbers are preceded by a V. The V Code conditions in *DSM-III* and their numbers include "Malingering" (V65.20), "Borderline Intellectual Functioning; (V62.89), "Academic Problem" (V62.30), "Occupational Problem" (V62.20), "Uncomplicated Bereavement" (V62.82), "Marital Problem" (V61.10), "Parent-Child Problem" (V61.20), and others. Organizations that make *third-party payments* tend to reject reimbursement claims for treatments of these conditions if they are the sole reasons for treatment.

vegetative signs: Behavior in which there is little indication of mental activity. The person is passive, mute, unresponsive to the environment, and not inclined to move. This behavior is often symptomatic of *organic mental disorders* and some types of *schizophrenia.*

vendor: One who sells a product or service. Because they are paid to provide social services, social workers and their agencies are referred to as vendors by insurance companies and other third-party funding organizations.

vendor payments: Money a government agency or insurance company pays to a social agency, institution, or independent professional to provide services. The U.S. federal government uses the term primarily to apply to payments made to professionals or agencies on behalf of people who can't afford to pay for the services in question themselves. The largest vendor payment system of this type in the United States is *Medicaid.*

vendorship: The practice of providing goods and services for specific fees that are charged either to the consumer or to third parties. In social work, the vendorship model is practised primarily by private social work practitioners, proprietary workers, and even traditional social agencies selling specific professional services to individuals and groups and being reimbursed for each unit of service by the consumer or by such third parties as health insurance companies, government agencies, or business organizations.

venereal diseases: Infections acquired through sexual contact and the exchange of body fluids; these may include *gonorrhea, syphilis,* genital *herpes,* and *AIDS.*

ventilation: In the worker-client therapeutic relationship, the process of permitting the client to express feelings during the description of the problem situation. According to psychosocial theorists, this releases or discharges emotions that have built up and caused the individual to have internal stress and conflict. It is also referred to as *catharsis.* See also *purposeful expression of feelings.*

Veterans Administration (VA): The federal organization established in 1920 (as the U.S. Veterans' Bureau and renamed in 1930) to provide for the health, educational, and welfare needs of former military service personnel. The VA administers hospitals for the physically and mentally ill, maintains programs of financial assistance and personal social services, establishes loans and insurance services, and offers training and rehabilitation programs and many other services.

vicarious learning: In *behavior modification,* the premise that a client's desired behavior is strengthened through observing someone else being rewarded for that behavior; a form of imitation or *modeling.*

vice: Criminal activity including prostitution, pornography, gambling, sales of illegal drugs or contraband, and other behaviors that are made illegal because they offend the community's moral standards.

victim blaming: A philosophy or orientation that attributes complicity to the person who is harmed by some social phenomenon. For example, a woman who is raped or sexually harassed is accused of seducing the attacker; an abused spouse is accused of being masochistic and encouraging the abusive action; or a poor person is accused of being too lazy to work.

victim compensation: Public payment in cash or service to people who are judged to have been harmed as a result of another's negligence or criminal activity.

victimology: The study of people who are harmed, usually by sociocultural phenomena, and the conditions in which the harm takes place.

Vietnam veterans: Military personnel who served in Vietnam during the protracted war that ended in 1974. Many American veterans of this war have experienced considerable difficulties in readjusting to life in the United States and thus have needed help from social workers, vocational counselors, physicians, and other professionals. These difficulties have been attributed or related to such factors as the lack of popular support for the war and its participants, "losing" the war, poor postwar economic conditions supposedly resulting in reduced veterans' services, the widespread use of drugs, and the use of defoliants such as *Agent Orange,* which may be carcinogenic. See also *Veterans Administration (VA)* and *posttraumatic stress disorder.*

violence: Severe and intense exercise of force and power, usually resulting in injury or destruction. The term "crimes of violence" pertains to those crimes in which physical harm occurs or is threatened, such as murder, rape, or assault and battery.

visiting teacher service: Programs within the educational system in which professionals in *school social work* provide personal social services to students and their families and help acquaint the schools with the special needs of these families. Originally these services were provided by educators, but eventually professional social workers assumed these duties in many school districts. The National Association of Visiting Teachers, which was established in 1916, was absorbed into the *American Association of Social Workers (AASW)* as the School Social Work Section in 1921.

VISTA: Volunteers in Service to America, the program established in 1964 as part of the *Economic Opportunity Act,* designed to bring volunteers into those urban and rural areas of the

United States that are experiencing economic and cultural deprivation. Often called the "Domestic Peace Corps," the workers help with training, socialization, and development of resources. VISTA is now part of the federal government's *ACTION* program.

vital signs: Indicators (such as pulse, respiration, temperature, and movement) that the body is alive and functioning.

vital statistics: Official demographic data pertaining to the incidence of marriages, divorces, births, deaths, health statuses, diseases, causes of death, and so on.

vivisection: Experimentation on living animals to study biological and behavioral responses to various conditions.

vocational guidance: Assisting people in the systematic process of locating suitable employment. The activities inherent in such assistance include delineating qualifications and possible job opportunities and helping individuals determine if they have the aptitude and qualifications for a job, helping them find the training necessary to do a job, and counseling about how to apply for a position.

vocational rehabilitation: Training people who are physically or mentally handicapped so they can do useful work, become more self-sufficient, and be less reliant on public financial assistance. *Block grants* and other funding through the U.S. *Department of Health and Human Services (HHS)* goes to states to facilitate specific vocational rehabilitation programs. The U.S. *Veterans Administration (VA)* also works with state agencies for the training of handicapped veterans.

Voluntary Action Centers (VAC): See *volunteerism*.

voluntary associations: Organizations whose funding comes from private contributions and whose goals are to provide health, social, and other services to the disadvantaged outside government auspices. Voluntary associations tend to specialize in particular needs and services. These include health and hospital support (for example, the American Cancer Society, the American Heart Association, and the National Kidney Foundation); help for specific groups (for example, *Big Brothers/Big Sisters of America* and the

National Shut-In Society); church-related organizations (for example, *Catholic Charities USA* and *Lutheran Social Services*); and community fund-raising groups (for example, the *United Way*).

volunteer: One who offers to serve, of his or her own free will, usually without financial compensation. See also *volunteerism*.

volunteerism: The mobilization and utilization of unpaid individuals and groups to provide human services outside the auspices of government agencies. This term also pertains to the ideologies of *self-help groups, mutual aid groups, self-help organizations,* and *philanthropy.* The U.S. government maintains, in its *ACTION* programs, the Office of Volunteer Liaison to help coordinate some of these efforts throughout the nation. Other organizations that serve the same purpose include the National Self-Help Clearinghouse, the National Self-Help Resource Center, and the National Center for Voluntary Action, which promoted the national network of local Voluntary Action Centers (VAC).

Volunteers in Service to America: See *VISTA*.

voter registration drives: A strategy used by social activists, community organizers, and other social workers to strengthen the power and influence of a community or segment of the population by encouraging and facilitating the enrollment of eligible citizens to permit them to vote in subsequent elections.

voucher system: A method of subsidizing a person's social service, health care, and other needs on the open market. Typically, in this system, a poor person is given vouchers, often in the form of redeemable stamps or coupons, worth a certain amount of money as long as they are spent on a specified service or product. Among the most common of these systems are *food stamps,* tuition grants, and housing subsidy checks.

voyeurism: A *psychosexual disorder* characterized by repetitive looking at unsuspecting people who are undressed or engaged in sexual activity. Popularly referred to as Peeping Tomism, this activity is the preferred source of sexual excitement for voyeurs. People who enjoy watching or observing others in everyday situations are sometimes informally referred to as voyeurs.

W

wage controls: Government regulations that limit the amount of increase or decrease in money that employers can pay to their workers. The stated purpose is usually to control inflation and increase employment. This policy is often accompanied by *price controls*.

WAIS test: See *intelligence quotient (IQ)*.

War on Poverty: The name President Lyndon B. Johnson used for the plans and programs established during his administration to encourage economic well-being, equal opportunity for all, and the *Great Society*. The war was to be fought primarily through the programs of the *Economic Opportunity Act* of 1964. This included a major revision of the *Social Security Act*, including greatly extended coverage, *VISTA*, the *Job Corps, Head Start*, the Legal Services Corporation, and the *Community Action Program*.

WCTU: See *temperance movement*.

welfare: A condition of physical health, emotional comfort, and economic security; also, the efforts of a society to help its citizens achieve that condition. The term is also used popularly as a synonym for *public assistance* or other programs that provide for the economic and social service needs of the poor.

welfare backlash: Resistance and opposition by some citizens and groups to public expenditures for the poor, often manifested in such social movements as "taxpayer revolts" and in political pressure to eliminate funding for some welfare programs.

welfare reform: Various efforts to change the way social welfare programs are administered, funded, and used. Some reformers seek more stringent rules to discourage people from obtaining assistance. Others advocate elimination of bureaucratic obstacles and any *means tests*. Some advocate replacing the entire welfare system with a *guaranteed annual income* for all people that would meet each person's minimal requirements. The welfare reform proposals listed in this dictionary include the *Family Assistance Plan*, the *guaranteed annual income*, the *negative income tax*, the *Newburgh welfare plan*, and *workfare*.

welfare rights: The view that public assistance and other social services are entitlements available to any of a nation's citizens. Welfare rights organizations say that among the rights of welfare recipients are confidentiality of personal information from welfare investigators, greater availability of information about the benefits for people who are eligible, increased accessibility of welfare offices (nearer to transportation routes, open longer hours, shorter waiting lines, and so on), and more equitable distribution of services and funds.

welfare state: A nation or society that considers itself responsible for meeting the basic educational, health care, economic, and social security needs of its people.

whistle-blowing: Alerting those in positions of higher authority in an organization about the existence of practices that are illegal, wasteful, dangerous, or otherwise contrary to the organization's stated policies. Some organizations, such as the U.S. government, encourage whistle-blowing by maintaining toll-free hot lines for anonymous tipsters and by protecting whistle-blowing employees from subsequent retribution from their superiors.

white-collar crime: Nonviolent illegal acts typically committed by businesspeople, public officials, and more affluent members of society. Such offenses include embezzlement, fraud, forgery, tax evasion, fraudulent use of credit cards, stock manipulation, bribery, and computer crime. The cost to society of white-collar crime is many times greater than the costs of street crime.

white flight: A lay term used to describe demographic patterns of racial resegregation in residential neighborhoods. The pattern is said to begin in some neighborhoods when one or more black families establish residence. Some white families who fear the possibility of negative economic or social conditions or who are racist move away precipitously. Many homes thus become vacant and then become occupied by more black families. The pattern continues as more white families leave, or "flee."

White House conferences: Formal meetings, convened by the U.S. president, of the nation's leaders in various social welfare and health fields to discuss specified social problems and potential solutions. The prototype conference was President Theodore Roosevelt's 1909 White House Conference on Child Welfare, which led to the development of the U.S. *Children's Bureau.* Subsequent conferences have focused on problems of aged Americans, health care, and families, and most have culminated in new laws and programs designed to resolve some of the problems addressed.

WIC program: The Special Supplemental Food Program for Women, Infants, and Children, assistance services under the auspices of the U.S. Department of Agriculture, designed to protect women, infants, and children who are identified as being at risk of nutritional deficiency due to inadequate income.

whooping cough: See *pertussis.*

widowhood: The stage of life following the death of one's spouse.

"wild analysis": The expression used primarily by psychotherapists with a Freudian orientation to describe a therapist's poorly planned verbalizations and idiosyncratic approaches to therapy.

withdrawal: A pattern of removing oneself physically or psychologically from other people or circumstances that are found to be disturbing.

withdrawal symptoms: The physical and emotional reactions of a person who has discontinued the use of certain drugs or alcohol to which he or she has been addicted or habituated. The individual may experience such reactions as tremors, pain in the digestive system, d.t.'s, convulsions, fears and panic disorders, acute anxiety, and mood swings.

Women for Sobriety: The national self-help organization, with chapters in many localities, whose members are mostly women with drinking problems. The members believe that women alcoholics have different needs and problems than do their male counterparts and thus need their own organization for combating the problem. They meet regularly to provide mutual support, inspiration, and information about dealing with specific problems of alcoholism.

Women's Bureau, U.S.: The organization within the U.S. *Department of Labor* whose primary concern is the working conditions of women.

It administers a variety of programs to see that these conditions are favorable. Other programs of the Women's Bureau include helping *displaced homemakers*, teenaged mothers, women of color and other minority status, and child care services.

workers' compensation: Programs—funded by employers, insurance companies, and government —to pay employees for some part of the cost of occupational diseases and injury. Most industrial countries have uniform national programs for such reimbursement. However, in the United States the programs are primarily established under state law and thus vary widely as to the amount of compensation and the conditions under which it is to be awarded. In most states the benefits are underwritten through private insurance companies whose premiums are paid by employers. The specific awards are usually under the scrutiny of state boards and federal *Department of Labor* supervision.

workfare: The proposal by various economists, social planners, and politicians to discourage able-bodied people from receiving welfare benefits. It would establish programs and facilities in the public and private sectors so that these people could earn some of their benefits through work. See also *workhouse.*

work force: Those who are employed in a given organization or industry.

workhouse: An *indoor relief* form of "assistance," common in various countries in the eighteenth century, in which poor people who received help had to live and work in special facilities. The government contracted with private individuals to feed and house these people in exchange for the work that they could do. The programs, which housed infants, children, the aged, handicapped, and diseased as well as able-bodied adults, were phased out in the late eighteenth century in favor of slightly more humane *almshouses* and *outdoor relief* programs.

Work Incentive program (WIN): The 1967 revisions in the *Aid to Families with Dependent Children (AFDC)* program that permitted and encouraged mothers receiving AFDC payments to work. Since 1986 the program has been within the *Family Services Administration (FSA)* of the U.S. *Department of Health and Human Services (HHS).* Formerly, in the AFDC program, all of an employed mother's earnings were subtracted from the amount she could receive in AFDC benefits. WIN permitted these mothers to retain part of the money they earned without losing their AFDC money. The legislation also encouraged development of day care centers and job training programs. Some critics say the program coerces some AFDC families by terminating assistance to those who refuse job or training opportunities.

work incentives: Benefits, requirements, or special aid to encourage people to seek and remain in suitable employment and to encourage employer organizations to hire and keep people on the job. Work incentives for individuals include such programs as *day care*, higher wages (made possible by government subsidy), reducing or terminating welfare payments for those who refuse to work, and improvements in the work environment. Work incentives for employer organizations include tax breaks for hiring and retaining specified numbers or categories of people (as in *experience ratings*), direct payments to subsidize wages paid, and stimulation of the general economy to enable the organization to employ more workers.

working class: The *socioeconomic class*, according to many sociologists, whose family members tend to hold steady employment in industry and blue-collar jobs and who have relatively modest incomes, limited education, and aspirations and values that tend to be oriented toward maintaining security and preserving their current lifestyles.

working poor: Employed people whose assets and incomes from their jobs are so low that they fall below the *poverty line*.

working through: In the worker-client *relationship*, the process of mutually exploring a problem until there is agreement about the solution and the means to achieve it. In psychoanalytic theory, the term refers to those processes that enable infantile and repressed unconscious material to be made conscious so it can be analyzed in therapy.

workplace: The setting in which one's employment or other work activity occurs.

work release program: A system whereby an inmate of a correctional or other institution is permitted to leave the facility regularly to maintain his or her paid employment. Often this program is used in conjunction with a *halfway house* so that the inmate has greater local access to the job and greater opportunity to reenter society when the required period of *incarceration* is concluded.

Works Progress Administration (WPA): A *New Deal* employment program established in 1935 under the leadership of social worker Harry Hopkins, chief of the *Federal Emergency Relief Administration (FERA)* and the *Civil Works Administration (CWA)*; it provided jobs for over 8 million people during its existence. Federal funds were used in building parks, bridges, roads, and airports and in sponsoring the work of artists, musicians, writers, and scholars. The program was renamed the Work Projects Administration in 1939. The WPA was disbanded in 1943 when employment conditions changed as a result of World War II.

World Health Organization (WHO): The United Nations agency established in its present form in 1948, with headquarters in Geneva, Switzerland, whose purpose is the "attainment by all peoples of the highest possible level of health." It sponsors medical research, health education, disease prevention programs, and the standardization of health and mental health statistics throughout the world.

"worthy poor": The term once used to describe people who were poor because they were widowed, handicapped, or had experienced unexpected economic reversals. They were considered to be honest, motivated to contribute, and basically hardworking. This term was used, mostly before the twentieth century, to distinguish those people who "deserved" assistance from those who did not, or the *unworthy poor*. Although the term is no longer used, many people still believe the concept. See also *victim blaming*.

Wyatt v. Stickney: The 1971 legal ruling in Alabama declaring that mental patients who had been committed on civil grounds have the constitutional right to receive such individual treatment as will give them a realistic opportunity to be cured or to improve their mental condition.

XYZ

xanthines: A group of drugs, related to *amphetamines* and *cocaine,* that act as central nervous system stimulants; caffeine is a common example.

X chromosome: One of the two human sex chromosomes, whose pairing (XX for females, XY for males) determines an individual's sex. See also *Y chromosome.*

xenophobia: Persistent, intense, and unreasonable fear of strangers or foreigners.

"YAVIS client": A term including the acronym for "young, attractive, verbal, intelligent, and sexy," which refers to the type of person some psychotherapists seem to prefer treating, even though other clients may be in greater need.

Y chromosome: One of the two human sex chromosomes, whose pairing (XX for females, XY for males) determines human sexuality. See also *X chromosome.*

youth service organizations: Privately funded and administered federated organizations, usually with chapters or recreational facilities in most communities in the United States, whose purpose is to help young people achieve their developmental potentials. They are particularly geared toward educationally oriented recreation, handicrafts, and sports activities designed to help youngsters keep physically fit and emotionally healthy while learning social skills, practical coping strategies, and moral conduct. Among the many groups of this type are the Boy Scouts of America, the Boys Clubs of America, the Girls Clubs of America, the Girl Scouts of the U.S.A., the *YMCA,* the *YWCA,* the *YM/YWHA,* the Campfire Girls, and many others.

YMCA: Young Men's Christian Associations, the worldwide group of organizations devoted to the physical, intellectual, social, and spiritual well-being of young men. No longer limited to young people, Christians, or even men in some localities, the YMCA was first established in London in 1844 and in the United States in 1851.

YM-YWHA: Young Men's and Young Women's Hebrew Associations, organizations in communities with significant Jewish populations, designed to provide young people with education, recreation, and social and spiritual opportunities.

YWCA: Young Women's Christian Associations, the worldwide group of organizations devoted to educating young women spiritually, socially, and physically. They originated in boarding houses for young women in London in 1855, and in 1877 a number of these organizations formed the YWCA.

zeitgeist: From the German for "spirit of the time," the characteristic feelings or thoughts of a people in a given period of time.

zero-based budgeting: In social administration, the process of evaluating the entire future plan for the financial operation of the organization without reference to past expenditures. Each new financial plan starts from zero. Thus, the organization does not simply study whether to increase or decrease funds for each of its units but considers the objectives of the organization and means of achieving them.

zero population growth: A movement that advocates population stability so that the birthrate equals the death rate. Advocates suggest that this is to be achieved through improved sex education, contraception, family planning, and sometimes tax penalties for those who have more children than prescribed. A formal organization, also known as Zero Population Growth, was established in 1968 and promotes these goals.

zero sum orientation: In social planning, budgeting, and management, the perspective that the available resources are relatively fixed so that an increased expenditure of funds or resources in one sector must be accompanied by a commensurate decrease of funds or resources in another.

zoning: Municipal rules about the use of land and the types of structures permitted on it.

Milestones in the Development of Social Work and Social Welfare

MILESTONES IN THE DEVELOPMENT OF SOCIAL WORK AND SOCIAL WELFARE

B.C.

1750: In Babylonia, King Hammurabi issues his code of justice, which includes a requirement that the people help one another during times of hardship.

1200: In Israel, the Jewish people are told that God expects them to help the poor and disadvantaged.

500: Philanthropy, from the Greek word for "acts of love for mankind," is institutionalized in the Greek city-states. Citizens are encouraged to donate money, which is used for the public good. Parks are built, and food, clothing, and other goods are kept in public facilities to be used for those in need.

300: In China, the *Analects* of Confucius declare humans to be social beings bound to one another by *Jen,* a form of sympathy that is often expressed through helping those in need.

100: In Rome, the *annona civica* tradition—in which patrician families distribute free or low-cost grain to all Roman citizens in need—is well established.

A.D.

30: Jesus Christ teaches that people's love for one another is God's will. He emphasizes the importance of giving to the less fortunate ("Inasmuch as ye have done it unto one of the least of these my brethren, ye have done it unto me").

313: Christianity is legalized by the Roman emperor Constantine. The more affluent converts can donate funds openly, and the Church is able to use these funds to care for the poor.

400: "Hospitals" are developed and extended throughout India. These facilities provide shelter for poor and disabled homeless people and resemble almshouses rather than modern hospitals.

542: Hospitals similar to those in India have spread to China and the Middle East and now make their first appearance in Europe. The first Hôtel Dieu ("house of God") is established in Lyons, France, and is staffed primarily by religious workers and volunteers.

650: The followers of the Prophet Muhammad are told they have an obligation to the poor and that paying a *zakat* ("purification") tax to care for the poor is one of the Five Pillars (obligatory duties) of Islam.

1084:   Almshouses for the poor and handicapped, similar to the hospitals in France, are established in Canterbury, England.

1100:   The Roman Church issues the *Decretum,* a compilation of its canon law, which includes an elaborate discussion of the theory and practice of charity. It states that the rich have a legal and moral obligation to support the poor.

1348:   The social system of feudalism begins to break down, partly because of bubonic plague, which kills nearly one-third of the population of Europe. Without the protection of the barons and lords, the serfs and peasants are at the mercy of economic and military threats.

1349:   The Statute of Labourers is issued in England, requiring people to remain on their home manors and work for whatever the lords want to pay. Begging and almsgiving is outlawed except for the aged and those unable to work. For the first time, a distinction is made between the "worthy poor" (the aged, handicapped, widows, and dependent children), and the "unworthy poor" (able-bodied but unemployed adults).

1526:   Juan Luis Vives, a Spaniard living in northern Europe, develops a plan for organized relief. It includes registering the poor, raising private funds to help them, and creating employment for the able-bodied poor. Many of his ideas were later used in European cities and influenced the Poor Laws in England and colonial America in the next century.

1531:   England's first statute dealing with poor relief is issued. It empowers local justices to license certain people (the aged and handicapped) to beg in their own neighborhoods, and to give harsh punishment to any unlicensed beggars. To implement this law, the justices had to develop criteria and procedures for deciding which persons to license. Thus, each applicant had to be evaluated by representatives of the justices.

1536:   The Henrician Poor Law, also known as the Act for the Punishment of Sturdy Vagabonds and Beggars, is established. The government of Henry VIII classifies different types of poor people and establishes procedures for collecting voluntary donations and disbursing these funds to the poor. The law requires that these procedures be carried out at the local rather than the national level. It also acknowledges that the state rather than the Church or volunteers must play some role in caring for the poor.

1572:   England can no longer depend on voluntary contributions to care for its poor. A national tax, the Parish Poor Rate, is levied to cover these costs. This is accompanied by a register of persons needing relief. It also recognizes that not all able-bodied poor people are lazy. Funds left over from poor relief are used to create jobs for the able bodied.

1601:   The Elizabethan Poor Law is established. Built on the experiments of the earlier Henrician Poor Law (1536) and the Parish Poor Rate (1572), this legislation becomes the major codification of dealing with the poor and disadvantaged for over 200 years. It also becomes the basis for dealing with the poor in colonial America. The Poor Law keeps the administration of poor relief at the local level, taxes people in each parish to pay for their own poor, establishes apprentice programs for poor children, develops workhouses for dependent people, and deals harshly and punitively with able-bodied poor people.

1625:   Father Vincent de Paul (canonized as Saint Vincent de Paul in 1737) establishes seminaries, religious orders, and charitable organizations to care for the poor of France and is the founder of organized charity in Europe. In many of those nations that do not become Protestant during the Reformation, the Church rather than the state retains more responsibility for the care of the poor.

1642:　Plymouth Colony enacts the first poor law in the New World, based on the Elizabethan Poor Law of 1601.

1650:　The influence of Luther, Calvin, and others has become established and manifested as the Protestant ethic, a philosophy that becomes influential in England, parts of Europe, and American colonies. It emphasizes self-discipline, frugality, and hard work and leads many of its adherents to frown on those who are dependent or unemployed.

1657:　The first private welfare organization in America, known as Scots' Charitable Society, is established in Boston.

1662:　The Law of Settlement and Removal is established in England as one of the world's first "residency requirements" in determining eligibility to receive help. Municipal authorities are authorized to help only poor local citizens and to expel from their jurisdictions anyone else who might become dependent for assistance. This law causes authorities to evaluate people as to the likelihood of their becoming poor. Thus, though the law is basically harsh and punitive, some efforts to look at the causes of poverty are codified.

1697:　The workhouse system is developed in Bristol and soon spreads throughout England and parts of Europe. It is designed to keep down poor taxes by denying aid to anyone who refuses to enter a workhouse. These institutions are usually managed by private entrepreneurs who contract with the legal authorities to care for the residents in exchange for using their work. Residents—including very young children, the handicapped, and very old people—are often given minimal care and are worked long hours as virtual slaves.

1729:　Ursuline Sisters of New Orleans establish America's first residential institution for orphaned children.

1773:　The colonies' first hospital for the mentally ill is established in Williamsburg, Virginia.

1782:　The Gilbert Act is passed in England, enabling humanitarians, appalled by the exploitation of workhouse residents, to institute reforms in many English jurisdictions. Many workhouses are closed, assistance to the poor in their own home is established, and children under 6 are placed with families. Many private entrepreneurs are replaced by municipal employees as managers of the remaining workhouses.

1790:　The first publicly funded orphanage in the United States is established in Charleston, South Carolina.

1795:　The Speenhamland system is inaugurated. In the English district of Speenhamland a "poverty line" is developed, and some workers are made eligible for subsidization whenever their wages are below this amount. The amount is based on the price of bread and the worker's number of dependents. As prices increase or wages decline, the public treasury makes up the difference.

1798:　The U.S. Public Health Service is established.

1819:　Scottish preacher and mathematician Thomas Chalmers assumes responsibility for Glasgow's poor. He develops private philanthropies to help meet the economic needs of the poor and organizes a system of volunteers to meet individually and regularly with disadvantaged people to give them encouragement and training.

1824: The Bureau of Indian Affairs is established. It is the first federal organization to attempt to provide direct assistance in the welfare of some Americans.

1833: Antoine Frédéric Ozanam establishes the Saint Vincent de Paul Society in Paris, using lay volunteers to provide emergency economic and spiritual assistance to the poor.

1834: The new Poor Law is established in England to reform the Elizabethan Poor Law (1601). The underlying emphasis of the new law is on self-reliance. Public assistance is not considered a right, and government is not seen as responsible for the unemployed. The principle of "less eligibility" (a recipient of aid can never receive as much as does the lowest-paid worker) is enforced.

1835: The Reverend Joseph Tuckerman, a Unitarian minister who is influenced by the reports of Thomas Chalmers's work in Scotland, organizes the Boston Society for the Prevention of Pauperism. This organization uses many of Chalmers's principles of individualized work with poor families, volunteer visitors, coordinated fundraising, and social action. Tuckerman's organization is influential in the subsequent development of the Charity Organization Societies.

1843: Robert Hartley, using the teachings of Thomas Chalmers, Joseph Tuckerman, and French philanthropist Baron de Gerando, establishes the New York Association for Improving the Condition of the Poor. Soon imitated in many other American cities, the association stresses character building as a way to end poverty. Volunteers, usually middle-class Protestant laypersons, work to get poor people to abstain from alcohol, become more self-disciplined, and acquire the work ethic.

1844: The first YMCA is established in London, England.

1845: As a result of the social movement led by Dorothea Dix, the first state asylum for the mentally ill is established in Trenton, New Jersey. Soon her efforts convince many other states to build mental hospitals.

1848: Feminists from throughout the United States convene at Seneca Falls, New York, to declare the goal of equal rights for women and to establish the philosophy and objectives of the women's movement, including suffrage, equal opportunities in education and jobs, and legal rights.

1853: The Reverend Charles Loring Brace, concerned about the plight of New York's street children and children living in almshouses, organizes the Children's Aid Society. The society transports thousands of children every year to the West to live with rural families.

1854: Congress, pressured by Dorothea Dix's movement on behalf of the mentally ill, allocates funds and land to build mental hospitals. President Franklin Pierce vetoes the legislation, saying that charity is the province of the states and localities.

1862: Congress establishes the U.S. Department of Agriculture. The Homestead Act is passed, giving 160 acres of unoccupied public land to any American citizen who agrees to live on it for five years.

1863: Massachusetts establishes a state board of charities to investigate and supervise its almshouses, prisons, and mental institutions. Other states soon follow suit.

The Red Cross is established in Switzerland by writer Jean Henri Dunant, and soon there are Red Cross organizations in many other nations.

1864:   French sociologist and engineer P. G. Frédéric Le Play completes the first scientific study of poverty—its extent, causes, consequences, and possible solutions.

1865:   At the end of the Civil War, the United States establishes its first federal welfare agency, the Freedmen's Bureau, to provide temporary relief, education, employment, and health care for the newly released slaves.

1869:   In London the first Charity Organization Society is established. Formally named the "Society for Organising Charitable Relief and Repressing Mendicity," the society works to coordinate efforts at fundraising and to disburse funds in a systematic fashion. Volunteers are recruited to befriend applicants for assistance, make individual assessments of the reasons for their poverty, and help correct those reasons.

1870:   Social Darwinism gains influence. Herbert Spencer's thesis was that "survival of the fittest" should apply to human society and that poverty was merely an aspect of natural selection. Helping the poor, it was believed, would make them lazy and nonindustrious.

The Fifteenth Amendment to the U.S. Constitution is ratified, guaranteeing each citizen (not including women) the right to vote, regardless of race, color, or previous condition of servitude.

1872:   The Freedmen's Bureau is abolished.

Charles Loring Brace publishes *The Dangerous Classes of New York and Twenty Years' Work Among Them*, which raises U.S. consciousness about the plight of the urban poor.

1874:   Members of private charity organizations, religious agencies, and public officials from several northeastern states begin meetings to discuss their mutual concerns. These meetings lead to the establishment of the National Conference of Charities and Corrections (later named the National Conference on Social Welfare).

1877:   Using the London organization as his model, the Reverend S. Humphreys Gurteen establishes America's first Charity Organization Society (COS) in Buffalo, New York. Volunteer workers dispense advice rather than money to the poor and information about them to philanthropists and private relief agencies. A sign at the doorway of the Buffalo COS reads "No relief here!" Within a decade, COSs are established in most larger cities and many are giving direct financial relief to the needy.

1878:   The Reverend William Booth reorganizes his East London Revival Society as the Salvation Army.

1883:   In newly united Germany, Chancellor Otto von Bismarck establishes a national health insurance system and, shortly thereafter, accident insurance and old age and invalid insurance programs. This system becomes a model for social security programs in many other nations, excluding Great Britain and the United States.

1884:   Toynbee Hall, the first settlement house, is established in London by Vicar Samuel A. Barnett. The settlement movement spreads quickly, and facilities are developed in most larger British and American cities. Their philosophy is to eliminate the distance between socioeconomic classes by locating settlements in working-class neighborhoods where ideas and information can be exchanged.

1886:   Stanton Coit, who had resided in Toynbee Hall, opens America's first settlement house, the Neighborhood Guild, in New York. Eventually more than 400 houses are established. Their residents are involved in social advocacy, group work, and community development.

1889:   In Chicago, Jane Addams and Ellen Gates Starr open Hull House, which becomes one of the most influential social settlement houses in the United States.

1890:   The Consumer's League is established in England and, later, in the United States. Its purpose is to fight for better conditions in the work environment and safer products for the public. In the United States, the National Consumer's League, under the leadership of social worker–lawyer Florence Kelley, establishes local chapters in most larger communities and leads successful campaigns to abolish child labor practices and to achieve minimum wages and shorter working hours as well as safe and effective consumer products.

1894:   Amos G. Warner's *American Charities*—the first U.S. social welfare textbook—is published.

1896:   In *Plessy v. Ferguson*, the U.S. Supreme Court upholds the "separate but equal" doctrine, which gives legal sanction to segregated schools and other facilities.

1898:   The first school for social workers is established. The New York School of Philanthropy (later to become the Columbia University School of Social Work) grows out of a series of summer workshops and training programs for volunteers and friendly visitors and offers a one-year educational program. Faculty member and COS administrator Mary E. Richmond publishes *Friendly Visiting Among the Poor.*

1899:   The American Hospital Association (AHA) is established to develop and maintain standards in the nation's health care facilities.

1900:   Educator Simon N. Patten coins the term "social workers" and applies it to friendly visitors and settlement house residents. He and Mary Richmond dispute whether the major role of social workers should be advocacy or delivering individualized social services.

1902:   Homer Folks, founder and head of the New York State Charities Aid Association, publishes *Care of Destitute, Neglected and Delinquent Children.* His philosophy becomes influential in subsequent child welfare goals and methods.

1903:   Graham Taylor and others establish the Chicago School of Civics and Philanthropy, which eventually becomes the University of Chicago School of Social Service Administration.

1905:   A social service department is established in Massachusetts General Hospital in Boston to help patients deal with the social problems of their illnesses. Within the next decade, more than 100 hospitals hire hospital social workers.

1907:   Psychiatric social work begins at Massachusetts General Hospital when social workers are hired to work with mentally ill patients.

1909:   The National Association for the Advancement of Colored People (NAACP) is founded. Social workers Mary White Ovington and Henry Moskowitz and others help organize blacks and whites to establish this voluntary organization oriented toward the protection of the legal and social rights of blacks and other minorities.

President Theodore Roosevelt convenes the first White House conference, bringing together social workers and other leaders to discuss the problems of America's children.

1910: Several states pass "workmen's compensation laws" to protect wage earners from the economic risks of injury or unemployment. By 1920 all but six states have some form of workers' compensation program.

1911: Great Britain passes the National Insurance Act, which organizes a health and compensation program paid for by contributions from workers, employers, and the public.

Several organizations whose purpose is to improve social conditions for black Americans living in cities merge, to become the National Urban League.

1912: The U.S. Children's Bureau is created, headed by social worker and former Hull House resident Julia Lathrop.

1913: The U.S. Department of Labor is created, primarily to promote the welfare of American workers; the U.S. Department of Commerce is established.

1914: The Harrison Narcotics Act becomes U.S. law, establishing the government organization later known as the Bureau of Narcotics; the act makes the sale and use of certain drugs a criminal offense.

1915: In an address to the National Conference on Social Welfare, Abraham Flexner declares that social work has not yet qualified as a profession, especially because its members do not have a great deal of individual responsibility and because it still lacks a written body of knowledge and educationally communicable techniques.

1917: Mary Richmond publishes *Social Diagnosis.* Social workers use her book as a primary text and as an answer to Flexner.

The first organization for social workers is established. The National Social Workers Exchange exists primarily to process applicants for social work jobs. Later the group becomes the American Association of Social Workers (AASW).

1918 The American Association of Hospital Social Workers (AAHSW) is formed as the first specialty within the new field. The organization is renamed the American Association of Medical Social Workers (AAMSW) in 1934. Ida M. Cannon, director of medical social work at Massachusetts General Hospital, delineates the principles of medical social work.

Smith College, Northampton, Massachusetts, establishes the first training program for psychiatric social workers.

1919: The 17 schools of social work that exist in the United States and Canada form the Association of Training Schools for Professional Social Work to develop uniform standards of training and professional education. This group is later renamed the American Association of Schools of Social Work (AASSW), eventually becoming the Council on Social Work Education (CSWE).

Social workers employed in schools organize as the National Association of Visiting Teachers.

The Charity Organization Societies (COS) become oriented increasingly toward helping families. Many local societies change their names to Family Welfare Agency. The National Alliance for Organizing Charity is renamed the American Association for Organizing Family Social Work. By 1946 this organization is known as the Family Service Association of America (FSAA), renamed Family Service America (FSA) in 1983.

1920: The Child Welfare League of America (CWLA) is formed.

The National Conference of Catholic Charities is established.

The Nineteenth Amendment to the U.S. Constitution gives women the right to vote.

1921: The American Association of Social Workers (AASW) is created.

The U.S. Sheppard-Towner Act goes into effect. Federal funds are granted to state health departments to provide for the pre- and postnatal health care of needy mothers and infants. Nearly 3,000 child and maternal health centers are established nationwide, and the nation's infant and maternal mortality rates drop significantly. Nevertheless, the program is dropped in 1929.

Social work educator Eduard C. Lindeman publishes *The Community,* in which the basic concepts of community organization are delineated.

1923: Clara Kaiser begins teaching the first social work course in social group work at Western Reserve University in Cleveland.

The Tufts Report on social work education is completed *(Education and Training for Social Work,* by James H. Tufts), formally delineating the components necessary to provide adequate education for social workers. The report recommends training students in bringing about improvements in society as well as in individuals.

1926: The American Association of Psychiatric Social Workers (AAPSW) is founded, as social work increasingly comprises caseworkers and clinical practitioners.

The U.S. Veterans Bureau (now Veterans Administration [VA]) begins employing social workers in its hospitals.

1928: The Milford Conference convenes to discuss whether social work is a disparate group of technical specialties or a unified profession with integrated knowledge and skills. The conclusion is that social work is one profession with more similarities than differences among its specialties. In 1929 the report of the conference is published as *Social Case Work: Generic and Specific.*

1929: The stock market crashes, heralding the Great Depression.

1930: The American Public Welfare Association (APWA) is established.

Virginia Robinson, who with Jessie Taft developed the "functional school" of social casework, publishes the first comprehensive text to integrate social and psychodynamic concepts, *A Changing Psychology in Social Casework.*

Grace Coyle publishes the first comprehensive text on group work, *Social Process in Organized Groups.*

1931: Social worker Jane Addams becomes corecipient of the 1931 Nobel Peace Prize.

1933: President Franklin D. Roosevelt proclaims a "New Deal" for Americans and establishes major social welfare programs to combat poverty and unemployment. Programs include the Civilian Conservation Corps (CCC), the Civil Works Administration (CWA), the Federal Emergency Relief Administration (FERA), and later the Works Progress Administration (WPA). Social workers Harry Hopkins and Frances Perkins are appointed to the highest relevant positions, Hopkins as head of FERA and Perkins as U.S. Secretary of Labor (the first woman to head a cabinet department).

Through FERA, Harry Hopkins establishes a federal grant program establishing public assistance offices in the states. Each office has to have at least one trained social worker on its staff.

1934:   Puerto Rico passes a law regulating social work practice. This is the first time social work is legally regulated in any U.S. state or territory.

1935:   The U.S. Social Security Act is signed into law. It includes a workers' retirement insurance program and coverage for dependent survivors and disabled workers. The act also establishes a federal welfare program that helps states pay for and administer programs in Old Age Assistance, Aid to the Blind, Aid to Dependent Children, and General Assistance for needy people who do not qualify for other forms of help.

Social worker Jane Hoey is appointed head of the U.S. Bureau of Public Assistance. She influences the state departments of public assistance so that qualified applicants for help receive counseling as well as income maintenance. She sees to it that professional social work education is a requirement for public assistance administrators.

Alcoholics Anonymous (AA), the nation's first self-help organization, is established in Akron, Ohio, and becomes the prototype for many other self-help groups such as Gamblers Anonymous, Narcotics Anonymous, and Parents Anonymous (for those who abuse their children).

1936:   Social group workers begin regular meetings and form an association that later becomes the American Association of Group Workers (AAGW).

1937:   The American Association of Schools of Social Work (AASSW) declares that beginning in 1939 the requirement for social work accreditation will be a two-year master's degree program. The MSW becomes a requirement to be considered a professional social worker.

1938:   The Federal Housing Administration (FHA) begins its home-loan guarantee program to encourage home ownership.

1939:   The Lane Report (*The Field of Community Organization*, by Robert P. Lane) presents a systematic and comprehensive description of the roles, activities, and methods in the field of community organization. The work built on previous studies by Eduard C. Lindeman in his 1921 book, *The Community*, and Jesse F. Steiner's 1930 book, *Community Organization*.

1940:   Mary Parker Follett's posthumous book *Dynamic Administration* is published; it becomes an influence in the field of social welfare administration.

1941:   The Fair Employment Practices Committee (FEPC) is established to monitor and correct discrimination practices in the U.S. labor market. FEPC is abolished in 1945.

1942:   The Beveridge Report is issued in Great Britain, recommending an integrated social security system that attempts to ensure cradle-to-grave economic protections for its citizens. Many of the report's recommendations go into effect after World War II.

1943:   Social agencies begin charging modest fees for clients who can afford them.

The Marsh Report is issued in Canada. Based partly on Britain's Beveridge Report, it establishes the guidelines for the Canadian social welfare system.

1945:   World War II ends. On October 24, the United Nations is established.

The GI Bill is implemented. The program is designed primarily to provide educational and vocational training opportunities for returning veterans of World War II.

California becomes the first state to pass a social work regulatory act, a registration law.

1946: Great Britain establishes its National Health Service.

After meeting in special study groups since 1936, social group workers formally organize as the American Association of Group Workers (AAGW). ASCO, the Association for the Study of Community Organization, is established.

The National Mental Health Act is passed, establishing the National Institute of Mental Health (NIMH) and encouraging states, through grants, to develop and upgrade community and institutional mental health services. The Hill-Burton Act (P.L. 79-725) is passed, providing federal funds to develop new hospital facilities.

The School Lunch program is established, finally making permanent temporary measures developed in the 1930s. Cash and commodities are supplied to the states, municipalities, and schools to ensure that poor children have adequate midday nutrition.

1949: The Social Work Research Group (SWRG) is formally established.

1950: The first licensing for independent social work practice goes into effect in San Diego.

1952: The Council on Social Work Education (CSWE) is formed through a merger of the American Association of Schools of Social Work (AASSW) and the National Association of Schools of Social Administration (NASSA)—the two competing organizations that had been setting standards for schools of social work. CSWE is soon granted the authority to accredit graduate (MSW) schools of social work.

The McCarran-Walter Act (P.L. 82-414) is enacted to codify the requirements for immigration and naturalization into the United States. The law includes a quota system that permits many more people from northern European nations to come to the United States than people from Asia, Africa, or Latin America.

1953: The U.S. Department of Health, Education, and Welfare (HEW) is established.

1954: The U.S. Housing Act (P.L. 83-560) becomes law, establishing a massive urban renewal program in most American communities.

In social casework, the so-called "diagnostic" and "functional" schools begin to merge and lose their separate identities. The functional school had been oriented toward a highly focused, goal-oriented approach to casework intervention. The diagnostic school had been influenced by Freudian theory, but adherents of this approach develop more of a psychosocial orientation in the 1950s.

In *Brown v. Board of Education of Topeka, Kansas*, the U.S. Supreme Court rules that racial segregation in public schools is unconstitutional.

1955: On October 1, the National Association of Social Workers (NASW) is created through the merger of seven organizations—the American Association of Social Workers (AASW), plus the American Association of Medical Social Workers (AAMSW), the American Association of Psychiatric Social Workers (AAPSW), the National Association of School Social Workers (NASSW), the American Association of Group Workers (AAGW), the Association for the Study of Community Organization (ASCO), and the Social Work Research Group (SWRG). Membership is limited to members of the seven associations and subsequently to master's degree–level workers graduating from accredited schools of social work.

1957:   Ernest Greenwood's article "Attributes of a Profession" appears in the July issue of *Social Work*. It describes a profession as having a systematic body of theory, authority, functional specificity, community sanction, a code of ethics, and an integrated set of norms.

1958:   NDEA, the National Defense Education Act (P.L. 85-864), is established, providing federal aid to all levels of public and private education in the United States. The act stressed education in math, sciences, and foreign languages and gave extensive funding for low-interest student loans.

1961:   Unemployed parents may be included in Aid to Families with Dependent Children (AFDC) payments in states that elect to include them.

Rhode Island becomes the third jurisdiction to pass a regulatory law for social workers.

The White House Conference on Aging develops plans for effective care for the nation's elderly. Its work leads to the 1965 Older Americans Act (P.L. 89-73).

1962:   NASW organizes the Academy of Certified Social Workers (ACSW), restricted to NASW members with accredited MSW degrees, two years' agency experience under certified social work supervision, and adherence to the NASW Code of Ethics. ACSW membership requirements are subsequently revised to include testing and professional recommendations.

CSWE recognizes community organization as a legitimate specialization for social work education.

Congress passes the Manpower Development and Training Act (P.L. 87-415), a full-scale government training program to return displaced and unemployed workers to new fields.

President John F. Kennedy signs into law the social security amendments (P.L. 87-543), which provide greatly increased federal support for states to employ social workers and others. The workers would provide counseling and training to help people get off the welfare rolls.

1963:   In *Gideon v. Wainwright*, the U.S. Supreme Court rules that all defendants in criminal cases have the right to free legal counsel.

The Joint Commission on Mental Illness and Health issues its findings. President Kennedy signs into law the Community Mental Health Centers Act (P.L. 88-164), which funds development of mental health centers, training programs, and outpatient treatment programs.

1964:   President Lyndon B. Johnson launches the Great Society programs. With legislation in the Economic Opportunity Act (P.L. 88-452) and the Civil Rights Act (P.L. 88-352), the resulting program include the Job Corps, Operation Head Start, VISTA, the Neighborhood Youth Corps, and the Community Action program. Federal funding is also employed to train thousands of social workers and end the social work manpower shortages. Racial discrimination in public places is made illegal.

The Food Stamp program (P.L. 88-525) is enacted. Recipients are required to purchase coupons that are redeemable in food stores. A family of four with a monthly income of $140 could buy $166 worth of coupons for $37.

1965:   More Great Society programs and organizations are enacted and implemented, including Medicare, Medicaid, the Older Americans Act (P.L. 89-73), and the Elementary and Secondary Education Act (P.L. 89-10). The Department of Housing and Urban Development is established. The Voting Rights Act (P.L. 89-110) becomes law. Wilbur Cohen, a social worker and economist who helped found NASW and served on the committee to create the Social Security Act, is appointed Secretary of the U.S. Department of Health, Education, and Welfare (HEW), which is to administer most of the Great Society programs.

1966: The U.S. Supreme Court issues the *Miranda* decision, requiring that police inform a suspect of his or her constitutional rights before questioning.

1967: The Social Security Act is amended to include a Work Incentive Program (WIN) designed to encourage AFDC recipients to work without losing most of their benefits.

Amendments (P.L. 90-36) to the Social Security Act separate the welfare system's income maintenance features from personal social services. Clerks can replace professionals in administering the income maintenance program. Social workers are only needed to provide personal social services; thus, their role in public welfare is greatly diminished.

In the *Gault* decision, the U.S. Supreme Court determines that juveniles have the same constitutional rights as do adults. The juvenile court system, which had minimized the adversary process and used social workers as advocates and probation officers, is greatly curtailed.

1968: The Kerner Commission (National Advisory Commission on Civil Disorders) issues its report, blaming white racism and limited opportunities for blacks as major causes of the strife and rioting in urban ghettos. The Omnibus Crime Control and Safe Streets Act (P.L. 90-351) is passed and establishes the Law Enforcement Assistance Administration (LEAA) to help state and municipal governments control crime, rehabilitate offenders, recruit and train corrections officers and police, and improve correctional facilities.

The Office of Economic Opportunity and War on Poverty programs start to dismantle. Within the next three years, many programs are abolished and others are downgraded and placed within other federal agencies, especially in the Community Service Administration.

The National Association of Black Social Workers (NABSW) is established; the National Association of Puerto Rican Social Service Workers (NAPSSW) is founded; and the Asian American Social Workers (AASW) is formed.

1969: Membership in NASW, once restricted to MSWs, is opened to social workers with qualified bachelor's degrees. The NASW Delegate Assembly approves the resolution to pursue licensing of social work practice within each state.

President Richard M. Nixon proposes the Family Assistance Plan to reorganize the nation's welfare program. The plan, which proposes a minimum guaranteed annual income and incentives to encourage people to work, is not enacted.

1970: The National Indian Social Workers Association (NISWA) is created.

1971: The National Federation of Societies for Clinical Social Work (NFSCSW) is established.

NASW establishes ELAN, the Educational Legislative Action Network. Its political action functions are later achieved by local NASW chapters and by other NASW bodies at the national level.

ACTION is established as an independent federal umbrella agency that includes, among others, the Peace Corps, VISTA, and the Foster Grandparent program.

1972:   The Supplemental Security Income Program (SSI; P.L. 92-603) is enacted, which combines and federalizes public assistance for the adult poor aged, blind, and disabled. Sex discrimination in federally assisted educational programs is abolished.

1974:   Personal social services, work training, housing and community development, and juvenile justice and delinquency programs become law. The amendment to the Social Security Act known as Title XX becomes the major source of funds for personal social services. Each state is reimbursed by the federal government for helping individuals to achieve economic self-support and independence, preventing and remedying neglect and abuse, and reducing and preventing improper institutional care. CETA (the Comprehensive Employment and Training Act; P.L. 93-203) provides job opportunities and education for disadvantaged people. Section 8 of the Housing and Community Development Act (P.L. 93-383) helps low-income people live in housing provided by the private sector at fair market value. The Equal Credit Opportunity Act (P.L. 93-495) prohibits discrimination in credit based on gender or marital status, among other criteria.

1975:   The Education for All Handicapped Children Act (P.L. 94-142) becomes law, ensuring that the nation's public schools will provide equal educational opportunities for handicapped and learning-disabled youngsters.

1976:   NASW establishes PACE (Political Action for Candidate Election).

1977:   President Jimmy Carter proposes a thorough revision of the nation's social welfare system with a Jobs and Income Security program, which fails to gain approval in Congress and is abandoned when he is not reelected.

1979:   The U.S. Supreme Court rules that welfare benefits must be paid to families left needy by the mother's loss of her job, just as to families in which the father becomes unemployed.

The NASW Delegate Assembly approves the profession's new Code of Ethics.

1980:   The U.S. Department of Health and Human Services (HHS) is established when the Department of Health, Education, and Welfare (HEW) is divided. The U.S. Department of Education is established as an independent cabinet-level department.

The British government's Barclay Report is completed, defining the roles and tasks of social workers in public assistance and personal social services. It states that social workers should be more involved in social care planning and counseling, promoting community networks, negotiating, and social advocacy.

The Child Welfare Act (P.L. 95-266), which reorganizes the nation's system of providing for the welfare of its children, becomes law. Subsidized adoptions, changes in foster home care, and day care facilities are developed. The Parental Kidnapping Prevention Act (P.L. 96-611) clarifies laws pertaining to parental custody rights and obligations and helps state and local law enforcement agencies coordinate their efforts to reunite children with their custodial parents.

1981:   The Omnibus Budget Reconciliation Act (P.L. 97-35) and the social service block grants are established to fund social service programs at the state level with reduced federal scrutiny and funding and to decentralize social service programs to states.

1982:   The proposed Equal Rights Amendment for sexual equality fails to be ratified by two-thirds of the states by the deadline required by law.

The Job Training and Partnership Act (P.L. 97-300) and the Emergency Job Bill (P.L. 97-404) are enacted. This legislation replaces many CETA public service job-training programs and seeks to encourage state governments and private industry to train the needy for suitable employment. The Tax Equity and Fiscal Responsibility Act (P.L. 97-248) is enacted, cutting back social service funding.

1983:   NASW establishes the National Peer Review Advisory Committee and trains social workers to evaluate the work of other social workers to promote accountability and to meet quality control requirements of government and third-party funding organizations. The CSWE issues a Curriculum Policy Statement for baccalaureate as well as master's degree programs in social work education. BSW education is recognized as the first level of professional social work education.

1986:   The Gramm-Rudman-Hollings federal budget reduction law (P.L. 99-177) is implemented, requiring automatic cutbacks in expenditures for social service and other programs if budget limits are exceeded.

The Family Services Administration (FSA) is created as a unit within the U.S. Department of Health and Human Services (HHS). It consolidates the six major federal low-income programs (AFDC, WIN, Community Services Block Grants, Low-Income Home Energy Assistance, Refugee Assistance, and the Child Support Enforcement program).

1987:   The NASW Center for Social Policy and Practice is established to coordinate the exchange of information, education, and policy formulation pertaining to social work and social welfare in the United States.

NASW
Code of Ethics

THE NASW CODE OF ETHICS

Preamble

This code is intended to serve as a guide to the everyday conduct of members of the social work profession and as a basis for the adjudication of issues in ethics when the conduct of social workers is alleged to deviate from the standards expressed or implied in this code. It represents standards of ethical behavior for social workers in professional relationships with those served, with colleagues, with employers, with other individuals and professions, and with the community and society as a whole. It also embodies standards of ethical behavior governing individual conduct to the extent that such conduct is associated with an individual's status and identity as a social worker.

This code is based on the fundamental values of the social work profession that include the worth, dignity, and uniqueness of all persons as well as their rights and opportunities. It is also based on the nature of social work, which foster conditions that promote these values.

In subscribing to and abiding by this code, the social worker is expected to view ethical responsibility in as inclusive a context as each situation demands and within which ethical judgement is required. The social worker is expected to take into consideration all the principles in this code that have a bearing upon any situation in which ethical judgement is to be exercised and professional intervention or conduct is planned. The course of action that the social worker chooses is expected to be consistent with the spirit as well as the letter of this code.

In itself, this code does not represent a set of rules that will prescribe all the behaviors of social workers in all the complexities of professional life. Rather, it offers general principles to guide conduct, and the judicious appraisal of conduct, in situations that have ethical implications. It provides the basis for making judgements about ethical actions before and after they occur. Frequently, the particular situation determines the ethical principles that apply and the manner of their application. In such cases, not only the particular ethical principles are taken into immediate consideration, but also the entire code and its spirit. Specific applications of ethical principles must be judged within the context in which they are being considered. Ethical behavior in a given situation must satisfy not only the judgement of the individual social worker, but also the judgement of an unbiased jury of professional peers.

This code should not be used as an instrument to deprive any social worker of the opportunity or freedom to practice with complete professional integrity; nor should any disciplinary action be taken on the basis of this code without maximum provision for safeguarding the rights of the social worker affected.

The ethical behavior of social workers results not from edict, but from a personal commitment of the individual. This code is offered to affirm the will and zeal of all social workers to be ethical and to act ethically in all that they do as social workers.

The following codified ethical principles should guide social workers in the various roles and relationships and at the various levels of responsibility in which they function professionally. These principles also serve as a basis for the adjudication by the National Association of Social Workers of issues in ethics.

In subscribing to this code, social workers are required to cooperate in its implementation and abide by any disciplinary rulings based on it. They should also take adequate measures to discourage, prevent, expose, and correct the unethical conduct of colleagues. Finally, social workers should be equally ready to defend and assist colleagues unjustly charged with unethical conduct.

Summary of Major Principles

I. THE SOCIAL WORKER'S CONDUCT AND COMPORTMENT AS A SOCIAL WORKER
   A. *Propriety.* The social worker should maintain high standards of personal conduct in the capacity or identity as social worker.
   B. *Competence and Professional Development.* The social worker should strive to become and remain proficient in professional practice and the performance of professional functions.
   C. *Service.* The social worker should regard as primary the service obligation of the social work profession.
   D. *Integrity.* The social worker should act in accordance with the highest standards of professional integrity.
   E. *Scholarship and Research.* The social worker engaged in study and research should be guided by the conventions of scholarly inquiry.

II. THE SOCIAL WORKER'S ETHICAL RESPONSIBILITY TO CLIENTS
   F. *Primacy of Clients' Interests.* The social worker's primary responsibility is to clients.

G. *Rights and Prerogatives of Clients.* The social worker should make every effort to foster maximum self-determination on the part of clients.

H. *Confidentiality and Privacy.* The social worker should respect the privacy of clients and hold in confidence all information obtained in the course of professional service.

I. *Fees.* When setting fees, the social worker should ensure that they are fair, reasonable, considerate, and commensurate with the service performed and with due regard for the clients' ability to pay.

III. The Social Worker's Ethical Responsibility to Colleagues

J. *Respect, Fairness, and Courtesy.* The social worker should treat colleagues with respect, courtesy, fairness, and good faith.

K. *Dealing with Colleagues' Clients.* The social worker has the responsibility to relate to the clients of colleagues with full professional consideration.

IV. The Social Worker's Ethical Responsibility to Employers and Employing Organizations

L. *Commitments to Employing Organizations.* The social worker should adhere to commitments made to the employing organizations.

V. The Social Worker's Ethical Responsibility to the Social Work Profession

M. *Maintaining the Integrity of the Profession.* The social worker should uphold and advance the values, ethics, knowledge, and mission of the profession.

N. *Community Service.* The social worker should assist the profession in making social services available to the general public.

O. *Development of Knowledge.* The social worker should take responsibility for identifying, developing, and fully utilizing knowledge for professional practice.

VI. The Social Worker's Ethical Responsibility to Society

P. *Promoting the General Welfare.* The social worker should promote the general welfare of society.

The NASW Code of Ethics

I. The Social Worker's Conduct and Comportment as a Social Worker

A. *Propriety.* The social worker should maintain high standards of personal conduct in the capacity or identity as social worker.

1. The private conduct of the social worker is a personal matter to the same degree as is any other person's, except when such conduct compromises the fulfillment of professional responsibilities.

2. The social worker should not participate in, condone, or be associated with dishonesty, fraud, deceit, or misrepresentation.

3. The social worker should distinguish clearly between statements and actions made as a private individual and as a representative of the social work profession or an organization or group.

B. *Competence and Professional Development.* The social worker should strive to become and remain proficient in professional practice and the performance of professional functions.

1. The social worker should accept responsibility or employment only on the basis of existing competence or the intention to acquire the necessary competence.

2. The social worker should not misrepresent professional qualifications, education, experience, or affiliations.

C. *Service.* The social worker should regard as primary the service obligation of the social work profession.

1. The social worker should retain ultimate responsibility for the quality and extent of the service that individual assumes, assigns, or performs.

2. The social worker should act to prevent practices that are inhumane or discriminatory against any person or group of persons.

D. *Integrity.* The social worker should act in accordance with the highest standards of professional integrity and impartiality.

1. The social worker should be alert to and resist the influences and pressures that interfere with the exercise of professional discretion and impartial judgement required for the performance of professional functions.

2. The social worker should not exploit professional relationships for personal gain.

E. *Scholarship and Research.* The social worker engaged in study and research should be guided by the conventions of scholarly inquiry.

1. The social worker engaged in research should consider carefully its possible consequences for human beings.

2. The social worker engaged in research should ascertain that the consent of participants in the research is voluntary and informed, without any implied deprivation or penalty for refusal to participate, and with due regard for participants' privacy and dignity.

3. The social worker engaged in research should protect participants from unwarranted physical or mental discomfort, distress, harm, danger, or deprivation.

4. The social worker who engages in the evaluation of services or cases should discuss them only for the professional purposes and only with persons directly and professionally concerned with them.

5. Information obtained about participants in research should be treated as confidential.

6. The social worker should take credit only for work actually done in connection with scholarly and research endeavors and credit contributions made by others.

II. The Social Worker's Ethical Responsibility to Clients

F. *Primacy of Clients' Interests.* The social worker's primary responsibility is to clients.

1. The social worker should serve clients with devotion, loyalty, determination, and the maximum application of professional skill and competence.
2. The social worker should not exploit relationships with clients for personal advantage, or solicit the clients of one's agency for private practice.
3. The social worker should not practice, condone, facilitate, or collaborate with any form of discrimination on the basis of race, color, sex, sexual orientation, age, religion, national origin, marital status, political belief, mental or physical handicap, or any other preference or personal characteristic, condition, or status.
4. The social worker should avoid relationships or commitments that conflict with the interests of clients.
5. The social worker should under no circumstances engage in sexual activities with clients.
6. The social worker should provide clients with accurate and complete information regarding the extent and nature of the services available to them.
7. The social worker should apprise clients of their risks, rights, opportunities, and obligations associated with social service to them.
8. The social worker should seek advice and counsel of colleagues and supervisors whenever such consultation is in the best interest of clients.
9. The social worker should terminate service to clients, and professional relationships with them, when such service and relationships are no longer required or no longer serve the clients' needs or interests.
10. The social worker should withdraw services precipitously only under unusual circumstances, giving careful consideration to all factors in the situation and taking care to minimize possible adverse effects.
11. The social worker who anticipates the termination or interruption of service to clients should notify clients promptly and seek the transfer, referral, or continuation of service in relation to the clients' needs and preferences.

G. *Rights and Prerogatives of Clients.* The social worker should make every effort to foster maximum self-determination on the part of clients.

1. When the social worker must act on behalf of a client who has been adjudged legally incompetent, the social worker should safeguard the interests and rights of that client.

2. When another individual has been legally authorized to act in behalf of a client, the social worker should deal with that person always with the client's best interest in mind.

3. The social worker should not engage in any action that violates or diminishes the civil or legal rights of clients.

H. *Confidentiality and Privacy.* The social worker should respect the privacy of clients and hold in confidence all information obtained in the course of professional service.

1. The social worker should share with others confidences revealed by clients, without their consent, only for compelling professional reasons.

2. The social worker should inform clients fully about the limits of confidentiality in a given situation, the purposes for which information is obtained, and how it may be used.

3. The social worker should afford clients reasonable access to any official social work records concerning them.

4. When providing clients with access to records, the social worker should take due care to protect the confidences of others contained in those records.

5. The social worker should obtain informed consent of clients before taping, recording, or permitting third party observation of their activities.

I. *Fees.* When setting fees, the social worker should ensure that they are fair, reasonable, considerate, and commensurate with the service performed and with due regard for the clients' ability to pay.

1. The social worker should not divide a fee or accept or give anything of value for receiving or making a referral.

III. THE SOCIAL WORKER'S ETHICAL RESPONSIBILITY TO COLLEAGUES

J. *Respect, Fairness, and Courtesy.* The social worker should treat colleagues with respect, courtesy, fairness, and good faith.

1. The social worker should cooperate with colleagues to promote professional interests and concerns.

2. The social worker should respect confidences shared by colleagues in the course of their professional relationships and transactions.

3. The social worker should create and maintain conditions of practice that facilitate ethical and competent professional performance by colleagues.

4. The social worker should treat with respect, and represent accurately and fairly, the qualifications, views, and findings of colleagues and use appropriate channels to express judgements on these matters.

5. The social worker who replaces or is replaced by a colleague in professional practice should act with consideration for the interest, character, and reputation of that colleague.

6. The social worker should not exploit a dispute between a colleague

and employers to obtain a position or otherwise advance the social worker's interest.

7. The social worker should seek arbitration or mediation when conflicts with colleagues require resolution for compelling professional reasons.

8. The social worker should extend to colleagues of other professions the same respect and cooperation that is extended to social work colleagues.

9. The social worker who serves as an employer, supervisor, or mentor to colleagues should make orderly and explicit arrangements regarding the conditions of their continuing professional relationship.

10. The social worker who has the responsibility for employing and evaluating the performance of other staff members, should fulfill such responsibility in a fair, considerate, and equitable manner, on the basis of clearly enunciated criteria.

11. The social worker who has the responsibility for evaluating the performance of employees, supervisees, or students should share evaluations with them.

K. *Dealing with Colleagues' Clients.* The social worker has the responsibility to relate to the clients of colleagues with full professional consideration.

1. The social worker should not solicit the clients of colleagues.

2. The social worker should not assume professional responsibility for the clients of another agency or a colleague without appropriate communication with that agency or colleague.

3. The social worker who serves the clients of colleagues, during a temporary absence or emergency, should serve those clients with the same consideration as that afforded any client.

IV. THE SOCIAL WORKER'S ETHICAL RESPONSIBILITY TO EMPLOYERS AND EMPLOYING ORGANIZATIONS

L. *Commitments to Employing Organization.* The social worker should adhere to commitments made to the employing organization.

1. The social worker should work to improve the employing agency's policies and procedures, and the efficiency and effectiveness of its services.

2. The social worker should not accept employment or arrange student field placements in an organization which is currently under public sanction by NASW for violating personnel standards, or imposing limitations on or penalties for professional actions on behalf of clients.

3. The social worker should act to prevent and eliminate discrimination in the employing organization's work assignments and in its employment policies and practices.

4. The social worker should use with scrupulous regard, and only for the purpose for which they are intended, the resources of the employing organization.

V. THE SOCIAL WORKER'S ETHICAL RESPONSIBILITY TO THE SOCIAL WORK PROFESSION

M. *Maintaining the Integrity of the Profession.* The social worker should uphold and advance the values, ethics, knowledge, and mission of the profession.

1. The social worker should protect and enhance the dignity and integrity of the profession and should be responsible and vigorous in discussion and criticism of the profession.
2. The social worker should take action through appropriate channels against unethical conduct by any other member of the profession.
3. The social worker should act to prevent the unauthorized and unqualified practice of social work.
4. The social worker should make no misrepresentation in advertising as to qualifications, competence, service, or results to be achieved.

N. *Community Service.* The social worker should assist the profession in making social services available to the general public.

1. The social worker should contribute time and professional expertise to activities that promote respect for the utility, the integrity, and the competence of the social work profession.
2. The social worker should support the formulation, development, enactment, and implementation of social policies of concern to the profession.

O. *Development of Knowledge.* The social worker should take responsibility for identifying, developing, and fully utilizing knowledge for professional practice.

1. The social worker should base practice upon recognized knowledge relevant to social work.
2. The social worker should critically examine, and keep current with, emerging knowledge relevant to social work.
3. The social worker should contribute to the knowledge base of social work and share research knowledge and practice wisdom with colleagues.

VI. THE SOCIAL WORKER'S ETHICAL RESPONSIBILITY TO SOCIETY

P. *Promoting the General Welfare.* The social worker should promote the general welfare of society.

1. The social worker should act to prevent and eliminate discrimination against any person or group on the basis of race, color, sex, sexual orientation, age, religion, national origin, marital status, political belief, mental or physical handicap, or any other preference or personal characteristic, condition, or status.
2. The social worker should act to ensure that all persons have access to the resources, services, and opportunities which they require.
3. The social worker should act to expand choice and opportunity for all persons, with special regard for disadvantaged or oppressed groups and persons.

4. The social worker should promote conditions that encourage respect for the diversity of cultures which constitute American society.
5. The social worker should provide appropriate professional services in public emergencies.
6. The social worker should advocate changes in policy and legislation to improve social conditions and to promote social justice.
7. The social worker should encourage informed participation by the public in shaping social policies and institutions.

ABOUT THE AUTHOR

Robert L. Barker is on the social work faculty of the National Catholic School of Social Service, Catholic University of America, in Washington, D.C. He also maintains a private practice in marital and family therapy in suburban Maryland. His MSW is from the University of Washington, and his DSW is from Columbia University. He is editor in chief of the *Journal of Independent Social Work* and author of numerous articles and twelve books, including *Social Work in Private Practice: Principles, Issues, and Dilemmas, Treating Couples in Crisis: Fundamentals and Practice in Marital Therapy,* and *The Business of Psychotherapy.* His next two books, *The Green-eyed Marriage: Overcoming Jealous Relationships* and *The Resource Book,* will be published in 1987 by Free Press (Macmillan Publishing Co.) and Haworth Press, respectively.